# CROSS-BORDER INTERNET DISPUTE RESOLUTION

The Internet has the potential to increase the number of cross-border disputes between a wide range of different users. For many Internet disputes, the use of online dispute resolution (ODR) becomes critical. ODR uses information technology (such as expert systems) and Internet communication applications (such as webforms or web filing platforms) to resolve disputes outside the courts. Although ODR is a progeny of alternative dispute resolution (ADR), using some of the same processes such as mediation and arbitration, ODR is different in that it adds new and transformative technology and processes. This book sets out the process standards with which ODR (and in particular online arbitration) should comply, shows how these standards can be implemented in the real world and considers applicable law and enforcement, thus providing a blueprint of how online arbitration processes should be devised.

JULIA HÖRNLE is a Senior Lecturer at the Centre for Commercial Law Studies, School of Law, Queen Mary University of London.

# CROSS-BORDER INTERNET DISPUTE RESOLUTION

JULIA HÖRNLE

CAMBRIDGE
UNIVERSITY PRESS

CAMBRIDGE UNIVERSITY PRESS
Cambridge, New York, Melbourne, Madrid, Cape Town, Singapore, São Paulo, Delhi

Cambridge University Press
The Edinburgh Building, Cambridge CB2 8RU, UK

Published in the United States of America by Cambridge University Press, New York

www.cambridge.org
Information on this title: www.cambridge.org/9780521896207

First published 2009

Printed in the United Kingdom at the University Press, Cambridge

*A catalogue record for this publication is available from the British Library*

*Library of Congress Cataloguing in Publication data*
Hörnle, Julia, 1970–
Cross-border internet dispute resolution / Julia Hörnle.
p.   cm.
Includes bibliographical references and index.
ISBN 978-0-521-89620-7 (hardback)
1. Electronic commerce – Law and legislation.    2. Dispute resolution (Law) – Automation.
3. Due process of law.    4. Electronic commerce – Law and legislation – Great Britain.
5. Dispute resolution (Law) – Great Britain.    I. Title.
K564.C6H67     2009
343.09′944 – dc22     2008049237

ISBN 978-0-521-89620-7 hardback

# CONTENTS

# ILLUSTRATIONS

# TABLES

# TABLE OF CASES

## World Intellectual Property Organization (WIPO)

# TABLE OF UK STATUTES

# TABLE OF UK STATUTORY INSTRUMENTS

# TABLE OF EUROPEAN COMMUNITIES LEGISLATION AND DOCUMENTS

## Recommendations

# TABLE OF FOREIGN STATUTES

## Australia

New South Wales Commercial Arbitration Act 1984
    s. 38   163
    s. 42   118

## Belgium

Judicial Code
    Art. 1701(5)   143
    Art. 1704(1)(i)   143

## China

Arbitration Law 1994
    Art. 34   118
    Art. 54   143
    Art. 58(6)   118

## France

Code Civile
    Art. 2061   174
Code Commerciale
    Art. 631   174
Nouveau Code de Procédure Civile
    Art. 1458   59
    Art. 1460(1)   58
    Art. 1471   143
    Art. 1476   59
    Art. 1496   62, 64, 68
    Art. 1502(c)   164

## Germany

Arbitration Act 1998
    §1032(1)   59
    §§1035–1036   118

# TABLE OF TREATIES AND CONVENTIONS

# ACKNOWLEDGEMENTS

This book is the result of four years of research for a PhD dissertation, which I successfully submitted in December 2007.

My greatest debt in producing this book is owed to the two supervisors of my doctoral research, Professor Chris Reed and Professor Ian Walden at the Centre of Commercial Law Studies, who first introduced me to the subject of Internet law seven years ago when I switched from legal practice to academia. Without their inspiration, enthusiasm, patience and criticism, this book would never have been produced. The subject of ODR was first brought to my attention by Arthur Marriott QC, who kindly trusted me to write a chapter on this subject for *Bernstein's Handbook of Arbitration and Dispute Resolution Practice*, and to whom I really owe the initial idea for this book. I was also influenced by my involvement in the UN Expert Group in ODR and the debates at the ODR Conference in London, which Gregory Hunt and I organised in 2004. Professor Ethan Katsh, Dr Thomas Schultz, Colin Rule, Mirèze Philippe and Professor Louise-Ellen Teitz have all contributed to my thoughts. I would like to thank my partner Sean, who has put up with my working during the small hours on many occasions and who has selflessly supported me during this time. Finally, and most importantly, I must mention my parents; without their role-model, encouragement and love, this book would not have been written.

# ABBREVIATIONS

| | |
|---|---|
| AAA | American Arbitration Association |
| ABA | American Bar Association |
| ADNDRC | Asian Domain Name Dispute Resolution Centre |
| ADR | alternative dispute resolution |
| B2B | business to business |
| B2C | business to consumer |
| BEUC | Bureau Européen des Unions de Consommateurs (European Consumer Organisation) |
| C2C | consumer to consumer |
| CCLS | Centre for Commercial Law Studies, Queen Mary University of London |
| CIArb | Chartered Institute of Arbitrators |
| CIETAC | China International Economic and Trade Arbitration Commission |
| CISAS | Communication and Internet Services Adjudication Scheme |
| CPR | International Institute for Conflict Prevention & Resolution |
| DIS | Deutsches Institut für Schiedsgerichtsbarkeit |
| DOC | US Department of Commerce |
| DTI | UK Department of Trade and Industry |
| ECC-Net | European Consumer Centre Network |
| ECHR | European Convention for the Protection of Human Rights and Fundamental Freedoms (or European Convention on Human Rights) |
| ECJ | European Court of Justice |
| EComHR | European Commission of Human Rights (before the 1998 reforms) |
| ECtHR | European Court of Human Rights |
| EEA | European Economic Area |
| EU | European Union |

| | |
|---|---|
| FOS | Financial Ombudsman Service |
| FSA | Financial Services Authority |
| FTC | US Federal Trade Commission |
| GAFTA | Grain and Feed Trade Association |
| IBA | International Bar Association |
| ICAC | International Commercial Arbitration Court (Moscow) |
| ICANN | Internet Corporation for Assigned Names and Numbers |
| ICAS | Independent Consumer Arbitration Service |
| ICC | International Chamber of Commerce |
| ICDR | AAA International Center for Dispute Resolution |
| ICSID | International Center for the Settlement of Investment Disputes |
| ICT | information and communications technology |
| IP | intellectual property |
| ISP | Internet service provider |
| LCIA | London Court of International Arbitration |
| LMAA | London Martitime Arbitration Association |
| NAF | National Arbitration Forum |
| ODR | online dispute resolution |
| OECD | Organisation for Economic Co-operation and Development |
| OFT | UK Office of Fair Trading |
| OOO | Online Ombudsman Office |
| Otelo | Office of the Telecommunications Ombudsman |
| UDRP | Uniform Domain Name Dispute Resolution Procedure |
| UNCITRAL | United Nations Commission for International Trade Law |
| URL | uniform resource locator |
| WIPO | World Intellectual Property Organization |
| WIPO Center | WIPO Arbitration and Mediation Center |

# 1

# Introduction

It is the year 1532. Michael Kohlhaas, described as an honest and law-abiding Brandenburg merchant,[1] is on his way with his merchandise to an important trade fair, across the border, in the town of Leipzig. Unfortunately, he does not get beyond the border post to Saxony as the local squire has two of his horses seized and beats up his stable boy. Michael Kohlhass misses the fair and loses the opportunity to sell his merchandise. He seeks redress against the squire's arbitrary and unlawful conduct: however, the local court in the principality denies him any form of civil remedy. In his frustration, he gathers a gang of rebels and seeks revenge. He starts to burn down and pillage houses in the Saxon squire's town and eventually commits murder. As the story progresses, Michael Kohlhaas' crusade becomes more and more excessive. He loses his wife, his possessions and finally his life when he is arrested and executed some eight years later.

The story of Michael Kohlhaas and his frustrated quest for justice are proverbial in Germany, and reflect how, in an extreme case, an unresolved dispute can slowly and incrementally escalate to a cross-border bloodshed. If he had obtained a remedy at the outset, the bloodshed and destruction in the story could have been avoided. This story is relevant to the Internet, since the Internet brings a variety of persons interacting from different countries into conflict with each other, sometimes without access to redress through the state courts.

As the reader will be aware, Internet applications such as email, commercial websites (E-commerce) and marketplaces (e.g. online auctions), content-sharing websites (e.g. video- or photo-sharing websites), social networking sites (such as MySpace, Facebook or LinkedIn), collaborative websites (e.g. wikis and blogs) and virtual worlds (such as SecondLife or World of Warcraft) allow users to interact directly with each other and exchange and share information regardless of their physical, geographical

---

[1] The story is told in a novella by Heinrich von Kleist (1777–1811).

1

location. This allows individuals (whether as consumers or active participants) to make international transactions and to become international
publishers. The Internet can thus be described as a powerful communications medium that allows data exchanges in various media formats
between a wide range of different users situated in distant locations.

As such, the Internet has the potential to lead to a multitude of international cross-border disputes. The reader may imagine, for example, a
defendant in state A collecting and using personal information uploaded
on a social networking site by an individual in state B for advertising or
harassment of the claimant, giving rise to a privacy infringement claim.
The individual in state B may not have the means to pursue a claim in
state A or to enforce it there. Another example would be an individual in
state C uploading a video or photo on a website hosting and/or streaming
this content worldwide, and a person in state D claiming that this activity
infringed his or her copyright or that this content contained defamatory
statements. A third example could be a consumer in state E buying goods
or services from a website operated by a company established in state F,
but the goods and services turning out to be defective. The reader may
think of similar examples. A moment's search for other examples indicates that, in practice, an endless variety of cross-border Internet disputes
can arise. Cross-border disputes pose a challenge for national courts, a
challenge that this book is attempting to address.

This book examines how cross-border Internet disputes can be resolved
fairly, outside the courts. The aim of the book is to develop a fair model
for the resolution of such Internet disputes, piecing together different
methods of dispute resolution into one jigsaw puzzle.

As a preliminary step to building this jigsaw puzzle, the book explores
the meaning of fairness in dispute resolution. It then considers different
methods and mechanisms for dispute resolution. It contains a detailed
exploration of the role of payment service providers, and focuses on the
roles played by mediation and arbitration. It considers the use of online
technology for mediation and arbitration, obviating the need for the
parties and lawyers to meet face-to-face and leading to more efficient
information processing, thereby reducing cost and delay in dispute resolution (see Chapter 5 on online dispute resolution (ODR)). The book
then describes existing ODR schemes and their advantages.

The next question is how ODR for Internet disputes should be structured. Binding dispute resolution and enforceability in cross-border cases
are important for Internet disputes, and can be provided by online arbitration. Therefore this book proceeds to examine in great detail the legal

issues surrounding online arbitration. It looks at questions of applicable law and due process in arbitration, and covers the legal issues surrounding business-to-consumer (B2C) arbitration, comparing the European approach to that in the United States. The book also contains a detailed analysis of domain-name dispute resolution, and considers to what extent this dispute resolution model could serve as a model for other types of Internet disputes, and suggests improvements.

The reader will find in the concluding chapter a model of dispute resolution that encourages the use of online arbitration for Internet disputes but, where there exists a substantial power imbalance between the disputants (such as the traditional B2C paradigm), subjects traditional commercial arbitration to more stringent due process standards for disputes. Finally, the book concludes by discussing different options of how these stricter standards should be implemented in practice.

It is hoped that this book contributes to the existing debate on dispute resolution for the Internet by synthesising recent thinking on due process in arbitration with the problem of dispute resolution on the Internet and Internet regulation. The story is told from the viewpoint of Internet law and the specific challenges that the Internet poses for dispute resolution, but the reader will also find a very detailed, rigorous and practical analysis of ADR and arbitration law as relevant for the analysis of Internet disputes. The result is a theory of how the traditional arbitration model needs to be adapted to suit the challenges posed by the Internet, and how these adaptations can be implemented.

The research focuses mainly on English and US law.[2] These jurisdictions have been chosen as it is there that the debate on ADR and arbitration is most developed. In some instances the book also uses a wider comparative approach, drawing on the laws of other jurisdictions by way of example to illustrate particular points, where relevant. The law is up to date until 1 January 2008.

---

[2] Looking mainly at federal law and only some state law.

# 2

## The concepts of fairness

An appreciation of unfairness develops early. A child of five, perhaps younger, is likely to know the meaning of unfairness . . . What any child might have more difficulty in doing is to give expression to the converse notion, the idea of fairness. Unfairness shouts out. Fairness goes unremarked.

(J. G. Riddall, *Jurisprudence* (London: Butterworths, 1999), 196)

### 2.1 Introduction

This book is concerned with the fair resolution of Internet disputes. It is therefore necessary to define procedural fairness at the outset.[1]

It is first necessary to distinguish procedural fairness from distributive fairness. The latter is concerned with the allocation of resources,[2] whereas procedural fairness is not concerned with the outcome of the allocation but rather the procedure of getting there.[3] Therefore, a theory on dispute resolution (such as the one set forth in this book) is about procedural fairness.

Fairness is an extremely amorphous and elusive notion, and it is frequently used in an emotive way. While most people have an instinctive idea about a procedure being 'unfair' or 'unjust', it is much more difficult to build a comprehensive concept of the converse: fairness in dispute resolution.

---

[1] The terms 'fair', 'just', 'fairness' and 'justice' are used interchangeably in this book – it seems that there is little difference in meaning; see also H. L. A. Hart, *The Concept of Law*, 2nd edn (Oxford: Clarendon Press, 1994), 158: 'most of the criticisms made in terms of just and unjust could almost equally well be conveyed by the words "fair" and "unfair".'

[2] Such as property rights and their limitation, contractual entitlements and obligations, social security, etc. Distributive justice is concerned with the fair allocation of resources.

[3] A. Tschentscher, 'The Function of Procedural Justice in Theories of Justice', in K. Röhl and S. Machura (eds.), *Procedural Justice* (Aldershot: Ashgate, 1997), 105–19, 105–6.

This chapter builds a concept of fairness using the building blocks of the traditional principle of due process,[4] and relates this to general theories of procedural fairness. In doing this, the theory of fairness adopted in this book leans heavily on Rawls' theory of justice. However, before looking at Rawls' theory and legal due process, the following section starts by deliberating on the elements of procedural fairness in a more general manner.

## 2.2 Definition of fairness in dispute resolution

By way of an overview, this section puts forward that procedural fairness in dispute resolution should consist of three main principles: (i) equal treatment; (ii) a rational approach to decision-making (adjudication,[5] such as litigation or arbitration) or to negotiation (and mediation); and (iii) effectiveness, which in turn consists of general access and mechanisms to counter-balance existing procedural inequalities between the parties (the 'counterpoise').

### 2.2.1 Equal treatment of the parties

The notion of equal treatment has been at the core of fair treatment.[6] A dispute resolution process that disadvantages one of the parties, that prevents only one of the parties from advancing any evidence or that involves a decision-maker who is biased towards one of the parties is self-evidently unfair.

While equal treatment is an obvious ingredient of fairness, it is only part of the picture. In addition, there must be a qualitative element to dispute resolution.

---

[4] The phrases 'due process' and 'natural justice' are used interchangeably with the same meaning. 'Due process' is more commonly used in the United States, and 'natural justice' more commonly in the English legal tradition; see H. J. Friendly, 'Some Kind of Hearing' (1975) 123 *University of Pennsylvania Law Review* 1267–317, 1276.

[5] The term 'adjudication' is used in this book as a neutral term to mean a form of dispute resolution involving a third party making a decision binding on the parties, and is to include arbitration, ombudsmen and litigation, rather than in the meaning of 'expert determination'.

[6] Riddall, *Jurisprudence*, 197.

### 2.2.2 A rational approach to dispute resolution

The second element of procedural fairness in dispute resolution is taking a rational approach to solving a dispute.

For Lon Fuller, the defining characteristic of adjudication, particularly compared to other forms of social ordering such as voting, is participation by presenting proofs and reasoned argument, and he therefore posits that the results from adjudication are subject to a high standard of rationality.[7]

Dispute resolution consists of fact-finding processes, problem-solving and law application.[8] These processes should be governed by logic and reason, so that no irrelevant considerations are taken into account.[9]

Applying the law in a rational manner also means that like cases should be treated in a like manner. Logic in applying and interpreting the law should determine when two factual scenarios are the same and should be treated the same and when two factual scenarios are different and should be treated differently.[10] Hence rationality implies a degree of regularity in the application of law.[11] This is encapsulated by the principle of the rule of law. H. L. A Hart points to this close connection between due process and proceeding by rule.[12]

Fact-finding processes should be in accordance with logic and be accurate, for a decision based on wrong facts is by definition unfair. Therefore a rational approach to dispute resolution additionally involves a degree of accuracy as to the factual basis of any decision.[13]

### 2.2.3 Effectiveness

A third element of procedural fairness in dispute resolution is the effectiveness of the procedure. Effectiveness means that a procedure leads to a decision or solution of a dispute. It consists of two elements: (i) access and (ii) the counterpoise.

---

[7] L. Fuller, 'The Forms and Limits of Adjudication' (1978–1979) 92 *Harvard Law Review* 353–409, 364, 366 and 370.

[8] As to the different types of dispute resolution and the processes they involve, see 4.2.

[9] W. Park, *Procedural Evolution in Business Arbitration* (Oxford University Press, 2006), 54.

[10] Hart, *The Concept of Law*, 159, 'Hence justice is traditionally thought of as maintaining or restoring a *balance* or *proportion*, and its leading precept is often formulated as "Treat like cases alike"; though we need to add to the latter "and treat different cases differently".'

[11] See also Fuller, 'The Forms and Limits of Adjudication', 380–1.

[12] Hart, *The Concept of Law*, 160.

[13] The *Oxford English Dictionary* accords the expression 'fair and square' the meaning 'with absolute accuracy, honestly and straightforwardly'.

## Access

If a dispute resolution procedure is so cumbersome, drawn out and expensive that a decision or solution is never reached, or is reached only after excessive cost and delay, this would mean that such a procedure is not fair.[14] This is encapsulated in the saying 'justice delayed becomes justice denied'.

## Counterpoise

While the principle of access looks at effectiveness of the procedure itself, the counterpoise takes into account obstacles to effective participation that are not inherent to the procedure but which arise from a party's inability to take part in the procedure on an equal footing. Thus the counterpoise is concerned with pre-existing power imbalances between the parties, and consists of measures to reduce them. Formal equal treatment of the parties by the judge/mediator/arbitrator and a rational approach to dispute resolution are necessary (but not sufficient) if the parties cannot participate in the dispute resolution process on an equal footing because of pre-existing procedural power imbalances. For example, if one party has no access to legal advice, no experience in litigation and no financial resources to fight a case, he or she would be less equipped to take part in a dispute resolution procedure than the other party.[15]

In particular, power imbalances are a problem for effectiveness since it is more likely that the dominant party imposes its terms on the weaker party.[16] Furthermore, the dominant party is less likely to agree to *binding* dispute resolution in the first place if the weaker party is the claimant.[17]

Therefore it must be recognised that there should be some counterpoise to pre-existing power imbalances for the purposes of dispute resolution to enable equal participation by both parties.[18]

---

[14] EU Recommendation 98/257/EC, Principle IV: 'Effectiveness'; see also the jurisprudence of the European Court of Human Rights (ECtHR) finding that excessive delay is a breach of the right to a fair trial under ECHR, Art. 6(1); see, for example, *Hentrich* v. *France*, A Series No. 296-A (1994) 18 EHRR 440.

[15] See 3.5 (power in dispute resolution).   [16] See 6.4.2 (party autonomy).   [17] See 8.2.

[18] M. Cappelletti, 'Alternative Dispute Resolution Processes within the Framework of the World-Wide-Access-to-Justice Movement' (1993) 56 *The Modern Law Review* 282–96, 283; G. Petrochilos, *Procedural Law in International Arbitration* (Oxford University Press, 2004), 128–9; L. Nader, 'Alternatives to the American Judicial System', in L. Nader, *No Access to Law* (New York, NY: Academic Press, 1980), 3–53, 29 and L. Nader and C. Shugart, 'Old Solutions for Old Problems', in L. Nader, *No Access to Law* (New York, NY: Academic Press, 1980) 57–102, 64–5.

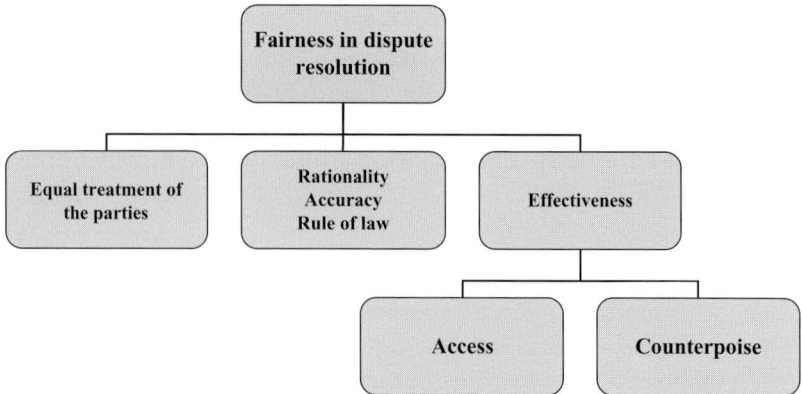

**Fig. 1.** Fairness definition: illustrating the main principles of fairness in dispute resolution.

### 2.2.4 Conclusion

This section has introduced a concept of fairness in dispute resolution consisting of three main principles, those being equal treatment, rationality and effectiveness. Effectiveness is concerned with access and a counterpoise to existing procedural inequalities, as illustrated in Fig. 1. All three principles must be met to some minimum level to achieve fairness in dispute resolution.

In the following sections, this conceptualisation will be deepened by synthesising the traditional notion of due process and Rawls' theory of justice and Habermas' ideas about fair participation.

## 2.3 Process values and forms of procedural justice

Having enumerated the principles that make up the concept of procedural fairness, it may be worthwhile to pause for a moment and consider process values more generally. Process values are legal principles governing procedures (such as a rule against torture, for example). Process values have been extensively discussed in literature under the question of whether they are important values in their own right or whether they are only important to the extent that they lead to a good outcome (such as a fair decision or a fair settlement). In other words, the question to be answered is whether process values are to be judged according to the results they produce or whether they have a value independent of any result they engender.

## 2.3.1 Process values

Some US scholars have argued[19] that particular features of legal processes are 'process values', independent of whether or not these features contribute to better outcomes of legal processes. They argue that an infringement against such values would be wrong, even if the infringement leads to a 'good outcome'. The rationale behind this argument is that its verity is reflected in the saying 'the ends do not always justify the means'. In other words, adherents to the theory of process values argue that certain features of legal processes must not be changed, even if they have no apparent positive effect on the outcome.

It is submitted that this vague concept of 'process values' is not particularly helpful.[20] The notion of 'process values', in fact, only describes the problem of balancing conflicting results caused by different processes. While the ends may not always justify the means, the means can *only* be judged by the effects they cause (balancing the intended results and the unintended effects). For example, if we imagine a (truthful) confession resulting from torture, it could (superficially) be argued that an unfair procedure (torture) has lead to a fair result (ascertainment of the truth), or that the apparently fair (intended) result does not make the unfair procedure fair. In fact, the torture has not only lead to a fair result but also to unintended unfair results, in the sense that the torture left the tortured person psychologically and physically injured, and upset the confidence in the legal system. Hence the positive and negative results of the procedure have to be carefully balanced. A recent case in 2003[21] has renewed the discussion about whether torture could ever be justified, and undermines the absolute nature of process values. The case involved a law student named Magnus Gäfgen, who kidnapped a boy from a banker's family for a ransom. When the police arrested and interviewed Gäfgen, they thought

---

[19] R. S. Summers, 'Evaluating and Improving Legal Processes – A Plea for "Process Values"' (1974) 60 *Cornell Law Review* 1–52; M. H. Redish and L. C. Marshall, 'Adjudicatory Independence and the Values of Procedural Due Process' (1986) 95 *Yale Law Journal* 455–505, 482–91; G. Richardson and H. Genn, 'Tribunals in Transition: Resolution or Adjudication' [2007] *Public Law* 116–41, 120.

[20] D. J. Galligan, *Due Process and Fair Procedures* (Oxford: Clarendon Press, 1996), 9; even John Allison, who supports the notion of 'process values', admits: 'These values are a bit more slippery than instrumental ones such as accuracy, efficacy and efficiency . . . their amorphous nature also makes them less susceptible to consensus' ('A Process Value Analysis of Decision-Maker Bias: The Case of Economic Conflicts of Interest' (1995) 32 *American Business Law Journal* 481–540, 499).

[21] See the article by Jochen Bittner in *Die Zeit*: www.zeit.de/2003/31/urteil_280703?page=all [1 April 2008].

that the victim might still be alive and would have to be found very quickly to save his life. When Gäfgen showed reluctance to admit the location of his victim, the police threatened to cause him considerable pain. Gäfgen revealed the location of the victim and it turned out that he had murdered the boy. These illegal police tactics caused a loud outcry in Germany, and demands were made that torture should never be used, regardless of the circumstances. However, the discussion largely overlooked the fact that the threat of torture in this case was not used to obtain a confession for conviction (which would have been inadmissible in court) but in order to save another person's life. Balancing the boy's right to life with the right to bodily integrity of the accused may lead to the conclusion that torture could be justified in some very rare and extreme cases (albeit that it is far from clear whether torture is effective).

Legal processes are never an end in themselves but are designed to lead to particular results (such as, e.g., ascertaining the truth or the correct and fair application of the law to the facts). The aim of a fair procedure is not the process itself but the fact that it leads to a fair result, and it is the result by which the procedure is judged.[22] Where a process has been tainted with unfairness (e.g. a biased judge), the result will be unfair, since there is a *risk* that the outcome may have been affected, since it cannot be shown with certainty whether or not the outcome was in fact affected, and since trust in the integrity of the legal system has been undermined.[23] In other words, procedures have an instrumental or defining function: they serve the purpose of making the process and its result fair.[24] This cannot be more clearly expressed than through Rawls' concept of procedural justice, which will be discussed in the next section.

### 2.3.2 The Rawlsian concept of procedural justice

John Rawls has distinguished between four forms of procedural justice.[25] For the first two forms (perfect procedural justice and imperfect procedural justice) it is clear what the *fair* outcome of the procedure would be, and the purpose of the procedure is to achieve or approximate this outcome. In other words, for perfect and imperfect procedural justice it can be objectively ascertained *a priori* what a fair outcome is, and the procedure is *instrumental* in achieving this.

---

[22] See also Galligan, *Due Process and Fair Procedures*, 65.
[23] *R v. Sussex Justices, ex parte McCarthy* [1924] 1 KB 256 (Divisional Court), and see 6.3.
[24] Galligan, *Due Process and Fair Procedures*, 62.
[25] J. Rawls, *A Theory of Justice*, revised edn (Oxford University Press, 1999), 74–5, 176.

In particular, for cases of *perfect* procedural justice, the procedure, if properly applied, realises the fair outcome. An illustration of this is the rule applied between two persons sharing a cake, where one person cuts the cake into two pieces and the other chooses which piece he or she takes. In this case the fair outcome is equal treatment, and this is achieved by the cake-cutter having an incentive to cut two pieces as equal as possible. In cases of *imperfect* procedural justice, the procedure has only an approximating function. In other words, the procedure merely increases the chances of the fair outcome. Examples for this are fact-finding procedures in civil and criminal trials, where part of the fair outcome is finding the facts of what happened. These procedures are called imperfect because the rules of evidence only imperfectly lead to the truth: 'the characteristic mark of imperfect procedural justice is that while there is an independent criterion for the correct outcome, there is no feasible procedure which is sure to lead to it'.[26]

By contrast, for the other two forms of procedural justice (pure and quasi-pure procedural justice), rules *define* the outcome as being fair. From merely looking at the outcomes of these procedures, it is not discernible as to whether or not the outcomes are fair – there is no independent criterion to assess whether or not the result is fair. In other words, it is the design of the procedural rules and their correct application that define the outcome as being fair.[27]

*Pure procedural justice* defines an outcome as fair, for example a game of chance allocating statistically equal chances of winning or losing to each participant. While it cannot be said that it is fair that this or the other participant wins, provided the rules have properly been applied, the outcome will be fair. *Quasi-pure procedural* rules also define the outcome as fair, but the rules might be contentious, as it is not statistically verifiable whether or not they lead to a fair result. According to Rawls, the function of quasi-pure procedural justice is to define the limits of discretion of a decision-maker for the selection of an outcome, which is merely one fair outcome of many possible other fair outcomes.[28]

Applying Rawls' conceptualisation to dispute resolution, dispute resolution involves both fact-finding processes and processes requiring the exercise of discretion, such as contract bargaining (e.g. in mediation) and law application (e.g. in adjudication, such as arbitration or before an ombudsman), for the latter to the extent that the application of law

---

[26] *Ibid.* 75.    [27] Galligan, *Due Process and Fair Procedures*, 62.
[28] Rawls, *A Theory of Justice*, 176.

involves a power of discretion, for example in the interpretation of the law.

The fact-finding part of the processes should be governed by rules of imperfect procedural justice to ensure that there is a great likelihood that the facts are found out correctly. However, contract bargaining and the exercise of discretion in applying and interpreting law require procedural rules to define them as fair, as it is impossible to discern from the outcome itself whether or not a particular interpretation of the law is fair or unfair.[29]

Lisa Bingham, in her examination of the fairness of arbitration awards in employment arbitration, emphasises the difficulty of measuring the fairness in terms of distributive justice of the outcome and accuracy of fact-finding and law application in dispute resolution: 'accuracy, both positive in the sense of correct fact finding and normative in the sense of correct application of decision standards is notoriously hard to measure in any dispute resolution process'.[30] For this reason, the standard of fairness has to be measured by the procedure. Lon Fuller also argues that the procedure of participation by presenting proofs and reasoned arguments by both parties *defines* the fairness and integrity of adjudication.[31]

Imperfect procedural justice and quasi-pure procedural justice both deal with deficiencies in human knowledge – the procedure is instrumental in filling this gap in human knowledge. In other words, we have no way to find the absolute factual accuracy; nor have we any means of ascertaining what the right decision is in the sense of normative regularity. We only have procedures, which we have good reason to believe will lead to the right result. This deficiency of knowledge explains the importance of public confidence in legal procedures and notions such as 'justice must be seen to be done'.[32]

In conclusion, rather than defining absolute procedural values (such as process values), it is more helpful to regard dispute resolution processes as governed by two types of procedural rules: (i) rules that are *instrumental* in establishing the truth underlying factual disputes and (ii) rules that *define* the boundaries of a fair exercise of discretion in applying and interpreting the law. The next section explains how due process realises both these functions.

---

[29] Allison, 'A Process Value Analysis of Decision-Maker Bias', 493.
[30] L. Bingham, 'On Repeat Players, Adhesive Contracts, and the Use of Statistics in Judicial Review of Employment Arbitration Awards' (1998) 29 *McGeorge Law Review* 223–59, 257–9.
[31] Fuller, 'The Forms and Limits of Adjudication', 364.
[32] Galligan, *Due Process and Fair Procedures*, 66 and 72.

## 2.4 Due process

John Rawls considers the principle of due process[33] as critical for securing the greatest equal liberty of citizens.[34] He maintains that 'even in a well-ordered society the coercive powers of government are to some degree necessary for the stability of social co-operation'.[35] Hence it is critical that these coercive powers are exercised in an impartial manner and in accordance with the rule of law.[36]

The notion of due process (or natural justice) comprises two fundamental principles: the principle that no-one should be a judge in his or her own cause (meaning that judges should be independent and impartial) and the principle of a fair hearing (meaning that each party should have an equal opportunity to present evidence and law).[37]

The purpose of the principle of impartiality is to ensure that the judge treats the parties equally, maintains an open mind and does not take into account irrelevant considerations,[38] hence contributing to equal treatment and the rationality of the decision and thereby to the fairness of the decision. An impartial mind is also required to ascertain the facts accurately, and is therefore a rule of imperfect procedural justice. However, it is also a rule of quasi-pure procedural justice in that it means that the judge applies his or her discretion without prejudgement or prejudice and therefore defines any resulting interpretation of the law as fair.

Similarly, the purpose of the principle of a fair hearing[39] is to ensure that each party participates in the process and has an opportunity to present their side of the case, thereby ensuring equality between the parties and rationality of the ensuing decision, and hence, ultimately, fairness. Furthermore, a fair hearing is instrumental to finding the facts underlying the case, and can therefore be described as a rule of imperfect procedural justice. However, to the extent that the parties present legal arguments, the principle of fair hearing also leads to a balanced application of discretion; it is therefore also a rule of quasi-pure procedural justice.

While due process is concerned with equal treatment, it ignores pre-existing inequalities between the parties. It gives each party a formally

---

[33] See Chapter 6.     [34] Rawls, *A Theory of Justice*, 210–11.     [35] *Ibid.* 211.
[36] *Ibid.* 210; for the argument that arbitration is coercive and should therefore comport with notions of due process, see 6.2.5.
[37] S. H. Bailey, J. P. L. Ching, M. J. Gunn and D. C. Ormerod, *Smith, Bailey and Gunn: On the Modern Legal System*, 4th edn (London: Sweet & Maxwell, 2002), 280, 1315; See also Chapter 6.
[38] See further at 6.3.     [39] See 6.4.

equal opportunity to participate but ignores any difference in the parties' *actual ability* to participate.

## 2.5 The difference principle: counter-balancing existing inequalities

John Rawls in his contract theory establishes two main principles for ensuring fairness in a well-ordered society.[40] As has been mentioned, the first principle is that of the greatest possible equal liberty, conferring equal basic rights and duties on all individuals. The second principle has two limbs, i.e. that there should be fair equality of opportunity and that the interests of the most disadvantaged groups of society should be advanced to close the gap between the most disadvantaged and the most advantaged: 'social and economic inequalities, for example inequalities of wealth and authority, are just only if they result in compensating benefits for everyone, and in particular for the least advantaged members of society'.[41]

John Rawls argues that these two principles would be chosen as the governing principles of justice by the imaginary founders of society (he calls this the 'original position'), if they were not acting in their own self-interest. This absence of self-interest could be guaranteed by the founders wearing what he calls the 'veil of ignorance' (i.e. they would not know their position in society, which groups or class they would belong to). Rawls uses this fiction of the 'veil of ignorance' (which is in itself an example of quasi-procedural justice) to convince us that the resulting principles are fair.[42]

Although equality is stipulated as a principle, it is also significant that Rawls acknowledges that equality cannot be achieved by mere equal treatment. Rawls' second principle demonstrates that it is necessary to counterbalance the inequalities existing in real societies. Hence in a Rawlsian sense, fairness is more than mere equal treatment. This argument that fairness transcends mere equality is a very important contribution to the conceptualisation of fairness.

Likewise, for Jürgen Habermas the defining (quasi-procedural) determinant of fairness is equal participation in legal discourses. This equal participation is more than the formal equality we have found in the notion of due process. In Habermas' view, it is critical that the parties can participate on an equal footing in legal processes.[43]

---

[40] Rawls, *A Theory of Justice*, 53.     [41] *Ibid.* 13.     [42] *Ibid.* 118–22.
[43] J. Habermas, *Faktizität und Geltung* (Frankfurt am Main: Suhrkamp, 1992), 187 and 516.

Habermas, like Rawls, effectively argues that power imbalances must be levelled out through procedural fairness,[44] and he expressly refers to Rawls' quasi-procedural justice.[45] However Habermas assumes that this is less important for adjudication, for the reason that judicial proceedings have institutionalised fair participation of both parties.[46] Habermas distinguishes between *negotiations* that *require* procedures to ensure that all interests are represented, that power imbalances are levelled out and that coercive powers do not prejudice the outcome,[47] and *judicial proceedings*, which have institutionalised due process.[48] Judicial proceedings define and limit the space in which the argumentation takes place; participation, roles, issues and the processes forming opinions and decisions are regulated. These procedural regulations are necessary to endue judicial proceedings with quasi-procedural justice.[49] Habermas, like Rawls, argues that equal participation of the parties has to be guaranteed through procedural rules.

For dispute resolution, Rawls' and Habermas' theories mean that due process (as defined above: equal treatment and rationality) in itself is not sufficient. It is not sufficient to merely ensure that the parties are treated equally and that decisions are rational, accurate and according to the rule of law. In addition, in cases in which a significant power imbalance exists between the parties, fairness means that measures must be taken to redress this power imbalance to ensure equal participation by the parties. Therefore the principle of due process in dispute resolution is a *sine qua non* condition, but is not sufficient to guarantee fairness of procedures. Additional steps must be taken to redress power imbalances. This requirement of a counterpoise to existing power imbalances is an important aspect of fairness, one which is neglected if one merely focuses on due process.

Various methods can be used to redress such power imbalances, the most important of which are legal aid or other mechanisms that give the disadvantaged party greater access to redress (such as small claims procedures in consumer cases). Many of these mechanisms will be of a distributive nature (such as legal aid). A detailed discussion of these distributive mechanisms is outside the scope of this book, which instead focuses on procedural rules in extra-judicial dispute resolution.

---

[44] *Ibid.* 205.    [45] *Ibid.* 220.

[46] *Ibid.*; similar reasoning can be found in Fuller, 'The Forms and Limits of Adjudication', 366–7.

[47] Habermas, *Faktizität und Geltung*, 218.    [48] *Ibid.* 219.    [49] *Ibid.* 220.

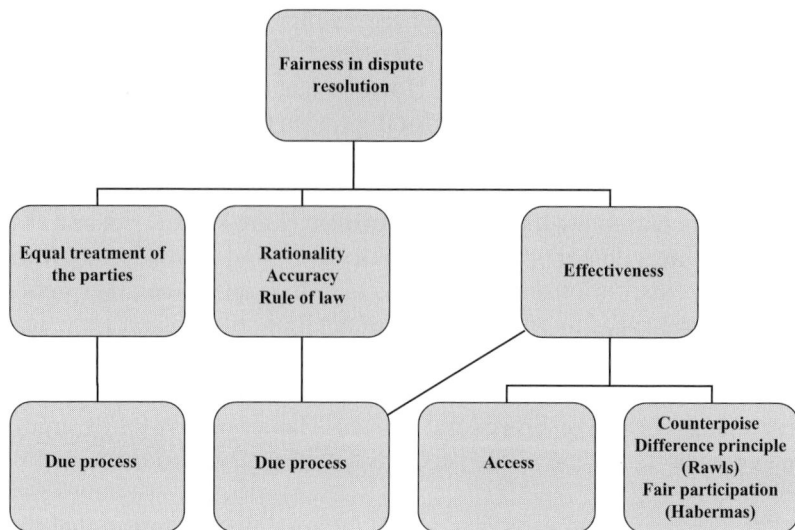

**Fig. 2.** The three elements of fairness in relation to due process and Habermas' and Rawls' theories.

Furthermore, this book only considers power imbalances in dispute resolution. It does not examine the existence of power imbalances generally, nor whether and how the substantive law (such as consumer-protection law) should address or redress such power imbalances.

Chapter 3 discusses power imbalances in the context of Internet disputes. It considers the factors giving power in dispute resolution and puts forward general criteria for legally determining the presence of a power imbalance between disputants. However, it would be costly and cumbersome to carry out such an assessment on a case-by-case basis for each dispute *ex post*. The approach has to be a general, *ex ante* approach, which establishes an irrebuttable presumption that a power imbalance is present if the parties have a certain status. This is the approach taken in consumer-protection law, and will be further discussed in Chapter 3.[50]

Figure 2 illustrates how the three elements of fairness discussed in the first section relate to due process and Habermas' and Rawls' theories.

The next question is how the three elements of fairness relate to each other. The more all three elements of fairness could be augmented at the same time, the fairer the ensuing procedure would be. Regrettably, this may not be possible, as the next section will explain.

---

[50] See 3.6.

## 2.6 The inherent conflict between due process and effectiveness

It is posited here that an inherent conflict exists between due process and effectiveness (access and the counterpoise). Due process require-ments make legal procedures more elaborate and more strategic, involv-ing the expenditure of precious resources and time, and are therefore apt to render legal processes lengthy and costly. They are thus likely to reduce the effectiveness of dispute resolution. Increased costs and delay not only make procedures less effective and less accessible but may also reinforce existing power imbalances.[51] Increased costs and delay put the stronger party at an advantage and the weaker party at a disadvantage. Therefore, a high degree of due process in legal procedure necessitates even greater efforts at providing access and a counterpoise to existing inequalities. If such efforts are not made, a higher degree of due process may well be counter-productive for fairness. Since there is a limit to the extent to which it is possible to use resources to increase access and to counter-balance existing inequalities, there is, logically, also a limit to due process.

This conflict is reflected in Axel Tschentscher's criticism of Habermas' discourse theory and Rawls' contract theory. He argues that they are unrealistic in practice. Factually existing inequalities in society make equal and non-coercive participation in legal processes impossible.[52]

This conflict is also the underlying cause for the difficulty of balancing funding and fairness of dispute resolution procedures. If the procedure is expensive, access is restricted (in particular for a party with few resources, such as a consumer) or the cost might be disproportionate to the value of the claim. If the procedure is initiated, set-up, designed, financed and subscribed to by one stakeholder only (such as a business association in B2C disputes), it is likely that the procedure may not be neutral, and will be contrary to due process requirements. In the reverse, a procedure with limited due process that is fast and cheap is likely to be 'rough justice' and is likely to infringe on due process principles.

William Park tells the anecdote of a shoe shop in Boston that displayed a notice in a window listing the following characteristics of its service: 'fast service', 'low price' and 'high quality', with the caption 'pick any two'.[53]

---

[51] See 3.5 for power in dispute resolution.
[52] Tschentscher, 'The Function of Procedural Justice' 114–15; see also H. J. Friendly, 'Some Kind of Hearing', 1276.
[53] Park, *Procedural Evolution in Business Arbitration*, 50.

The same applies to dispute resolution.[54] Hence the challenge is to find the 'right' balance between due process and effectiveness.

However, in the reverse, it is also true to say that if effectiveness can be increased (e.g. through state funding[55] or through technology[56]) more due process can be afforded. Hence it can be argued that measures should be taken to increase both due process and effectiveness; this will be discussed in Chapter 8.[57]

## 2.7 Conclusion

This brief chapter has advanced the proposition that fairness consists of three fundamental principles – due process and access and a counterpoise – to reduce pre-existing inequalities. Traditionally, the notion of due process has ensured that the parties are treated equally and that dispute resolution is a rational, accurate and regular process. However, in the twentieth century there has been some emphasis on power imbalances and the need to equalise pre-existing inequalities, as, for example, espoused in Rawls' difference principle. If one accepts that fairness requires due process, access and a counterpoise to pre-existing inequalities, a conflict results. If due process is increased, access is likely to be reduced and a greater counterpoise is required. This chapter has shown that there is an inherent conflict between due process, which tends to make dispute resolution less accessible and less effective, which requires that access to dispute resolution is increased. Therefore the challenge of any fair dispute resolution system is to find the 'right' balance between these principles. There is a wide range of methods that might be used to increase access and to reduce pre-existing inequalities; this book will look at one particular method: Chapter 5 discusses the potential of ODR to increase access to justice and its ability to act as a counterpoise against existing procedural power imbalances. This book will also show in Chapters 6 and 7 that concerns exist as to whether ODR complies with due process requirements. However, before these aspects of fairness are debated and weighed up, it will be expedient to demonstrate why alternative dispute resolution (ADR) and ODR are needed for Internet disputes in the first place. This will be the task of the next chapter.

---

[54] *Ibid.* 48–50.     [55] See 8.5 on the need for a subsidy from general taxation.
[56] See 5.5 on online dispute resolution (ODR) and access to justice.
[57] See 8.2 and 8.5.

# 3

## Internet disputes

If there is a technological advance without a social advance, there is, almost automatically, an increase in human misery.

(Michael Harrington, 1928–89)

### 3.1 Introduction

The purpose of this chapter is to circumscribe the types of disputes this book is concerned with. It starts by conceptualising the characteristics underlying the Internet and why this makes the resolution of Internet disputes difficult. The chapter then discusses the nature of the Internet as a powerful multi-media communications channel, which has enabled individuals and consumers to take part in international interactions, cross-border E-commerce, international publishing and the distribution of user-generated content on an unprecedented scale. By way of illustration, this chapter sketches some typical international disputes that arise (or hypothetically may arise) on the Internet. This leads to a concern about cross-border disputes involving individuals, their access to cross-border litigation, and power imbalances, where one party has many more resources for disputing than the other.

### 3.2 Characteristics of the Internet

By way of an overview, this section briefly outlines the main characteristics of the Internet, and assesses the implications of these characteristics for Internet disputes.

Before discussing the characteristics of the Internet, a definition of the term 'Internet' is called for. The Internet essentially is a medium for communications that allows data exchanges between computers across the world. The Internet consists of hardware, a set of protocols called the TCP-IP set of protocols and various software applications such as the

World Wide Web, email, peer-to-peer file-sharing systems, ftp and news-groups, which allow computers (and ultimately the persons sitting behind these computers) to communicate with each other.[1] The technology of the Internet connects networks of networks of computers worldwide. It is important to point out that the phrase 'on the Internet' (just like the phrases 'on the television' or 'on the telephone') does not relate to a particular place but to a communications medium for the provision or collection of data.[2]

### 3.2.1  Location irrelevant for functionality

The Internet is a transnational communications medium that enables the seamless exchange of information through various applications (such as email or the World Wide Web) across national borders at a high speed.

Location is irrelevant for the functionality of applications used on the Internet. In principle, information on a networked computer can be exchanged with any other networked computer, regardless of its geographical location. The reason for this is that the Internet-protocol address system used to locate computers on the Internet is not structured according to geographic or political borders.[3] In other words, the logic underlying the Internet-protocol address system is not congruent with geographical borders. For this reason, the Internet can be described as 'borderless' or ubiquitous, and the location of computers on the Internet is irrelevant for both receiving/accessing and providing/sending information.

David Johnson and David Post in their famous article 'Law and Borders – the Rise of Law in Cyberspace', have emphasised the borderless nature of the Internet:

> Cyberspace has no territorially based boundaries, because the cost and speed of message transmission on the Net is almost entirely independent of physical location. Messages can be transmitted from one physical location

---

[1] Sometimes the word 'Internet' is used in a loose sense to refer to the World Wide Web, but strictly speaking this is incorrect, and I avoid such use of the word.
[2] See C. Reed, *Internet Law*, 2nd edn (Cambridge University Press, 2004), 8–13.
[3] D. Johnson and D. Post, 'Law and Borders – the Rise of Law in Cyberspace' (1996) 48 *Stanford Law Review* 1367–402, 1370–71; J. Reidenberg, 'Governing Networks and Rule-Making in Cyberspace' (1996) 45 *Emory Law Journal* 911–30, 913–14; H. Perritt, 'The Internet is Changing the Public International Legal System' (1999–2000) 88 *Kentucky Law Journal* 885–955, 886–8.

to any other location without degradation, decay or substantial delay, and without any physical cues or barriers.[4]

Also, Christopher Marsden writes:

> The ubiquity, rapid penetration and commonplace necessity of international data flows over digital communications networks . . . combined with the economic and social effects of such flows, makes the Internet the paradigm of globalisation: it was 'born global'.[5]

This ubiquity of the Internet is limited in some parts of the world by the conditions of the infrastructure, which are not the same in each country (fixed/mobile telephony, affordability of Internet access, broadband availability). However, provided there is capacity to access the network, communication is not contingent on physical proximity between sender and recipient. The Internet enables communication over large distances at low cost.

The borderless nature of the Internet means that more interactions and transactions are involving parties located in different jurisdictions. Therefore there is a likelihood of a greater number of small-value, cross-border disputes. For such disputes, it is difficult and complex to find a competent court, determine the applicable law and ensure enforcement.

### 3.2.2 Difficulty of establishing location of Internet users

Internet-protocol addresses, URLs (Uniform Resource Locators) and email addresses are opaque in the sense that they do not necessarily reveal the location or identity of the person operating the computer(s) thus identified on the Internet.

Any particular access point on the Internet is identified by an Internet-protocol address. Internet-protocol addresses contain four numbers, each in the range of 0 to 255, separated by a dot. Internet-protocol addresses are not structured according to geographic locations. Therefore an Internet-protocol address does not by itself disclose the geographical location of a user.

---

[4] Johnson and Post, 'Law and Borders', 1370–1.

[5] C. Marsden, 'Introduction: Information and Communications Technologies, Globalisation and Regulation', in C. Marsden (ed.), *Regulating the Global Information Society* (London: Routledge, 2000), 1–40, 2.

However, it should be pointed out that, as a reaction to the difficulty of determining the location of Internet users, technologies have been developed that look up the likely location of the user from that user's Internet-protocol address.[6] Since Internet-protocol addresses have been allocated in blocks, it is possible for such technologies to map most Internet-protocol addresses. Some editorials have argued that this development means that borders are returning to the Internet.[7] However, this is an exaggeration – it is debatable how accurately geolocation tools can predict the location of a computer connected to the Internet,[8] and they are not used for all Internet interactions and transactions.

Domain names do not reveal much about the user's location. A domain name is an alphanumeric label corresponding to an Internet-protocol address.[9] Domain names were introduced because they were easier to remember than a string of Internet-protocol numbers. URLs (locating a resource on the World Wide Web, such as www.iana.org/root-whois/tm.htm) and email addresses (such as a.name@qmul.ac.uk) are based on domain names. Domain names are hierarchical. The last suffix such as .edu or .uk is the top-level domain, which can either be generic (such as .edu, .com, .biz, .museum, .pro, .name, .aero, .int, .net, .org) or country-specific (so-called 'country-code' domain names, such as .uk). However, even a country-code top-level domain name does not necessarily indicate that the registrant of that name is located in that country. Some country-code top-level domain registries (such as that of Turkmenistan[10]) register non-resident users for their country-code top-level domain.

This difficulty of establishing a user's location means that users interact and transact without being aware of the geographical location of each other. If a dispute arises, they may have to face the fact that their

---

[6] Examples are www.quova.com and www.digitalenvoy.net [1 April 2008].

[7] B. Tedeschi, 'E-Commerce: Borders Returning to the Internet', *New York Times* (2 April 2001); 'Putting It in Its Place', *The Economist* (9 August 2001).

[8] In *LICRA and UEJF v. Yahoo! Inc and Yahoo France*, Tribunal de Grande Instance de Paris, 20 November 2000, the appointed expert panel found that Internet-protocol mapping is about 70 per cent accurate (mapping the Internet-protocol addresses to a particular country). For a more detailed description of geolocation tools and their limitation, see ITAA, *E-Commerce Taxation and the Limitations of Geolocation Tools*, available from www.itaa.org/taxfinance/docs/geolocationpaper.pdf [1 April 2008].

[9] W. Black, 'The Domain Name System', in L. Edwards and C. Waelde, *Law & the Internet*, 2nd edn (Oxford: Hart Publishing, 2000), 125–32, 125–6.

[10] .tm is popular for trademark domain names; anyone can register. See the .tm Registry website: www.nic.tm [1 April 2008].

counter-party(ies) is (are) unexpectedly located in another jurisdiction or many locations, as the case may be.

Twinned to the question of location is the question of identity. The only trace a user leaves is anything they choose to disclose about themselves and their Internet-protocol address, neither of which are, in many cases, sufficient to establish a person's identity.[11] The recipient of an Internet communication cannot presume that the sender is the person he/she claims to be. Attributes of a person such as his or her name and geographical address are more difficult to assess and verify in an Internet communication than in face-to-face communication. Some Internet interactions (such as postings on discussion boards) are routinely carried out under a pseudonym. These factors mean that for many claimants in Internet disputes, it may be difficult to establish the defendant's identity and to trace his or her whereabouts and assets, which is clearly a prerequisite to starting proceedings. While tracing the defendant is an important practical, preliminary aspect of dispute resolution, it is not a point directly related to the dispute resolution procedure; hence, the question of how to establish a person's identity on the Internet will not be further discussed in this book.

### 3.2.3 Increase in transnational contacts – a quantitative and qualitative change

To some extent, international trade, shipping, aviation and 'older' communications media (telex, telephone and fax) have also crossed borders and therefore have posed a challenge to dispute resolution. However, the Internet multiplies and amplifies that challenge as it allows for many more multi-media applications. Unlike 'older' communications media, such as telephone and fax, the Internet allows for truly *multi*-media applications. Not just voice, not just text, but images, graphics, video, audio, music and software can be transferred from any computer to any other computer on a connected network.

In the offline world, international trade and international publishing traditionally were largely confined to 'sophisticated' business or professional people. By contrast, on the Internet, anyone can publish on an

---

[11] Some access providers allocate Internet-protocol addresses dynamically so that several connections share it. If the access provider keeps a record as to which connection used which Internet-protocol address at which time, it is possible to trace the connection. Furthermore, several users might share one connection, or several persons may have access to that same connection.

international scale,[12] and consumers and small-business entities, such as sole traders, can buy/sell directly from/to an individual located abroad.[13] The Internet has lowered barriers to transactions and interactions by lowering communication costs and other transaction costs (such as those associated with payment).

Moreover, the arrival of the Internet, and in particular the World Wide Web, is changing the distribution and communication patterns of trade. In the pre-Internet age, consumers mostly bought from retail suppliers located in their own country, and cross-border transactions were largely confined to organised business-to-business (B2B) distribution.

Now, consumers can easily buy goods and services directly from a vast network of foreign suppliers on the Web. Likewise, a small business may procure its input requirements through a B2B exchange from a small or large player located on the other side of the planet.

For business on the Internet, the costs of setting up an international business, which previously has required the establishment of branches and agencies in different countries, are almost the same as for a purely local one. This is even more so if the Internet business sells digitalised products (i.e. information products downloaded via the Web) and if it uses automated decision-making and processing.[14] Therefore these low barriers of entry and access have enabled even very small businesses to offer their goods and services on a global scale to small and large players alike. In addition, auction platforms such as eBay enable consumers (and small businesses) to sell internationally on a large scale. Social networking sites such as Facebook or MySpace and game providers such as Second Life also enable transnational interactions between individuals.

Thus it seems fair to state that the Internet has intensified international contacts and transactions at and between all levels. This entails a greater number of cross-border disputes involving small businesses, consumers and other non-professional, 'unsophisticated' parties. Therefore the Internet gives rise to many disputes with a significant power imbalance between the parties.

---

[12] A. Reed, 'Jurisdiction and Choice of Law in a Borderless Electronic Environment', in Y. Akdeniz, C. Walker and D. Wall (eds.), *The Internet Law and Society* (Harlow: Longman, 2000), 79–106, 104; L. Edwards, 'Defamation and the Internet', in L. Edwards and C. Waelde, *Law & the Internet*, 2nd edn (Oxford: Hart Publishing, 2000), 249–73, 250.

[13] V. Heiskanen, 'Dispute Resolution in International Electronic Commerce' (1999) 16 *Journal of International Arbitration* 29–44, 29–30; I. Lloyd, *Legal Aspects of the Information Society* (London: Butterworths, 2000), 268.

[14] Reed, *Internet Law*, 5.

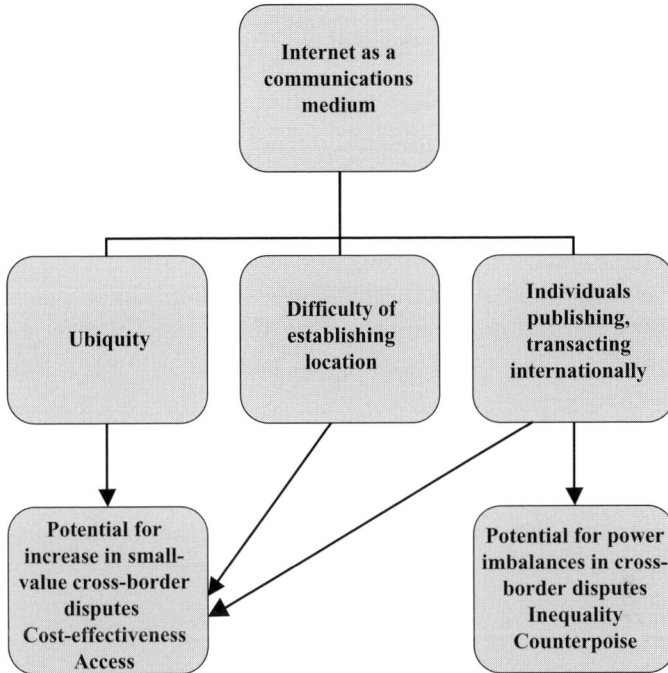

**Fig. 3.** Characteristics of the Internet and implications for Internet disputes.

### 3.2.4 Conclusion: the implications for Internet disputes

The characteristics of the Internet that inform this discussion are its borderless, ubiquitous nature, the difficulty of establishing a user's location and the fact that it allows direct, multi-media communications and transactions between individuals on a global basis. It follows from these characteristics that the Internet is causing an increase in cross-border disputes, a number of which will be of small value and/or involve a significant power imbalance between the parties. In other words, there are three features that cause issues for dispute resolution: (i) parties located in two different jurisdictions, (ii) the small value of the dispute, and (iii) power imbalances. In many Internet disputes, these factors are combined.

Figure 3 illustrates the characteristics of the Internet and their implications for disputes. Power imbalances are a matter of concern, as they infringe the equality principle, the significance of which has been discussed in Chapter 2.[15] It is the function of the following sections of this chapter

---

[15] See 2.2 and 2.5.

to describe and illustrate the types of cross-border Internet disputes that give rise to significant power imbalances.

## 3.3  Examples of Internet disputes

In this book, Internet disputes are disputes connected to the use of the Internet in a *wide sense*. This includes *all* disputes arising from the parties communicating, interacting or transacting through the Internet, as well as disputes about the technology itself (such as disputes about the registration of domain names). Thus the phrase 'Internet disputes' encompasses all types of private disputes based on actionable rights and entitlements.

For the purposes of this book, E-commerce disputes are a subcategory of Internet disputes, i.e. disputes of a commercial nature, which are based on a contractual relationship between the parties. Depending on the nature of the parties to the dispute, a further distinction can be made between B2B, B2C and consumer-to-consumer (C2C) E-commerce disputes.

Clearly the phrase 'Internet disputes' is indeterminate. An endless variety of disputes occur on the Internet or about the Internet. Since this book is concerned with the fairness of dispute resolution, the task is to describe and illustrate the types of 'Internet disputes' giving rise to concerns about fairness. As has been outlined in the preceding section, these are, particularly, Internet disputes where the parties are of significantly unequal power, and/or the parties are located in two different jurisdictions. Hence this book ignores Internet disputes where the disputants are fairly sophisticated business parties, even if both parties are in different jurisdictions, as such disputes can be and are, in practice, resolved by traditional litigation or arbitration. This section briefly illustrates examples of the disputes this book is most concerned about.

### Example 1

A sole trader in Nigeria concludes a contract with a large company – manufacturing locally in China and trading internationally – for some widgets through a B2B E-commerce trading platform. The widgets are defective and the sole trader seeks redress for breach of contract.

### Example 2

A consumer in Chile enters into a contract with a large US travel company for a cruise holiday through an E-commerce website. However, the cruise is cancelled at the last minute and the deposit of $2000 has not been refunded. The consumer seeks a refund of the deposit paid.

## Example 3

The owner of a bricks and mortar shop located in Dublin (sole trader) has named her shop 'Crate & Barrel', and she also operates a website connected to her shop under the domain www.crateandbarrel.biz. A large US company running an extensive chain of stores present in most states of the US claims infringement of their US federal trademark in the same name, and commences infringement proceedings against the unincorporated Irish trader before a US district court. The owner cannot afford litigation in the United States, and the US district court enters default judgment in favour of the US corporation. The domain name is transferred to the US corporation.[16]

## Example 4

A US-based corporation publishes a video clip on an interactive, online news platform, accusing a named Egyptian civil servant of belonging to a terrorist organisation. The Egyptian individual seeks redress for defamation.

## Example 5

A US citizen uploads potentially defamatory comments about an internationally famous Australian film star on his own website. These comments are copied and downloaded widely and thus propagated on a global basis. The film star commences proceedings against the US citizen before his local Australian court for defamation.

## Example 6

A large Russian company illegally hacks into the server of an English inventor in order to obtain confidential, sensitive information. The English inventor seeks redress for damages arising from this unlawful action.

Chapter 8[17] will return to these examples and consider if and to what extent the model of dispute resolution developed in this book can provide a fair resolution of such disputes.

All six examples of Internet disputes involve parties in two different jurisdictions whose contact is enabled and intermediated by the Internet.

---

[16] See *Euromarket Designs Inc* v. *Crate & Barrel Ltd and Peters*, 96 FSupp2d 824.
[17] See 8.2.1.

It is unlikely that these parties would have come into conflict in the offline, pre-Internet world. Five of the examples pitch an individual against a large incorporated organisation, either as claimant or defendant. These examples illustrate the cross-border nature of some Internet disputes coupled with a power imbalance between the parties. The examples mentioned are not limited to contractual disputes but include tortious and other disputes.

The next question is whether the argument set forth in this book covers disputes between individuals (such as, but not limited to, a C2C dispute). These disputes are less problematic from the point of view of fairness,[18] as it is less likely that there is a significant power imbalance between the parties.[19] The lack of a power imbalance makes it more likely that the parties can successfully use ADR/ODR to solve their dispute. However, even if there is no pre-existing power imbalance between the parties, in small-claims, cross-border Internet disputes, the parties will have no, or limited, access to the courts. This means that they have no recourse to effective dispute resolution, which leads to unfairness.[20] Since ADR/ODR operates in the 'shadow of the law',[21] this will impact on the effectiveness and fairness of extra-judicial dispute resolution. Therefore such Internet disputes between individuals are included in this book, and the model outlined in Chapter 8[22] will include them.

### 3.4 Contract and tort

Only courts have coercive powers. Extra-judicial means of dispute resolution require an agreement between the parties to participate.[23] This agreement can be concluded before or after the dispute has arisen. Parties to a contract may well incorporate a clause about dispute resolution in their contract, thereby binding themselves to participate in dispute resolution long before a dispute arises. By contrast, parties to a tort dispute frequently have had no previous relationship or contact with each other, which raises the question of how these parties can agree to extra-judicial dispute resolution. In some instances the parties may agree to use such dispute resolution after the dispute has arisen, but in other instances this is unlikely. If the weaker party is a claimant who cannot afford litigation, it is unlikely that the stronger defendant will agree to use other forms of settlement, as in examples 1, 2, 4 and 6. By not agreeing to use

---

[18] See Chapter 2.     [19] See 3.5.     [20] See 2.2.3.
[21] See 4.2.1.     [22] See 8.6.     [23] See 4.2.

alternative forms of dispute resolution, the defendant can effectively stall the claimant's attempts to obtain redress.

However, there might be models other than a bilateral agreement to bind a defendant to extra-judicial dispute resolution. For example, if the unlawful act is committed using technology controlled by a third-party intermediary, such as a platform provider, this third party may bind the users of that technology to take part in extra-judicial dispute resolution.[24] Therefore the use of extra-judicial dispute resolution is not limited to contractual disputes.

## 3.5  Power in dispute resolution

A power imbalance essentially arises if one party has significantly more power than the other. This imbalance raises the question of what gives power in dispute resolution.

Power manifests itself in different forms, and power relationships are frequently complex. Power itself is affected by the perception the parties have of their own power and that of the other party.[25]

This section considers the meaning of power in dispute resolution and negotiation of legal relationships, suggesting that three main factors can be distinguished: (i) resources, (ii) whether a party is a repeat player and (iii) vulnerability.

### 3.5.1  Resources

One obvious factor is a party's resources to fight a case or negotiate a contract. By way of illustration, this encompasses financial resources, human resources, legal know-how, access to internal or external legal advice (in particular on foreign law) and the ability to engage top lawyers in the relevant jurisdiction(s).[26]

### 3.5.2  'Repeat player' effect and power

Marc Galanter has coined the term 'repeat player' for parties who have been regularly involved in similar types of disputes. This can be contrasted with the 'one-shotters', for whom the dispute at issue is the only dispute

---

[24]  See 8.2.1.
[25]  H. Brown and A. Marriott, *ADR Principles and Practice*, 2nd edn (London: Sweet & Maxwell, 1999), 479.
[26]  Brown and Marriott, *ADR Principles and Practice*, 479; Nader and Shugart, 'Old Solutions for Old Problems', 64–5.

of that kind they have ever been involved with.[27] The repeat players are at a substantial advantage, for several reasons:[28]

(i) They have acquired legal knowledge and access to specialist lawyers through their previous involvement.
(ii) They have knowledge and experience of the relevant dispute resolution processes and institutions.
(iii) They benefit from economies of scale in their dispute resolution practice.
(iv) They can engage in strategic behaviour by settling some cases but not others, thereby creating precedents favourable to them.
(v) They can engage in lobbying activities to change the law in their favour.
(vi) They have informal continuing relationships with the relevant institutions and have established a client relationship with such institutions.

For these reasons, repeat players have strategic advantages and more power in their disputes with one-shotters.[29] Lisa Bingham in her empirical study of 1998 comparing the statistics of non-repeat and repeat appointments of arbitrators by employers, has clearly shown that employers are at an advantage over employees where they make repeat appointments.[30]

The next question is: who are the typical repeat players in Internet disputes? In the examples mentioned above, it seems that the 'bigger' party is likely to be a repeat player, in the sense that they are more frequently involved in similar disputes. In examples 1 and 2, the large manufacturer of widgets or a large travel company is more likely to have encountered similar complaints by other sole traders or consumers. Large and sophisticated owners of intellectual property (IP), such as a trademark registration (example 3), are likely to defend their rights on a regular basis and have strategies in place for doing so.[31] Finally, large publishers of news are

---

[27] M. Galanter, 'Why the "Haves" Come Out Ahead: Speculations on the Limits of Legal Change' (1974) 9 *Law and Society Review* 95–160, 97.
[28] Galanter, 'Why the "Haves" Come Out Ahead', 103; Bingham, 'On Repeat Players', 240–4.
[29] See also 6.6.1.
[30] Bingham, 'On Repeat Players', 236–9; see also A. S. Rau, 'Integrity in Private Judging' (1997) 38 *South Texas Law Review* 485–539, 524.
[31] However, this does not mean that the more powerful player (in terms of size and resources) is always the repeat player; one could think about an individual, who is a serial cybersquatter, registering the domain names of various large entities and hence getting involved in various pieces of litigation or other domain-name dispute resolution.

periodically sued for defamation and will likewise have strategies in place for defending themselves against such suits (example 4). If one party pays for dispute resolution and regularly appoints the arbitrator or mediator, this also causes a 'repeat player' effect.[32]

### 3.5.3 Vulnerability

The relative importance of the case for each party is another factor.

One party may only be marginally concerned by the result of the dispute resolution or contract negotiation, whereas the other may be crippled by an adverse resolution or the failure to reach an agreement.[33] In other words, the parties may have very different stakes: for one party the outcome is critical, for the other the stake (and risk) is small. If this is the situation, the party for whom the outcome is critical is more vulnerable and therefore has less power.

Conversely, one party may be more vulnerable than the other for exactly the opposite reason: the stake is so small that it is inefficient to invest many resources, with the consequence that the other party is not held liable for its breach or infringement. This is the case in many consumer claims, where individual consumers may not bother to pursue a claim as the stake is too small.

Vulnerability can be a complex factor and can include emotional aspects (such as one party's desire to seek justice or revenge), which are impossible to quantify and which play a role in disputes regardless of the status of the parties. Therefore vulnerability is difficult to assess. Furthermore, vulnerability as a factor can only be assessed on a case-by-case basis. However, general assumptions based on the preponderance of power in certain relationships have to be made if a workable definition for power imbalances is to be found. Generally speaking, a party with fewer resources and who is a single-shot player is likely to be more vulnerable for the reason that he or she has more at stake. For this reason it is suggested here that these two factors – financial resources and 'repeat player' status – are more reliable (if perhaps stereotypical) than an assessment of the vulnerability of a party.

---

[32] R. Reuben, 'Constitutional Gravity: A Unitary Theory of Alternative Dispute Resolution and Public Civil Justice' (2000) 47 *UCLA Law Review* 949–1104, 1063–6; see 6.3.2.

[33] Brown and Marriott, *ADR Principles and Practice*, 479.

## 3.6  Definition of relevant disputes in respect of the parties

As has already been pointed out in Chapter 2,[34] this book suggests that the presence of power imbalances cannot be assessed on a case-by-case basis. Therefore it is necessary to develop general categories, linked to the status of the disputants, that are presumptive of the presence of a power imbalance.

The closest existing legal paradigm to the issues examined here is that of consumer-protection laws. If one party satisfies the legal definition of the status 'consumer', and the other party satisfies the legal definition of the status 'business', there is a legal presumption that a power imbalance exists, and hence consumer-protection law applies as a mandatory form of law. As a consequence, special rules protecting consumers apply in certain defined B2C relationships. In this section the definition of 'consumer' under different laws will be examined, and it will be argued that this definition needs widening for the purposes of this book on Internet dispute resolution.

### 3.6.1 Meaning of 'consumer' under different laws and regulations

Under English law, the definition of what amounts to a B2C relationship varies between different pieces of legislation in a piecemeal fashion. From summarising the thrust of these different pieces of legislation, essentially two components[35] can be distinguished:

(i)  Generally speaking, the consumer must be an individual who does not act in a business capacity.[36] Some legislation, however, includes unincorporated business entities (such as a sole trader or a partnership) in the definition of a consumer,[37] and there is case law[38] suggesting

---

[34]  See 2.5.

[35]  Some legislation merely requires that the goods or services supplied must be intended for private, non-business use, i.e. a company can be a consumer under this definition: Unfair Contract Terms Act 1977, s. 12(1)(c); this is not required if the consumer is an individual: s. 12(1A).

[36]  Unfair Contract Terms Act 1977, s. 12(1)(a); Directive 93/13/EEC on Unfair Terms in Consumer Contracts, Art. 2(b); E-commerce Directive 2000/31/EC, Art. 2(e); Distance Selling Directive 1997/7/EC, Art. 2(2) and Jurisdiction Regulation EC/44/2001, Art. 15(1).

[37]  An example is s. 189 of the Consumer Credit Act 1974: the term 'individual' includes an unincorporated body, such as a partnership.

[38]  *R&B Customs Brokers Co Ltd v. United Dominions Trust Ltd* [1988] 1 WLR 321 (CA), 330.

that even a company can act as a consumer under the Unfair Contract Terms Act 1977.[39]

(ii) Conversely, the supplier must act in a business capacity.[40] It seems that for the purposes of civil liability, this criterion is interpreted widely. There is no need for the transaction to be an integral part of the business, in the sense that the business trades in the type of goods or services sold. Hence a fisherman selling his boat was acting in the course of business.[41] Generally speaking, there are no limitations to the size of the entity of the supplier, and the definition of the business party includes natural persons (such as sole traders and traditional partnerships) as well as incorporated entities such as companies.

The traditional B2C paradigm just described can be criticised on three grounds.

The first criticism is that it is problematic to subject all businesses, regardless of their size and operation, to the same types of consumer-protection rules. However, this criticism is probably slightly less important in the context of fairness of dispute resolution mechanisms, and

---

[39] This is clear from s. 12(1)(a) of the Unfair Contract Terms Act 1977, but if the party is not an individual, then, according to s. 12(1)(c), the goods must be of a type ordinarily supplied for private use and consumption. An example of this would be a company buying drinks or a car for their employees' private use. Also, s. 90 of the English Arbitration Act 1996 includes companies not acting in a business capacity when protecting consumers against unfair arbitration clauses; see the discussion at 7.2.2. By contrast, European legislation makes clear that a consumer must be a *natural* person acting for purposes that are outside his or her trade, business or profession: see Directive 93/13/EEC on Unfair Terms in Consumer Contracts, Art. 2(b); E-commerce Directive 2000/31/EC, Art. 2(e); Distance Selling Directive 1997/7/EC, Art. 2(2); Art. 15(1) of the Jurisdiction Regulation EC/44/2001 only refers to 'persons', not *natural* persons; however, the ECJ has made clear that only natural persons are protected by the consumer provisions in the Jurisdiction Regulation: see Case C-150/77, *Bertrand* v. *Ott* [1978] 1431 (ECJ), para. 22 and also Case C-269/95, *Benincasa* v. *Dentalkit* [1997] ECR I-3767 (ECJ), para. 17. Similarly, the ECJ has also found that the notion of 'consumers' does not extend to legal persons in the context of Directive 93/13/EC: Joined Cases C-451 and 452/99, *Cape SNC* v. *Idealservice SRL* [2003] 1 CMLR 42 (ECJ), para. R1. The tendency is that under EU legislation, the notion of consumers has a narrower meaning: see, for example, the case of C-464/01, *Johann Gruber* v. *Bay Wa AG*, OJ C57/1 of 5 March 2005. In that case, the ECJ found that in the context of the Brussels Convention, where the contract is for goods partly intended for private and partly for trade purposes, the consumer provisions only apply if the trade purpose is so limited as to be negligible. Contrast this with the case of *R&B Customs Brokers Co Ltd* v. *United Dominions Trust Ltd*, 330, in which the court said that in the case of mixed use, the business use only prevails if there is a high degree of regularity of the business use.

[40] For example, s. 12(1)(b) of the Unfair Contract Terms Act 1977.

[41] *Stevenson* v. *Rogers* [1999] 2 WLR 1064 (CA), 1039–42, but cf. ECJ jurisprudence.

more important in the context of a discussion on substantive consumer-protection laws.[42]

The second criticism is that the criteria are sometimes inaccurate in assessing power imbalances. An example of this would be a hypothetical case of an extremely wealthy and sophisticated consumer who contracts with a sole trader. In *Standard Bank of London Ltd* v. *Apostolakis*, two high-net-worth individuals (husband and wife) entered into an investment contract to acquire foreign currency worth US $7 million, and the court found that they acted as consumers.[43] The problem this illustrates is the general proposition that it is impossible to find general criteria for assessing power relationships that fit all individual cases. However, legal criteria have to rely on generalised assumptions, without which it would be impossible to formulate policy principles.

The third and most important criticism is that the scope of the traditional consumer paradigm should be widened for this discussion of fairness in the resolution of Internet disputes. The traditional paradigm would only apply to example 2 above, and would ignore all other power imbalances.

It is interesting to note that in two recent ombudsman dispute resolution schemes, the class of eligible complainants has been widened to include not only individual consumers but also small businesses. In the Ombudsman scheme for the resolution of disputes between communication service providers and their customers, set up by the Communications Act 2003, small business customers, defined as those with no more than ten employees, can also file a complaint under the scheme.[44] In the Financial Ombudsman Service scheme, as far as it relates to financial services, an eligible complainant includes a business that has a group annual turnover of less than £1 million, a charity that has an annual income of less than £1 million, and a trust that has a net asset value of less than £1 million.[45] Furthermore, it is stated expressly that a complainant can be a sole trader, company or partnership.[46]

The Chartered Institute of Arbitrators (CIArb) has also set up a special arbitration procedure for disputes between a company and a small

---

[42] The only significant burden imposed on businesses in the model proposed at 8.6 is that the 'stronger' party would be bound by the arbitration clause and should pay a greater share of the costs of dispute resolution.

[43] [2000] ILPr 766 (Comm), 772.

[44] Communications Act 2003, s. 52(6)(b); see Chapter 8.

[45] Financial Services Handbook, r. 2.4.3.     [46] *Ibid.* r. 2.4.4.

business[47] or individual consumer.[48] These examples also indicate that the paradigm has to be widened.

By contrast, for complaints relating to consumer credit, which have been heard by the Financial Ombudsman Service (FOS) since April 2007, the definition of eligible complainant is narrower: only unincorporated entities and partnerships with up to three partners can use this complaint service.[49] This is similar to the definition put forward in the next section.

### 3.6.2 A preliminary definition: widening the scope

The main conclusion from the discussion of the B2C paradigm is that it is unsuitable for this discussion of fairness in the resolution of Internet disputes. It is too narrow to deal with power imbalances in the resolution of Internet disputes. For the model proposed in this book, the scope here should be wider and should encompass both contract and tort disputes. Moreover, the subject matter of Internet disputes is wider, not merely including disputes about commoditised, consumer goods and services but also a whole variety of other issues; hence why the traditional B2C paradigm does not fit well.

For the purposes of this book, the definition of power imbalances in Internet disputes should be restricted to disputes where one party is an individual[50] and the other party is a corporate entity.[51] For this definition, it is irrelevant whether or not the individual acts for private, non-profit purposes or acts in the course of a trade, business or profession. The criterion for the 'stronger' party should be that this party is incorporated, i.e. a legal person. The assumption made here is that entities above a certain size and sophistication are likely to be incorporated. Arguably this definition should also include incorporated partnerships. Unincorporated partnerships should be treated as natural persons.

This definition of relevant power imbalances is admittedly crude, but it has the beauty of clarity and simplicity. It would not catch power imbalances between individuals and between incorporated entities, but the assumption here is that power imbalances between such entities are, relatively speaking, less severe than those between individuals and corporations. The definition would falsely catch disputes if, for example,

---

[47] Defined as a business with no more than ten employees.
[48] (ICAS) Rules, r. 1.1; the rules are available from www.idrs.ltd.uk/Consumer/PDF/ ICAS_Rules_Application.pdf [1 April 2008].
[49] Financial Services Handbook, r. 2.4.3.     [50] A natural person.     [51] A legal person.

a company and an individual are of equal power in dispute resolution, which is assumed to be comparatively rare.

An alternative approach would be to define the business entity by setting threshold values relating to its power (e.g. market capitalisation of a company, turnover, size of employees, number of offices), but it is submitted here that this is likely to be complicated, unclear and equally inaccurate.

Thus redefined, the definition would capture the power imbalances in examples 1, 2, 3, 4 and 6. It would not apply to example 5 (involving a dispute between two individuals), but this result is probably correct, as it would be impossible to encapsulate the respective 'power' of individuals by legal rules.

### 3.6.3 The definition of relevant Internet disputes and its purpose

The definition of relevant Internet disputes for the purposes of the argument in this book is as follows: disputes directly resulting from one party's activities or both parties' interaction on the Internet, if at least one party is an individual.[52] The main concern of this book is with such disputes between a corporate entity and an individual, because of the presumed power imbalance.

As has already been pointed out in the previous chapter 2,[53] this book is only concerned with fair dispute resolution, not with power imbalances generally. Hence the purpose of the definition of relevant Internet disputes is not to define or redefine the scope of substantive laws protecting the weaker party. The argument presented here is not about widening the law on consumer protection but is merely to discuss a model incorporating fair procedural rules for the resolution of Internet disputes.

However, it should be pointed out that there is no clear dividing line between substantive and procedural issues. One area of overlap is the area of applicable law, and in particular the question: which situations do mandatory laws, protecting the weaker party in the situation of a power imbalance, apply?[54]

Furthermore, where both parties are individuals, there may not be a power imbalance (as just defined in 3.6.2). However, if the claim is small, the parties may not be able to litigate.[55] Hence there is lack of access

---

[52] This includes, but is not limited to, B2C disputes.     [53] See 2.5.     [54] See 4.3.5.
[55] See further, 3.9.

(second principle of fairness as discussed in Chapter 2[56]) and therefore such disputes are included in the model discussed in Chapter 8.[57]

The model in the book therefore applies to cross-border Internet disputes where the parties are either an individual pitched against a corporate entity or both individuals.

### 3.7 Definition of relevant disputes in respect of the size of the claim

The main issue in this book is the fact that the parties to an Internet dispute are likely to be located far from each other, possibly in different jurisdictions. This factor increases the cost and complexity of Internet dispute resolution. It has its greatest impact on small disputes, as here the costs of resolution may easily be disproportionate to the value of the claim.[58]

As has been mentioned in Chapter 1, this relationship refers to the *value of the claim* in dispute. A small-claims dispute involves a claim in a cross-border Internet dispute where the costs of litigation and enforcement across a border make it disproportionately expensive to do so. This raises the question of what falls in the category of small disputes. In the United Kingdom, the fee for the domestic small-claims track, triggering a less formal court procedure, is £5,000.[59] Since cross-border disputes are more expensive to litigate and to enforce, it is likely that the figure which amounts to a 'small' international dispute is considerably higher.[60] Under the proposed European Small Claims Procedure, the value of small claims is even smaller, i.e. €2,000.[61] These limits give some guidance as to the relevant values in litigation. The model developed in Chapter 8 will

---

[56] See 2.2.3.    [57] See 8.6.

[58] A study commissioned by the European Commission found that, on average, the total cost of realising a cross-border claim by litigation in the EU was €2,489 (about £1,673) (proceedings at the defendant's residence); see H. von Freyhold, V. Gessner, E. Vial and H. Wagner (eds.), *Cost of Judicial Barriers for Consumers in the Single Market, A Report for the European Commission* (Zentrum für Europäische Rechtspolitik an der Universität Bremen, October/November 1995), 123, Table. Since this study is more than ten years old, it is likely that this figure has since risen. For disputes involving a country outside the EU, this figure will be substantially more.

[59] Civil Procedure Rules 1998 (SI 1998/3132), r. 27.1(2).

[60] In the *Euromarket Designs Inc* case, the English judge mentioned that the parties had already incurred more than £100,000 in costs up until the preliminary hearing on jurisdiction: *Euromarket Designs Inc v. Peters and Crate & Barrel Ltd* [2001] FSR 20 (ChD), para. 8.

[61] About £1,344; see Proposal for a Regulation establishing a European Small Claims Procedure, 15 March 2005, COM(2005) 87 final, Art. 1(1).

distinguish between, and adopt different solutions for, small disputes on the one hand, and large disputes on the other. At that point, it will also outline and develop value limits specific to online arbitration.[62]

## 3.8 Chargebacks and refunds by payment service providers

This book will demonstrate the need for online arbitration for certain Internet disputes. The argument is that for Internet disputes held out of court, ADR mechanisms are crucial. This argument will be further refined in Chapters 4 and 5, explaining that online arbitration can provide a suitable, binding form of dispute resolution for some disputes.

However, it should be pointed out at the outset that a subset of Internet disputes, i.e. consumer E-commerce disputes involving certain forms of payment mechanism, may, in some circumstances, be resolved by intervention of the payment service provider. Chargebacks and refunds by payment service providers are free to the individual user and may provide redress to *consumers*.[63] Hence this section briefly describes these mechanisms and points out that where such mechanisms are available and effective, online arbitration may not be necessary.

### 3.8.1  Credit-card chargeback and joint liability

The first of these interventions by payment service providers is the mechanism of chargebacks by credit-card issuers, which are partly backed up by legislation in the United Kingdom providing for statutory joint liability, and by EU and UK legislation dealing with fraudulent transactions. Credit cards are currently the most common form of payment for B2C E-commerce transactions.[64]

### Credit-card chargeback explained

A credit-card chargeback is essentially a reversal of a payment instruction moving from the credit-card holder to the credit-card issuer, and down the chain to the merchant bank and the merchant, re-crediting the holder's credit-card account and cancelling a credit on the merchant's account.

---

[62] See 8.5.      [63] Not to all individuals in Internet disputes, though!
[64] OECD, *Online Payment Systems for E-Commerce* (2006 Report) (18 April 2006).

There may be many reasons for a credit-card chargeback, such as processing errors, authorisation issues or duplication, but in the context of
this book, disputes and fraud are the only two reasons of interest.

A chargeback mechanism essentially allows an individual, *after* having
authorised payment for goods or services via a credit card, to reverse
payment if the trader is in breach of contract (such as non-delivery of
goods or goods being defective or not as described) or if the payment
has been made fraudulently. Credit-card chargeback is based on and
established by the rules of the major credit-card networks, such as Visa[65]
and Mastercard.[66]

## UK joint liability for breach of contract and misrepresentation

In the United Kingdom, legislation goes much further in relation to credit
cards issued by domestic providers. It not only provides for chargeback
of the purchase price to the consumer but, in the case of the supplier's
breach of contract or misrepresentation, it also gives the consumer a right
to pursue the credit-card issuer for damages or any other remedy available.
Such damages may vastly exceed the amount of the purchase price paid.
Section 75(1) of the Consumer Credit Act 1974 provides that the credit-
card issuer is jointly liable with the seller for breaches of contract and
misrepresentation, provided that the cash price for the goods or services
is in the range of £100–£30,000.[67]

In a landmark ruling, the Court of Appeal has recently clarified the
jurisdictional scope of these provisions: they also apply in respect of
consumers entering into Internet (and other) transactions with foreign
suppliers, irrespective of the place where the transaction was entered into
and irrespective of the location of the supplier.[68] The Court of Appeal
held that s. 75(1) applied to *all* supply transactions where the consumer
uses a credit card regulated by the Consumer Credit Act 1974, even if
the supply transaction was concluded abroad or with a foreign supplier.[69]

---

[65] See Visa, *Rules for Visa Merchants – Card Acceptance and Chargeback, Management Guidelines*, 2006 edition (VRM 08.12.06), Section 6, 69ff., available from
http://merchants.visa.com/ds/pdfs/Card_Acceptance_and_Chargeback_Guidelines.pdf [1
April 2008].

[66] Mastercard, *Merchant Rules Manual*, Chapter 3, available from www.mastercard.com/
us/wce/PDF/MERC-Entire_Manual.pdf [1 April 2008].

[67] Consumer Credit Act 1974, s. 75(3)(b).

[68] *Office of Fair Trading* v. *Lloyds TSB* [2007] QB 1 (CA), 29, 40.

[69] *Ibid.* para. 122.

This decision has been upheld by the House of Lords, dismissing an appeal against the Court of Appeal decision in its entirety.[70]

The main issue in the case was whether s. 75(2), which confers a right of indemnity on the creditor to recoup the loss suffered in satisfying the liability and the costs of defending the action brought by the consumer, would lead to extra-territorial application of the Act in cases where the supplier is located abroad.[71] The Court of Appeal and the House of Lords rejected this reasoning on the basis that the primary purpose of s. 75 was to provide additional protection to consumer debtors under domestic credit agreements,[72] and that the creditors' right under s. 75(2) to recover against the supplier was merely ancillary to that primary object.[73] Furthermore, the Court of Appeal and House of Lords found that there was nothing in s. 75 that justified a distinction to be drawn between domestic and foreign supply transactions.[74] Finally the Court of Appeal also rejected the argument that the practical difficulties that a creditor may face in enforcing a claim against a foreign supplier are insurmountable. The Court of Appeal found that these problems are not so great as to conclude that Parliament can be presumed to have intended to exclude foreign transactions from the scope of the Consumer Credit Act 1974. The court held that the difficulties of enforcing an indemnity claim against a supplier abroad is part of the price credit-card issuers have to pay for the benefits obtained by allowing such cards to be used abroad.[75] Lord Hope, in the House of Lords, expressly said that 'the creditor is in a better position than the debtor, in a question with a foreign supplier, to obtain redress. It is not to be assumed that the creditor will always get his money back. But, if he does not, the loss must lie with him as he has the broader back.'[76]

This decision is highly significant for Internet disputes based on contractual claims or misrepresentation involving consumers. If a UK consumer has paid for an E-commerce transaction by credit card, claims breach of contract or misrepresentation and merely wishes to rescind the contract, he or she can rely on s. 75(1) of the Consumer Credit Act 1974, even if the supplier is located abroad. Section 75(1) therefore provides

---

[70] *Office of Fair Trading* v. *Lloyds TSB* [2007] 3 WLR 733 (HL), 735 (Lord Hoffmann), 737 (Lord Hope), 747 (Lord Mance).
[71] *Office of Fair Trading* v. *Lloyds TSB* [2007] QB 1 (CA), paras. 77ff.
[72] *Ibid.* paras. 76, 120 and [2007] 3 WLR 733 (HL), 735 (Lord Hoffmann), 737 (Lord Hope).
[73] *Ibid.* paras. 88, 120 and (HL), 735 (Lord Hoffmann), 737 (Lord Hope), 746 (Lord Mance).
[74] (CA), para. 120 and (HL), 746–7 (Lord Mance).
[75] (CA) para. 87; similarly, in the House of Lords, Lord Mance at 743.
[76] [2007] 3 WLR 733 (HL), 737.

statutory backing to credit-card chargebacks against foreign suppliers. Since many, if not most, consumer E-commerce transactions are now paid for by credit card, this statutory backing of the mechanism entitles the consumer to fast and effective relief.

If the consumer in this situation claims damages (over and above the purchase price), he or she is entitled to sue the UK-based credit-card issuer, obviating the need to sue the foreign supplier and/or enforce a judgment abroad. In this case, s. 75(1) relieves the consumer of the burden of cross-border litigation and shifts that burden to the creditor. Nevertheless, the consumer would have to litigate, and online arbitration may be more cost-effective than court litigation.[77]

Furthermore, s. 75(1) does not apply if the purchase price is £100 or less.[78] Many consumer E-commerce transactions are of very small value and will slip underneath this threshold. In these low value transaction cases, consumers have to rely on the rules of chargeback established by the credit-card networks discussed above.[79]

Finally, where the consumer uses a credit card to transfer money to a payment service provider (such as PayPal),[80] and the payment provider then, in turn, transfers the money to the seller of the goods or services, it is doubtful whether the consumer can achieve a chargeback on the basis of the seller's breach of contract or misrepresentation. Arguably, if the payment service provider is not in breach of contract, it is irrelevant that the goods or services were defective. In this scenario the payment service provider is the supplier, not the provider of the goods and services, and chargeback may not be available.

### Protection against fraudulent misuse of all payment cards

Section 83 of the Consumer Credit Act 1974 provides that a credit-card holder is not liable for the fraudulent misuse of a credit card.[81] Hence, within the confines of this provision, there is a legal obligation on credit-card issuers to provide a chargeback mechanism in the case of fraudulent abuse. For payment cards other than credit cards used for E-commerce (and other forms of distance selling), reg. 21 of the Consumer Protection (Distance Selling) Regulations 2000 (SI 2000/2334) provides that the

---

[77] See 5.5.  [78] Consumer Credit Act 1974, s. 75(3)(b).  [79] See 3.8.1.
[80] As to payment service providers, see 8.2.
[81] Similar provisions for all other types of banking cards are contained in the UK *Banking Code* (Version March 2005), para. 12.12, available from www.bankingcode. org.uk/pdfdocs/BANKING%20CODE.pdf [1 April 2008].

consumer should be able to reverse a payment or obtain a full refund in the case of fraudulent use of his or her payment card. Moreover, reg. 21(3) provides that the burden of proof of showing that the use was not authorised rests with the payment-card issuer.

These provisions implement legislation within the EEA Member States, providing that card issuers must cancel/re-credit payments made as a result of the fraudulent use of all payment cards in connection with a distance-selling transaction, including Internet transactions.[82]

### Conclusion as to chargebacks

In E-commerce transactions paid by credit card, the credit-card charge-back mechanism effectively shifts the power from the merchant (who usually demands prepayment for goods and services) to the consumer (who can use the mechanism to receive back that payment). A credit-card chargeback may avoid a dispute between the consumer and merchant and provide the consumer with a remedy. In this scenario it obviates the need for dispute resolution from the credit-card holder's (consumer's) point of view. However, to the extent that the credit-card chargeback system is abused by card holders, there is still a need for dispute resolution from the merchant's point of view. Furthermore, as has been pointed out, chargeback may not always be available.

### 3.8.2  PayPal

Other payment mechanisms may provide some form of complaints assistance or mediation. An example of this is PayPal, an eMoney provider, transferring money between two account holders, whose services have gained prominence through its use by buyers and sellers on the online auction provider eBay.[83]

PayPal essentially deals with two types of disputes: (i) where goods have not been delivered and (ii) where goods do not match their description, i.e. false description of goods.[84] Its 'Buyer Protection Programme' works at three levels.

---

[82] See Distance Selling Directive 1997/7EC, Art. 8. There are no harmonised EU-wide provisions on joint liability of supplier and credit-card issuer.

[83] PayPal is now owned by eBay.

[84] PayPal, *Buyer Complaint Policy* (Version 7 June 2007), para. 1, available from www.paypal.com/uk/cgi-bin/webscr?cmd=p/gen/ua/policy_buyer_complaint-outside [1 April 2008].

Firstly, at the informal level, PayPal obliges buyers to file a dispute and use an online platform to negotiate a solution with the seller, and in some instances PayPal may recommend a solution to the parties (mediation).[85]

Secondly, if the dispute cannot be solved this way, PayPal allows buyers to file a formal complaint, and it will investigate (e.g. check the seller's tracking system in the case of non-delivery of goods) and may order the seller to make a refund from his or her PayPal account (if the goods have been falsely described, it may order the buyer to return the goods first), provided there are sufficient funds in the seller's PayPal account to make such a refund.[86] In its terms and conditions, PayPal expressly provides that it retains the right to freeze any payments made into the seller's account on complaint by the buyer.[87] However, if the seller has already redeemed the payment, PayPal will not be able to order a refund.[88]

Finally, for certain transactions, PayPal provides (limited) insurance.[89]

It should be noted that PayPal's 'Buyer Protection Programme' is limited, as it only applies to tangible goods that can be delivered in the post.[90] Furthermore, its refund policy for goods significantly not as described only applies to eBay transactions,[91] and its insurance policy is limited to certain eBay sellers possessing a good track record.[92]

### 3.8.3 Conclusion

The intervention of payment service providers in the form of credit-card chargebacks and buyer-protection programmes is apt to provide a remedy for consumer buyers in many E-commerce disputes, especially those of small value. Therefore such mechanisms and programmes have, in practice, an extremely important role to play in E-commerce consumer protection. However, their reach is limited. Firstly, they only apply to disputes where the remedy is the reversal of the payment. Secondly, as discussed, the application of the various schemes is limited.[93] They form

---

[85] *Ibid.* paras. 2 and 3.   [86] *Ibid.* para. 6.
[87] PayPal, *User Agreement*, para. 10, available from www.paypal.com/uk/cgi-bin/webscr?cmd=p/gen/ua/policy_pbp-outside [1 April 2008].
[88] *Ibid.* para. 6.
[89] See the PayPal buyer protection policy (Version 11 January 2007) in the *User Agreement*, para. 13, available from www.paypal.com/uk/cgi-bin/webscr?cmd=p/gen/ua/policy_pbp-outside [1 April 2008].
[90] PayPal, *Buyer Complaint Policy*, para. 1.   [91] *Ibid.* para. 1.   [92] *Ibid.* para. 3(a).
[93] Credit-card chargebacks apply to credit cards, not debit cards; the protection under the distance-selling regime discussed above only applies to fraudulent abuses, not breach of contract; the PayPal programme is limited to tangible goods etc.

one piece in the intricate jigsaw of dispute resolution on the Internet.[94] Finally, in the context of an argument on the fair resolution of Internet disputes, it also has to be pointed out that they do not provide for due process and a fair hearing. Saying that chargebacks provide a remedy to buyers in E-commerce transactions in many instances is not the same as saying that they provide a fair means of dispute resolution. Hence, despite the availability of a chargeback to the buyer, in some instances the merchant supplier may need a means of dispute resolution in order to obtain payment or recoup the goods.

### 3.9 The jurisdictional challenge of the Internet

Global interactions on the Internet lead to an increase in international contacts and hence ample opportunities for cross-border disputes and conflicts between various type of disputants. This creates the jurisdictional challenge for the Internet.

The problems private international law creates for the Internet have been discussed elsewhere in literature.[95] The consequence of these problems is that cross-border litigation and enforcement are so expensive and time-consuming that access to this form of dispute resolution is barred but for the largest claims, and that for small claims the costs and delay of cross-border litigation are frequently not proportionate to the remedy eventually obtainable. As this topic has been treated elsewhere, it is not necessary (and for lack of space also not possible) to make this argument in detail again here.[96]

---

[94]  See the model in 8.6.

[95]  R. Schu, 'The Applicable Law to Consumer Contracts Made over the Internet: Consumer Protection through Private International Law?' (1997) 5 *International Journal of Law and Information Technology* 192–229; M. Burnstein, 'A Global Network in a Compartmentalised Legal Environment', in K. Boele-Woelki and C. Kessedjian (eds.), *Internet: Which Court Decides? Which Law Applies?* (The Hague: Kluwer Law International, 1998), 23–34; H. Perritt, 'Dispute Resolution in Cyberspace: Demand for New Forms of ADR' (2000) 15 *Ohio State Journal on Dispute Resolution* 675–703; Reed, *Internet Law*; Reed, 'Jurisdiction and Choice of Law'; L. Gillies, 'European Union: Modified Rules of Jurisdiction for Electronic Consumer Contracts' (2000) 17 *Computer Law & Security Report* 395–8; J. Hörnle, 'Private International Law and E-Finance: The European Perspective' (2001) 8 *The EDI Law Review* 209–29; H. Kronke, 'Applicable Law in Torts and Contracts in Cyberspace', in K. Boele-Woelki and C. Kessedjian (eds.), *Internet: Which Court Decides? Which Law Applies?* (The Hague: Kluwer Law International, 1998), 65–87.

[96]  The author's chapter for the forthcoming 2009 edition of L. Edwards and C. Waelde, *Law & the Internet*, 3rd edn (Oxford: Hart Publishing, forthcoming 2009) deals with these problems in detail.

Academic scholars,[97] policy-makers[98] and legal practitioners[99] have demanded the use of alternative forms of dispute resolution. For this reason this book focuses on ODR as a way forward for the resolution of Internet disputes.

Not just in the context of E-commerce but more generally, there is a noticeable tendency to overcome the cost factor of (even merely domestic) litigation by the use of ADR. Since the introduction of the Civil Procedure Rules, the English courts are under an obligation to encourage ADR,[100] if appropriate, and the courts are empowered to impose cost penalties on parties who unreasonably refuse to participate in ADR.[101] Furthermore, the courts have recognised the validity and enforceability of ADR clauses in commercial contracts.[102]

## 3.10 Conclusion

This chapter has explained the characteristics of the Internet that make it more likely than before the use of the Internet became widespread that individuals become embroiled in cross-border disputes. This involvement of individuals in international disputes leads to concerns about access to and power imbalances in dispute resolution and, hence, to concerns about fairness. As to power imbalances, this chapter has described the notion of power in dispute resolution and concludes that this is an extremely multifaceted concept, but that an important role is played by access to

---

[97] A. Patel, 'Consumer Protection and Redress – The Wider Context' (2000) 3 *Electronic Business Law* 9–10; L. Gillies, 'A Review of the New Jurisdiction Rules for Electronic Consumer Contracts within the European Union' [2001] *Journal of Information Law & Technology* (eJournal, available from www2.warwick.ac.uk/fac/soc/law/elj/jilt [8 July 2008]); Heiskanen, 'Dispute Resolution in International Electronic Commerce', 38ff.

[98] E-commerce Directive 2000/31/EC Art. 17, published in OJ L178/1 of 17 July 2000, encourages the Member States to establish fair out-of-court dispute resolution mechanisms.

[99] J. Gunn and W. Roebuck, 'White Paper on Alternative Dispute Resolution in a Supply Chain Transformed by On-Line Transactions' (May 2001), available from the eCentre, Legal Advisory Group.

[100] Civil Procedure Rules 1998 (SI 1998/3132), Part 1.4(2)(e); *Cowl* v. *Plymouth City Council* [2002] 1 WLR 803 (CA).

[101] Civil Procedure Rules 1998 (SI 1998/3132), Part 44.5; *Dunnett* v. *Railtrack* [2002] 2 All ER 850 (CA); *Royal Bank of Canada* v. *Secretary of State for Defence* [2003] EWHC 1841 (ChD), unreported, paras. 11–13; *Burchell* v. *Bullard* [2005] EWCA Civ 358; but cf. *Hurst* v. *Leeming* [2003] 1 Lloyd's Rep 379 (ChD), where the refusal to mediate was justified, on the basis that there was no real prospect of success, at 381.

[102] *Cable & Wireless Plc* v. *IBM* [2002] 2 All ER 1041 (Comm) – upholding the validity of an ADR clause.

resources and the 'repeat player' effect. In order to simplify the extremely complicated concept of power paradigms, a presumption has been introduced that power imbalances are likely to exist for Internet disputes in the relationship between a corporate entity and an individual.

This chapter has explained that the discussion is not limited to E-commerce disputes, but that a wide approach is taken that includes all disputes arising from interactions mediated by the Internet, including disputes about domain names. It has been acknowledged that some B2C E-commerce disputes (a subset of Internet disputes relevant to this book) can be solved by intervention of payment service providers.

In summary, the main focus of the book is on cross-border Internet disputes where: (i) one party is a corporate entity and the other party is an individual, and (ii) there is no access to the courts, due to costs. However, the scope of this book also encompasses disputes between individuals where there is no access to the courts for the same reason.

This chapter has also briefly explained that cross-border litigation is complicated and expensive and will therefore not be suitable for many Internet disputes. ADR may provide the way forward, and the next chapter will look at ADR and its significance.

# ADR and applicable law

Those, who in quarrels interpose,
Must often wipe a bloody nose.

(John Gay, 1685–1732)

## 4.1 Introduction

The function of this chapter is to explain the meaning of alternative dispute resolution (ADR). This serves as background to the discussion of ODR in the following chapter. This chapter concentrates on the two main forms of ADR (mediation and arbitration), discussing their main characteristics, function and limitations. In doing so, this chapter explains why only arbitration is to be regarded as a true alternative to litigation, and why mediation is, in its nature, a sort of filter for disputes, a complementary rather than independent form of dispute resolution.

One way to deal with disputes is through adjudication.[1] The essence of adjudication is to have a neutral third person decide whether the second person should give the disputed something to the first person or do what the first person demands. The adjudicator thereby defines the first person's legal rights and entitlements.[2]

Alternatively, the first person may want to bargain with the other person. Bargaining by its very nature involves the first person persuading the second person that it is in his or her interests to give to the first person what they wish to obtain, or to do what the first person wants him or her to do.[3]

---

[1] Adjudication includes litigation, arbitration and ombudsmen. The term 'adjudication' is used in this book as an overarching term to mean a form of dispute resolution involving a third party making a decision binding on the parties.

[2] Lon Fuller argues that it is the very essence of adjudication that it ultimately defines rights and entitlements; see Fuller, 'The Forms and Limits of Adjudication', 369.

[3] There are different strategies for negotiation, for example strategies focusing on positions and strategies focusing on interests. The Harvard Negotiation Project has developed a

Between the opposite ends of the spectrum of formality (namely bargaining and litigation) lies a range of dispute resolution mechanisms that involve a neutral third party but which are kept outside the courts. These mechanisms are called alternative dispute resolution (ADR).

## 4.2 ADR

ADR is a collective expression for all dispute resolution mechanisms that interpose a neutral third party but which are outside the courts, and is a synonym for extra-judicial or 'out-of-court' dispute resolution.[4] In this book the term includes other adjudicative techniques such as arbitration.[5] Figure 4 illustrates the relationship between different forms of dispute resolution.

The adjective 'alternative' in ADR connotes that ADR was conceived to be an alternative to the state court system. In the 1970s and 1980s, the ADR movement (consisting, to a large part, of academic scholars) advocated the increasing use of ADR and conceptualised ADR as a distinct subject in response to deficiencies in the official court system, particularly in the US.[6] However, it should be pointed out that the mechanisms of arbitration and mediation had been used long before in various contexts.[7]

---

negotiation method, focusing on interests, called 'principled negotiation', a method from which mediation has greatly benefited; see below.

[4] G. Kaufmann-Kohler and T. Schultz, *Online Dispute Resolution: Challenges for Contemporary Justice* (The Hague: Kluwer Law International, 2004), 6; C. Rule, *Online Dispute Resolution for Business* (San Francisco, Calif.: Jossey-Bass, 2002), 13; Brown and Marriott, *ADR Principles and Practice*, 12; H. Genn, *The Central London County Court Pilot Mediation Scheme Evaluation Report* (London: Lord Chancellor's Department, July 1998), para. 1.1.1.

[5] Some authors exclude all adjudication/arbitration from the scope of ADR: see N. Vidmar, 'Procedural Justice and Alternative Dispute Resolution', in K. Röhl and S. Machura (eds.), *Procedural Justice* (Aldershot: Ashgate, 1997) 121–36, 121; K. Mackie, D. Miles, W. Marsh and T. Allen, *The ADR Practice Guide* (London: Butterworths, 2000), 9.

[6] Kaufmann-Kohler and Schultz, *Online Dispute Resolution*, 6; Rule, *Online Dispute Resolution for Business*, 15. Roger Fisher and William Ury first published their famous book, *Getting to Yes: Negotiating an Agreement Without Giving In*, 2nd edn (London: Random House, 1992), in 1974; see also Laura Nader's *No Access to Law: Alternatives to the American Legal System* (New York, NY: Academic Press, 1980); C. Menkel-Meadow, 'Toward Another View of Legal Negotiation: The Structure of Problem-Solving' (1983–1984) 31 *UCLA Law Review* 754–842.

[7] Many authors cite arbitration between merchants in Mediaeval Europe as the origin of contemporary arbitration, but arbitration was also known in Roman times. The first English arbitration statute dates from 1698, and one of the oldest arbitration institutions was the LCIA, founded in 1892; see for more detail, A. Redfern and M. Hunter, *Law and Practice of International Commercial Arbitration*, 4th edn (London: Sweet & Maxwell, 2004), 3–6. Mediation, as an informal dispute resolution process, has, in one form or another, been practised in all societies.

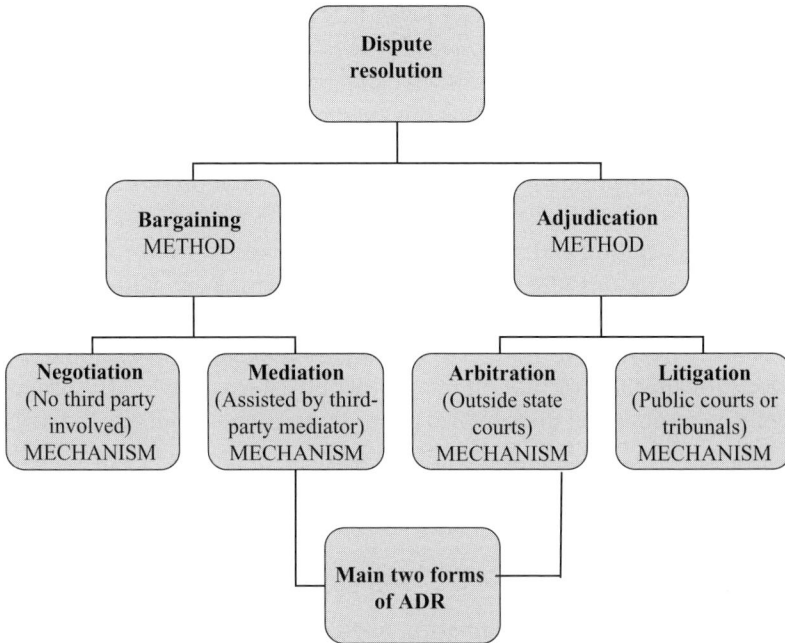

**Fig. 4.** Illustrating the basic methods and mechanisms of dispute resolution.

The foundation of all ADR processes is the agreement of the parties to submit their dispute to the neutral third party – this consent is necessary for all dispute resolution mechanisms outside the courts.[8]

The advantages of ADR are that the parties (at least in theory) have more control over the process, and it has been shown in empirical research that process control is important for the parties' satisfaction with the dispute resolution process;[9] the parties to ADR can choose the procedure to be used and influence the procedural rules. Furthermore, the parties select the arbitrator(s) or the mediator(s). The parties may well choose someone with expertise in the subject matter of the dispute, and they will select someone they trust, hence creating legitimacy for the process. In some cases the parties' preference may be for confidentiality,[10] which ADR, but

---

[8] Consent signifies the waiver of the right to go to court; see 6.2.5 and 7.2.
[9] Vidmar, 'Procedural Justice and Alternative Dispute Resolution', 125; P. Houlden, S. La Tour, L. Walker and J. Thibaut, 'Preferences for Modes of Dispute Resolution as a Function of Process and Decision Control' (1978) 14 *Journal of Experimental Social Psychology* 13–30, 26–7.
[10] See 6.6.

not the public state courts, can provide. Finally, in most cases ADR is more informal, and in some cases also cheaper.[11]

In addition, mediation has further advantages over adjudication (both litigation and arbitration) in that it is even more informal, can resolve (or even remove) the dispute by more creative and efficient solutions, and it is, at least in principle, less confrontational, thus preserving existing relationships (if applicable).[12]

While arbitration and mediation are the two basic forms of ADR, there are many variations and hybrid forms, such as med-arb (using the two forms consecutively), expert evaluation (mediation with an expert issuing a recommendation) or mini-trial (having a senior figure recommending a decision after representation of argument by the parties).[13] However, a detailed discussion of these hybrid forms and variants is outside the scope of this book, which will instead focus on the two main forms of ADR: mediation and arbitration.

### 4.2.1 Mediation

#### Mediation explained

Mediation is a form of dispute resolution whereby a third-party mediator brokers a settlement between the parties. It is essentially a process of negotiation, which is structured and influenced by the third-party mediator. His or her role in negotiation is to facilitate the parties' endeavour to reach a settlement through a series of joint meetings and private meetings with each party separately ('caucuses').[14]

The parties can agree to submit their dispute to mediation either before or after the dispute arises. A mediation agreement is not a mere agreement

---

[11] The degree of informality in ADR varies, and so does the cost. Whereas judges are paid by the state, arbitrators and mediators will charge their time to the parties, a factor that makes ADR potentially more expensive than litigation. However, to the extent that ADR uses shorter procedures and less evidence than the courts, it may be cheaper. The role of using technology and the resulting efficiency is explained at 5.5.1 and 5.5.2.

[12] Despite these advantages, it seems that take-up of a voluntary option to mediate a dispute is low among parties in civil disputes, about 5 per cent during the Central London County Court Pilot Mediation Scheme: Genn, *Evaluation Report*, paras. 1.1.4, 2.1.1 and 2.1.2; S. Merry and S. Silbey, 'What Do Plaintiffs Want? Reexamining the Concept of Dispute' (1984) 9(2) *Justice System Journal* 151–78, 152.

[13] See Brown and Marriott, *ADR Principles and Practice*, 17–19.

[14] Brown and Marriott, *ADR Principles and Practice*, 127; Mackie, Miles, Marsh and Allen, *The ADR Practice Guide*, 11.

to negotiate[15] but is binding on the parties, if the parties' obligations are sufficiently clear.[16] In *Cable & Wireless Plc* v. *IBM*, a mediation clause was held to be enforceable since it referred to an institution and specified procedure, and the court held that the parties' obligation was to participate in the process of initiating the mediation, selecting a mediator and presenting the mediator with the case and relevant documents.[17]

A distinction is usually made between facilitative and evaluative mediation. The former mode is slightly more limited in that the mediator merely assists the parties in finding their own agreement, without making recommendations or suggestions. In the latter mode the mediator evaluates the parties' respective positions and makes a recommendation as to the terms of the settlement. Such recommendations may be based on the mediator's view of the legal merits of the case or, in a non-legalistic, pragmatic context, on the mediator's view of what are reasonable terms of settlement.[18]

It should also be pointed out that a settlement agreement is a contract, and as such cannot directly be enforced before the courts as a court order. Hence, in the case of non-compliance with a settlement, the deprived party would have to start court proceedings to enforce contractual entitlements.[19]

The distinctive feature of mediation is that the parties *agree* the terms of their settlement. A mediator does not impose a decision or solution on the parties. The parties initially only agree to participate in the procedure, but ultimately decide during the process if they settle, and on what terms. The parties can discontinue the process at any stage and 'walk away'. They are not bound until they have completed a binding settlement agreement, and in this sense mediation is a voluntary process.[20] Even mediation under a binding mediation agreement is voluntary, as the obligation is limited to initiating and attempting the process.[21]

---

[15] Not enforceable under English law: *Courtney and Fairbairn Ltd* v. *Tolaini Brothers (Hotels) Ltd* [1975] 1 WLR 297 (CA), 301.

[16] *Cable & Wireless Plc* v. *IBM* [2002] 2 All ER 1041 (Comm), paras. 23–4, 34.

[17] *Ibid.* paras. 24, 29.

[18] Mackie, Miles, Marsh and Allen, *The ADR Practice Guide*, 5 11–12, 49.

[19] Unless the settlement was reached in the context of pending litigation, in which case, in England, it can be drawn up as a consent order (or 'Tomlin' order, after the case of *Tomlin* v. *Standard Telephones and Cables* [1969] 3 All ER 201 (CA)).

[20] Brown and Marriott, *ADR Principles and Practice*, 129.

[21] *Cable & Wireless Plc* v. *IBM* 16, paras. 22, 29.

From this description it should be clear that the goal of mediation is an agreed settlement, not a decision about each party's rights and entitlements, as in adjudication. Therefore the goal of mediation is fundamentally different from that of adjudication, and this is further discussed in the next section.

### How mediation works, and its purpose

As has been discussed above, negotiation advances by the parties considering and measuring up their respective interests, albeit each from their own subjective perspective. This statement equally rings true for mediation, which, as has been pointed out above, is a form of third-party assisted negotiation.

One measurement of the parties' respective interests is an assessment of their legal rights and entitlements. In other words, the parties' rights and entitlements inform their respective interests to settle or not to settle. Both parties are likely to consider what would happen if they could not reach agreement, and this entails an evaluation of how an adjudicator would decide the case.

However, collaterally, the parties will also weigh up access to and the costs of adjudication.[22] These costs include the delay involved and expense of adjudication, emotional factors and the fact that an adjudicator is restricted to particular remedies, whereas a settlement agreement may contain a variety of solutions.[23] Hence a party usually will be prepared to accept slightly less than they would obtain through adjudication, or a party usually will be prepared to give slightly more than they would have to, if ordered by an adjudicator, taking into account the costs of adjudication. However, these factors depend on each party's subjective perception of the merits of the case and the costs of adjudication, as both factors are impossible to predict with certainty. Hence the more risk-adverse person is likely to be in a disadvantaged bargaining position.[24]

Conversely, if it is clear that one party has no access to binding and coercive adjudication (since the costs vastly exceed the value of the claim),

---

[22] See also R. Mnookin and L. Kornhauser, 'Bargaining in the Shadow of the Law: The Case of Divorce' (1979) 88 *The Yale Law Journal* 950–97, 971–2.

[23] See the music band example in the text below. A court of law can only award the remedies provided for by law.

[24] Mnookin and Kornhauser, 'Bargaining in the Shadow of the Law', 979.

the other party (if defendant) may not be prepared to settle at all, or the other party (if claimant) may obtain a settlement exceeding any adjudicated decision.[25] As will be seen below, this raises serious questions of availability of redress and fairness.

By way of illustration, if each party bears its own costs, the claimant's desire to settle could be expressed as $S > A - CC$ ('S' standing for settlement, A being the adjudicated decision and CC the claimant's costs). The defendant's desire to settle could be expressed as $S < A + CD$ (CD standing for the costs of the defendant). Therefore, if the claimant's costs are very high, the claimant will be prepared to settle low. If the defendant's costs are very high, the claimant can obtain a settlement substantially exceeding the adjudicated decision. However, in a court system, where the winner pays the loser's cost, assuming that it is clear that the claimant will win, the respective settlement desires would be $S > A$ (claimant) and $S < A + CC + CD$ (defendant). Hence, if the costs of either party are very high, the claimant could obtain a settlement vastly exceeding the adjudicated decision. Under English civil procedure, either party can make an offer to settle. If the offeree does not accept the offer but does not succeed in obtaining a better bargain at trial, that party will be responsible for the offeror's costs incurred after the offer has been made.[26] The defendant could use a Part 36[27] offer to prevent the claimant from using its bargaining power to obtain a settlement vastly exceeding the likely adjudicated decision. Conversely, if there is a chance that the claimant may lose the case and bear the whole costs $(CC + CD)$, the defendant may be less likely to settle at the likely adjudicated decision. Again, the claimant in that case could use the Part 36 offer to put pressure on the defendant. Hence, under English civil procedure rules, there are mechanisms to level out the unfair bargaining power derived from the cost risk. However, this system is not perfect, as courts rarely award the whole costs to the winning parties, and litigation is very expensive; this may lead a risk-averse party to settle well below or above the adjudicated decision.

So, two important factors in mediating a solution to a dispute are the perceived outcome of adjudication balanced with the feasibility and costs

[25] Menkel-Meadow, 'Toward Another View of Legal Negotiation', 834.
[26] Civil Procedure Rules 1998 (SI 1998/3132), Part 36.
[27] Offers to settle under the English Civil Procedure Rules 1998 (SI 1998/3132).

involved in adjudication.[28] This is the meaning of the phrase 'mediation takes place "in the shadow of the law"'.[29]

However, it should also be pointed out that, in some disputes, factors other than those related to the feasibility and outcome of adjudication strongly influence the parties' respective interests in negotiation and mediation.

If the dispute is genuinely about one single issue, such as how much compensation should a perpetrator of a tort pay to the victim, then there is little scope for aligning the parties' interests through a compromise other than a linear solution, whereby the parties meet somewhere between the claimant's monetary demands and the defendant's offer to pay compensation.

Conversely, many disputes will involve multiple issues, and the parties' preferences for each issue can be adapted to achieve the solution optimal for both parties.[30] In fact, the most important task of mediation is to find such an optimal solution, satisfying as many interests of the parties as possible.

This becomes clearer if one makes a distinction between positions and interests. A position is what the party says he or she wants, whereas his or her interests are the motivation behind that position. If a different position equally satisfies the underlying interest, parties may well be able and willing to change their position. Roger Fisher and William Ury argue that reconciling interests works much better than reconciling positions, as for every interest there might exist more than one position, and frequently a different position than the one initially taken satisfies both parties' respective interests.[31]

One famous and simple example[32] of this is the story of two children arguing about who should have the last orange in the fruit bowl. A parent adjudicating this 'case' might merely focus on the question of which of the two children has a better entitlement to the orange, for example one

---

[28] E. Clark, G. Cho and A. Hoyle, 'Online Dispute Resolution: Present Realities, Pressing Problems and Future Prospects' (2003) 17(1) *International Review of Law, Computers & Technology* 7–25, 16.

[29] Coined by the Mnookin and Kornhauser article, 'Bargaining in the Shadow of the Law', 968; see also Menkel-Meadow, 'Toward Another View of Legal Negotiation', 766.

[30] Brown and Marriott, *ADR Principles and Practice*, 130; Menkel-Meadow, 'Toward Another View of Legal Negotiation', 795; L. Fuller, 'Mediation – Its Forms and Functions' (1971) 44 *Southern California Law Review* 305–39, 316–17.

[31] Fisher and Ury, *Getting to Yes*, 42–3.

[32] Menkel-Meadow, 'Toward Another View of Legal Negotiation', 771, or see Fisher and Ury, *Getting to Yes*, 41, 58–9.

child may have eaten three oranges already, whereas the other child has had none. By contrast, mediating between the children might involve an examination of the reasons why each child wants to have the orange. The first child might want to have the orange in order to grate the rind for making a cake, whereas the other child may want to eat the flesh, in which case an obvious solution has been found that fully satisfies both children's interests underlying the demand to have the orange.

Another less theoretical but anecdotal example may further support and illustrate this argument. In one case solved by mediation, the claimant had ordered a jazz music band for a corporate entertainment function from the defendant's agency business organising such events. Through a series of unlikely and unfortunate events (rather than the defendant's incompetence), she had to cancel the band's performance at the last minute. It seemed that under the terms of the contract she was likely to be in breach of contract, and a court would have been likely to award damages. However the claimant agreed to attempt mediation and was persuaded that the breach had not occurred because of the negligent or careless operation of the defendant's business but because of a series of unfortunate events. Hence the claimant agreed to have a certain number of free performances in lieu of compensation (but exceeding in monetary value the amount of damages) he was likely to receive from a court. This solution satisfied the interests of both parties: the defendant was spared negative publicity, did not have to pay damages and costs and obtained a satisfied customer, whereas the claimant obtained something of greater value than the monetary compensation he would have been entitled to.

However, again, this solution only worked because of the particular circumstances of the case. It worked for the reason that the defendant trusted the claimant to render satisfactory performances in the future, and for the reason that he happened to require further, regular performances after the cancelled one.

Clearly, only some disputes lend themselves to such neat solutions. It is argued here that it is exactly the function of mediation to find out the parties' respective interests and align the resulting preferences in such a way that the solution satisfies each party's interests. However, not all disputes can be solved in this way. In some factual scenarios, the underlying interests of the parties cannot be aligned, and it is therefore necessary to resort to adjudication.[33]

---

[33] See, along similar lines, H. Edwards, 'Alternative Dispute Resolution: Panacea or Anathema?' (1986) 99 *Harvard Law Review* 668–84, 678 – he points out that the 'broken

In the literature on the purpose of mediation and its value, the debate is largely bipolar and focuses on an either/or approach – mediation is either a 'good institution' or a 'bad institution'.

Some authors[34] argue that mediation is preferable to adjudication for the reason that it makes eminent sense to base dispute resolution on the parties' interests rather than on their legal rights or entitlements. These authors point to the advantages of mediation, such as preservation of ongoing relationships,[35] parties having greater control over their dispute and the availability of more flexible solutions tailored to the parties' needs, and possibly, in some instances, reduced costs.

Other authors,[36] by contrast, argue that adjudication according to law is preferable, as mediation may lead a party to renounce his or her rights and entitlements.

These authors also argue that mediation is contrary to the notion of justice and fairness.[37] At first glance it may indeed seem that mediation is contrary to fairness, as mediation is partly an irrational process, not entirely based on the parties' rational arguments about facts and law but on bargaining about interests.[38] This involves strategic behaviour and inducing the opponent, regardless of the quality of his or her arguments, to agree to a settlement. This aspect of mediation may enhance power imbalances between the parties.[39] Habermas, for example, argues that the outcomes of negotiation processes[40] are less fair than those reached through court procedures, which have institutionalised due process.[41]

It is argued here that the apparent conflict between these opposing views can be resolved if one regards mediation not as an alternative but as complementary to adjudication.

---

telephone' theory of disputes is wrong: disputes are not only about miscommunication; some conflicts may not be solved through mere realignment of interests.

[34] Menkel-Meadow, 'Toward Another View of Legal Negotiation', 757; Mackie, Miles, Marsh and Allen, *The ADR Practice Guide*, 14–15; Cappelletti, 'Alternative Dispute Resolution Processes', 289–90.

[35] Mediation tends to adopt a problem-solving approach and is frequently less confrontational; Brown and Marriott, *ADR Principles and Practice*, 131.

[36] Vidmar, 'Procedural Justice and Alternative Dispute Resolution', 123; Galligan, *Due Process and Fair Procedures*, 16 and 276; O. Fiss, 'Against Settlement' (1984) 93 *Yale Law Journal* 1073–90, 1085–6; M. Galanter and M. Cahill, 'Most Cases Settle: Judicial Promotion and Regulation of Settlements' (1994) 46 *Stanford Law Review* 1339–91, 1364 and 1385–6.

[37] *Ibid.*; see also 2.5.    [38] Fuller, 'Mediation', 367.

[39] Genn, *Evaluation Report*, paras. 7.7.5–7.7.6.    [40] He speaks about negotiation generally.

[41] Habermas, *Faktizität und Geltung*, 218–19; Fuller, 'Mediation', 366–7, and see 2.5. The problem with this argument is that, in practice, strategic behaviour in litigation and the costs of litigation also increase power imbalances between the parties.

Mediation is not about fair resolution[42] of disputes.[43] The function of mediation is to attempt to analyse the parties' interests underlying their position and to reformulate their preferences in such a way that the dispute is removed. Therefore mediation is about removing disputes, not about solving them fairly. In the example of the children fighting about an orange, it is irrelevant whether it is fair or not that the child who is allowed to eat the last orange's flesh has already consumed three oranges, whilst the child who wants to bake the cake has eaten none. The fact that the child baking the cake merely wishes to use the rind has completely removed the dispute. Hence fairness in mediation is limited to enabling communication between the parties and reformulating positions, and does not involve designing procedures to enable the fair resolution of disputes.

However, mediation becomes unfair if one party feels pressurised in accepting a compromise that does not reflect that party's interests nor that party's rights and entitlements.[44] This is more likely to occur if adjudication is not available or accessible because of the costs of adjudication discussed above. In other words, a lack of accessible and affordable adjudication affects the fairness of mediation. Hence access to adjudication guards against unfairness in mediation.

Furthermore, mediation does not always lead to a settlement, for two reasons. Firstly, as has just been discussed, mediation only works if the circumstances of the case lend themselves to a compromise.[45] Secondly, as has been discussed in the previous section, mediation is voluntary, not coercive, and for this reason it cannot provide an avenue of redress for all cases since a party can terminate the process at any stage. In other words, mediation does not obviate the need for binding adjudication in some cases.

---

[42] It has been argued above that the purpose of mediation is to remove the dispute between the parties rather than to solve it fairly. This purpose can be jeopardised if a mediator is biased, for example. In fact, neutrality of the mediator is a value asserted but rarely measured – pointed out by S. Cobb and J. Rifkin, 'Practice and Paradox: Deconstructing Neutrality in Mediation' (1991) 16 *Law and Social Inquiry* 25–63, 39. There are other due process issues such as accountability and confidentiality; see P. Robinson, 'Centuries of Contract Common Law Can't Be All Wrong' [2003] *Journal of Dispute Resolution* 135–73, 164; see also US Uniform Mediation Act 2001, § 6, and EU Mediation Directive 2008/52/EC of 21 May 2008, OJ L136/3 of 24 May 2008 Art. 7. However, as this book focuses on arbitration, these issues are not discussed here.

[43] Menkel-Meadow, 'Toward Another View of Legal Negotiation', 816, and Fuller, 'Mediation', 307–8.

[44] Vidmar, 'Procedural Justice and Alternative Dispute Resolution', 124; Galligan, *Due Process and Fair Procedures*, 274–9; O. Fiss, 'Against Settlement', 1076–8.

[45] Galligan, *Due Process and Fair Procedures*, 274–6.

For these reasons, in this argument only arbitration is regarded as a true alternative to litigation.

In conclusion, the argument advanced here is that mediation should be provided in conjunction with adjudication, rather than as an alternative to adjudication.[46] Mediation should be attempted before adjudication (unless it is obvious that it will fail). As a preliminary process, it has a very important and useful filtering function. It filters out those disputes that lend themselves to a compromise, removing those disputes and thereby making adjudication unnecessary. However, it is crucial that adjudication is available and accessible for those disputes not lending themselves to compromise.

### 4.2.2 Arbitration

Arbitration is a form of private adjudication whereby a neutral third party, the arbitrator,[47] chosen and paid by the parties, makes a binding and enforceable decision (called an award) as to how the dispute should be resolved. The arbitrator will usually decide the case according to authoritative standards set by the applicable law(s).[48] Therefore, as in litigation, the arbitrator will hear evidence to establish the facts and decide on the relevant law. However, unlike litigation, the procedure used to arrive at the award is more flexible and is usually determined by the parties (principle of party autonomy).[49]

The basis of the arbitrator's jurisdiction is the parties' agreement to submit the dispute (or disputes of this type) to arbitration. The agreement to arbitrate is the cornerstone of arbitration. There can be no arbitration without agreement.[50] One exception to this is statutory arbitration, in

---

[46] See also Edwards, 'Alternative Dispute Resolution', 668–84, 675.

[47] Or a panel of (usually three) arbitrators.

[48] See applicable law at 4.3; the arbitrator's duty to give reasons at 6.5.

[49] English Arbitration Act 1996, ss. 1(b) and 34(1); French Nouveau Code de Procédure Civile, Art. 1460(1); German Arbitration Act, § 1042(3), and Japanese Arbitration Act 2003, Art. 26(1); party autonomy is discussed at 6.2.5 and 6.4.2.

[50] Redfern and Hunter, *Law and Practice of International Commercial Arbitration*, 6–7, 9 and 155; J. D. M. Lew, L. A. Mistelis and S. M. Kröll, *Comparative International Commercial Arbitration* (The Hague: Kluwer Law International, 2003), 3–4, 99; English Arbitration Act 1996, s. 30(1), which requires, as one of the prerequisites to the tribunal's jurisdiction, a valid arbitration agreement, and New York Convention, Art. II(1), which states that the contracting states should recognise an arbitration agreement in writing, and provides in Art. V(1)(a) that recognition and enforcement may be refused if there is no valid arbitration agreement; *Harry L. Reynolds* v. *International Amateur Athletic Federation* (1996) XXI *Yearbook Commercial Arbitration* 715 and *Oberlandesgericht (Court of Appeal)*, Rostock,

England recognised according to ss. 94 to 98 of the English Arbitration Act 1996.

This arbitration agreement can be made either before or after the dispute has arisen, and it is binding on the parties. If one party starts court proceedings in a dispute within the remit of the arbitration agreement and the other party objects, the court stays proceedings.[51]

Unlike mediation, arbitration is mandatory, i.e. once the parties have submitted to arbitration they cannot withdraw from the process. If the respondent refuses to participate in the arbitration, the arbitrator may issue a default award.[52]

The arbitration award can be directly enforced, similar to a judgment.[53] Hence, unlike mediation, arbitration is coercive. Furthermore, the New York Convention[54] provides that, subject to narrow exceptions,[55] contracting states must enforce a foreign arbitration award.[56] The widespread ratification of the New York Convention[57] ensures that arbitration awards are enforceable across most borders, unlike court judgments, for which the enforcing party has to rely on notions of comity in the enforcement jurisdiction or a bilateral or multilateral enforcement treaty.

An arbitration award is also final in the sense that awards have *res judicata* effect, i.e. once an award has been made, and unless the award is successfully challenged, the same matter cannot be brought before a court or arbitration tribunal again.[58]

Therefore, in contrast to mediation, arbitration is binding and mandatory, leading to a directly enforceable award with *res judicata* effect. Because of these characteristics of arbitration, compared to the characteristics of mediation discussed above, only arbitration can be a true alternative to litigation as a binding and enforceable avenue for redress for Internet disputes.

---

22 November 2001, No. 1 Sch. 03/00, reported in (2004) XXIX *Yearbook Commercial Arbitration* 732.

[51] English Arbitration Act 1996, s. 9(4); French Nouveau Code de Procédure Civile, Art. 1458; German Arbitration Act, § 1032(1); Japanese Arbitration Act 2003, Art. 14(1).

[52] English Arbitration Act 1996, s. 41(4); German Arbitration Act, § 1048; Japanese Arbitration Act 2003, Art. 33.

[53] English Arbitration Act 1996, s. 66; French Nouveau Code de Procédure Civile, Art. 1476; German Arbitration Act, § 1055; Japanese Arbitration Act 2003, Art. 45(1).

[54] 330 UNTS 3, adopted on 10 June 1958, entered into force on 7 June 1959.

[55] New York Convention, Art. V.    [56] New York Convention, Art. III.

[57] On 12 September 2007, 142 states had ratified the New York Convention.

[58] English Arbitration Act 1996, s. 58(1); Redfern and Hunter, *Law and Practice of International Commercial Arbitration*, 459.

## 4.3 Applicable law

It has been argued in this chapter generally that mediation operates in the shadow of the law, and that a binding form of resolution is required to complement mediation. For disputes internal to one jurisdiction, litigation complements mediation. For international cross-border Internet disputes, mediation should be complemented by arbitration as a binding form of extra-judicial dispute resolution, which has *res judicata* effect and which, thanks to the New York Convention, can be easily enforced across national borders.[59]

Since arbitration is mainly based on decisions founded on legal rules and standards, in cross-border Internet disputes it is necessary to answer the question of which legal rules apply or should apply.

### 4.3.1 Law of the arbitration agreement, the lex arbitri and applicable law distinguished

In arbitration, the question of 'which law applies' can be raised in three different contexts: (i) the law of the submission agreement or arbitration clause itself in deciding its validity and scope; (ii) the law of the seat of the arbitration, which provides the procedural framework for the arbitration; and (iii) the law applicable to the substantive issues between the parties (the applicable law). The main focus of this section is on item (iii), applicable law, but the other aspects should be mentioned briefly.

As to item (i), this will frequently be the same as item (iii) if the parties have made an express choice and the agreement to arbitrate is contained in a clause of the main agreement between the parties.[60] However, some courts have found that the scope and validity of the arbitration agreement (whether contained in a submission agreement or a clause) should be governed by the law of the seat.[61] The courts in the place of enforcement, if this is in a state being a contracting state to the New York Convention,

---

[59] See 6.2.6, 6.7 and 8.4.3.

[60] *Union of India* v. *McDonnell Douglas Corp* [1993] 2 Lloyd's Rep 48 (Comm), 49–50; *Sonatrach Petroleum Corporation (BVI)* v. *Ferrell International Ltd* [2002] 1 All ER 627 (Comm), para. 32; see *Hanseatisches Oberlandesgericht* (Court of Appeal), Hamburg, 24 January 2003, No. 11 Sch. 06/01, reported in (2005) XXX *Yearbook Commercial Arbitration* 509, para. 16; C. M. V. Clarkson and J. Hill, *The Conflict of Laws*, 3rd edn (Oxford University Press, 2006), 252.

[61] Case No. T1881–99, *Bulgarian Foreign Trade Bank Ltd* v. *Al Trade Finance Inc* (2001) XXVI *Yearbook Commercial Arbitration* 291 (Swedish Supreme Court), Judgment of 27 October 2000; *XL Insurance Ltd* v. *Owens Corning* [2000] 2 Lloyd's Rep 500 (Comm), 508; Clarkson and Hill, *The Conflict of Laws*, 252.

would have to examine validity in conformity with the provisions of that convention and international public policy.

As to item (ii), the *lex arbitri* establishes the procedural framework of the arbitration[62] and attaches the arbitration to a jurisdictional forum.[63] The New York Convention still refers to the *lex arbitri* as the 'law of the country where the arbitration took place'[64] or as the 'law of the country where the award is made'.[65] This actual territorial connection between the *lex arbitri* and the place where the actual arbitration is taking place is, as a matter of fact, becoming more and more tenuous, as with modern air travel and instant communication the arbitration may be held in more than one place and also, with online arbitration, in no particular place at all. Therefore modern arbitration legislation and rules usually provide that the *lex arbitri* is chosen by the parties in their agreement to arbitrate. The parties can also empower the arbitral institution (if any) or the tribunal to designate the seat.[66] Therefore the seat of arbitration is now a designated place rather than the actual territory in which the arbitration takes place. Since the seat and hence the *lex arbitri* can be agreed by the parties, the choice of the procedural law is much more flexible than in litigation and hence more suitable to international, cross-border disputes.

The law applying to the substantive issues in dispute is probably more contentious, and the parties may find it harder to agree the applicable law. For this reason the remainder of this section focuses on applicable law.

### 4.3.2 Options

Before discussing how the applicable law is determined, it might be useful to consider the different options amongst which a choice must be made.

---

[62] The principle of party autonomy in arbitration means that the parties can, to a large extent, determine the procedure they wish to follow; see Chapter 6.

[63] Some scholars have argued that international commercial arbitration should be delocalised, i.e. only controlled by the courts at the place of enforcement; see, for example, J. Paulsson, 'Delocalisation of International Commercial Arbitration: When and Why It Matters' (1983) 32 *International and Comparative Law Quarterly* 53–61. However, this is only possible if the *lex arbitri* does allow for this; see Redfern and Hunter, *Law and Practice of International Commercial Arbitration*, 108.

[64] New York Convention, Art. V(1)(d).     [65] New York Convention, Art. V(1)(a) and (e).

[66] English Arbitration Act 1996, s. 3 provides that the seat is designated by the parties or by the arbitral or other institution or person vested by the parties with powers in that regard, or by the arbitral tribunal if so authorised by the parties. The UNCITRAL Rules, Art. 16(1) go even further, by stipulating that if the parties cannot agree on the seat, the arbitral tribunal will make the choice for them, and so does the UNCITRAL Model Law in Art. 20(1). Similarly, the ICC Rules, which state in Art. 14(1) that the place of arbitration will be fixed by the ICC's Court of Arbitration if the parties have not agreed.

Firstly, in most cases the applicable law will be the law of a particular jurisdiction (either a national, state or federal law). Applying the law of a jurisdiction has the advantage that this constitutes a developed, mature legal system that is geared up to provide an answer for any legal problem, and that such a system is capable of interpretation by lawyers trained in it, thereby providing reasonable certainty.[67]

Secondly, the applicable law may consist of international law[68] or an aspect of international law, such as the general principles of international law.[69] Applying international law to a dispute has the reverse advantage to applying the law of a particular jurisdiction: it is inherently more abstract and flexible and may appear neutral, but may lack certainty and may not be subject-specific. International law is not designed to answer detailed, specific questions of contract law.[70]

Thirdly, the applicable law may be transnational law[71] such as the UNIDROIT[72] Principles,[73] the Lando Principles,[74] CISG[75] or *Lex Mercatoria*.

---

[67] Redfern and Hunter, *Law and Practice of International Commercial Arbitration*, 115.

[68] English Arbitration Act 1996, s. 46 only allows the tribunal to apply international law if the parties have agreed not to apply the law of a particular jurisdiction. German Arbitration Act 1998, § 1051(2) takes an even more conservative approach: it only allows the application of international law if the parties have expressly agreed that international law should apply. By contrast, French Nouveau Code de Procédure Civile, Art. 1496 allows the tribunal discretion: in the absence of choice, the tribunal can apply any rules it considers appropriate.

[69] Statute of the International Court of Justice, Art. 38(1)(c) refers to the 'general principles of law recognised by civilised nations' as a source of law to fill any gaps in international law. These are common themes and principles appertaining to many different legal orders; see M. N. Shaw, *International Law*, 5th edn (Cambridge University Press, 2003), 94; R. Wallace, *International Law*, 4th edn (London: Sweet & Maxwell, 2002), 22–3.

[70] Redfern and Hunter, *Law and Practice of International Commercial Arbitration*, 120–1.

[71] See fn. 68, above.

[72] UNIDROIT, set up in 1926, is the International Institute for the Unification of Private Law, an independent intergovernmental organisation with its seat in Rome.

[73] *UNIDROIT Principles of International Commercial Contracts*, 2004 edn, containing general contract rules for international commercial agreements, available from www.unidroit. org/english/principles/contracts/principles2004/blackletter2004.pdf [1 April 2008].

[74] *The Principles of European Contract Law*, formulated by the independent Commission on European Contract Law (available from http://frontpage.cbs.dk/law/commission_ on_european_contract_law [23 July 2008]).

[75] 1489 UNTS 25567, 1980 United Nations Convention on Contracts for the International Sale of Goods (or 'Vienna Convention'), governing aspects of the international sale of goods, where both parties are in contracting countries or where they have chosen CISG as applicable law.

*Lex Mercatoria* is a modern version of the mediaeval law merchant, consisting of rules and practices of the international business community/ communities. It proceeds by comparing different national systems to extract common denominators,[76] and by looking at international law – such as the UNIDROIT principles, the general principles of international law mentioned above and trade usages (including codes of conduct) – to close any gaps.[77]

Some scholars have accumulated lists of rules and principles,[78] whereas others have adopted a functional approach.[79] Under this latter approach, *Lex Mercatoria* is merely a method for finding the appropriate rule for the actual problem in question.[80] Some scholars and practitioners have been sceptical or even hostile towards this method, doubting the existence of *Lex Mercatoria* as an identifiable body of law to which reference can or should be usefully made.[81]

Finally, in rare cases the tribunal may be empowered to decide the case without applying any particular body of law, on the basis of what is fair and reasonable, *ex aequo et bono*.[82] This is not further discussed here.

In litigation, the courts are limited to applying the law of a particular jurisdiction to the substantive issues in dispute. By contrast, in arbitration a wider range of options exists, including international and transnational law, giving the tribunal greater discretion and flexibility.

### 4.3.3 Determination of the applicable law

#### Choice of law

The principle of party autonomy in arbitration means that the parties can choose the law applicable to the substantive issues of the contract, and they can expressly avail themselves of any of the options listed

---

[76] Critical on this basis, see L. J. Mustill, 'The New Lex Mercatoria – The First Twenty-Five Years' (1987) 4(2) *Arbitration International* 86–119, 92.

[77] Lew, Mistelis and Kröll, *Comparative International Commercial Arbitration*, 454.

[78] See, for example, the *Central Transnational Law Digest & Bibliography* by Klaus Peter Berger, available from www.tldb.net [1 April 2008].

[79] Redfern and Hunter, *Law and Practice of International Commercial Arbitration*, 131–2.

[80] E. Gaillard, 'Transnational Law: A Legal System or a Method of Decision-Making' (2001) 17(1) *Arbitration International* 59–71, 64 and 69.

[81] Mustill, 'The New Lex Mercatoria', 92; F. A. Mann, 'The Proper Law in the Conflict of Laws' (1987) 36 *International Comparative Law Quarterly* 437–53, 448.

[82] English Arbitration Act 1996, s. 46. German Arbitration Act 1998, § 1051(3) only allows the tribunal to act as *amiable compositeur* if the parties have agreed this expressly.

above.[83] This is subject to public-policy concerns and the principle of mandatory laws discussed below.[84]

## No choice of law

If the parties have made no discernable choice at all, there are two possibilities of how to deal with this situation.[85] The applicable law could either be determined according to conflicts-of-law rules,[86] for example by deciding to which jurisdiction the dispute is most closely connected,[87] or by giving the arbitral tribunal a wide discretion in determining the rules and standards according to which it decides the dispute.[88] Whether the tribunal has to decide according to conflicts-of-law rules or whether it has a discretion concerning the question of the most appropriate rules to apply to the substantive issues in dispute depends on the arbitration law at the seat of arbitration or on the rules of the arbitration institution.

If a tribunal decides that it has to apply 'traditional' conflicts-of-law analysis, it will have to apply the law of a jurisdiction to which these conflicts-of-law rules point. For this, it will have to decide which jurisdiction's conflicts-of-law rules to refer to. In Europe, the law applicable to contracts has, of course, been harmonised in the Rome Convention, now the Rome I Regulation, which the UK has opted out of.[89] Article 1(2)(e) of that Regulation provides that it does not apply to arbitration agreements (same as Art. 1(2)(d) of the Rome Convention). However, most scholars have interpreted this exception narrowly, meaning that the conflicts-of-law rules in the Rome Convention/Regulation do not apply to the submission agreement itself but do apply to the determination of the law applicable to the substantive issues.[90] Article 4(1) sets out the applicable

[83] Lew, Mistelis and Kröll, *Comparative International Commercial Arbitration*, 413; Redfern and Hunter, *Law and Practice of International Commercial Arbitration*, 111–12; English Arbitration Act 1996, s. 46(1); German Arbitration Act 1998, § 1051(1); UNCITRAL Model Law, Art. 28(1); French Nouveau Code de Procédure Civile, Art. 1496; Japanese Arbitration Act 2003, Art. 36(1).

[84] See 4.3.5.    [85] The parties may not have been able to agree a 'neutral' applicable law.

[86] UNCITRAL Model Law, Art. 28(2) and English Arbitration Act 1996, s. 46(3): 'the tribunal shall apply the conflict of law rules which it considers applicable' (not necessarily English conflicts-of-law rules).

[87] Japanese Arbitration Act 2003, Art. 36(2); German Arbitration Act 1998, § 1051(2); Swiss Federal Law on Private International Law 1987, Art. 187(1).

[88] French Nouveau Code de Procédure Civile, Art. 1496; 1998 ICC Rules, Art. 17(1).

[89] Rome Convention of 19 June 1980 on the Law Applicable to Contractual Obligations, OJ C027 of 26 January 1998; Regulation (EC) No. 593/2008 of 17 June 2008, OJ L177/6 of 4 July 2008.

[90] Report by M. Giuliano and P. Lagarde on the Rome Convention, *Report on the Convention on the Law Applicable to Contractual Obligations*, OJ C282 of 31 October 1980, para. 5;

law of the party effecting the characteristic performance (Art. 4(2)), such as the seller, service provider or distributor. Articles 4(3) and 4(4) refer to the country with which the contract has the closest connection.

By contrast, if the arbitration tribunal can freely decide which rules to apply to the substantive issues, it is not bound by the results of conflicts-of-law analysis, and, more importantly, it is not restricted to referring to the law of a particular jurisdiction but may additionally or alternatively apply transnational rules of law.[91]

Finally, if the parties cannot agree on a choice of law, the question arises as to whether the parties are allowed to confer a power on the tribunal to make this choice for them, by providing, for example, 'that the arbitration tribunal may apply any rules it deems applicable'. Some arbitration laws, even if they do not generally confer discretion on the tribunal to determine applicable law without a conflicts-of-law analysis, allow the parties to expressly empower the tribunal to do so.[92]

### 4.3.4 Conclusion: the challenge of applicable law

Applicable law is important in two respects. For cross-border Internet disputes, determining applicable law in court proceedings involves considering localisation factors, and is therefore complex. Since arbitration, like litigation, is based on legal rules and standards, the question arises as to whether finding the applicable law poses a similar challenge.

This section has shown that arbitration takes a more flexible and pragmatic approach than litigation. In arbitration, the choice is not limited to the law of a particular legal system but may encompass international and transnational legal rules and trade usages, if the parties provide for this. Furthermore, in some jurisdictions the arbitration tribunal is empowered with wider discretion in deciding which rules to apply. However, since this book is concerned with fairness in online arbitration, it should also examine whether applicable law in arbitration raises fairness issues.

---

Clarkson and Hill, *The Conflict of Laws*, 256; P. North and J. Fawcett, *Cheshire and North's Private International Law*, 13th edn (London: Butterworths, 1999), 548–9; Redfern and Hunter, *Law and Practice of International Commercial Arbitration*, 112, 144; same applies for the Regulation.

[91] Under the Rome Regulation/Convention, the law to be applied must be the law of a state, not transnational law; see D. McClean and K. Beevers, *Morris on the Conflicts of Law*, 6th edn (London: Sweet & Maxwell, 2005), 339.

[92] English Arbitration Act 1996, s. 46(1)(b); UNCITRAL Model Law, Art. 28(1).

### 4.3.5 Mandatory laws

Clearly the determination of which laws and legal standards are applied to a dispute may be decisive for the outcome, and may therefore be a crucial and hotly disputed question between the parties. Fairness issues may arise if, in a situation of power imbalance, the 'weaker' party is deprived of mandatory laws designed to protect this 'weaker' party and counterbalance the weaker bargaining position of that party.[93] This 'deprivation' may arise because of an express choice-of-law clause inserted by the 'more powerful' party or because of the tribunal not applying the mandatory law, in the absence of an express choice.

### Mandatory laws explained

The legal concept of mandatory laws in private international law is, of course, wider than merely counter-balancing power differentials between unequal contracting parties. Mandatory rules are *all* rules of a legal system that cannot be derogated from by contrary contractual provision[94] or, in the international context, that cannot be avoided by an express choice of law[95] in the contract and overriding provisions of the applicable law

---

[93] See 2.2.3 and 2.5; EC Recommendation 98/257/EC, Principle V; S. Ware, 'Default Rules from Mandatory Rules: Privatizing Law through Arbitration' (1999) 83 *Minnesota Law Review* 703–54, 726.

[94] Definition in Rome Regulation and the Convention, Art. 3(3); these are 'internal mandatory rules'.

[95] Generally speaking, it seems that before many US courts, the principle of the overriding effect of mandatory laws is much narrower. (US doctrine does not express the principle by using the concept of mandatory laws, but in terms of policy. Thus the comparison has to be made by analogy.) The US Restatement Second Conflict of Laws provides in § 187(2)(b) that if there is an express or implicit choice of law by the parties, this choice will be overridden by the law applicable in the absence of choice, if (and only if) this chosen law is contrary to a fundamental policy of the state providing the applicable law in the absence of choice, and if that state has a materially greater interest than the state providing the chosen law in the determination of the particular issue. This principle is narrower than Art. 9(1) of the Rome Regulation as it only refers to the law applicable in the absence of choice rather than any foreign mandatory law that has a close connection to the issues, and as it only applies where the parties have made a choice of law. With regard to choice-of-law clauses in the standard terms of consumer contracts (or other contracts where there is a substantial power imbalance), the United States applies the doctrine of adhesion contracts. Choice-of-law clauses contained in adhesion contracts are usually upheld, unless there is substantial injustice to the 'weaker party'; see Comment to § 187 in Restatement Second Conflict of Laws. This is in marked contrast to Art. 6 of the Rome Regulation (Art. 5 of the Rome Convention). Adhesion contracts are also discussed, in relation to consumer arbitration clauses, at 7.2.3.

identified by conflicts-of-law rules.[96] The rationale for mandatory laws is the protection of the public interest overriding party autonomy in contract and, in a conflicts-of-law situation, the recognition that states other than that providing the applicable law may have a public interest in regulating the situation.[97] Mandatory laws embody state, economic or social policy, such as exchange regulations, foreign export prohibitions, import regulation, competition and antitrust law, or mandatory rules that protect the weaker party in consumer, employment, insurance, and commercial agents/landlord and tenant relationships.[98]

There are two types of mandatory laws.[99] The first type is the mandatory law of a country that is closely connected to the issues in dispute, but whose law is not the applicable law. Here the mandatory law is a foreign law, different from the applicable law and foreign to the forum. For this type, it is necessary to examine the nature of the law itself to see whether it is intended not to be derogated from, and to analyse whether there is a sufficient connection to the issues in dispute.[100]

The second type is the limitation of the applicable law by the public policy of the forum. This, in turn, can take two forms. Firstly, the court may consider and apply mandatory norms of the forum itself,[101] and secondly, the court may refuse to apply a particular aspect of the applicable law on the grounds of incompatibility with the public policy of the forum.[102]

### Applicability of mandatory laws in arbitration of Internet disputes

Having (very) briefly sketched the concept of mandatory law in conflicts-of-law theory, and in particular its implementation in the Rome Convention/Regulation, it is necessary to return to the question on which this book focuses: namely, whether an arbitration tribunal (as opposed to a public court) would have to apply mandatory law to Internet disputes in order to redress power imbalances.

---

[96] 'International mandatory laws'; N. Voser, 'Mandatory Rules of Law as a Limitation on the Law Applicable in International Commercial Arbitration' (1996) 7 *American Review of International Arbitration* 319–57, 321; Clarkson and Hill, *The Conflict of Laws*, 257, North and Fawcett, *Cheshire and North's Private International Law*, 576.

[97] Clarkson and Hill, *The Conflict of Laws*, 195–6; North and Fawcett, *Cheshire and North's Private International Law*, 576.

[98] Voser, 'Mandatory Rules of Law', 325.      [99] Clarkson and Hill, *The Conflict of Laws*, 195.

[100] See, for example, Rome Regulation, Arts. 3(3) and 9(1) and Rome Convention, Art. 7(1), generally providing for the application of this type of mandatory law; however, this provision does not apply in the United Kingdom: see Contracts (Applicable Law) Act 1990, s. 2(2). Subject-matter specific mandatory laws are contained in Art. 6 (B2C contracts) (Art. 5 of the Rome Convention).

[101] Rome Regulation, Art. 9(2); Rome Convention, Art. 7(2).

[102] Rome Convention, Art. 16.

It should be remembered that the central concern of this book is of Internet disputes between parties subject to a power imbalance, and for the purpose of this book this power imbalance has been defined as a corporate entity–individual paradigm.[103]

Traditionally, international commercial arbitration has been conceived to be a form of dispute resolution between business parties of (very) roughly equal bargaining power.[104] Thus it is not surprising that questions of power imbalances, such as in B2C relationships, have not been central to the doctrines pertaining to international commercial arbitration. The online arbitration of Internet disputes introduces a new paradigm here.[105]

To what extent arbitration tribunals should take into account mandatory laws is not entirely clear.[106] Some argue that since arbitration is of a private nature, being founded on the agreement of the parties and being carried out by a private tribunal, the principle of party autonomy should play a greater role than in litigation, and that therefore no regard should be had to mandatory rules (other than those of the law chosen by the parties).[107] Furthermore, as far as the second type of mandatory laws (i.e. the public policy of the forum) is concerned, it can be argued that, due to the private nature of the tribunal, there is no forum and hence no obligation to apply these types of mandatory rules, unless they amount to international public policy.[108]

This argument is not convincing; in the opinion of the author and many scholars, it should be rejected.[109]

---

[103] See 3.6.3.

[104] This conception is, of course, a generalisation; to what extent this has been historically accurate will not be further examined here.

[105] See 3.2.

[106] English Arbitration Act 1996, s. 46; German Arbitration Act 1998, § 1051; French Nouveau Code de Procédure Civile, Art. 1496 – all silent on the issue of mandatory laws.

[107] Lew, Mistelis and Kröll, *Comparative International Commercial Arbitration*, 420–1, in particular para. 17–30: 'There is no basis for a tribunal to ignore the express choice of the parties because it determines that there is a contrary mandatory rule in one of these national laws.'

[108] Lew, Mistelis and Kröll, *Comparative International Commercial Arbitration*, 420; Voser, 'Mandatory Rules of Law', 330.

[109] Voser, 'Mandatory Rules of Law', 331, 336–7 and 342–3; P. Mayer, 'Mandatory Rules of Law in International Arbitration' (1986) 1 *Arbitration International* 274–93, 285; D. Hochstrasser, 'Choice of Law and "Foreign" Mandatory Rules in International Arbitration' (1994) 11 *Journal of International Arbitration* 57–86, 84–5; M. Blessing, 'Mandatory Rules of Law Versus Party Autonomy in International Arbitration' (1997) 14 *Journal of International Arbitration* 23–40, 31–2 (subject to conditions); A. Lowenfeld, 'The Mitsubishi Case: Another View' (1986) 2 *Arbitration International* 178–90, 186–7.

The first reason for this rejection is specific to the narrow focus of the book, i.e. it has to be seen in the specific context of Internet disputes. Arbitration as adjudication according to laws and legal rules should include those fundamental public-policy values agreed in a democratic state; otherwise it loses its legitimacy as a legal process. To this, one could object that the mandatory rules of the law chosen by the parties or that apply in the absence of choice would apply. However, this objection does not hold up against the fairness argument made in Chapter 2, i.e. that fairness requires that power imbalances be actively counter-balanced. If a stronger party directs its activities towards the territory of the weaker party and then imposes a choice of law on the weaker party, the mandatory rules of the weaker party's jurisdiction should apply in order to achieve this counter-balance.[110]

The second reason is that if mandatory law were not applied to arbitration, courts and policy-makers would ensure that areas of law containing mandatory laws would not be subject to arbitration. In other words, the consequence of a finding that mandatory rules are inapplicable before arbitration tribunals would be that certain subject matter, governed by mandatory rules, would have to stay outside the ambit of arbitration. The fact that disputes involving laws designed to promote public-interest objectives (such as competition-law disputes) are now considered arbitrable means that mandatory rules must apply.[111] In fact, this argument could be a political tool to obtain agreement for the new conflicts-of-law rule for arbitration of Internet disputes proposed in this book. The bargain could be to allow consumer arbitration more generally, against the concession that the mandatory laws in the individual's location apply if the corporate entity directed its activities there.[112]

The other two reasons relate to the nature of arbitration as private or public, which will be discussed in greater detail in Chapter 6.[113]

Arbitration fulfils the same *function* as court proceedings, i.e. adjudicating a dispute according to laws and legal rules, and hence the same considerations of public interest as are reflected in the mandatory rules

---

[110] EC Recommendation 98/257/EC, Principle V; Ware, 'Default Rules from Mandatory Rules', 726; see also Regulation (EC) No. 593/2008 of 17 June 2008, OJ L177/6 of 4 July 2008.

[111] *Mitsubishi Motors Corp* v. *Soler Chrysler-Plymouth Inc*, 473 US 614; 629 105 SCt 3346, 87 (1985), where the US Supreme Court enforced an arbitration clause in a dispute involving antitrust law; Swiss Federal Supreme Court Decision BGE 118 II 193 (1992), where the court decided that the arbitration tribunal had to take into account EC competition law; Voser, 'Mandatory Rules of Law', 330; Lowenfeld, 'The Mitsubishi Case', 186–7.

[112] See Chapter 8.    [113] See 6.2.5.

themselves and their applicability should apply. This reason essentially is based on an argument that there should be no discrimination between litigation and arbitration, since both forms of adjudication fulfil a public *function.*

Finally, arbitration can also not be said to be entirely private, since the courts support arbitration through their supervisory and enforcement jurisdiction; this public element means that the principle of party autonomy may well have to be balanced with the public interest.

For these reasons, it is argued in this book that party autonomy should be restricted to the extent that mandatory laws apply, at least in Internet disputes, if the conditions for their application are fulfilled.

## Mandatory rules applied in practice

It should be mentioned that while the applicability of mandatory laws in arbitration is not settled, tribunals will consider mandatory laws in some situations as a practical matter, in order to avoid a challenge of the award at the seat or on the basis that it is against the public policy of the enforcing court, but this is usually limited to international public policy.[114]

Furthermore, in the specific context of B2C contracts, arbitration tribunals in the EU may (although their obligation is unclear) decide to apply mandatory laws. Some jurisdictions impose restrictions on consumer arbitration, with the consequence that an arbitration clause in a consumer contract is invalid, and hence the parties have to litigate.[115] However, if the arbitration clause is valid and the dispute arbitrable, the question arises as to whether an arbitration tribunal would apply the specific mandatory laws contained in Art. 5 of the Rome Convention or Art. 6 of the Rome Regulation. If the tribunal chooses to determine applicable law according to the conflicts-of-law rules of a contracting state to the Rome Convention or the Rome Regulation for those Member States who have not opted out,[116] the answer to this question is yes. Article 5(2) of the

---

[114] If England is the seat of arbitration under s. 68 of the English Arbitration Act 1996 (serious irregularity), or in the enforcement court under Art. V(2) of the New York Convertion. However, the latter only applies if the transnational or international public policy of the enforcement court contradicts the applicable law and will be used sparingly; see, for example, the Swiss Federal Supreme Court Decision BGE 120 II 155 (1994); see also 6.2.6 and 6.7. This consideration, of course, only applies if there is a conflict between the applicable law and the mandatory law at the seat or at the place of enforcement; it does not apply if the conflict arises with another state, such as the consumer's country of residence; Voser, 'Mandatory Rules of Law', 335.

[115] See 7.2.

[116] As has been pointed out above, tribunals have a power of discretion in this matter. If the tribunal applies the conflicts-of-law rules of a state who is not a party to the Rome

Rome Convention provides that the mandatory consumer-protection law of the country of the consumer's country of residence applies if the contract was preceded by advertising or a specific invitation in the consumer's country of residence, and the consumer took the steps to conclude the contract there. The Rome Regulation applies the mandatory consumer protection law of the consumer's country of residence, if the supplier directs its activities there (Arts. 6(1)(b), 6(2)).

### Conflicts-of-law rule on mandatory laws for Internet disputes

For the model in Chapter 8,[117] it is argued here that mandatory rules should be applied (on a similar basis as in Art. 5(2) of the Rome Convention) but modified in three respects.

Firstly, the concept of mandatory laws as expressed in Art. 5 of the Rome Convention is unsatisfactory. If the contract contains an express choice of law other than the law of the consumer's residence, Art. 5(2) of the Rome Convention and Art. 6(2) of the Rome Regulation envisage that a mix of the chosen law and the consumer's law applies – the consumer's law to the extent that it is mandatory, and the chosen law for the issues where the consumer's law is non-mandatory. If the contract does not contain a choice of law, Art. 5(3) of the Rome Convention and Art. 6(1) of the Rome Regulation provide that the consumer's law shall govern all aspects. It would be simpler and clearer to provide – whether or not the contract contains a choice of law – that the law of the consumer's country of residence should apply to all aspects of the dispute *if* the contract is a relevant consumer contract.[118]

Secondly, the B2C relationship paradigm is unsatisfactory and should be extended to incorporated entity–individual relationships. In other words, the conflicts-of-law rules should not be limited to disputes between business and consumers but should apply where there is an Internet dispute between a corporate entity and an individual. This will not be discussed further, as this argument has already been made in Chapter 3.[119]

An important distinction has to be made here between: (i) the relevant connection of the mandatory law to the situation of the dispute, and (ii) the scope of the mandatory law itself. The connection is the conflicts-of-law rule, stating in what circumstances the mandatory law overrules the

---

Convention, or applies transnational rules directly, so that the Rome Convention/Regulation obviously does not apply.

[117] See 8.3.1.

[118] See EU Commission Proposal for a Regulation on the Law Applicable to Contractual Obligations (Rome I) COM(2005) 650 of 15 December 2005, Art. 5(1), which was not adopted in the Regulation.

[119] See 3.6.3.

otherwise applicable law, which is essentially the trigger for the application of the mandatory law. The scope of the mandatory law is the provision or definition in the mandatory law itself describing when it is applicable, such as the definition as to who is a 'consumer' in a consumer-protection law. For a mandatory law to be applicable, it has to pass two gateways: (i) the conditions for applicability under the conflicts-of-law rule, and (ii) the conditions of the mandatory law itself. Since this book is not concerned with substantive matters, it only examines the former.

Thirdly, the wording concerning the relevant connecting factors in the Rome Convention/Regulation is unclear in its application to Internet disputes, and should be improved in the proposed conflicts-of-law rule.

First of all, if, on an objective assessment of the online activity (such as selling goods or services on a website), this is targeted at a particular location, the mandatory laws of that targeted jurisdiction should prima facie apply.

However, additionally, the issue is essentially one of fair risk allocation. It could be argued that an incorporated entity actively seeking to enter into contracts with individuals in foreign jurisdictions via the Internet should comply with the mandatory laws applying to these individuals at their place of residence, and that the cost of this compliance is a concomitant factor directing commercial activities abroad.

The issue is that corporate entities are legitimately concerned about how to limit the risk of being prosecuted or sued for not complying with the laws of numerous jurisdictions when using a communications medium that is essentially global. One way of limiting this risk would be to target only those jurisdictions with whose laws a corporate entity wishes to comply, and therefore the issue is how to identify its individual client's location. As has been discussed in Chapter 3,[120] establishing the location of a person communicating via the Internet with certainty is a difficult and expensive (albeit not insurmountable) task. Hence to impose a burden on the corporate entity to establish the location of its individual customers with certainty would be too harsh.

Secondly, in light of this, it should be stipulated that the corporate entity may take some measures towards establishing the location of its customers by simply asking the customer to identify his or her location. If the customer then misleads the corporate entity as to location, he or she should lose the protection of the mandatory laws at the customer's location, and the law of the corporate entity should apply. Therefore a corporate entity can protect itself by enquiring about a customer's

---

[120]  See 3.2.2.

location before the transaction is completed, and the mandatory law of the individual customer's residence should apply if the corporate entity has directed its activities to that state, unless the customer has misled the corporate entity about his or her location.[121] Such a conflicts-of-law rule has the advantage that the customer's location is made transparent with simple means, and that it protects the trader from unwittingly contracting with an individual in a jurisdiction it is trying to avoid.

## 4.4 Conclusion

This chapter provides the background for the argument that a variant of arbitration, i.e. online arbitration, should be considered to be the main *binding* form of dispute resolution for Internet disputes.

This chapter has looked at the two main forms of ADR – mediation and arbitration – and has explained their function and significance. Mediation (being a voluntary, non-coercive form of dispute resolution, based on consensus between the parties and not leading to a directly enforceable result) cannot be regarded as a true replacement for adjudication. Therefore it has been argued that mediation is only fair if the parties have access to adjudication, as otherwise a compromise may be based on a party's desperation rather than a consideration of the merits of a case. This argument does not detract from the significance of mediation as an important method to filter out disputes lending themselves to a compromise.

Having singled out arbitration as the primary form of *binding* dispute resolution for Internet disputes, this chapter also had to deal with applicable law. Since arbitration is adjudication based on law, in cross-border Internet disputes it is necessary to determine the applicable law. This chapter has shown that arbitration tribunals have adopted a more flexible approach to this issue, in particular by relying on notions such as *Lex Mercatoria*. However, this approach is not suitable where the application of a foreign law or mercantile rules would deprive an individual, as the weaker party, of the protection of national mandatory laws, such as consumer-protection laws. This chapter therefore argues that mandatory laws valid at the location of the individual should be adopted by the schemes of online arbitration (which are part of the model outlined in Chapter 8) if the corporate entity has directed its activities to that jurisdiction, unless the individual has misled as to his or her location.

The next step in the progression of the book is to show how technology can be used to transform ADR into ODR.

---

[121] Similarly, see the EU Commission Proposal for a Regulation on the Law Applicable to Contractual Obligations (Rome I) COM(2005), 650 of 15 December 2005, Art. 5(2).

# 5

# ODR and access

I have a spelling checker
It came with my PC;
It plainly marks for my revue
Mistakes I cannot sea.
I've run this poem threw it,
I'm sure your pleased too no,
Its letter perfect in it's weigh,
My checker tolled me sew.

(Janet Minor, US poet)

## 5.1 Introduction

This chapter looks at online forms of mediation and arbitration and variants of the main forms of ADR and how they have been transformed by ODR. This chapter essentially focuses on the online dimension of extra-judicial dispute resolution, defining the meaning of the phrase 'online dispute resolution' and its significance for the fair resolution of Internet disputes. This chapter explains the different forms of ODR and the technology currently being used or developed for dispute resolution. Its main argument is that ODR is more than mere online ADR. The technology has a transforming effect – it makes dispute resolution for Internet disputes more effective and hence more accessible, thus contributing to fairness.[1]

## 5.2 Definition of ODR

The adjective 'online' refers to the use of computer and Internet technology, best described by the phrase 'information and communications

---

[1] See 2.2.3.

technology' (ICT). ODR is therefore dispute resolution carried out by combining the information processing powers of computers with the networked communication facilities of the Internet. For the purposes of this book, the following simple and short definition is proposed: 'ODR is a collective noun for dispute resolution techniques outside the courts using ICT and, in particular, Internet applications.'

The benefits of using such technology are so crucial to the understanding of the significance of ODR that the technology has been referred to as the 'fourth party'.[2]

The phrase 'ODR' as used in this book encompasses processes that are conducted completely online (without the parties ever meeting face to face) as well as processes that are completed only partly online.[3] ODR is based on variations of mediation and arbitration, as described in the previous chapter, but new and innovative variants have developed, as will be seen in the next section.

## 5.3 Forms of ODR

### 5.3.1 Brief overview

The first experiments in extra-judicial ODR were made during 1996 and 1997 in the US and Canada.[4] Most of these were initially university projects that evolved into commercial ventures. The European Commission and national governments in Europe and beyond have strongly advocated the

---

[2] E. Katsh and J. Rifkin, *Online Dispute Resolution* (San Francisco, Calif.: Jossey-Bass, 2001), 93.

[3] *ABA Task Force on Electronic Commerce and Alternative Dispute Resolution, Final Report August 2002*, as updated on 28 October 2002 (on file with author); M. Conley-Tyler, 'One Hundred and Fifteen and Counting: The State of Online Dispute Resolution 2004', in M. Conley-Tyler, E. Katsh and D. Choi (eds.), *Proceedings of the Third Annual Forum on Online Dispute Resolution 2004*, available from www.odr.info/cyberweek2004_library.php [1 April 2008]; L.-E. Teitz, 'Providing Legal Services for the Middle Class in Cyberspace: The Promise and Challenge of Online Dispute Resolution' (2001) 70 *Fordham Law Review* 985–1016, 991; S. Schiavetta, 'The Relationship between e-ADR and Article 6 of the European Convention of Human Rights Pursuant to the Case Law of the European Court of Human Rights' [2004] (1) *Journal of Information Law and Technology*, available at www2.warwick.ac.uk/fac/soc/law/elj/jilt/2004_1 [1 August 2008].

[4] The *Online Ombuds Office* (mediation, University of Massachusetts), out of which eventually developed the *Squaretrade* venture – see www.squaretrade.com [1 April 2008]; and see the *Cybertribunal* (University of Montreal), out of which later developed e-Resolution, a commercial venture that, albeit well known, ceased operations in December 2001.

use of ODR systems for consumer disputes.[5] While this is a continuously developing field, ODR is far from merely a theoretical concept – it is already relevant to dispute resolution practice. Melissa Conley-Tyler, in her survey in July 2004, counted 115 ODR services worldwide.[6]

Traditional offline arbitration and mediation institutions[7] have been focusing on the possibilities raised by online technology. Furthermore, some statutory dispute resolution schemes that use ODR have been established.[8] Recent years have also seen an amount of private entrepreneurial activity in the ODR field,[9] albeit with mixed results, only some of which seem to have established a viable business model in the long run.[10]

### 5.3.2 Case study: Austrian Internet Ombudsman

An interesting project in the ODR context is the Austrian Internet Ombudsman,[11] founded in 1999. Consumers can bring disputes against

---

[5] E-commerce Directive 2000/31/EC of 8 June 2000, Art. 17; the European Commission has funded a consumer mediation project called ECODIR – see www.ecodir.org [1 April 2008]; see also OECD, 'Guidelines for Consumer Protection in the Context of Electronic Commerce' (9 December 1999), Section B, available from www.oecd.org/document/51/0,2340, en_2649_34267_1824435_1_1_1_1,00.html [1 April 2008]; see the documentation regarding the workshop organised by the US DOC and FTC in June 2000: *Alternative Dispute Resolution for Consumer Transactions in the Borderless Online Marketplace*, available from www.ftc.gov/os/2000/02/altdisputeresolutionfrn.htm [1 April 2008]; a good overview of early private and public initiatives in this field is provided by A. Wiener, 'Regulations and Standards for Online Dispute Resolution', dated 15 February 2001 (on file with author).

[6] Conley-Tyler, 'One Hundred and Fifteen and Counting', 1.

[7] ICC Court of Arbitration's online filing platform, 'NetCase', at www.iccnetcase.org; the Electronic Case Facility (ECAF) of the WIPO Center at www.wipo.int/amc/en/ecaf/index.html; the AAA's online filing platform, WebFile, at https://apps.adr.org/webfile; Consensus Mediation's e-Mediator scheme at www.consensusmediation.co.uk/e-mediator.html; and the ADR Group's online mediation platform at www.adrgroup.co.uk/online-dispute/online-dispute-res.htm [1 April 2008].

[8] See, for example, CISAS for disputes between communication service providers and their customers, discussed at 8.2.2; Otelo, also discussed at 8.2.2 (www.otelo.org.uk); FOS, discussed in Chapter 8 (www.financial-ombudsman.org.uk) [1 April 2008].

[9] *Squaretrade*: www.squaretrade.com/cnt/jsp/index.jsp; *Cybersettle*: www.cybersettle.com/info/about/company/overview.aspx; i-courthouse: www.i-courthouse.com/main.taf?&redir=0 [1 April 2008].

[10] Conley-Tyler, 'One Hundred and Fifteen and Counting', Appendix 3; two prominent providers, Online Resolution (http://onlineresolution.com) and eResolution (www.theregister.co.uk/2001/12/04/eresolution_quits_domain_arbitration) [1 April 2008] ceased operation in 2003 and 2001 respectively.

[11] See www.ombudsmann.at; see also www.ecin.de/news/2003/12/09/06515 [1 April 2008].

business,[12] arising from E-commerce, before this ombudsman service. Only consumers can make a complaint and initiate the procedure, not businesses.[13]

In 2006, the Internet Ombudsman service worked on 4,750 complaints, with the total of claims amounting to €609,000 (about £412,969).[14] This equals an average claim of €128 (about £87). Hence this ombudsman scheme covers mainly small claims.

The procedure is a two-step one, consisting of online mediation and an online recommendation. At the first stage, the Ombudsman mediates between the parties. If this does not lead to a settlement, and if both parties agree to a second stage, the Ombudsman makes a recommendation.[15] The process uses an online platform and electronic file.[16]

The Austrian ombudsman service is not mandatory. Consumers can choose it by initiating a claim. The company against whom a claim is made is asked whether or not it wishes to participate in the procedure. Some companies may have agreed to take part before the dispute, by signing up to the Eurolabel Code of Conduct and trustmark scheme.[17] This does not make online arbitration generally obligatory, but, for a business which has opted to become a member of Eurolabel before the dispute arose and who has been certified in Austria, it does require participation in the Internet Ombudsman procedure.[18] Such a business would have to accept a recommendation made by the Internet Ombudsman service at the second stage of the procedure.[19]

For other companies, participation is based on voluntary agreement after the dispute has arisen. However, the Internet Ombudsman publishes the names of companies – against whom multiple complaints have

---

[12] The Internet Ombudsman offers conciliation services only for C2C disputes.
[13] See www.ombudsmann.at/ombudsmann.php/cat/21/title/H%E4ufige+Fragen [1 April 2008].
[14] See www.ombudsmann.at/ombudsmann.php/cat/3/title/News [1 April 2008].
[15] Confirmed by email by the Austrian Ombudsman (on file with author).
[16] See www.ombudsmann.at/ombudsmann.php/cat/21/title/H%E4ufige+Fragen [1 April 2008].
[17] See www.euro-label.com [1 April 2008]; see also 8.2.1.
[18] See www.ombudsmann.at/ombudsmann.php/cat/21/aid/59/title/Wie+l%E4uft+das+ Streitschlichtungsverfahren+beim+Internet+Ombudsmann+ab%3F and www. guetezeichen.at [1 April 2008].
[19] See www.guetezeichen.at [1 April 2008]; Verfahrensrichtlinien (Procedural Rules), para. 16(3), available from www.guetezeichen.at/kriterien/Verfahrensrichtlinien.pdf [1 April 2008]; the Internet Ombudsman had 127 Eurolabel cases in 2006.

been made and who have consistently refused to take part in dispute resolution – on its website.[20] Furthermore, the procedure will only continue to the second stage if both parties agree to this. In particular, the ombudsman only makes a recommendation if both parties agree to this.[21]

As to the jurisdiction of the Internet Ombudsman, this is only available to consumers who are resident in Austria and who complain against a business that is established within an EU Member State.[22]

The ombudsman service is free for the user – both the consumer and the company concerned. The parties only have to pay their own costs (if any). The parties may have legal representation, but this is not required as the Internet Ombudsman gives guidance to the parties during the procedure.[23] The costs of the Internet Ombudsman are born by Austrian public funds, through the Austrian Institute for Applied Telecommunication,[24] the Federal Ministry for Social Services and Consumer Protection[25] and the Federal Work Commission.[26] It has also received funding from the European Commission and the Austrian Internet Privatstiftung.

The Austrian Internet Ombudsman is an example of a current application of ODR for Internet disputes. The final chapter of this book will draw some lessons from this scheme. However, it should also be pointed out that, in some ways, the model, based on the discussions in this book (and which is outlined in Chapter 8), is quite different.[27]

## 5.4 Technologies used

This section briefly describes the technologies used in online mediation and online arbitration.

---

[20] See www.ombudsmann.at/ombudsmann.php/cat/21/title/H%E4ufige+Fragen [1 April 2008].

[21] *Ibid.*

[22] *Ibid.*; confirmed by email by the Austrian Ombudsman (on file with author).

[23] See www.ombudsmann.at/ombudsmann.php/cat/21/title/H%E4ufige+Fragen [1 April 2008].

[24] Österreichisches Institut für Angewandte Telekommunikation (ÖIAT).

[25] Bundesministerium für Soziales und Konsumentenschutz (BMSK).

[26] Bundesarbeitskammer.

[27] The Austrian Internet Ombudsman is not compulsory, and it seems to cover small consumer claims. This book is concerned with a wider range of disputes and power imbalances that go beyond small consumer claims.

### 5.4.1 Online mediation

Mediation[28] consists of a neutral third party brokering a settlement between the disputants. For this, communication between the mediator and each party, and between the parties, is crucial. In online mediation,[29] the mediator assists the parties in negotiating their dispute using electronic communication such as email or specially designed websites that provide virtual rooms in which the parties can communicate online.[30]

Email can provide a fast, easy to use, readily available and convenient method of communication and negotiation. Email can be supplemented by other means of communication such as instant messaging, the telephone and face-to-face meetings.

Intelligent filing forms ('dynamic forms') on the Web utilise the experience accumulated on particular types of disputes and allow the parties to file the statement of case and defence online. Such online forms are ordinarily easier to complete than offline forms as they change depending on the information entered. For example, if the claimant classifies the type of dispute as 'non-delivery of goods', the questions the form asks are tailored to this particular type of dispute.[31]

Alternatively or additionally, the parties and the mediator may use an online platform.[32] This is a computer that is linked to the Internet which hosts a set of linked pages containing instructions and information. Such an online platform is interactive: it allows the parties to post material, view postings and respond to postings. The online platform may contain various technologies allowing for written communication and discussions, as well as voice- or video-conferencing.

Furthermore, it is possible to segment the online platform into spaces, such that Space A is only accessible to one party and the mediator, Space B is only accessible to the other party and the mediator, and Space C is accessible to both parties and the mediator. Spaces A and B could be used for virtual private caucuses, and Space C for public discussions.

---

[28] See 4.2.1.

[29] See www.consensusmediation.co.uk/e-mediator.html or www.conciliaonline.net/concilia/default.asp?idtema=4 [1 April 2008].

[30] L. Ponte and T. Cavenagh, *Cyberjustice* (New Jersey, NJ: Pearson Prentice Hall, 2005), 63.

[31] See, for example, the AAA's WebFile or the form used by Otelo: http://oteloapp.otelo.org.uk/tkwebflow/flow.aspx?f=OteloInternetComplaint&template=otelowebtpl&xsl=Otelowebdtree [1 April 2008].

[32] For example, see the platform used by the ADR Group: www.adrgroup.co.uk/online-dispute/online-dispute-res.htm [1 April 2008].

In this way, the platform can be used to replicate the traditional three-room procedure by the use of virtual meetings on an online platform. The mediator and the parties in an online mediation can be simultaneously in Spaces C and A/B, thus being in a joint meeting and caucus at the same time. This would be impossible in real-world, offline mediation.[33]

Another obvious advantage of such virtual meetings is that they can be held at a distance, obviating the need to travel, and if the meetings are held asynchronously, whenever the participant in the mediation has a convenient moment.

The disadvantage of a virtual meeting is that the meeting is deprived of non-verbal communication such as postures, gestures, facial expressions and tonality of voice. It is often said that the lack of non-verbal communication makes it harder for the mediator to establish the parties' trust and confidence in the procedure.[34] However, this disadvantage must be balanced against the opportunities computer communication offers.[35]

Computer-aided communication is not limited to text and words but can be enhanced by other forms of visual expression such as the imaginative use of images, graphics, shapes and symbols. For example, as a means of encouragement, colourful graphics could illustrate to the parties the progress they have made in their rapprochement. Symbols and colours could be used to represent emotions. Thus, face-to-face communication is replaced by 'screen-to-screen' communication. This, however, requires mediators to adapt their communication skills from face-to-face interaction to screen-to-screen interaction.[36]

Finally, translation software[37] supports the translation of documents, an important factor in international, multilingual disputes.

---

[33] Rule, *Online Dispute Resolution for Business*, 72.
[34] Kaufmann-Kohler and Schultz, *Online Dispute Resolution*, 23; Rule, *Online Dispute Resolution for Business*, 66–7; L. Gibbons, R. Kennedy and J. Gibbs, 'Cyber-Mediation: Computer-Mediated Communications Medium Massaging the Message' (2002) 32 *New Mexico Law Review* 27–72, 43; H.-J. Fietkau argues that face-to-face communication is a complex process that cannot be satisfactorily reproduced in textual communication: see his chapter 'Unscharfe Kommunikation und verzerrte Entscheidungen in der Online Mediation', in O. Märker and M. Trénel, *Online Mediation* (Berlin: Edition Sigma, 2003), 82–104, 89–90.
[35] R. Gordon, 'The Electronic Personality and Digital Self' [February/April 2001] *Dispute Resolution Journal* 8–19; Kaufmann-Kohler and Schultz, *Online Dispute Resolution*, 23 and Rule, *Online Dispute Resolution for Business*, 66–7 – better reflection, less provocation and intimidation through distance; Gibbons, Kennedy and Gibbs, 'Cyber-Mediation', 43.
[36] Katsh and Rifkin, *Online Dispute Resolution*, 132–4.
[37] An example of free translation software can be found at http://babelfish.altavista.com/tr [1 April 2008].

### 5.4.2 Automated negotiation – negotiation assistance

Another useful ODR mechanism, which can be deployed in conjunction with online mediation, is negotiation software, which assists the parties in refining their interests. An example for this is the Smartsettle software,[38] which, with the help of a mediator, allows users to analyse their bargaining positions by evaluating and prioritising their negotiation objectives and by calculating (through an algorithm) the outcome most efficient for *all* parties.

The procedure has been influenced by modern negotiation theory, which moves away from position bargaining and towards principled negotiation based on each party's underlying interests, discussed in the preceding chapter.[39] Ernest Thiessen has described this procedure as 'working towards the goal of Pareto efficiency in negotiation'.[40]

Each party first states their initial position (without making demands) and identifies the underlying interests. From this, the software lists all issues, whether qualitative or quantitative, in a neutral manner. The mediator then helps the parties to further refine their underlying interests, priorities and the relative importance of each issue, as well as such matters as what they would expect from litigation (in other words, their best alternative to a negotiated agreement[41]). If the parties wish, this information can be kept confidential and will not be disclosed to the other side. The software then generates various packages, trading off the various issues against each other, calculating the most efficient allocation of interests on the different issues. In this way (it is claimed), the most efficient solution can be found.

### 5.4.3 Automated negotiation – blind bidding

A second form of automated negotiation is blind bidding,[42] which can also be used in conjunction with online mediation. Automated settlement systems are a highly innovative form of ODR, suitable for settling monetary claims[43] (i.e. where liability is not disputed, only the amount of damages payable). The process involves the parties making successive blind bids, which are then entered into a form on a secure website. 'Blind'

---

[38] See www.smartsettle.com [1 April 2008].    [39] See 4.2.

[40] E. Thiessen and J. McMahon, 'Beyond Win-Win in Cyberspace' (2000) 15 *Ohio State Journal on Dispute Resolution* 643–67, 666.

[41] See 4.2.1.    [42] See Cybersettle: www.cybersettle.com/info/main.aspx [1 April 2008].

[43] Kaufmann-Kohler and Schultz, *Online Dispute Resolution*, 19.

means here that the bids are not disclosed to the other party, hence offers and demands remain confidential, so as to not prejudice future negotiations.[44] Once the bids are within a certain range of each other, settlement will automatically be reached, for the median amount. The process is driven by software so that no human third party is directly involved, and is therefore particularly cost-effective. The software keeps offers confidential until they come within the range. Communication applications such as email and Web-based platforms support the settlement process. Such software can assist in avoiding posturing and conflicts 'over the last few pennies'.[45]

### 5.4.4 Online juries / mock trials

Online summary jury trials[46] or mock trials are an ODR mechanism whereby a jury of peers makes a non-binding determination of the issues via a website. The parties upload their respective pleadings and evidence onto the site, and the 'jurors' can ask questions and render an online verdict, recommending how the dispute should be solved. The neutral third party is replaced by a number of volunteering Internet users acting as if they were the jury in a truncated civil court trial by posting their questions and verdicts onto the website. This ODR mechanism assists the parties in their negotiations for a settlement by reality-testing their positions against the supposed common sense of the volunteers forming 'the jury'. The mock jury is claimed to reflect the likely behaviour of a real jury, and takes into account the US constitutional preference for jury trials in civil cases.[47]

### 5.4.5 Online arbitration

Online arbitration replicates the offline, traditional fact-finding and decision-making processes that are constituent of arbitration online by using ICT for communication and information processing.

One extremely useful online information-processing technique for arbitration is electronic file management, especially for complex, large-scale arbitration. Electronic file management means that all documents

---

[44] Ponte and Cavenagh, *Cyberjustice*, 44.
[45] Rule, *Online Dispute Resolution for Business*, 61.
[46] See, for example, www.i-courthouse.com [1 April 2008].
[47] Brown and Marriott, *ADR Principles and Practice*, 371 (mock trials).

pertaining to the case in question are stored electronically in a systematic order. Electronic file-management software permits individual documents or passages to be easily retrieved, displayed or printed, browsed, cross-referenced, compared, annotated and searched for keywords. Electronic file management reduces the time wasted in searching for documents, and it avoids the carrying of large amounts of paper. Cross-referencing allows the linking of text (e.g. in the pleadings) to evidence or law. It may also be combined with diary-management functions, such as automatically sending out notices of filing deadlines, and can be integrated with word-processing functions so that the database generates procedural documents, notices, etc.

Electronic file management is already widely used in practice, whether it is only used internally by the dispute resolution institution or externally accessed by the parties and arbitrators via an online platform (described in the next paragraph).

In terms of online techniques, the next step forward is an online platform,[48] which is normally combined with electronic file management. This allows the parties and arbitrators to upload documents directly onto a structured website – using a unified filing system – via a secure connection.[49] An online platform is a website for document management, which creates one central, unified case database, allowing the parties, the arbitrators and the administrator to upload, view, browse, search and retrieve documents.[50] The platform may also contain an electronic diary and an electronic secretariat, which automatically records the filing of documents and automatically, at the required date, sends out certain standard documents such as acknowledgements, receipts or certain notices. Furthermore, the online platform can additionally allow for electronic payment of arbitration fees by credit card. However, online filing may

---

[48] See ICC Court of Arbitration's online filing platform, NetCase, at www.iccnetcase.org/Netcase/init.do; Electronic Case Facility (ECAF), WIPO Center's online filing platform at www.wipo.int/amc/en/ecaf/index.html; the AAA's online filing platform, WebFile, the online filing platform for .eu disputes, at www.adreu.eurid.eu/arbitration_platform/overview/index.php; online filing platforms for mediation – see the Consensus Mediation's e-Mediator scheme, at www.consensusmediation.co.uk/e-mediator.html; and the ADR Group's platform, at www.adrgroup.co.uk/online-dispute/online-dispute-res.htm [1 April 2008].

[49] M. Philippe, 'NetCase: A New ICC Arbitration Facility' [2004] (Special Supplement) *ICC International Court of Arbitration Bulletin* 53–61, 54.

[50] *Ibid.*

entail security risks, and precautions must be taken against unauthorised access.[51]

In this context, it is interesting to look at the results of a user survey conducted by the American Arbitration Association (AAA) in 2004. They asked the users of their online filing platform, WebFile, for what purposes did they use the WebFile; the result was that only 16.2 per cent of users completed the entire arbitration process online.[52] This may indicate that users do not entirely trust or are not entirely familiar with online platforms as yet. However, 61 per cent of users said that if the other party suggested using the online platform, they would in principle agree to use it for some part of the procedure.[53]

Concerning communication applications for online arbitration, interactive, synchronous discussion applications such as instant messaging and online chat can be used. However, relying on purely text-based communication has significant disadvantages for the reality of the communication, such as the assessment of non-verbal cues (i.e. body language), which has already been discussed in relation to mediation above. This is particularly significant for the cross-examination of witnesses and the assessment of a witness' credibility.

Instead, means of visual distance communication, such as Web- and video-conferencing, may be used to replace traditional face-to-face hearings. The great advantage of Web- and video-conferencing is that witnesses, parties and arbitrators do not need to travel, thus reducing time wasted and cost. However, the issue is to what extent it is possible for the tribunal to assess the credibility of a witness giving testimony via video link? This depends to a large extent on the quality of technology used. This means, in particular, that the connection needs to avoid delays and interruptions, and the witness must be clearly seen and heard. The physical demeanour and tone of voice should be easily detectable to assess the credibility of the witness. For example, it might not be apparent if a witness blushes because the colour resolution of the monitor is not sufficient. Therefore the hardware used should be suitable, and the connection should be of sufficient capacity.[54] Also, it may be difficult to make direct

---

[51] Such as encryption for transmission, passwords for authentication, virus protection and firewalls. If these protections are taken, online platforms are safer than unprotected email; see Philippe, 'NetCase', 54.

[52] Debi Miller-Moore's presentation at the Joint Conference of CCLS and CIArb, London, on 6 September 2004.

[53] *Ibid.*     [54] A dedicated link or broadband might not be available in all countries.

eye contact, as the camera and the displaying screen are not in the same place.[55]

It is sometimes discussed to what extent a witness giving oral, filmed testimony can be manipulated; for example, it could be that there is someone prompting or coaching the witness what to say. This person would stand in front of the witness and not be captured by the camera, which is directed at the witness. In order to avoid coaching of the witness, the picture should cover the whole room at the witness end, which necessitates at least two cameras. There is also the issue of identification of the witness. Therefore, most weight can be given to evidence via video link if both parties are represented, or if a member of the tribunal is present at either end of the link. However, this might not always be possible. Alternatively, a trusted third party – such as a law firm, an arbitral institution, a notary or a court – could be used.

It is now fairly common in adjudicative proceedings to examine and cross-examine a witness by two-way video link, for example where it is impractical for the witness to travel to a hearing venue. This allows the evidence to be given directly to the tribunal without the witness having to travel far. Also, the rules of civil procedure (e.g. in England and Wales and the US) allow for this under certain circumstances.[56]

In addition to seeing the faces of the persons communicating, evidence may have to be visually presented. Such a functionality may be provided by shared collaborative workspaces, which are online communication applications that not only allow the parties and the arbitrator to communicate through synchronous chat and to see each other through Web- and video-conferencing but that, in addition, provide a facility to share visual information by displaying and manipulating a graphic interface, where a multitude of people see the same objects roughly simultaneously.[57] This could be a 3D image of an object that can be rotated or zoomed in and out

---

[55] Gibbons, Kennedy and Gibbs, 'Cyber-Mediation', 34.

[56] Civil Procedure Rules 1998 (SI 1998/3132), Part 32, r. 32.3 or CPR PD 32, Annex 3, by leave of the court; it is pointed out, however, that evidence by video link may be of a lesser quality, and that hence convenience and fairness should be balanced; see CPR PD 32, Annex 3, para. 2. In *Polanski* v. *Condé Nast Publications* [2005] HRLR 11 (HL), the House of Lords restored an order allowing the claimant to give evidence by means of a video link from France. The court argued that evidence given by video-conferencing can be tested adequately (per Lord Nicholls, paras. 14, 27: 'seeking a VCF order is not an indulgence'). See also the US Federal Rules of Civil Procedure, r. 43(a).

[57] D. Protopsaltou, T. Schultz and N. Magnenat-Thalmann, 'Taking the Fourth Party Further? Considering a Shared Virtual Workspace for Arbitration' (2006) 15(2) *Information & Communications Technology Law* 157–73, 160–2 and 165.

by each participant in turn, or it could be a drawing board used for graphical illustration. It can be used, for example, to enable the participants to view pieces of evidence or illustrate an argument. Since arbitration is based on the establishment of facts, shared collaborative workspaces can be important for each party explaining, arguing and illustrating their case. The use of collaborative workspaces in arbitration increases understanding of factual issues and thereby makes the process quicker and more efficient.[58]

## 5.5 Transformative power of ODR

As the preceding discussion has shown, ODR is derived from and based on variants of the two main forms of ADR: mediation and arbitration. From a superficial point of view, it may seem that different forms of ODR are mere transplants of ADR into the online environment; in other words, ODR replicates ADR online. This superficial observation is fallacious in the same way as the argument that, for all forms of motorised transport, the horse that drew the cart has merely been replaced by an engine, but that the transportation itself has not changed. To say that ODR is merely online ADR would similarly underestimate the transformative power of the technology.

### 5.5.1 Technology as the fourth party in ODR

Ethan Katsh and Janet Rifkin have expressed the critical role of technology and coined the metaphor of the 'fourth party':

> The fourth party does not except in a few well-defined instances such as blind-bidding, *replace* the third party. But it can be considered to *displace* the third party in the sense that new skills, knowledge and strategies may be needed by the third party. It may not be coequal in influence to the third party neutral, but it can be an ally, collaborator, and partner.[59]

This expression signifies that the technologies used are not merely subordinate tools in the same way that a pen and paper pad are for recording an award or mediation settlement. The metaphor expresses that the input of the technology is not subsidiary to that of the 'third party', but that

---

[58] *Ibid.* 162.
[59] Katsh and Rifkin, *Online Dispute Resolution*, 93–4; the first two parties being the disputants, the third party the mediator/arbitrator.

the 'fourth party' is influential in shaping the process and in assisting the parties to reach a solution of their dispute. The implication from this metaphor is that ODR is fundamentally changing the ways disputes are solved. Firstly, ODR is changing the underlying ADR processes,[60] and new dispute resolution mechanisms, such as blind bidding,[61] having no equivalent in the offline world, have evolved through the use of ICT for dispute resolution. Secondly, and more importantly, ODR has a transformative power. How and why this transformative power takes effect is explained in this section.

## Overcoming distances

The use of online distance communication (email, bulletin boards, chat, Web- and video-conferencing, online collaborative workspaces, etc.) obviates the need for face-to-face meetings in mediation or arbitration hearings. This means that the parties, their representatives, witnesses, experts and the third parties need not travel. Furthermore, to the extent that asynchronous communication on an online platform is used, the parties also need not meet at the same time, thus avoiding co-ordination of busy schedules. If documents are filed on an online platform, they can be accessed from anywhere, as the Internet is ubiquitous. These features of ODR overcoming distances reduce costs and delay, making dispute resolution cheaper, quicker and more accessible.[62]

## Empowering communication

One aspect of ODR is improving communication in dispute resolution processes. The technology aids the understanding of what a person is alleging or explaining by visualisation (such as in collaborative workspaces) or by providing access to knowledge resources (such as legal databases and case-management systems, for example hypertext linking text with legal authority or evidence). Such technologies make the speaker more effective and more persuasive, and will potentially lead to fairer outcomes that are more firmly grounded in law and evidence.

---

[60] See M. Philippe, 'Where is Everyone Going with Online Dispute Resolution?' (2002) 2 *International Business Law Journal* 167–210, 168.

[61] See the preceding section.

[62] Kaufmann-Kohler and Schultz, *Online Dispute Resolution*, 76; Gordon, 'The Electronic Personality and Digital Self', 10–11; Gibbons, Kennedy and Gibbs, 'Cyber-Mediation', 42–3; Clark, Cho and Hoyle, 'Online Dispute Resolution', 9.

## Saving human labour cost

The automation of certain functions previously performed manually may lead to cost-savings and may make dispute resolution cheaper. However, technologies replacing human intelligence by artificial, computer intelligence[63] are limited. Evaluating complex factual evidence and applying law to such complex factual scenarios (as in arbitration), or finding a solution that satisfies the needs of both parties (as in mediation), still, at present, have to be performed by a trained arbitrator or mediator,[64] whose services have to be paid for. However, artificial intelligence is used in smaller tasks such as online forms (legal expert systems, where the form responds to the user's input by categorising the dispute and asking the questions relevant to the type of dispute), in automated negotiation systems (calculating the solution satisfying most interests of the parties), automated diary-management functions (e.g. sending out notifications and registering any filings made by the parties to an arbitration), in legal research (through natural-language searches) and automated translation software (but automated translation is not as good as that performed by a human translator).

## Psychological effect of online communication – dealing with negative emotions

Changing communication patterns from face-to-face to online, textual or Web- and video-conferencing communication has ramifications for its emotional effect on the parties or their representatives. It has already been pointed out[65] that mediators and arbitrators have experienced problems in establishing trust in ODR, and that the loss of non-verbal cues in textual

---

[63] Webopedia defines artificial intelligence as 'the branch of computer science concerned with making computers behave like humans'. Two branches of artificial intelligence are of particular relevance here: expert systems, which are designed to make decisions in real-life scenarios, and natural-language systems, designed to make computers understand natural, human language. R. Susskind defines artificial intelligence as 'the design, development and implementation of computer systems that can perform tasks and solve problems of a sort for which human intelligence is normally thought to be required', in *Transforming the Law* (Oxford University Press, 2000), 162.

[64] S. Ross Saxer, 'One Professor's Approach to Increasing Technology Use in Legal Education' (1999–2000) 6 *Richmond Journal of Law and Technology* 21–57, 35; A. Lodder and J. Zeleznikov, 'Developing an Online Dispute Resolution Environment: Dialogue Tools and Negotiation Support Systems in a Three Step Model' (2005) 10 *Harvard Negotiation Law Review* 287–337, 291.

[65] See 5.4.1.

communication has to be compensated for by different forms of graphic signs employed online.

Conversely, distance can have a positive effect. It has been reported from mediators' personal experience that distance leads to a cooling down of acrimonious emotions, and that asynchronous communication gives the party a chance to reflect. Likewise, textual communication may give opportunities for mediators to rephrase the parties' aggressive communication, thereby preventing an escalation of the dispute and speeding up its resolution.[66]

Another example of the positive impact of ODR on communication patterns is the use of automated negotiation software, which prevents posturing 'over the last few pennies', as discussed above.[67]

### Jurisdictional problems overcome in cross-border disputes

ODR, like ADR, being extra-judicial, avoids any arguments between the parties as to which state court is competent. The determination of which court is competent can be complex, time-consuming and expensive. All of this is avoided through ODR.[68] However, issues of applicable law nevertheless arise for online arbitration, but these have been discussed in the previous chapter and need not be repeated here.

### Faster information processing

A final point is that ICT enables processing of larger amounts of information in shorter spaces of time than if carried out by humans. Electronic-document management and information-retrieval systems are examples of this. Faster information processing makes dispute resolution more efficient, reducing delay and costs.

### 5.5.2 *Transformative power: greater access to justice*

The features of ODR discussed above have the potential to transform dispute resolution by enabling access to justice at a much greater scale. ODR improves dispute resolution processes by making them more efficient, reducing delay and costs. These characteristics are not merely incidental: if dispute resolution is cheaper and quicker, this means that persons with

---

[66] Rule, *Online Dispute Resolution for Business*, 66 and 72; Gordon, 'The Electronic Personality and Digital Self', 10–11; Gibbons, Kennedy and Gibbs, 'Cyber-Mediation', 33 and 43; Clark, Cho and Hoyle, 'Online Dispute Resolution', 9.
[67] See 5.4.3.     [68] Clark, Cho and Hoyle, 'Online Dispute Resolution', 9.

limited resources may have access to ODR. The use of ICT in dispute resolution therefore widens access.[69] In other words, the transformative power of ODR widens access *to justice*. ODR is an important breakthrough in reducing pre-existing power imbalances (as conceptualised as the third element of procedural fairness in Chapter 2[70]), by providing access to efficient dispute resolution for disputants with limited resources.

## 5.6 Conclusion

This chapter argues that ODR transcends traditional ADR, so that ODR is not merely online ADR. As has been seen, new forms of ODR have been developed that have no offline equivalent. More importantly, the technologies used have transformative power, which can be harnessed to increase access to justice and reduce pre-existing inequalities between the parties. In this sense, ODR contributes to greater fairness in dispute resolution. This chapter explains that ODR provides powerful technology for increasing access to justice by reducing delay and lowering costs of dispute resolution through efficiency gains, overcoming geographical distances, solving jurisdictional issues and overcoming power imbalances. While this chapter shows that ODR does contribute to the second (access) and third (counterpoise) principles of procedural fairness, it has yet to be explored to what extent ODR complies with the first principle of due process. Since mediation has been shown to be a mere filter before adjudication, the discussion of due process in the next chapters will focus on arbitration.

---

[69] More generally, in relation to IT and law; see Susskind, *Transforming the Law*, 158.
[70] See 2.2.3.

# 6

# Arbitration and due process

> Convenience and justice are often not on speaking terms.
>
> (Lord Atkin in *General Medical Council* v. *Spackman* [1943] AC 627
> (HL), 638)

## 6.1 Introduction

This book develops a model for the fair resolution of Internet disputes. Since online arbitration has been suggested as the most important method to solve Internet disputes for the model, the fundamental question is whether the use of online arbitration based on the structures and principles of commercial arbitration is fair for these types of disputes and, to the extent that the answer to this question is 'no', how arbitration should be adapted for the purposes of this model.

This chapter concentrates on due process, which has been defined as a constituent element of fairness (alongside access and the counterpoise) in Chapter 2.[1] By way of reminder, Chapter 2 posits two elements of due process (equal treatment of the parties before an adjudicator and rationality, in the sense that the adjudicator must not take into account any irrelevant or irrational considerations).

This chapter applies these due process principles to arbitration. It starts by exploring the sources of law for due process in arbitration, and examines the elements of due process, contrasting litigation and arbitration. This chapter discusses the principles of impartiality and independence, fair hearing, the duty to give reasons, transparency and rights to an appeal or judicial review.

## 6.2 Sources of legal due process

Before the discussion can proceed, it is necessary to explain the sources of law for the due process requirements. The following sources of law

---

[1] See 2.5.

are relevant: professional codes of conduct, institutional (and other arbitration) rules, national arbitration legislation, common law, constitutional and human rights standards and international conventions and standards. As can be seen, these sources are a mixture of private and public law.

Arbitration as an out-of-court dispute resolution process is largely governed by contract and by the principle of party autonomy, conferring the parties with the freedom to fashion the arbitration procedures according to their needs. Notwithstanding this important principle of party autonomy, arbitration as a dispute resolution process is also governed by 'hard' public law in the shape of arbitration laws, which set the framework for the procedure. The courts at the parties' chosen seat may support and intervene in the process by rulings on the validity of the arbitration agreement, by staying legal proceedings in favour of arbitration, by appointing a tribunal, by rulings on subject-matter arbitrability, by the removal of an arbitrator, by compelling witnesses to attend or by allowing the challenge of an award. Furthermore, the courts at the place of enforcement may refuse enforcement of a foreign award for public-policy reasons. The sources of law discussed here reflect the hybrid nature of arbitration.

### 6.2.1 Professional codes of conduct and contract for arbitral services

The contracts between the parties, the arbitration institution and the arbitrator may impose an express duty on the arbitrator to act in accordance with due process principles (i.e. to act judicially), and a duty to exercise proper care and skill in carrying out his or her function.[2] Furthermore, an arbitrator who is also a member of a profession – such as a doctor, architect, engineer, accountant or lawyer – is under an implied duty to carry out their work (including any adjudication or valuation) to professional standards. In the United Kingdom, the Supply of Goods and Services Act 1982, s. 13 implies, in contracts for the supply of services, a duty to carry out the service with reasonable care and skill. In measuring the reasonableness of care and skill, the courts take into account the professional standards of the service provider.[3] A definition of such professional standards can be found in the regulations of the appropriate professional body. Such bodies may have formulated professional rules of conduct

---

[2] Redfern and Hunter, *Law and Practice of International Commercial Arbitration*, 284–5, 291.
[3] *Arenson* v. *Casson Beckman Rutley & Co* [1977] AC 405 (HL), deciding that an accountant could be liable for a negligent valuation of a shareholding: at 419, 425.

when their members are acting in the capacity of arbitrators.[4] In addition, there are codes of conduct or guidelines formulated by arbitration institutions or international associations,[5] which may be incorporated by reference in the contract between the parties and the arbitrator or may, at a minimum, as in the case of the IBA's (International Bar Association) guidelines, impose moral and ethical duties on arbitrators.

This raises the question of whether arbitrators are immune from suit. Under one school of thought, the arbitrator may be contractually liable for breach of the implied duties to act judicially and to exercise proper care and skill. Under another, the arbitrator carries out a judicial role and hence is immune from liability.[6] English law subscribes to the second school of thought, by granting a large degree of immunity to arbitrators and arbitral institutions. Neither the arbitrator nor the appointing institutions are liable for any act or omission in carrying out the arbitration, unless the claimant can show bad faith.[7] However, in this chapter, the focus is not so much on the arbitrator's or institution's liability for damages.[8] Due to the high hurdle of liability, the issues relating to the arbitrator's duty to comply with due process arise in the context of a challenge of the award or proceedings for the removal of the arbitrator, as these may be avenues of redress an aggrieved party may seek when evidence of bad faith is absent.

### 6.2.2 Institutional and other arbitration rules

Arbitration institutions – such as the AAA, International Center for the Settlement of Investment Disputes (ICSID), CIArb, China International Economic and Trade Arbitration Commission (CIETAC), International Chamber of Commerce (ICC), Deutsches Institut für Schiedsgerichtsbarkeit (DIS), AAA International Center for Dispute Resolution (ICDR), or London Court of International Arbitration (LCIA) – have issued rules

---

[4] See, for example, the English Law Society's *Guide to the Professional Conduct of Solicitors*, the ABA/AAA's *Code of Ethics for Arbitrators in Commercial Disputes* of 1 March 2004.

[5] ICDR's *Code of Ethics for Arbitrators in Commercial Disputes* of 1 March 2004; the AAA's *Standards of Ethics and Business Conduct*, available from www.adr.org [1 April 2008]; CIArb's *Code of Professional and Ethical Conduct* of September 2004, available from the Chartered Institute of Arbitrators and on file with the author; and the IBA *Guidelines of Conflicts of Interest in International Arbitration* of 22 May 2004, available from www.ibanet.org/publications/IBA_Guides_Practical_Checklists_Precedents_and_Free_Materials.cfm [1 April 2008].

[6] Redfern and Hunter, *Law and Practice of International Commercial Arbitration*, 285–7.

[7] English Arbitration Act 1996, s. 29.

[8] The question of immunity will not be further discussed.

of arbitration governing arbitration procedures carried out under the auspices of the respective institution. Even where the parties do not choose to submit their dispute to arbitration through an institution (i.e. in an ad hoc arbitration), the parties usually refer to a set of arbitration rules (such as the UNCITRAL (United Nations Commission for International Trade Law) Rules or some institutional rules) to govern the procedure. In either case, the rules are incorporated by reference into the arbitration agreement between the parties, the contract between the parties and the arbitrator and the contract between the institution and the arbitrator (if applicable). Hence the arbitrator, the parties and the institution are all contractually bound to comply with the rules, including any rules on due process.

This book also takes into account several important policy documents dealing with the issue of standards for online arbitration (and ODR/ADR more generally): European Commission Recommendation 98/257/EC and the guidelines of the American Bar Association (ABA) Task Force on E-Commerce and ADR,[9] the UK Office of Fair Trading's (OFT) Consumer Codes Approval Scheme[10] and the Due Process Protocol of the AAA.[11]

The 1998 EC Recommendation is addressed to the designers, operators and providers of arbitration for consumer disputes.[12] Hence its scope is limited to consumer disputes. It provides for seven general principles that should apply to binding dispute resolution:[13] (i) independence, (ii) transparency,[14] (iii) adversarial principle,[15] (iv) effectiveness,[16] (v) legality,[17] (vi) liberty[18] and (vii) representation.[19] These principles go some

---

[9] Available from the ABA website: www.abanet.org/dispute/documents/BestPractices-Final102802.pdf [1 April 2008].

[10] Consumer Code Approval Scheme, Core Criteria and Guidance November 2006, OFT 390.

[11] Available from www.adr.org/sp.asp?id=22019 [1 April 2008].

[12] Recommendation 98/257/EC, last sentence.

[13] This applies to arbitration and ombudsman schemes; see the Recitals to the Recommendation.

[14] This principle merely refers to information about the dispute resolution procedure.

[15] This refers to fair hearing in the sense discussed below at 6.4.

[16] Conglomerate of different aspects: no need for legal representation, procedure free of charge or moderate costs, no undue delay in the decision-making, judge taking an active role.

[17] Consumer must be protected by the mandatory law applying in the consumer's state of residence (see 4.3) and the duty to give reasoned decisions (see 6.5).

[18] The parties must have specifically agreed to the binding nature of the dispute resolution.

[19] Parties may choose to be legally represented.

way to establishing minimum standards but are very general and abstract, and do not address some of the weaknesses in respect of due process, such as the conflict between funding and independence, the detailed fair-hearing requirements, publication of awards and appeal systems. Hence it is suggested that the principles should be refined and developed along the lines discussed in this chapter and Chapter 8, to make them more useful and to avoid divergent interpretation by the Member States.[20] Ideally, the principles should be clothed in a regulation to make them binding on the Member States.

### 6.2.3 National arbitration legislation

National legislation is at the same time the most obvious and least obvious source of law in this discussion, most obvious in the sense that it is not surprising that sovereign states can and do legislate in their territory on any subject matter, whether this subject matter is in the realm of private contract law or not, and as the least obvious source of law for the resolution of cross-border disputes on the Internet. Indeed, the whole point of the discussion of due process in this chapter is to overcome the limitations of the rules of private international law as a species of national law. Yet it has to be acknowledged that regulation within a system of nation states is (still) carried out, to a large extent, at a national level, but in the field of arbitration, national laws have increasingly been assimilated due to the pressure exerted by the needs of the parties in commercial cross-border disputes.[21]

There is a convergence of different national rules in business arbitration. This convergence is caused by the quest to improve procedural rules and exchanges at all levels through academic debate, through discussions between the parties involved in a particular arbitration procedure or at the political level in international institutions such as UNCITRAL. Instrumental for convergence are the UNCITRAL Model Law[22] (upon which some states have modelled their legislation); arbitration rules (some of which have been drafted without reference to a particular seat); academic,

---

[20] See also BEUC (European Consumers' Organisation) position paper, 'Alternative Dispute Resolution' of 21 November 2002, BEUC/X/048/2002, 2 and 8.
[21] Redfern and Hunter, *Law and Practice of International Commercial Arbitration*, 77.
[22] Model Law on International Commercial Arbitration, adopted by UNCITRAL on 21 June 1985.

comparative texts elaborating standards for international commercial arbitration;[23] international practice; and, most importantly, international conventions[24] (which have limited the power of the national courts to refuse to enforce foreign arbitration awards).

Acknowledging the contribution and impact of international arbitration practice on national arbitration laws, however, should not be equated with ignoring the role of national arbitration laws, which are an important source of law, forming the interface for the different modes of regulation of arbitration.

National legislation on arbitration pursues two aims: (i) it draws the outer limits of arbitration, for example by defining what disputes can and cannot be brought to arbitration, and by imposing certain due process standards (mandatory provisions); and (ii) national arbitration Acts facilitate arbitration by providing default rules where the parties or arbitration rules have not addressed a matter, and by lending the courts' powers to the parties (e.g. by staying legal proceedings). National laws apply by virtue of the parties choosing the seat of the arbitration to be within the territory of the state, or by virtue of the fact that the award is to be enforced within the jurisdiction.

This chapter concentrates on due process requirements under English law and international commercial practice, referring to the English Arbitration Act 1996 as a starting point for the discussion, and making comparisons to the legislation of other jurisdictions where useful for the argument, without claiming to paint a complete picture of arbitration law in these jurisdictions. At some stages in the discussion, for the purposes of comparison, reference is made to US law and, in particular, the Federal Arbitration Act 1925.[25] In the United States, of course, a distinction has to be made between federal and state law, and arbitration laws can be found at both levels. The Federal Arbitration Act 1925 was enacted to overcome court rulings that were hostile to arbitration and which refused to order a stay of proceedings to enforce a pre-dispute arbitration agreement.[26] All fifty states and the District of Columbia have passed specific arbitration Acts, usually modelled on the 1920 New York Arbitration Law or the Federal Arbitration Act 1925.[27] Nevertheless, most arbitration law in the

---

[23] Redfern and Hunter, *Law and Practice of International Commercial Arbitration*; Lew, Mistelis and Kröll, *Comparative International Commercial Arbitration*.
[24] See 6.2.6.    [25] 9 USC.
[26] T. Carbonneau, *Cases and Materials on the Law and Practice of Arbitration*, 2nd edn (Huntington, NY: Juris Publishing, 2000), 50–1.
[27] Reuben, 'Constitutional Gravity', 976.

United States is federal law, because of the wide definition of commerce in the Federal Arbitration Act itself, and an even more elastic interpretation of the notion of interstate commerce by the US Supreme Court.[28] The Federal Arbitration Act 1925 essentially applies in a maritime transaction or in a contract evidencing a transaction involving commerce,[29] which is defined as 'commerce among the several States or with foreign nations, or in any Territory of the United States or in the District of Columbia'.[30] In the case of *Southland Corporation* v. *Keating*, the US Supreme Court extended the application of the Federal Arbitration Act 1925 to the state courts, and confirmed the validity of an arbitration clause in a contract governed by state law, where the state law was in conflict with the Arbitration Act.[31] The effect of this case law is that the Federal Arbitration Act 1925 now applies in federal question cases, diversity cases (in which state law applies) and in cases before the state courts, applying state law but linking to interstate commerce. Thomas Carbonneau even calls the Federal Arbitration Act 1925 the 'national American law of arbitration'.[32] Because of this supremacy of the Federal Arbitration Act 1925 over state arbitration law, the discussion of US law is largely restricted to the federal level.

### 6.2.4 English common law

Natural justice[33] is a time-honoured doctrine of the English common law that applies to all decision-making in judicial or administrative proceedings, affecting the rights, property or legitimate expectations of an individual.[34] It comprises two fundamental maxims guaranteeing equal

---

[28] Carbonneau, *Cases and Materials*, 1954–5; Reuben, 'Constitutional Gravity', 976, and 979–80.

[29] 9 USC, § 2.      [30] USC, § 1.

[31] 465 US 1, 14–16 (1984); see also *Doctor's Associates Inc* v. *Casarotto*, 517 US 681, 686–7 (1996); see also *Allied-Bruce Terminix Cos* v. *Dobson*, 513 US 265 (1995), concerning an arbitration clause in a termite protection agreement for a house – the court found that the Federal Arbitration Act 1925 displaces state law to the contrary. For a more recent case, see *Cooper* v. *MRM Investment Co*, 367 F3d 493, 498 (2004); however, not all questions pertaining to arbitration are governed by federal law – for example, the question whether the parties have concluded an arbitration agreement and whether the clause is conscionable may be determined by state contract law; see, for example, *Plaskett* v. *Bechtel International Inc*, D Virgin Islands 243 FSupp2d 334 (2003).

[32] Carbonneau, *Cases and Materials*, 57.

[33] It is roughly the equivalent to 'due process' in US parlance.

[34] G. Flick, *Natural Justice Principles and Practical Application*, 2nd edn (Sydney: Butterworths, 1984), 26–7.

treatment:[35] (i) *nemo judex in sua causa*[36] (impartiality and independence of the judge) and (ii) *audi alteram partem*[37] (fair hearing). This raises the question of whether *common-law* natural justice equally applies to ADR processes based, at least to some extent, on contractual relationships.

The next section discusses in detail whether *constitutional* (as opposed to common law) due process applies to private decision-making.

However, notwithstanding the recent incorporation of the European Convention of Human Rights (ECHR)[38] into UK law, the legal *tradition* of the United Kingdom is different from that of states such as the United States and other European countries where there is a written, higher-ranking constitution incorporating human rights standards, such as due process and the right to a fair trial, but only (at least directly) applying it to state actors.[39] Since the common law has developed incrementally, drawing analogies between cases, there was no need for such a bold differentiation between public and private law. English judges have simply stated that natural justice also applies to someone acting in a private but quasi-judicial function. Case law has long established that a private body, such as a sports club, may also be subject to the rules of natural justice when making a decision affecting a member based on contract.[40] This paved the way for applying the same principles to other private adjudicatory systems.[41] Hence it is clear that in the United Kingdom, the common-law rules of natural justice not only apply to public bodies or bodies exercising a public function but also to arbitration.[42]

## 6.2.5 Human rights standards

This section is about the right to a fair trial contained in the ECHR, and the due process standards enshrined in the US Constitution. The human rights contained in the ECHR and the US Constitution are primarily addressed to states, not private actors. Hence the main issue discussed in

---

[35] Bailey, Ching, Gunn and Ormerod, *Smith, Bailey and Gunn*, 1315; Flick, *Natural Justice Principles and Practical Application*, 26.

[36] No one may be a judge in his own cause.          [37] Hear the other side.

[38] ECHR of 4 November 1950, signed at Rome TS 71 (1953) Cmd 8969; ETS No. 5 1950.

[39] See 6.2.5.2.

[40] *Wood* v. *Woad* (1874) LR 9 Ex 190; *Calvin* v. *Carr* [1980] AC 574 (PC), 596; *R (Irvine)* v. *The Royal Burgess Golfing Society of Edinburgh* [2004] LLR 334 (Court of Session), para. 25; Flick, *Natural Justice Principles and Practical Application*, 32–3.

[41] For example, *R* v. *Gough* [1993] 97 Cr App R 188 (HL), 199; *AT&T* v. *Saudi Cable Co* [2000] 2 Lloyd's Rep 127 (CA), 138 (Potter LJ).

[42] See 6.3.2 and 6.4.2.

this section is the question of whether these human rights standards apply to arbitration as a private dispute resolution process.

## ECHR

For English law, in addition to the traditional principles of natural justice, another source of due process principles has been the ECHR, now incorporated into English law by the Human Rights Act 1998.[43] This section of the book also takes into account the interpretation of the ECHR by the Strasbourg institutions,[44] to which the English courts must pay heed.[45] If English law applies, the English courts have to read, interpret and apply English legislation (including the English Arbitration Act 1996) in accordance with the ECHR under s. 3(1) of the Human Rights Act 1998.

Article 6(1) of the ECHR reads:

> In the determination of his civil rights and obligations . . . everyone is entitled to a fair and public hearing within a reasonable time by an independent and impartial tribunal *established by law*.

This does not answer the question of whether the standards of due process established in the ECHR do apply to a private arbitration tribunal. It should first be noted that, prima facie, human rights instruments govern a state's relationship with its citizens (vertical effect) as opposed to the relationships between citizens (horizontal effect).[46] Hence it is far from obvious that the ECHR should apply in the private relationship between the arbitration tribunal and the parties.

In the context of English law, under s. 6(1) of the Human Rights Act 1998, any act of a public authority must be compatible with the ECHR, and a public authority includes a *court* or *tribunal*.[47] Hence, clearly, Art. 6(1) applies to the *courts* in proceedings related to arbitration,[48] albeit that occasionally the courts have, even here, found a waiver of

---

[43] Human Rights Act 1998, s. 1 and Schedule 1.

[44] That is, the EComHR and the ECtHR before the 1998 reforms, and now the ECtHR.

[45] Human Rights Act 1998, s. 2(1).

[46] A. Jaksic, *Arbitration and Human Rights* (Frankfurt am Main: Peter Lang, 2002), 60; see ECHR, Art. 1.

[47] Human Rights Act 1998, s. 6(2); an arbitration tribunal is unlikely to be a 'tribunal' within the meaning of the Human Rights Act 1998, which defines a tribunal as one 'in which legal proceedings can be brought' (s. 21).

[48] *North Range Shipping Ltd* v. *Seatrans Shipping Corporation* [2002] 1 WLR 2397 (CA), para. 27, confirmed in *CGU International Insurance Plc* v. *Astrazeneca Insurance Co Ltd* [2006] EWCA Civ 1340 (CA), Judgment of 16 October 2006, para. 59.

rights in respect of the court proceedings (e.g. regarding confidentiality[49]). The consequence of this is that if an English court is acting under its supervisory jurisdiction (where England is the seat of arbitration) or its enforcement jurisdiction (where England is the place of enforcement), the courts have an obligation to act in accordance with the ECHR. However, the issue here is whether the ECHR also applies to the arbitration tribunal itself – its not being a *public* tribunal or a *tribunal established by law*.

### The due process rule of the ECHR and its application to arbitration

The potential for arbitration to conflict with the right to a fair hearing in a court of law arises since a valid arbitration agreement blocks either party's way to obtain resolution of the dispute by the ordinary, 'proper' courts *established by law*. The reason for this is that arbitration agreements are binding (in the sense that the courts order a stay of legal proceedings[50]), and the ultimate award is also binding and enforceable.[51] Hence, in theory, an arbitration agreement may deprive a person of their right to a fair trial in a court, and hence to their entitlement under Art. 6(1) of the ECHR.

Because of the binding nature and finality of arbitration, the central question here is whether the due process rights enshrined in Art. 6(1) apply to arbitration.

Since the human rights standards espoused in the ECHR are primarily applicable to state actors, it is questionable whether these human rights standards can also be invoked in relationships between private parties.[52]

Unsurprisingly, there is no agreement on this complex question. Three theories can essentially be distinguished.[53] The first theory holds that the guarantee of a fair trial in Art. 6(1) applies directly to arbitration, the second theory, that it applies indirectly, and the third theory, that it does not apply at all.

Why is it important whether Art. 6(1) applies directly or indirectly? If Art. 6(1) applies directly, the guarantees contained in that Article

---

[49] *City of Moscow* v. *Bankers Trust Company* [2005] QB 207 (CA), para. 39.
[50] English Arbitration Act 1996, s. 9(4).   [51] English Arbitration Act 1996, s. 66(1).
[52] C. Jarrosson, 'L'Arbitrage et la Convention européenne des droits de l'Homme' [1989] *Revue de l'arbitrage* 573–607, 578–80.
[53] Aharon Barak, in his chapter on the horizontal effect of constitutional human rights, distinguishes four theoretical approaches. Apart from the non-applicability, direct and indirect applicability, he also mentions a judiciary model, where human rights are not applied to private actors as such but must be applied by the judiciary as an organ of the state. In my nomenclature, this would be subsumed under indirect applicability. See A. Barak, 'Constitutional Human Rights and Private Law', in D. Friedmann and D. Barak-Erez, *Human Rights in Private Law* (Oxford: Hart Publishing, 2001), 13–42.

apply fully, just as they apply to a court of law, and parties can invoke Art. 6(1) against each other. If Art. 6(1) only has indirect applicability, a party cannot rely directly on Art. 6(1) when challenging an award. Instead, the award has to be challenged on some other basis, such as a national arbitration law, and the courts then have an obligation to interpret this law in accordance with Art. 6(1). This indirect application clearly leaves scope for interpretation, so that not all guarantees apply, or if they do apply indirectly, only in modified form.

**Delegation theory** Some authors have argued that Art. 6(1) of the ECHR is *directly* applicable to an arbitration tribunal for the reason that the arbitration tribunal, in fact, carries out a quasi-judicial function, a function traditionally exclusively exercised by the courts and hence delegated to the arbitration tribunal by law. Because of this delegation of the judicial function, the arbitration tribunal would be subject to obligations of due process. Authors subscribing to this delegation theory, such as Jaksic, argue that:[54] 'Arbitration is adjudication of the dispute ending in a final and binding arbitral award, which is provided with *res judicata* effect. Although there are individuals who confer upon the arbitrators the power to resolve their dispute, arbitration is neither an isolated nor abstracted institution which should evade the applicability of human rights norms.'

Whether one finds the delegation theory persuasive depends on one's view of the nature of arbitration and one's view on whether dispute resolution is essentially a public or private function. If one regards arbitration as being driven by the preference of the parties, one could argue that the delegation theory ignores the significance of the contractual basis of arbitration. In this view, the delegation theory is unconvincing, as the state has not delegated its judicial function to the tribunal, but the parties have simply chosen to go to a private tribunal instead of the courts by concluding the arbitration agreement (opting out).

Conversely, if one regards arbitration as being driven by the lack of efficient public dispute-resolution processes, so that the only option is arbitration, then one could argue that states have failed to provide this public function and have instead chosen to delegate this function to a private tribunal. The argument here is that states have not enacted arbitration-friendly laws primarily for the reason that they respect individual freedom and party autonomy in contract law, but that states have been motivated

---

[54] Jaksic, *Arbitration and Human Rights*, 203; Schiavetta, 'The Relationship between e-ADR and Article 6?', para. 4.1.

by the recognition that if the cost of some dispute resolution is shifted to the private sector, the burden on the publicly financed courts is reduced.[55]

**Indirect applicability**    The second theory is that the ECHR is *indirectly* applicable. This theory recognises that the courts do not, in fact or in law, delegate their functions to an arbitration tribunal, and that arbitration is based on the parties' contractual choice. Nevertheless, this theory also accepts that arbitration is not entirely private; the courts are still involved in arbitration. The courts of the seat of arbitration or the courts at the place of enforcement have (albeit limited) jurisdiction to set aside or enforce an award, as the case may be. This (actual or potential) involvement of the courts – as organs of the state – means that the ECHR is (at least) indirectly applicable.[56]

**Direct or indirectly applicable**    It is submitted that the second theory (i.e. that Art. 6(1) of the ECHR is indirectly applicable) is the most convincing theory for voluntary arbitration. The first theory is not entirely convincing, where the parties had a choice to go to the courts and could have included a jurisdiction clause in their agreement but instead agreed to use arbitration. Conversely, direct applicability of the ECHR is appropriate in cases of compulsory arbitration (discussed below), as here the authority of the arbitration tribunal is not based on the parties' choice but on law.[57] Therefore, it is necessary to make a distinction between voluntary and compulsory arbitration.

**Distinction between voluntary and compulsory arbitration**    At times, it might be difficult to decide whether or not a party has submitted to

---

[55]  T. Carbonneau, 'Arbitral Justice: The Demise of Due Process in American Law' (1996) 70 *Tulane Law Review* 1945–67, 1958–9.

[56]  F. Matscher, 'Schiedsgerichtsbarkeit und EMRK', in N. Habscheid and D. Schwab, *Beiträge zum internationalen Verfahrensrecht und Schiedsgerichtsbarkeit* (Münster: Festschrift für Heinrich Nagel, 1987), 237; see also Redfern and Hunter, *Law and Practice of International Commercial Arbitration*, 77 and 493, and also Kaufmann-Kohler and Schultz, *Online Dispute Resolution*, 198; also W. Robinson and B. Kasolowsky, 'Will the United Kingdom's Human Rights Act Further Protect Parties to Arbitration Proceedings?' (2002) 18(4) *Arbitration International* 453–66, 460; A. Samuel, 'Arbitration, Alternative Dispute Resolution Generally and the European Convention on Human Rights' (2004) 21(5) *Journal of International Arbitration* 413–38, 416; Petrochilos, *Procedural Law in International Arbitration*, 130, 152–3; T. Shultz, 'Human Rights: A Speed Bump for Arbitral Procedures?' (2006) 9(1) *International Arbitration Law Review* 8–23, 15.

[57]  C. Liebscher, *The Healthy Award* (The Hague: Kluwer Law International, 2003), 74.

arbitration out of their own free will. In *Deweer* v. *Belgium*, a butcher was prosecuted for having sold pork and beef at too high a profit margin, and he was given the invidious choice between paying a fine in full settlement or having his shop closed whilst awaiting criminal prosecution. Unsurprisingly, he opted (under protest) for the former. The Court found that he had *not* voluntarily waived his right to go to court and hence had been deprived of his due process rights.[58] In *Thompson* v. *UK*,[59] the defendant of an absence-without-leave charge agreed to summary trial (as opposed to trial by court martial) by the commanding officer in circumstances where he was in the presence of the superior officer and was not informed about his rights, and the European Court of Human Rights (ECtHR) held that this was not a valid waiver.

By contrast, in *Le Compte, Van Leuven and de Meyere* v. *Belgium*, the ECtHR found that the applicants had not waived their right to a public hearing in disciplinary proceedings through their (compulsory) membership of a medical professional body.[60]

Also, in *Axelsson* v. *Sweden*, four taxi owners were members of a trade association, the Malmö Taxi Economic Association, which they *had* to be a member of if they wished to obtain business from the local taxi despatch. The membership agreement provided for arbitration of all disputes. The Commission found that this was a voluntary and valid waiver of their right to have their dispute heard by an ordinary court and hence found the complaint inadmissible.[61] Essentially, arbitration is voluntary and not compulsory if it is based on an agreement between the parties that was free from duress, undue influence or mistake, even if the arbitration was imposed by a private, monopolistic organisation and all persons wishing to undertake a certain activity (such as acting as football players' agent or driving a taxi) had to agree to it. Arbitration is only compulsory if it is required by law (such as a statutory requirement).[62]

If participation in the arbitration is not voluntary but compulsory (e.g. under a statute), the arbitral proceedings must comply in full with the due process rights set out in Art. 6(1), or be subject to review by a body (such as a court) that does.[63] The case of *Bramelid and Malmström* v.

---

[58] *Deweer* v. *Belgium* (1979–80) 2 EHRR 439 (ECtHR), 462–3.
[59] (2005) 40 EHRR 11 (ECtHR), para. 45.   [60] (1982) 4 EHRR 1 (ECtHR) 22.
[61] *Axelson* v. *Sweden* (EComHR), Admissibility Decision of 13 July 1990, No. 11960/86, available from the HUDOC database; *Stretford* v. *Football Association* [2007] All ER (D) 346 (Mar) (CA), Judgment of 21 March 2007, para. 49.
[62] *Stretford* v. *Football Association*, paras. 48–9 and 52.
[63] *Albert and Le Compte* v. *Belgium* (1983) 5 EHRR 533 (ECtHR), 545.

*Sweden* concerned mandatory arbitration to determine the price of shares that were compulsorily sold to the majority shareholder under Swedish company legislation. Here, the European Commission of Human Rights (EComHR) said that mandatory arbitration is permissible provided that there is recourse to a court, which has the power to review the case both as to facts[64] and law, in order to guarantee the due process rights granted by Art. 6(1).[65] This case has interesting consequences for court-mandated forms of ADR – here, the due process rights would have to be guaranteed in full, and Art. 6(1) is directly applicable.[66]

Having discussed the first two theories on the applicability of the ECHR, it remains to examine the theory that it does not apply at all.

**Absolute waiver theory**    The third theory is that the due process standards in the ECHR do not apply to arbitration at all, since the arbitration tribunal is not a tribunal established by law, and the arbitration agreement is a waiver of the right to go to court and the due process rights applicable to the courts.[67] The logic of the absolute waiver theory is that the arbitral tribunal derives its authority and mandate from the private agreement of the parties, and hence not from the state, and that, therefore, the ECHR is not applicable to this private, 'horizontal' relationship.[68] This theory is unconvincing and should be rejected for the following reasons.

Firstly, as has been discussed above in the context of the indirect applicability of the ECHR, states support arbitration and enforce arbitration awards, hence endorsing the process. Thus states' responsibility under Art. 6(1) is indeed engaged if they condone flagrant breaches of the ECHR by giving effect to arbitral awards that infringe fundamental principles of due process.[69]

Secondly, while it is clear that the arbitration agreement does in fact waive the parties' right to go to court, it does not logically follow that the

---

[64] See also *Le Compte, Van Leuven and de Meyere* v. *Belgium* (1982) 4 EHRR 1 (ECtHR), 22.

[65] *Bramelid and Malström* v. *Sweden* (1983) 5 EHRR 249 (EComHR), 258–9.

[66] Robinson and Kasolowsky, 'Will the UK's Human Rights Act Further Protect Parties to Arbitration Proceedings?', 455.

[67] Supporters of this absolute waiver theory do not necessarily argue that the absolute waiver does not imply that no due process rights apply to arbitration; it merely means that such rights are not based on Art. 6(1) of the ECHR.

[68] A view taken by C. Jarrosson in 'L'Arbitrage et la Convention européenne des droits de l'Homme', 573–607, 588–9; he concedes, though, that the ECHR may have some indirect influence on arbitrators.

[69] See, for example, *Bramelid and Malström* v. *Sweden*, a case in which one party had an opportunity to appoint an arbitrator, whereas the other did not. The EComHR found the case admissible.

parties have also waived all due process enshrined in Art. 6(1). Authors in favour of the absolute waiver theory quote the case of *Nordström-Janzen and Nordström-Lehtinen* v. *Netherlands*, where the EComHR emphasised that the parties had waived their due process rights: 'there was a renunciation by the parties of a procedure before the ordinary courts, satisfying *all* the guarantees of Article 6 of the Convention'.[70] However, the EComHR did *not* say that the parties therefore did not enjoy *any* of these guarantees.[71]

In fact, in the *Nordström-Janzen and Nordström-Lehtinen* case, the Commission examined to what extent the national legislative framework for arbitration allowed some control over the due process of arbitration, and found that this control existed and had been properly exercised.[72] Hence, in this case, the question was not whether the arbitration itself complied with Art. 6(1), but was instead whether the national courts were ensuring that in case of breach of due process, the award could be challenged. However, the Commission also stressed that the contracting states may decide themselves 'on which grounds an arbitral decision should be quashed', giving the state concerned a wide margin of discretion in applying the due process principles.[73] This case probably goes too far in leaving due process standards wholly to the national courts,[74] and has been contradicted by later decisions, such as *Suovaniemi*.[75]

The absolute waiver theory has not been confirmed by the jurisprudence of the Strasbourg institutions; for example, in the case of *Jakob Boss* v. *Germany*, the EComHR found that the fact that the parties have entered into an arbitration agreement:

> does not mean, however, that the respondent State's responsibility is completely excluded as the arbitration award had to be recognised by the German courts and be given executory effect by them. The courts thereby exercised a certain control and guarantee as to the fairness and correctness of the arbitration proceedings which they considered to have been carried out in conformity with fundamental rights and in particular with the right of the applicant company to be heard.[76]

---

[70] *Nordström-Janzen and Nordström-Lehtinen* v. *Netherlands* (EComHR), Admissibility Decision of 27 November 1996, No. 28101/95, available from the HUDOC database.
[71] Robinson and Kasolowsky, 'Will the UK's Human Rights Act Further Protect Parties to Arbitration Proceedings?', 462.
[72] *Ibid.*    [73] *Ibid.*
[74] Schiavetta, 'The Relationship between e-ADR and Article 6', 56.
[75] See below.
[76] Admissibility Decision of 2 December 1991, No. 18479/91, available from the HUDOC database.

In the *Suovaniemi* case,[77] the ECtHR expressly said that the fact that the parties had entered into an arbitration agreement and thereby validly *waived* their right to go to a public court did not mean that they had forsaken *all* due process rights (such as the right to an impartial arbiter).[78] The Court said that the very core of Art. 6(1) rights apply to arbitration.[79] In conclusion, the absolute waiver theory does not withstand scrutiny and should therefore be rejected.

**Significance of waivers**    Article 6(1) applies to arbitration, either directly (as in the case of compulsory arbitration) or indirectly (as in the case of voluntary arbitration). In other words, the arbitration agreement is considered to constitute a general waiver of the right to go to court but not of *all* due process rights enshrined in Art. 6(1).[80] The distinction between a waiver of the right to go to court and a *specific* waiver of due process rights is critical, and this distinction is not always clearly drawn in the discussion.

The fact that an arbitration agreement is not a general waiver of all due process rights does not necessarily mean that the parties cannot, in addition, renounce a specific right. To put it another way, in arbitration proceedings, two different types of waivers should logically be distinguished.[81] One type is the parties generally waiving their right to go to the ordinary courts to seek resolution of their dispute (i.e. the arbitration agreement).[82] The other type of waiver would be one or both parties specifically relinquishing a specific right in particular circumstances, such as a party, reaffirming or not opposing the nomination of a particular arbitrator in full awareness of a conflict of interest, which the arbitrator has previously disclosed to the parties.

As has been seen above, this distinction has never consistently and clearly been made in the jurisprudence of the ECtHR or the English courts.[83] The jurisprudence can be criticised because of this failure to distinguish between a general waiver not to go to court and a waiver of

---

[77] *Suovaniemi and Others* v. *Finland* (ECtHR), Admissibility Decision of 23 February 1999, No. 31737/96, available from the HUDOC database.

[78] *Ibid.* 5.        [79]  *Ibid.* 5.

[80] *Stretford* v. *Football Association* [2007] All ER (D) 346 (Mar) (CA), Judgment of 21 March 2007, para. 65.

[81] M. Kurkela, *Due Process in International Commercial Arbitration* (New York, NY: Oceana, 2005), 30–1.

[82] *Ibid.*

[83] *Nordström-Janzen and Nordström-Lehtinen* v. *Netherlands*; see also the case of *BLCT Ltd* v. *J Sainsbury Plc* [2004] 2 P&CR 3 (CA), 44.

a *specific* right. Hence a general waiver of the parties' right to go to court has, at times, been misused as justification for limiting due process rights in arbitration.[84]

**Requirements for waivers** A waiver 'must be supported by minimum procedural guarantees commensurate to the importance of the rights waived'.[85] Therefore, for a waiver to be valid, it must be clear and unambiguous,[86] as well as express[87] and informed,[88] and must not run counter to an important public interest.[89] This latter requirement suggests that not all rights can be completely waived (e.g. such as the rule against partiality), but this is a question on which there is no authority and which, ultimately, is not clear.[90] For a waiver to qualify as *informed*, it must be undertaken in full awareness of the legal implications. Agreement to this can be evinced (e.g. by the party entering into an arbitration agreement being legally advised).[91]

Similar jurisprudence can be found in England. The English courts also have consistently held that a waiver of an aspect of the right to a fair trial must be voluntary and fully informed.[92] In the Court of Appeal case of *Peter Smith* v. *Kvaerner*, Lord Phillips CJ observed: 'the party waiving should be aware of all the material facts, of the consequences of the choice open to him, and given a fair opportunity to reach an un-pressured decision'.[93] In that case, the Court of Appeal found that a waiver was not

---

[84] *Ibid.*

[85] *Suovaniemi and Others* v. *Finland*, 5; see also, for a recent criminal case, *Thompson* v. *UK* (2005) 40 EHRR 11 (ECtHR), para. 43.

[86] 'Unequivocal'; see *LeCompte, De Meyere, Van Leuven* v. *Belgium*, para. 59; *Håkansson and Sturesson* v. *Sweden* (1991) 13 EHRR 1 (ECtHR) 16; *Suovaniemi and Others* v. *Finland*, 5; *Thompson* v. *UK*, para. 43.

[87] *McGonnell* v. *UK* (2000) 30 EHHR 289 (ECtHR), para. 44; *Paul Stretford* v. *(1) Football Association Ltd (2) Barry Bright* [2006] EWHC 479 (Ch), para. 42.

[88] *Suovaniemi and Others* v. *Finland*, 6; *Thompson* v. *UK*, para. 44; *Paul Stretford* v. *(1) Football Association Ltd (2) Barry Bright*, para. 42.

[89] *LeCompte, De Meyere, Van Leuven* v. *Belgium*, para. 59; *Håkansson and Sturesson* v. *Sweden*, 16; *Suovaniemi and Others* v. *Finland*, 5; *Thompson* v. *UK*, para. 43; *Stretford* v. *Football Association*, para. 56.

[90] *Suovaniemi and Others* v. *Finland*, 5.

[91] *Ibid.* 6; cf. *Pfeifer and Plankl* v. *Austria* (1992) 14 EHRR 692 (ECtHR), para. 78 (no legal assistance hence waiver invalid).

[92] In the context of procedural rights in litigation: *R* v. *Bow Street Magistrate, ex parte Pinochet (No. 2)* [2000] 1 AC 119 (HL), 137 (Lord Browne-Wilkinson); *Millar* v. *Dickson* [2001] 1 WLR 1615 (HL), 1629 (Lord Bingham); *Peter Smith* v. *Kvaerner* [2006] EWCA Civ 242 (CA), para. 29.

[93] *Peter Smith* v. *Kvaerner*, para. 29.

valid, as it had not been fully informed and voluntary. Although the party later alleging bias had been informed of the judge's conflict of interest, he had not been fully informed of the consequences of objecting to the judge, and, in particular, he had not been told how quickly the case could be tried if it had to be listed again.[94] The Court of Appeal also found that the waiver was not voluntary, as his Counsel, in effect, advised him to waive this right.[95]

**Conclusion**   In summary, a minimum of procedural protection is guaranteed through the direct[96] or indirect[97] application of Art. 6(1). The absolute waiver theory is not supported by the jurisprudence of the Strasbourg institutions. It is also to be rejected on the grounds of principle in that it ignores the courts' involvement in arbitration and it illogically confuses the parties' waiver not to go to court with a waiver of all due process rights. Hence the fundamental principles of due process – such as equality of arms between the parties in the hearing, giving every party a reasonable opportunity to present their case under conditions that do not place that party at a significant disadvantage towards its opponent,[98] and the impartiality and independence of the arbitrator[99] – must be guaranteed despite the existence of a general agreement to arbitrate. By contrast, other due process rights, such as publicity[100] or the right to appeal, may be modified under the ECHR in voluntary, private dispute-resolution processes, simply because of the inherent nature of the particular private dispute-resolution process (general waiver).[101]

Nevertheless, the impact of the ECHR on due process has been extremely limited, and only very few of the cases in this area have been successful. One reason for this is that the parties can waive particular rights by a specific waiver.[102] An additional reason is that the indirect application of Art. 6(1) to arbitration gives only minimal protection, as the contracting states are allowed a wide margin of discretion, and usually the applicable arbitration law or *ordre public* already provides for such a minimum of rights (as does the English Arbitration Act 1996).[103]

---

[94]  *Ibid.* para. 31.     [95]  *Ibid.* paras. 32 and 37.

[96]  In the case of compulsory arbitration.     [97]  In the case of voluntary arbitration.

[98]  *Dombo Beheer BV* v. *Netherlands* (1994) 18 EHRR 213 (ECtHR), 230 – contrast this with *Jakob Boss* v. *Germany*.

[99]  *Suovaniemi and Others* v. *Finland*; ECtHR considered the impartiality question but found specific and unequivocal waiver.

[100]  *Nordström-Janzen and Nordström-Lehtinen* v. *Netherlands*.

[101]  See also the case of *BLCT Ltd* v. *J Sainsbury Plc* [2004] 2 P&CR 3 (CA), 44.

[102]  Samuel, 'Arbitration, ADR Generally and the ECHR', 416.     [103]  *Ibid.* 419.

## US constitutional due process standards

The notion of procedural due process as enshrined in the US Constitution fulfils an equivalent function to the notion of natural justice under the English common law.[104] The 5th[105] and 14th[106] Amendments guarantee that individuals may not be deprived of their life, liberty nor property without due process of law. The essential tenets of due process have been stated by the US Supreme Court in the seminal case of *Goldberg* v. *Kelly*.[107] They are: the right to an impartial judge,[108] notice of the case and the opportunity to be heard,[109] the right to present evidence,[110] the right to retain counsel[111] and the right to obtain a written statement of the decision with reasons.[112]

The due process clauses in the US Constitution are a restriction on government power and hence only apply to private actors if they can be brought within the confines of the state action doctrine. A private actor performs a state action if he or she carries out a public function and there is a close nexus to government administration.[113] The dominant view is that the extra-judicial resolution of disputes is not an exclusive governmental function, and hence arbitration is not 'state action'.[114] In numerous cases, US state[115] and federal[116] courts have held that arbitration is not state action even if awards are ultimately enforced by the courts. For example, in *Davis* v. *Prudential Sec Inc*, the court said 'that the mere confirmation of a private arbitration award by a district court is insufficient state action to trigger the application of the Due Process Clause'.[117] Hence the idea of indirect applicability of due process has not held sway with the US courts, and the traditional and dominant approach of US law has been bipolar; in other words, a black and white distinction is made between trial in the public courts (which is subject to constitutional due process) and arbitration (which is a private process and hence not subject to

---

[104] Friendly, 'Some Kind of Hearing', 1269 and 1277.
[105] Applying to federal government, its courts and agencies.
[106] Applying to state governments, agencies and courts.          [107] 397 US 254, 260–7 (1970).
[108] *Ibid.* 271.          [109] *Ibid.* 267–8.          [110] *Ibid.* 268.          [111] *Ibid.* 270.          [112] *Ibid.* 271.
[113] Reuben, 'Constitutional Gravity', 990.
[114] *Ibid.* 997; Friendly, 'Some Kind of Hearing', 1269 and 1277.
[115] *MedValUSA Health Programs Inc* v. *Memberworks Inc*, 273 Conn 634, 641–54.
[116] *Davis* v. *Prudential Sec Inc*, 59 F3d 1186, 1190–2 (11th Cir 1995); *Federal Deposit Ins Corp* v. *Air Florida Sys Inc*, 822 F2d 833, 842, fn. 9 (9th Cir 1987); *Elmore* v. *Chicago & Illinois Midland Ry Co*, 782 F2d 94, 96 (7th Cir 1986); *Austern* v. *Chicago Bd Options Exch Inc*, 716 FSupp 121, 125 (SDNY 1989); affirmed 898 F2d 882 2nd Cir), cert. denied 498 US 850 (1990).
[117] 59 F3d 1186, 1192 (11th Cir 1995).

constitutional process).[118] Furthermore, the arbitration agreement has traditionally been regarded as an absolute waiver of the right to a fair trial.[119] For example, in *Bowen* v. *Amoco Pipeline Company*, the US Court of Appeals for the 10th Circuit held that the defendant had voluntarily entered and participated in arbitration[120] and was hence barred from arguing a due process violation.[121] Because of the waiver, the court found it unnecessary to decide whether or not arbitration was state action.[122]

The reason for the bipolar approach of the US doctrine and the courts is that the formality of constitutional due process and the informality of arbitration are regarded as antithetical.[123] The upshot of this is that the due process clauses in the Constitution do not apply to arbitration. Of course, this does not mean that due process is inapplicable to arbitration – it only means that the US Constitution is not a source of law for due process requirements.

### 6.2.6 International conventions and standards

The most important international convention in this area is the 1958 New York Convention on the Recognition and Enforcement of Foreign Arbitral Awards.[124] This provides for the recognition and enforcement of international arbitration agreements[125] and the recognition and enforcement of foreign arbitral awards.[126] The New York Convention provides an exhaustive list of the grounds on which the contracting states can refuse to recognise and enforce a foreign award in their jurisdiction. Thereby it limits the contracting states' ability to refuse such enforcement. However, the New York Convention does contain the 'catch all' exception to enforcement:[127] public policy, in order to allow states a margin of discretion where enforcement would be contrary to fundamental values of the state in which enforcement is being sought. Nevertheless, states have accepted that the New York Convention has laid down a clear policy in favour of enforcement. Because of the recognition of the importance of

---

[118] Reuben, 'Constitutional Gravity', 953; Friendly, 'Some Kind of Hearing', 1269 and 1277.

[119] See, for example, cases where the arbitration agreement has been held to be a waiver of the 7th Amendment (right to trial by jury): *Dillard* v. *Merrill Lynch*, 961 F2d 1148, 1155 (5th Cir 1992); *Kimbrough* v. *Holiday Inn*, 478 FSupp 566, 577 (ED Pa 1979).

[120] In fact, it had compelled arbitration.    [121] 254 F3d 925, 940 (10th Cir 2001).

[122] *Ibid.*    [123] Reuben, 'Constitutional Gravity', 1046.

[124] 330 UNTS 3, adopted on 10 June 1958, entered into force on 7 June 1959.

[125] New York Convention, Art. II.    [126] New York Convention, Art. III.

[127] New York Convention, Art. V(2)(b).

arbitration for international trade, contracting states have exercised self-restraint and have limited the (potentially wide) public policy restriction normally applied to the enforcement of foreign judgments. As a result, the enforcement of arbitration awards is now governed by the more restricted notion of *international public policy*.[128] Hence interference by states with arbitration awards is limited to upholding the 'most basic notions of morality and justice',[129] and consequently refusal of enforcement is relatively rare.[130] It is precisely because of the limited interpretation of public policy that the New York Convention has facilitated the recognition and enforcement of awards. In this way, arbitration has overcome the limitations of private international law, and hence has proven to be more effective in the resolution of cross-border disputes than litigation. Hence, the New York Convention has had the dual effect of harmonising the standards for the enforcement of awards and making such enforcement easier.[131]

The question here is to what extent the New York Convention is a source of law for *due process*. From one perspective, one could say that the Convention limits due process in international commercial arbitration in that it potentially restricts the courts of the contracting states to refuse enforcement on the basis that due process has not been complied with by the foreign arbitral tribunal. However, looking at the grounds listed in Art. V and, in particular, Arts. V(1)(a),[132] V(1)(b),[133] V(1)(d)[134] and V(2)(b),[135] they are sufficiently wide to include various aspects of due process considerations. Article V(1)(b) is the main provision in this respect, as it allows refusal of recognition and enforcement where 'the party against whom the award is invoked was not given proper notice of the appointment of the arbitrator or of the arbitration proceedings or was otherwise unable to present his case'. Hence for most cases on due process it will not be necessary to invoke public policy. For example, in the case of *Generica Ltd* v. *Pharmaceuticals Basics Inc*, the US Federal Appeal Court

---

[128] Lew, Mistelis and Kröll, *Comparative International Commercial Arbitration*, 721, fn. 173 and 726–8.

[129] *Parsons & Whittemore Overseas Co Inc* v. *Société Générale de l'Industrie du Papier (RAKTA)*, 508 F2d 969, 974 (2nd Cir 1974).

[130] Lew, Mistelis and Kröll, *Comparative International Commercial Arbitration*, 724 and 726.

[131] Lew, Mistelis and Kröll, *Comparative International Commercial Arbitration*, 693.

[132] Invalid arbitration agreement.

[133] Party not given proper notice or unable to present its case.

[134] Arbitral authority or procedure not in accordance with the agreement of the parties or the law of the seat.

[135] Public policy of the enforcing state.

of the 7th Circuit held that the ground for refusal in Art. V(1)(b) corresponds to the general due process requirements under US law, consisting of 'adequate notice, a hearing on the evidence and an impartial decision by the arbitrator'.[136] This acknowledgement of the significance of due process in the New York Convention, and the subsequent interpretation of this Article by national court decisions, is an important source for the international law aspects of arbitration.

### 6.2.7  Conclusion

This section has discussed the following sources of law for due process: contractual provisions and rules of arbitral institutions, national arbitration laws, the common law, human rights law, and the New York Convention and international public policy. These sources of law are both of public and private origins and have a national and international dimension. As we have seen, human rights law has not had much influence in forming due process in arbitration, and most impulses for due process stem from national arbitration laws, the arbitral rules and the interpretation of the provisions of the New York Convention by the courts. The following sections contain a comparison of due process in litigation with due process in arbitration.

## 6.3  Impartiality and independence in adjudication

This chapter contains a discussion of constituent elements of due process, such as the impartiality and independence of the adjudicator(s), fair hearing, the duty to give reasons, transparency and the right of appeal.

### 6.3.1  Impartiality and independence of judges

The first principle of common-law due process – that no person shall be a judge in his or her own cause – means that an adjudicator in judicial or

---

[136] (1998) XXIII *Yearbook Commercial Arbitration* 1076, 1078–9; 125 F3d 1123, 1129–30 (7th Cir 1997); also in *Parsons & Whittemore Overseas Co Inc* v. *Société Générale de l'Industrie du Papier (RAKTA)*, where the 2nd Circuit said that 'this provision essentially sanctions the application of the forum state's standards of due process': 975. This is not in contradiction to the earlier finding that the due process requirements in the US Constitution do not apply to arbitration, as here the courts are dealing with the interpretation of the New York Convention and only using constitutional due process by way of analogy (i.e. the argument is not about whether arbitration is state action but about what the concept of due process means).

quasi-judicial proceedings should be impartial *and* independent.[137] This distinction between impartiality on the one hand and objective independence on the other has also been maintained by the Strasbourg institutions in their rulings on Art. 6(1) of the ECHR.[138]

This section discusses the traditional approaches to allegations of a *judge's* bias under the English common law, and the next section will discuss how these principles have been applied to *arbitrators*, both under the common law and arbitration-specific legislation and rules, contrasting the differences.

## Defining impartiality and independence

Impartiality in the context of judicial decision-making has been given the meaning 'absence of actual bias' (subjective), whereas independence has been taken to mean 'absence of appearance of bias' (objective), or in more modern terminology, 'absence of a relevant conflict of interest' under the English common law.

**Impartiality (no actual bias)**   Partiality or actual bias relates to the adjudicator's internal prejudices, prejudgement or predisposition towards one of the parties or the subject matter of the dispute. Thus partiality or actual bias is an abstract, *subjective* requirement referring to the judge's state of mind.

Partiality or bias means having an inclination for or against a party, taking into account irrelevant considerations and acting either out of self-interest or prejudice. Galligan emphasises the element of prejudging by a biased judge: 'The idea of prejudice as pre-judgment brings out well the core idea that to be biased is in some way to have judged the issue beforehand or to have judged it for reasons which are not the right reasons.'[139]

An allegation of partiality or actual bias would involve an examination of the subjective state of mind of the judge, which causes obvious problems of evidence and would be a serious allegation against the judge. Hence, in practice, partiality or actual bias is notoriously difficult to prove, and therefore a challenge of a ruling on these grounds has never been successful under English law.

---

[137] Bailey, Ching, Gunn and Ormerod, *Smith, Bailey and Gunn*, 280 and 1315.
[138] See, for example, *Pullar* v. *UK* (1996) 22 EHRR 391 (ECtHR), 402–3.
[139] Galligan, *Due Process and Fair Procedures*, 438.

**Independence (no appearance of bias)**    Because of this evidentiary concern, the courts have added the second requirement that judges must also be independent, and this second criterion of independence goes some way towards effectuating an absence of actual bias. Hence, in practice, the requirement that judges are independent is more important.

Independence is a factual concept, in that it means absence of an objectively ascertainable conflict of interest.[140] In the context of judicial decision-making in the English courts, the requirement is usually expressed as an absence of the appearance of bias or, in more recent decisions, an absence of conflicts of interest.

However, the question of what amounts to a relevant conflict of interest clearly is a *question of degree* – if the slightest possibility of bias were to be sufficient for a finding of non-independence, it would be difficult to find any adjudicator for many cases.[141] To answer this question, it is necessary to assess the risk of possible prejudice.

### Independence and the relevant risk assessment

Looking at the risk assessment from a more abstract point of view, the risk of bias depends on how directly the interest (or other predisposition) relates to the parties or subject matter of the decision to be made, and also how important the outcome is for the judge.[142] The test for this risk assessment has been succinctly expressed in the US Supreme Court case of *Tumey* v. *Ohio*, where a relevant conflict of interest has been described as a 'possible temptation to the average man as a judge'.[143]

Under the English common law, the courts have made a distinction between conflicts of interest that result in automatic disqualification of the judge (without further risk assessment) and conflicts of interest that are subject to a risk assessment (under the 'appearance of bias' argument).

**Automatic disqualification: more serious conflicts**    It has long been recognised by the English courts that a conflict of interest stemming from a financial interest in the subject matter of the dispute, such as shares in a

---

[140] *Ibid.* 438; Kaufmann-Kohler and Schultz, *Online Dispute Resolution*, 112; Jaksic, *Arbitration and Human Rights*, 253–4; Redfern and Hunter, *Law and Practice of International Commercial Arbitration*, 238–9; Lew, Mistelis and Kröll, *Comparative International Commercial Arbitration*, 258 and 260.

[141] Redish and Marshall, 'Adjudicatory Indepence', 492ff.

[142] Allison, 'A Process Value Analysis of Decision-Maker Bias', 514–17.

[143] *Tumey* v. *Ohio* 273 US 510, 522 (1927).

company, may lead to automatic disqualification of the judge.[144] However, this has now been widened to include other personal (non-financial) interests. The seminal case in this area is the *Ex parte Pinochet Ugarte* case,[145] concerning extradition proceedings, in the course of which the House of Lords had to decide on the question of state immunity granted to the former Chilean head of state. Amnesty International had been granted leave to act as an intervener in the proceedings. It transpired after the ruling that one of the Law Lords, Lord Hoffmann, was a director of the charity arm of Amnesty International, and the defendant petitioned the House of Lords to set aside the decision. The House of Lords unanimously granted the petition on the basis that Lord Hoffmann's link with Amnesty International was such that he should have automatically been disqualified from sitting in the case. In the *Ex parte Pinochet Ugarte* case, all five Law Lords held that there can be automatic disqualification of a judge, without having to show a real danger of bias, if the judge has a relevant interest in the outcome of the case.[146]

Automatic disqualification obviates the need to show that the interest was such as to be liable to influence the judge's decision.[147] Thus the House of Lords extended automatic disqualification of a judge with a relevant interest to non-pecuniary interests. This immediately raises the question of what kind of non-pecuniary interest would lead to disqualification.

On this matter, Lord Hutton stated that:

> I am of the opinion that there could be cases where the interest of the judge in the subject matter of the proceedings arising from his strong commitment to some cause or belief or his association with a person or body involved in the proceedings could shake public confidence in the administration of justice as much as the shareholding (which might be small) in a public company involved in litigation.[148]

In a similar vein, Lord Browne-Wilkinson regarded the promotion of a cause of a party as a relevant interest.[149] Thus it seems that, post the *Ex parte Pinochet Ugarte* case, the promotion of and strong commitment to a

---

[144] *Dimes v. Grand Junction Canal* (1853) 3 HL Cas 759 (HL), 793; *R v. Rand* (1866) LR 1 (QB), 230, 232.

[145] [2000] 1 AC 61.

[146] *Ibid.* 133 (Lord Browne-Wilkinson): 'once it is shown that the judge is himself a party to the cause, or has a relevant interest in its subject matter, he is disqualified without any investigation into whether there was a likelihood or suspicion of bias'; at 139 (Lord Goff): 'the relevant interest need not be a financial interest'.

[147] *Ibid.* 135.    [148] *Ibid.*    [149] *Ibid.*

particular cause or an association with one of the parties of the proceedings are non-pecuniary grounds leading to automatic disqualification without any further inquiry into the likelihood of bias.

**Lesser conflicts: appearance of bias**    Lesser conflicts of interest are subjected to a risk assessment. Generally speaking, conflicts of interest may stem from a relationship with a party (e.g. through friend- or kinship) or from the adjudicator's promotion of a particular cause.[150] Hence, usually for a finding of lack of independence, an objectively ascertainable conflict of interest or predisposition ('apparent bias') is necessary.

The leading case for the requirement of absence of apparent bias is the famous 1924 case of *R* v. *Sussex Justices, ex parte McCarthy*. In this case, Lord Hewart made the famous dictum that it is 'of fundamental importance that justice should not only be done, but should be manifestly and undoubtedly be seen to be done'.[151]

In this case, a solicitor was acting as a magistrates' clerk in a criminal case relating to a dangerous driving charge, and as solicitor for the plaintiff in the ensuing civil trial for damages against the same defendant. On the facts, it was clear that he had not advised the magistrates and, hence, had not influenced the magistrates' decision to convict the defendant.[152] Nevertheless, the defendant's conviction was quashed for the appearance of bias. The logic underlying this decision is the difficulty of proving or disproving actual bias, and that, therefore, as a matter of policy, it is undesirable and unhelpful to even pose the question of whether a person was, in fact, biased.[153] Even if one accepted that an appearance of bias was sufficient for challenging a decision, this still leaves open the question as to *how much* apparent bias is required before a decision is quashed. The case law after *R* v. *Sussex Justices, ex parte McCarthy* was conflicting as to the likelihood of bias required; in particular, some courts seemed to state

---

[150] Bailey, Ching, Gunn and Ormerod, *Smith, Bailey and Gunn*, 280 and 1315.
[151] *R* v. *Sussex Justices, ex parte McCarthy* [1924] 1 KB 256 (Divisional Court), 259.
[152] Although one could argue that his mere presence could have influenced the magistrates, this is not a point that was argued by the court.
[153] *R* v. *Sussex Justices, ex parte McCarthy*, 259; see the explanation for the appearance of bias rule in *R* v. *Gough* [1993] 97 Cr App R 188 (HL) 191 (Lord Goff); 202 (Lord Woolf). In more recent decisions, the courts refer to unconscious bias rather than appearance of bias; see Simon Browne LJ in the case *R* v. *Inner West London Council, ex parte Dallaglio* [1994] 4 All ER 139 (CA), 152, who said that the courts are 'no longer concerned strictly with the appearance of bias but rather with establishing the possibility there was actual although unconscious bias'; see also *AT&T Corporation* v. *Saudi Cable Co* [2000] 2 Lloyd's Rep 127 (CA), 136 (Lord Woolf).

that a mere suspicion of bias was sufficient to create an appearance of bias,[154] whereas others held that there must be a real likelihood of bias.[155]

This conflict was eventually resolved in favour of the latter concept by the leading House of Lords decision in *R v. Gough*.[156] In that case, one of the jurors in a criminal trial was the neighbour of the defendant's brother – albeit that she was not aware of this connection during the trial. Lord Goff stated that a mere suspicion of bias is not sufficient – there has to be a real danger of bias in the sense of a real possibility of bias.[157] The only exception to this was where the judge had a financial interest in the outcome; in such cases, bias is automatically presumed.[158] Hence the courts will now look at the likelihood of bias, rather than a mere theoretical appearance of bias.

In a similar vein, the ECtHR has held, in a case where one of the jurors in a criminal trial was an employee of one of the main prosecution witnesses, that the applicant's doubts about the juror's impartiality must be objectively justified. The ECtHR said that in each individual case it had to be examined as to whether there was a real risk that the familiarity would taint the impartiality of the tribunal member. The ECtHR by a majority of five votes to four found that there had been no breach of Art. 6(1), since the juror had been employed in a junior position, had had no involvement in the project concerned and, in fact, had been made redundant before the trial.[159]

By way of summary, if the judge has a significant financial or other direct and personal interest in the outcome, he or she will automatically

---

[154] Lord Goff in *R v. Gough*, 194 pointed out that 'following the Sussex Justices case, there developed a tendency for courts to invoke a test requiring no more than a suspicion of bias'; see, for example, *Metropolitan Properties Co (FGC) Ltd v. Lannon* [1969] 1 QB 577 (CA), 599, referring to the 'impression which would be given to other people' (Lord Denning); Danckwerts LJ and Edmund Davies LJ endorsed a reasonable suspicion of bias standard at 601–2 and 606.

[155] *R v. Camborne Justices, ex parte Pearce* [1955] 1 QB 41 (Divisional Court), 51–2; *R v. Barnsley County Borough Licensing Justices, ex parte Barnsley and District Licensed Victuallers Association* [1960] 2 QB 167, 186–7 (Devlin LJ).

[156] *R v. Gough* (HL) 194.   [157] *Ibid.* 198.

[158] *Ibid.* 195; *Dimes v. Grand Junction Canal* (1853) 3 HL Cas 759 (HL), 793; *R v. Rand* (1866) LR 1 (QB), 230, 232; see also the US Supreme Court case of *Tumey v. Ohio*, 522; Allison, 'A Process Value Analysis of Decision-Maker Bias', 515–16 argues that this harsher treatment of financial bias can be explained by the fact that it is easier to prove than prejudice, and because of the public's expectations; he argues that financial interests may, in fact, have less influence on a decision-maker than other interests. Of course, in the United Kingdom the *Ex parte Pinochet Ugarte* case has made clear that interests of a non-financial nature may also lead to automatic disqualification.

[159] *Pullar v. UK* (1996) 22 EHRR 391 (ECtHR), 405.

be disqualified; however, such extreme cases, exemplified by the *Ex parte Pinochet Ugarte* case, will be rare. In most cases, the interest will be more indirect and less substantial, so that a risk assessment in relation to the conflict of interest must be undertaken, and a judge's independence must be assessed by objective criteria.

### 6.3.2 Impartiality and independence of arbitrators

Unsurprisingly, national arbitration laws[160] and the rules of some of the most important arbitrational institutions[161] expressly provide that arbitrators must be independent and/or impartial. In addition, the rules of conduct governing the legal professions state that members of that profession must be impartial and independent and must not advise any party when acting as arbitrators.[162] Furthermore, it is a recognised fundamental principle of international arbitration law that arbitrators should be both impartial and independent.[163]

Nonetheless, the application of this general principle causes problems when applied to the manifold situations of alleged bias in which arbitrators may find themselves.

#### The English Arbitration Act 1996 and the common law

Looking at English law and, in particular, the English Arbitration Act 1996 in more detail, it provides first of all, in s. 1(a), that 'the object of arbitration is to obtain the fair resolution of disputes by an *impartial* tribunal without unnecessary delay and expense'. Most importantly, s. 24(1)(a) entitles a party to apply to the court to remove an arbitrator where circumstances exist that give rise to justifiable doubts as to his or

---

[160] For example English Arbitration Act 1996, ss. 24(1)(a), 33(1)(a) and 68(2)(a); German Arbitration Act 1998, §§ 1035 and 1036; US Federal Arbitration Act 1925, § 10(a)(2) ('evident partiality or corruption'); New South Wales Commercial Arbitration Act 1984, s. 42; Arbitration Law of the People's Republic of China 1994, Arts. 34 and 58(6); Japanese Arbitration Law 2003, Art. 18(1)(ii).

[161] ICC Rules, Arts. 7(1) and 11(1); AAA ICDR, Art. 7(1); AAA Commercial Arbitration Rules, rr. 17(a)(i) and 16; LCIA Rules, Art. 5(2); UNCITRAL Rules, Art. 9; WIPO Rules, Art. 22(a).

[162] Law Society's *Guide to the Professional Conduct of Solicitors*, 8th edn (London: Law Society, 1999), r. 22.02.

[163] Redfern and Hunter, *Law and Practice of International Commercial Arbitration*, 236; Lew, Mistelis and Kröll, *Comparative International Commercial Arbitration*, 255–6; IBA Guidelines of Conflicts of Interest in International Arbitration (22 May 2004), Part 1.1, available from www.ibanet.org/publications/IBA_Guides_Practical_Checklists_Precedents_and_Free_Materials.cfm [1 April 2008].

her impartiality.[164] Furthermore, s. 33 provides that the tribunal shall act fairly and impartially between the parties; non-compliance with this duty leaves any ensuing award open to challenge.[165] Although the English Arbitration Act 1996 does not refer to independence (only to impartiality), the right to challenge an arbitrator under the 1996 Act includes circumstances where the arbitrator cannot be considered to be independent, since an award can be challenged if there are objective circumstances that give rise to justifiable doubts as to the arbitrator's impartiality. This wording includes objectively ascertainable conflicts of interest and the 'real danger of bias' test established in *R* v. *Gough.*

It has been long established that a private body, such as a sports club, may also be subject to the rules of natural justice when making a decision affecting a member based on contract.[166] This paved the way for applying the same principles to private adjudicatory systems. Lord Goff in *R* v. *Gough* stated that the same standard of real danger of bias applies to all persons acting in a judicial capacity, whether they are adjudicating on the facts or on the law (i.e. judges, jurors, justices, tribunal members and arbitrators). Lord Goff has said, obiter, that the standard as to the likelihood of bias stemming from a conflict of interest is the same in arbitration and in court proceedings (i.e. whether there is a real danger of bias or a real possibility of bias).[167]

Furthermore, in the more recent case of *Laker Airways Inc* v. *FLS Aerospace Ltd*, Mr Justice Rix specifically held that the test in s. 24 of the English Arbitration Act 1996 is congruent with the test of real danger of bias established in *R* v. *Gough.*[168]

Likewise, in the case of *AT&T* v. *Saudi Cable Co*,[169] the Court of Appeal reiterated the dictum in *R* v. *Gough* that the test for bias applied to courts and arbitration tribunals in the same manner (i.e. the relevant test is whether there is a *real* danger that the arbitrator could be unconsciously biased).[170]

---

[164] *Norbrook Laboratories* v. *A Tank and Moulson* [2006] WL 1333300 (Comm) – the arbitrator was removed because of bias after contacting witnesses directly; see para. 156.

[165] Under s. 68(1).

[166] *AT&T* v. *Saudi Cable Co* [2000] 2 Lloyd's Rep 127 (CA), 138 (Potter LJ); *Wood* v. *Woad* (1874) LR 9 Ex 190; *Calvin* v. *Carr* [1980] AC 574 (PC), 596; *R (Irvine)* v. *The Royal Burgess Golfing Society of Edinburgh* [2004] LLR 334 (Court of Session), para. 25; Flick, *Natural Justice Principles and Practical Application*, 32–3.

[167] *R* v. *Gough* [1993] Cr App R 188 (HL), 199 – before the passing of the 1996 Act.

[168] *Laker Airways Inc* v. *FLS Aerospace Ltd* [1999] 2 Lloyd's Rep 45 (Comm), 49.

[169] [2000] 2 Lloyd's Rep 127 (CA).  [170] *Ibid.* 134–5 (Lord Woolf) and 138 (Potter LJ).

In the *AT&T* case, the chairman of an arbitration panel was a non-executive director of Nortel, a competitor to one of the parties in the dispute, AT&T. The dispute arose from a bid for a Saudi telecommunications project, which had been won by AT&T, whereas Nortel had been an unsuccessful bidder. AT&T was concerned about the risk of disclosure of confidential information to Nortel, in particular in view of future bids for Saudi projects. The Court of Appeal found that the fact that the arbitrator was a non-executive director of a competitor did not affect his independence, and that there was no real danger of unconscious bias.[171] Although the arbitrator's failure to disclose this interest to the parties at the outset did amount to a mishap in the procedure, the Court of Appeal denied that this was sufficient to set aside the award (particularly at this late stage, after millions of pounds had been spent in the proceedings).[172] The Court of Appeal agreed with the first-instance judge's assessment that the arbitrator's position as non-executive director would not have involved him in operational decisions by Nortel, and that it was therefore extremely unlikely that he would have disclosed any information, especially since such disclosure would have amounted to a serious breach of the arbitrator's duty of confidentiality. The chairman, given his experience and standing, would have been well aware of this duty.[173]

In summary, the courts have firmly established that the standards of impartiality and independence applied to arbitrators are equivalent to those applied to judges in the ordinary courts. As a matter of principle, the courts' insistence on equivalence is manifest.

### Important differences between arbitrators and judges

Nevertheless, by insisting on this principle, the English courts have turned a blind eye to the fact that there are important differences between the role played by arbitrators and that by judges. It is argued below in this chapter[174] that there are important differences between judges and arbitrators, and that the courts should acknowledge these differences by admitting that they apply[175] a lower standard to arbitrators than to judges.

By contrast to the English position, in the leading US case on the issue of arbitrator impartiality, the US Supreme Court has, albeit obiter, expressly recognised the difference between arbitrators and judges. In the United States, § 10 of the Federal Arbitration Act 1925 allows vacation

---

[171] *Ibid.* 136 (Lord Woolf) and 139 (Potter LJ).
[172] *Ibid.* 138 (Lord Woolf), 140 (Potter LJ) and 141 (May LJ).    [173] *Ibid.* 138.
[174] See the next section.    [175] See the discussion of the *Rustal* and *Bremer* cases below.

of the award only on the limited grounds of corruption, fraud, undue means or where there is *evident* partiality or corruption in the arbitrators, and the legislation does not expressly mention appearance of bias or lack of independence. Hence it may seem, at first sight, that under federal arbitration law, the test as to arbitrator bias is more restrictive and less protective than under the English common law.

However, the US Supreme Court, in the seminal *Commonwealth Coatings Corp* case,[176] held that any tribunal, whether it is a court of law or an arbitration tribunal, must not only be unbiased but must also *appear* to be unbiased.[177] The case concerned a claim for payment allegedly due for work carried out by a subcontractor against the prime contractor. The presiding arbitrator was an engineering consultant with a large business in Puerto Rico, and he had had sporadic but repeated business contacts with the prime contractor, generating fees of about US $12,000 over a period of four to five years, albeit no dealings in the year preceding the arbitration. The Supreme Court decided that this business relationship between the arbitrator and one of the parties was sufficiently significant to raise an appearance of bias (even though no actual bias was alleged), and that, as a consequence, the award should be vacated.

Mr Justice Black, who delivered the leading Opinion of the court, said[178] that, in principle, the same, if not higher, standards should apply to an arbitration tribunal compared to a court of law:

> It is true that arbitrators cannot sever all their ties with the business world, since they are not expected to get all their income from their work deciding cases, but we should, if anything, be even more scrupulous to safeguard the impartiality of arbitrators than judges, since the former have completely free rein to decide the law as well as the facts and are not subject to appellate review.

By contrast, the other two concurring judges, Mr Justice White and Mr Justice Marshall, found that arbitrators should not be held to the same standards as judges for the reason that:

> it is often because they are men of affairs, not apart from, but of the marketplace, that they are effective in their adjudicatory function . . . but it is enough for present purposes to hold, as the Court does, that where the arbitrator has a substantial interest in a firm which has done more than trivial business with a party, that fact must be disclosed.[179]

---

[176] *Commonwealth Coatings Corp* v. *Continental Casualty Co*, 393 US 145, 89 SCt 337 (1968).
[177] *Ibid*. 150.     [178] *Ibid*. 148–9.     [179] *Ibid*. 150, 152–3.

The dicta concerning the question of whether the same, higher or less stringent standards should be applied to arbitrators than to judges were ultimately obiter, as the court decided that, in this case, there was an appearance of bias. It is interesting that the court was badly divided over the question, with Mr Justice Black considering that the same, if not higher, standards should apply, whereas Justices White and Marshall held that the standards for arbitrators should be less stringent. This disagreement shows the difficulty of applying the same standards of impartiality and independence to arbitrators as those that apply to judges.

### Arbitrators as men or women of business

Even though the courts in England have held arbitrators to the same standards as judges as a matter of law, the question arises as to what extent is this possible *in practice*. It is argued here that, generally speaking, independence is more difficult to achieve in practice for arbitrators, as arbitrators are not civil servants or full-time adjudicators, unlike (most) judges, and they earn their living through some kind of commercial activity.[180] Hence they have business interests that may conflict with their adjudicatory role in some circumstances.[181] Arbitrators are frequently professionals or business people (such as lawyers, engineers, architects, surveyors, medical experts) and are chosen for the very reason of their knowledge and expertise in a given field.[182]

Conflicts may arise, in particular where specialist knowledge of a field is required, simply for the reason that the number of 'insiders', such as leading members of a particular trade association or experts in the field, is limited. As a consequence, the arbitrators, the parties' representatives, the parties' expert witnesses and the parties themselves may have pre-existing relationships or connections. Furthermore, for an arbitrator working for a large professional practice (such as a law, accountancy or construction firm), it is likely that one of his or her partners or associates may have had a business relationship with, or may even be acting for, one of the parties to the dispute in an unrelated matter.

Two cases illustrate this point. In the first case, *Rustal Trading Ltd* v. *Gill & Duffus SA*,[183] the arbitrator, a director of a sugar-trading company, had previously been a party to a protracted and acrimonious dispute involving allegations of fraud with a consultant of the claimant, Rustal

---

[180]  Rau, 'Integrity in Private Judging', 494–5.
[181]  Lew, Mistelis and Kröll, *Comparative International Commercial Arbitration*, 258.
[182]  Rau, 'Integrity in Private Judging', 494–5.    [183]  [2000] 1 Lloyd's Rep 14 (Comm).

Trading Ltd. The consultant acted as an important witness for Rustal in the arbitration in question. However, the court found that this was insufficient to establish a real danger of bias, saying that there was no reason to suspect that the arbitrator would, in fact, be predisposed against the witness' evidence.[184] The court pointed out that:

> if the arbitrators are themselves to be active traders there is every likelihood that at least one member of the tribunal will at some time have had commercial dealings with one or both parties to the dispute . . . The fact that those dealings had on occasions given rise to disputes would likewise not of itself provide grounds for doubting an arbitrator's impartiality. Disputes are part and parcel of commercial life in general and commodity trading is no exception.[185]

In a situation where a judge in an ordinary court had a pre-existing dispute with an important witness, this constellation would give rise to an appearance of bias, disqualifying the judge from sitting in the case. Because such a constellation is more likely to arise in the arbitration world, where arbitrators and expert witnesses share a common trading background, the courts seem to accept a lower standard regarding the question of appearance of bias.

In the second case used to illustrate the point, *Bremer Handlesgesellschaft mbH*, the claimant sought to challenge the appointment of one arbitrator to an appeal panel. Bremer was a seller in one of over a thousand Grain and Feed Trade Association (GAFTA) arbitrations arising from a US soya beans embargo. It argued that as the arbitrator was a director of a company whose parent company was a party involved in the soya beans embargo arbitrations, but allegedly as a buyer, there was a risk that the arbitrator may not be able to review the case without any bias. Bremer alleged that a precedent in favour of the buyers would be useful to the arbitrator's company; hence there was a conflict of interest giving rise to an appearance of bias. The Commercial Court and the Court of Appeal dismissed the complaint.[186] The complaint failed on factual grounds, as the complainant was not able to show that the parent company of the one on whose board the arbitrator sat was in fact buyer-oriented.[187] However, the Court of Appeal also said, obiter, that it found nothing objectionable

---

[184]  *Ibid.* 19.      [185]  *Ibid.* 18.

[186]  *Bremer Handelsgesellschaft mbH* v. *Ets Soules et Cie* [1985] 1 Lloyd's Rep 160 (QB); 2 Lloyd's Rep 199 (CA).

[187]  *Ibid.* 203.

about the fact that traders sit in arbitrations, as 'members of the Grain and Feed Trade Association are particularly concerned to have their disputes decided by arbitrators who were experienced both as arbitrators and above all as traders in that particular trade'.[188] Curiously, though, the Court of Appeal, obiter, approved the judge's finding that even if the parent company had been buyer-oriented, there would have been no risk of bias, as there was no evidence of any significant pattern in the outcome of the previous soya bean arbitrations on which that particular arbitrator sat. The reasoning behind this is not entirely logical, as the question of patterns of previous arbitrations relates to a showing of *actual* bias, whereas the claimants tried to show merely an *appearance* of bias. If the courts had found that the arbitrator's interest was too remote and indirect in any case to give rise to a real risk of bias, then it would have followed the same standard as that applied to judges. Instead, the Court of Appeal chose to emphasise that the arbitrator in the case was a trader, and that this was not objectionable, thereby implicitly applying a different standard than that applied to 'ordinary' judges. Hence certain predispositions do not disqualify arbitrators unless they reach a high intensity and actually blind the arbitrator as to the factual findings and applicable law.[189]

The conclusion from these cases is that a lower standard of impartiality is applied in arbitration than in litigation.

### Payment and the 'repeat player' syndrome

Arbitrators differ from judges in that they are paid by the parties, and not by the state, so that the arbitrator may, at least theoretically, be interested in repeat appointments. This is problematic if the parties are involved in the appointment of the arbitrator and the arbitrator expects repeat 'business' from one of the parties but not from the other.[190] Lisa Bingham, in her empirical study of 1998 comparing the statistics of non-repeat and repeat appointments of arbitrators by employers, has clearly shown that employers are at an advantage over employees where they make repeat

---

[188] *Ibid.* 204.     [189] Park, *Procedural Evolution in Business Arbitration*, 132.
[190] C. Partasides, 'International Commercial Arbitrations', in J. Tackaberry and A. Marriott, *Bernstein's Handbook of Arbitration and Dispute Resolution Practice*, 4th edn (London: Sweet & Maxwell, 2003), 651–706, 687; Rau, 'Integrity in Private Judging', 524; E. Thornburg, 'Going Private: Technology, Due Process and Internet Dispute Resolution' (Fall 2000) 34 *UC Davis Law Review* 151–220, 208; L. J. Gibbons, 'Private Law, Public "Justice": Another Look at Privacy, Arbitration and Global E-Commerce' (2000) 15 *Ohio State Journal on Dispute* Resolution 769–93, 780.

appointments.[191] Discussion of the 'repeat player' syndrome can be found in Chapter 3.[192]

## Appointment by the parties

Another related issue in relation to independence is that, in most cases, the parties appoint the arbitrator(s). If a panel of three arbitrators is appointed, it is common practice that each party appoints one arbitrator and the third arbitrator is then appointed in some other manner (such as being appointed by agreement of the party-appointed arbitrators) as neutral chairman.

The function of each party-appointed arbitrator in international commercial arbitration is to ensure that the cultural, linguistic and legal background of that party is properly understood by the tribunal. Hence, in the context of an arbitral tribunal with several arbitrators, it is necessary to distinguish between neutrality and impartiality. A party-appointed arbitrator is not neutral, but should act fairly and impartially between both parties.[193] This can cause problems where one party fails to appoint an arbitrator and the other party's appointed arbitrator acts as a single arbitrator.[194]

By contrast, in domestic US arbitration, the practice has been the reverse, in that a party-appointed arbitrator has been regarded as *not* being independent from the appointing party, and as acting more like a representative.[195] However, US practice is being influenced by international practice to the contrary.[196] The 'Code of Ethics' jointly promulgated by the AAA and the ABA states that, as a general rule, party-appointed arbitrators should be impartial and independent, unless the parties or the governing rules state otherwise.[197]

---

[191] Bingham, 'Private Law Public "Justice"', 236–9; see also Rau, 'Integrity in Private Judging', 524.

[192] See 3.5.2.

[193] Lew, Mistelis and Kröll, *Comparative International Commercial Arbitration*, 258–9.

[194] See BGH III ZR 332/99 of 1 February 2001, albeit in that case the German courts nevertheless enforced the English award, as the opposing party should have challenged the award earlier, before the courts at the seat.

[195] Rau, 'Integrity in Private Judging', 497–8; Redfern and Hunter, *Law and Practice of International Commercial Arbitration*, 237; Lew, Mistelis and Kröll, *Comparative International Commercial Arbitration*, 256. Subject to a duty not to mislead or harass the other party or engage in delaying tactics, the non-neutral arbitrator may be predisposed towards the appointing party; see ABA/AAA, *Code of Ethics*, Canon XA(1).

[196] Park, *Procedural Evolution in Business Arbitration*, 9.

[197] Under 'Note on Neutrality' and Canon X in ABA/AAA, *Code of Ethics*.

There seems to be a consensus, at least in international arbitration, that party-appointed arbitrators should be impartial, even though the party-appointed arbitrator cannot be said to be entirely neutral. However, as long as each party appoints an arbitrator, and there is a neutral chairman, this should not be seen as lowering standards of due process.

## Systemic bias

While bias is prohibited, doctrinal predisposition is a legal factor that an appointing party may take into account.[198] Such predisposition may have an impact on fairness. Systemic bias may arise from an arbitrator's belonging to a particular interest or stakeholder group or from repeat appointments by such a group,[199] or from the fact that one party appoints the arbitrator and pays for the procedure.[200]

Issues of systemic bias are extremely difficult to assess.[201] As Lisa Bingham has argued, 'statistical analysis may be useful to explore questions of structural bias stemming from the nature of the rules governing arbitration'.[202] However, she also points out that a substantive scanning of arbitration awards for systematic bias is difficult, as factual and legal accuracy are notoriously hard to measure.[203]

Systemic bias additionally refers to those leanings and propensities that *every* individual has, not because of a personal conflict of interest or a consciously adopted viewpoint, but as a result of belonging to a particular group or organisation or as a result of a particular attitude or predisposition. Hence systemic bias is caused by our outlook on life as influenced by our social background and milieu, and this, of course, includes our work environment, professional training and membership of professional organisations.[204] Lon Fuller tells the story of a three-judge court which had to adjudicate on the question of whether the criminal offence of threatening serious bodily harm to another person had been committed. The accused was a sailor in the navy, and the unrefuted witness statements showed that the accused had said to a fellow sailor: 'I'll stick a

[198] Park, *Procedural Evolution in Business Arbitration*, 9.
[199] Thornburg, 'Going Private', 209.
[200] See also T. Schultz, 'Does Online Dispute Resolution Need Governmental Intervention?' (2004) 6 *North Carolina Journal of Law & Technology* 71–106, 92–3.
[201] Thornburg, 'Going Private', 209.      [202] Bingham, 'Private Law, Public Justice', 253.
[203] *Ibid.* 257–8.
[204] Galligan, *Due Process and Fair Procedures*, 438; Rau, 'Integrity in Private Judging', 488 – he argues that this is unavoidable; see also J. Sternlight, 'Panacea or Corporate Tool?: Debunking the Supreme Court's Preference for Binding Arbitration' (Fall 1996) 74 *Washington University Law Quarterly* 637–712, 684–5.

knife in your guts and turn it round three times.' Lon Fuller wrily remarks: 'Two of the judges, who had spent their lives in genteel surroundings far from the waterfront, were with great difficulty persuaded by the third to acquit.'[205]

The arbitrator's professional or business background may mean that he or she belongs to a particular interest or stakeholder group that influences his or her view of a dispute, which favours one or the other party.[206] This is clearly not a problem if the parties both belong to the same interest group (e.g. both are members of the same trade association), and possibly less so if the interest group is not relevant to the dispute. Issues of systemic bias only arise if there is a substantial power imbalance between the parties, and the parties belong to two opposing interest groups whose interests clash in the particular dispute under arbitration. In order to illustrate this argument, one could imagine an arbitrator, who is a leading member of a consumer association, adjudicating a consumer-law dispute between a business and a consumer as sole arbitrator. Similar constellations can be made out (e.g. IP rights holder / user of IP, doctor/patient dispute or accident insurance company / claimants' association in personal injury cases) where the arbitrator belongs to one of the interest groups (e.g. to the association of IP rights holders, the medical profession or an association of personal injury claimants). In such cases, where a dispute involves opposing interest groups, the potential for systemic bias should be reduced by ensuring a balanced composition of the tribunal, including representation of both stakeholder groups on the tribunal and having a neutral chairman.

Independence standards for arbitrators attempt to draw the minute line between allowing for the general expertise and knowledge of arbitrators but prohibiting specific conflicts of interest and providing for a balanced composition of arbitration tribunals. For example, the AAA/ABA's Code of Ethics expressly recognises that arbitrators may have a business/ professional background, and states: 'Arbitrators do not contravene this [Code] if, by virtue of such experience or expertise, they have views on certain general issues likely to arise in the arbitration, but an arbitrator may not have prejudged any of the specific factual or legal determinations to be addressed during the arbitration.'[207]

---

[205] Fuller, 'The Forms and Limits of Adjudication', 391.
[206] This type of conflict of interest is also possible for judges in extreme cases; see the *Ex parte Pinochet Ugarte* case. However, because of arbitrators' involvement in commercial affairs, it is more likely that they belong to relevant interest groups.
[207] AAA/ABA, *Code of Ethics*, under 'Comment to Canon I'.

In commercial arbitration and other situations where there is no significant power imbalance between the parties, and where the parties have made a fully informed and voluntary decision to go to arbitration, this slight taint on arbitrators' independence is of less significance than in arbitrations where there is a power imbalance and/or one party had to agree to the arbitration clause in a non-negotiated contract. However, even in the context of commercial arbitration, Alan Redfern and Martin Hunter have pointed out that 'in the past there was probably too great an acceptance by the parties of manifestly dependent or biased arbitrators nominated by their opponents'.[208]

## Disclosure

Some may say that the issue of conflicts of interest is dealt with, in practice, by disclosure.[209] The arbitrator should disclose all matters that affect his or her independence from the parties, or that could cause a conflict of interest.[210]

In England, if the parties either expressly agree that the disclosed matters do not disqualify the arbitrator, or omit to challenge the arbitrator after a disclosure, the prejudiced party has waived his or her right to challenge the appointment of the arbitrator. As a consequence, a party may challenge the award after it has been rendered on the basis of lack of independence of the arbitrator only if the challenge is based on facts that the party did not know at the outset of or during the arbitration.[211]

This waiver doctrine would be in accordance with Art. 6(1) of the ECHR. In *Suovaniemi and Others* v. *Finland*, the ECtHR held that:

> the Contracting States enjoy considerable discretion in regulating the question on which grounds an arbitral award should be quashed, since the quashing of an already rendered award will often mean that a long and

---

[208] Redfern and Hunter, *Law and Practice of International Commercial Arbitration*, 245; see similar: Jaksic, *Arbitration and Human Rights*, 256–7; Samuel, 'Arbitration, ADR Generally and the ECHR', 414; Khawar Qureshi also points out that conflicts of interests have threatened the confidence in the arbitral process: K. Qureshi, 'Conflict of Interest' (2004) 154 *New Law Journal* 1400–1; Reuben, 'Constitutional Gravity', 984.

[209] Reuben, 'Constitutional Gravity', 1067; see also UNCITRAL Rules, Art. 9; ICC Rules, Art. 7(2); LCIA Rules, Art. 5(3).

[210] Redfern and Hunter, *Law and Practice of International Commercial Arbitration*, 242; Lew, Mistelis and Kröll, *Comparative International Commercial Arbitration*, 265; see also *Commonwealth Coatings Corp* v. *Continental Casualty Co*, 149 (Mr Justice Black) and 151 (Mr Justice White); see also UNCITRAL Model Law, Art. 12; see also the ABA *Guidelines*, Principle VI A(1)–VI A(3)(a) and (b).

[211] English Arbitration Act 1996, s. 73(1).

costly arbitral procedure will become useless and that considerable work and expense must be invested in new proceedings.[212]

By contrast, if the arbitration proceeds under the US Federal Arbitration Act 1925, the award can only be challenged *ex post*, although the challenging party should express his or her objection to the appointment of the arbitrator to make sure that the party has not waived his or her right to do so.[213]

However, it is important to point out that the arbitrator's obligation to disclose does not solve the question of under what circumstances should an arbitrator step down because of a relevant conflict of interest. If the arbitrator does not consider the disclosed conflict to warrant resignation, and only one of the parties challenges the independence of the arbitrator after disclosure, the question of whether or not the arbitrator is disqualified must be decided by the institution administering the arbitration or, ultimately, the courts.[214] The arbitrator's duty to disclose relevant conflicts of interest at the outset, while notably sensible, only has the effect that the issue of independence must be decided at an earlier stage in the arbitration, to avoid wasted costs and delay. It does not circumvent the question of standards of independence.

### 6.3.3 Conclusion

The conclusion here is that although, in theory, the English courts have pronounced that the same standards of impartiality and independence apply to arbitrators as to judges, the fact that arbitrators are part of a certain business community may in fact lead to the application of lower standards in respect of impartiality and independence.[215] Hence the English courts' rhetoric betrays the fact that lower standards are applied. The fact that the courts do not expressly recognise the differences between arbitrators and judges means that they never had a chance to address the issues arising from these differences.

---

[212] *Suovaniemi and Others* v. *Finland* (ECtHR), Admissibility Decision of 23 February 1999, No. 31737/96, 6, available from the HUDOC database; see also *Nordström-Janzen and Nordström-Lehtinen* v. *Netherlands* (EComHR), Admissibility Decision of 27 November 1996, No. 28101/95, available from the HUDOC database.

[213] This is a gap in the US Federal Arbitration Act 1925; see further Redfern and Hunter, *Law and Practice of International Commercial Arbitration*, 249.

[214] For example, English Arbitration Act 1996, s. 24(1)(a).

[215] This is similar to the findings in Park, *Procedural Evolution in Business Arbitration*, 137.

## 6.4 Fair hearing

The second principle of natural justice provides for a fair hearing. At a minimum, it requires prior notice of a claim to be given to a defendant, and the giving of a fair opportunity to each party to present his or her case to the decision-maker and rebut that of the opponent.[216] These minimum requirements apply, in principle at least, to both litigation and arbitration.[217] The purpose of the fair hearing principle is to ascertain what happened between the parties (fact-finding) and to evaluate these facts according to the applicable law.[218] As has been discussed in Chapter 2, the two main elements of fairness are equal treatment and rationality, and this is reflected in the fair hearing principle.[219]

### 6.4.1 Prior notice

Notice in good time[220] before the proceedings gives the defendant knowledge in advance of the considerations that, unless challenged, may lead to an adverse decision.[221] Therefore, an explicit disclosure of the 'substance of the matters on which the decision-maker intends to proceed' is central to the maxim.[222] Hence a party must be given adequate notice of any hearings in arbitration.[223] In addition, a party should properly be informed of the appointment of the arbitral tribunal.[224]

In the recent case of *Bernuth Lines Ltd* v. *High Seas Shipping Ltd*, the Commercial Court found that a notice of arbitration (and other arbitration documents) sent to the email address *info@bernuth.com* had

---

[216] *R (Irvine)* v. *The Royal Burgess Golfing Society of Edinburgh* [2004] LLR 334 (Court of Session), para. 33; *Calvin* v. *Carr* [1980] AC 574 (PC) 597; see also the US Supreme Court case *Joint Anti-Facist Refugee Committee* v. *McGrath*, 341 US 123, 171–2 (1950): 'notice of the case and an opportunity to meet it'.

[217] English Arbitration Act 1996, s. 33(1)(a); see also, for example, Recommendation 98/257/EC.

[218] Park, *Procedural Evolution in Business Arbitration*, 45; see also the discussion in Chapter 2.

[219] See 2.2, 2.3.2 and 2.4.

[220] *R* v. *Thames Magistrates' Court, ex parte Polemis* [1974] 2 Lloyd's Rep 16, 19.

[221] Flick, *Natural Justice Principles and Practical Application*, 51; Friendly, 'Some Kind of Hearing', 1280; New York Convention, Art. V(1)(b).

[222] Lord Mustill in *R* v. *Secretary of State for the Home Department, ex parte Doody* [1994] 1 AC 531 (HL), 560.

[223] J. Tackaberry and A. Marriott, 'General Principles', in J. Tackaberry and A. Marriott, *Bernstein's Handbook of Arbitration and Dispute Resolution Practice*, 4th edn (London: Sweet & Maxwell, 2003), 160–1.

[224] Redfern and Hunter, *Law and Practice of International Commercial Arbitration*, 491.

been validly served on the respondents.[225] The respondents had not, in fact, realised that arbitration proceedings were being held until they received a copy of the award in the post. The respondents used this email address for marketing and clerical purposes, and stated that they received a large amount of spam emails for this email address and hence had overlooked the emails pertaining to the arbitration. The Commercial Court refused to set aside the award, since this email appeared on the respondents' website and the respondents had entered this email in the Lloyd's Maritime Directory as their email address.[226] This argument is dubious, as it seems entirely reasonable that the respondents did not expect to receive important legal documents in an email account that by its very name seems to suggest that it was for inquiry purposes only. For litigation, Civil Procedure Rules 1998 (SI 1998/3132), r. 6.2(1)(e) and CPR Practice Direction 6 make clear that the electronic service is only valid where a party has agreed to such service in writing beforehand, and has specified an email address for this specific purpose.[227] In relation to arbitration, the Commercial Court expressly stated that these provisions are not the applicable benchmark, as here the parties are businessmen and/or are legally represented, so that any recognised means for effective business communication could be used for the service.[228] This case is interesting as it makes clear that a lower standard of notice applies to arbitration than to litigation.

### 6.4.2 Opportunity to present one's case and rebut that of the other party – fair hearing in a narrower sense

#### Fair hearing – the principle

The notion of a fair hearing under the common law has been shaped by the adversarial procedure. The basic principle can be formulated summarily as follows: each party must be given a fair and equal opportunity to argue his or her case, as to both matters of fact and law, and each party should also have a right to react to and rebut the submissions of the other party.[229]

In theory, under an adversarial procedure, each party should be able to gather as much evidence as possible, have access to all the documents

---

[225] [2005] EWHC 3020 (Comm), para. 34.     [226] *Ibid.* para. 34.     [227] *Ibid.* para. 3.1.

[228] *Ibid.* para. 28; s. 76(1) of the English Arbitration Act 1996 stipulates that the parties are free to agree the method of service, and s.76(3) states that any effective means of service will do.

[229] Flick, *Natural Justice Principles and Practical Application*, 69.

through disclosure and adduce pertinent evidence. Furthermore, in theory, each party has a right to call witnesses, including relevant experts, and to cross-examine the witnesses of the opponent.[230]

Clearly, in other jurisdictions, the inquisitorial approach, with the tribunal taking a more active approach in calling evidence (and deciding which evidence is to be called), may epitomise the concept of a fair hearing.[231] However, in civil-law systems, the maxims of *droit de la defense* and the *principe du contradictoire* impose similar requirements as the English maxim of fair hearing (i.e. the parties must have an opportunity to comment on and challenge each piece of evidence and each argument).[232]

For example, in *Paklito* v. *Klockner East Asia Ltd*, it was alleged by the claimant attempting to enforce a CIETAC award in Hong Kong that, under an inquisitorial system, there is no need to allow any cross-examination of an expert since the expert is appointed by the tribunal. The Supreme Court of Hong Kong disagreed and concluded, after hearing expert evidence on the questions of Chinese procedural law and the practice of CIETAC, that even under an inquisitorial procedure, the parties have a right to comment on the reports of the tribunal-appointed experts.[233]

### Amorphous nature of the requirements of fair hearing

A multitude of different procedural rights can be squeezed under the notion of a fair hearing – basically, every aspect of a party presenting or adducing evidence or law before a tribunal can be enshrined in the principle.

However, it is important to emphasise that not every restriction of a party in the conduct of his or her case necessarily amounts to a breach of that person's right to a fair hearing. The detailed requirements vary according to the nature of the tribunal and the courts' appraisal of what is appropriate in the circumstances,[234] so there is clearly a correlation

---

[230] Friendly, 'Some Kind of Hearing', 1282–6.

[231] Although it seems that there might be a general perception by the parties taking part in the dispute resolution that the adversarial procedure is fairer, as it allows the parties more control. This is the outcome of a 1978 study, which showed the same perception among common-law (England and the United States) and civil-law countries (Germany and France): E. A. Lind, B. E. Erickson, N. Friedland and M. Dickenberger, 'Reactions to Procedural Models for Adjudicative Conflict Resolution: A Cross-National Study' (1978) 22(2) *Journal of Conflict Resolution* 318–41, 335.

[232] Redfern and Hunter, *Law and Practice of International Commercial Arbitration*, 491.

[233] (1994) XIX *Yearbook Commercial Arbitration* 664, 666.

[234] Galligan, *Due Process and Fair Procedures*, 198; Flick, *Natural Justice Principles and Practical Application*, 47; Bailey, Ching, Gunn and Ormerod, *Smith, Bailey and Gunn*, 1315; *R* v.

between the nature of the tribunal and the issues at stake on the one hand, and the fair hearing requirements on the other.

In *R v. Commission for Racial Equality, ex parte Cottrell & Rohon*,[235] Lord Lane CJ said that there are degrees of justice – depending on the nature of the hearing and the seriousness of the penalties – that can be imposed.[236] In this case, the court found that the defendant, in an investigation by the Commission for Racial Equality, had no right to cross-examine the witnesses on whom the Commission was relying for its findings.[237] Lord Lane CJ cited[238] a passage in the judgment of Diplock LJ in *R v. Deputy Industrial Injuries Comr, ex parte Moore*, who had said that:

> technical rules of evidence form no part of the rules of natural justice. The requirement that a person exercising quasi-judicial functions must base his decision on evidence means no more than that it must be based on material which tends logically to show the existence or non-existence of facts relevant to the issue to be determined . . . It means that he must not spin a coin or consult an astrologer; but he may take into account any material which, as a matter of reason, has some probative value in the sense mentioned above.[239]

Due process is a flexible principle, whose precise meaning can only be ascertained on a case-by-case basis.[240] For example, the right to a fair hearing does not necessarily mean that it involves a right to make representations in person during an oral hearing, and hence the parties may be limited to written submissions.[241] Under the jurisprudence of the ECtHR, the right to a public hearing in Art. 6 of the ECHR normally requires an oral hearing in proceedings of a court or tribunal of first and only instance.[242] However, in appeal proceedings there may be less need

---

*Commission for Racial Equality, ex parte Cottrell & Rohon* [1980] 3 All ER 265 (QB), 271–3; *R v. Secretary of State for the Home Department, ex parte Doody*, 560; *R (Irvine) v. The Royal Burgess Golfing Society of Edinburgh* [2004] LLR 334 (Court of Session), para. 29.

[235] [1980] 3 All ER 265 (QB), 271–3.     [236] *Ibid.*

[237] See also Friendly's comment about administrative tribunals: 'in many such cases the main effect of cross-examination is delay' ('Some Kind of Hearing', 1285).

[238] *R v. Commission for Racial Equality, ex parte Cottrell & Rohon*, 272.

[239] *R v. Deputy Industrial Injuries Comr, ex parte Moore* [1965] 1 All ER 81 (CA), 94; this is the rationality element of fairness, discussed in Chapter 2.

[240] Park, *Procedural Evolution in Business Arbitration*, 51.

[241] *R (Irvine) v. The Royal Burgess Golfing Society of Edinburgh* [2004] LLR 334 (Court of Session) para. 33; Flick, *Natural Justice Principles and Practical Application*, 14–15; Friendly, 'Some Kind of Hearing', 1270.

[242] *Ekbatani v. Sweden* (1991) 13 EHRR 504 (ECtHR), 511; *Helmers v. Sweden* (1993) 15 EHRR 285 (ECtHR), 293–4; *Fischer v. Austria* (1995) 20 EHRR 349 (ECtHR), 364; *Regina*

for an oral hearing if the appellant has had an oral hearing at first instance and if the appeal only raises legal issues.[243] In the case of *BLCT Ltd* v. *J Sainsbury Plc*,[244] Arden LJ said that there is no general presumption under English law and Art. 6 of the ECHR that there should always be an oral hearing before a court. He found that whether or not an oral hearing is required depends on the nature of the application and, in particular, on whether factual issues or such issues as the credibility of witnesses are at stake.[245]

For any court or tribunal, the procedure adopted depends on the importance of the issues at stake, the value of the claims and the complexity of the issues involved.[246]

## Fair hearing in arbitration

Returning to the more specific question of fair hearing in arbitration, the principle that each party must be given a reasonable opportunity of putting his or her case, and dealing with that of the opponent, is equally well established.[247] For example, in Art. 34(2) of the UNCITRAL Model Law, an action for setting aside the award may be brought where 'the aggrieved party was not given proper notice of the appointment of the arbitral tribunal or the arbitral proceedings or was otherwise unable to present its case'.[248]

A good example of how the principle of fair hearing has been applied in international arbitration is the US case of *Iran Aircraft Industries* v. *Avco*. In this case, the US Court of Appeals for the 2nd Circuit refused to enforce an award by the Iran–US Claims Tribunal on the basis that the US company had been denied an opportunity to present its case. The tribunal had agreed at a pre-hearing conference that the US company would be allowed to present a summary of 'kilos and kilos of invoices' produced by an independent audit. Later, the tribunal dismissed the US company's claim for the reason that the evidence was insufficient. The US courts refused to enforce the award on the basis that the claimant

---

(*Hammond*) v. *Secretary of State for the Home Department* [2005] 3 WLR 1229 (HL), 1237–8.

[243] *Ibid.*     [244] [2004] 2 P&CR 3 (CA).     [245] *Ibid.* para. 37.

[246] Galligan, *Due Process and Fair Procedures*, 204; *R* v. *Commission for Racial Equality, ex parte Cottrell & Rohon* [1980] 3 All ER 265 (QB) 271–3; *R* v. *Secretary of State for the Home Department, ex parte Doody*, 560; *R (Irvine)* v. *The Royal Burgess Golfing Society of Edinburgh* [2004] LLR 334 (Court of Session), para. 29.

[247] English Arbitration Act 1996, s. 33; Redfern and Hunter, *Law and Practice of International Commercial Arbitration*, 490.

[248] See also New York Convention, Art. V(1)(b).

had been denied an opportunity to present its claim, as the tribunal had unwittingly misled the claimant as to the evidence to be presented.[249]

However, it is also apparent that the courts are slower to interfere with awards rendered by private bodies. In *Calvin v. Carr*, Lord Wilberforce expressly stated that 'While flagrant cases of injustice, including corruption or bias, must always be firmly dealt with by the courts, the tendency . . . should be to leave these to be settled by the agreed methods without requiring the formalities of judicial processes to be introduced'.[250]

In arbitration, it is possible for the parties to cut the cost and delay of adversarial processes in various ways, and limit the admissibility to the most relevant material.[251] The parties (or the institutional rules, by default) can, for example: restrict the length of the parties' written submissions by setting a word limit; limit or forgo disclosure; restrict the evidence adduced; renounce an oral hearing or cross-examination, proceed exclusively by written submissions;[252] or, conversely, limit themselves to an oral procedure. They can also limit the time allowed to prepare the case. Furthermore, it is possible to restrict the number of witnesses and, in particular, expert witnesses,[253] or decide not to call witnesses at all. Frequently, arbitrators appoint experts according to a secret, non-transparent procedure. Furthermore, they can adopt a more inquisitorial approach, where the witnesses are not examined by the parties but where the tribunal takes greater control of the procedure, decides which witnesses to hear (and not to hear) and puts the questions to the witnesses, if any.

Likewise, in the United States, the courts have stated that although the arbitration hearing must be fair and must comply with the basic notions of due process, the parties should not expect the same procedures as they

---

[249] 980 F2d 141 2nd Cir 1992); (1993) XVIII *Yearbook Commercial Arbitration* 596, 601–2.

[250] *Calvin v. Carr* [1980] AC 574 (PC), 593.

[251] Kurkela, *Due Process in International Commercial Arbitration*, 185.

[252] Under the English Arbitration Act 1996, s. 34(1) and (2)(h), there is no right to an oral hearing (i.e. neither party can insist on an oral hearing). If the parties cannot agree, the tribunal has a discretion to decide whether an oral hearing should be held. Contrast this position with UNCITRAL Model Law, Art. 24(1): 'unless the parties have agreed that no hearings shall be held the arbitral tribunal shall hold such hearings at an appropriate stage of the proceedings, if so requested by a party'. US federal courts have also held that the failure to conduct an oral hearing violates a party's due process rights: *Parsons & Whittemore Overseas Co Inc v. Société Générale de l'Industrie du Papier (RAKTA)*, 508 F2d 969 2nd Cir 1974).

[253] For example, *Egmatra AG v. Marco Trading Corporation* [1999] 1 Lloyd's Rep 862 (Comm), 866.

would find in a court.[254] For example, in *Generica Ltd* v. *Pharmaceutical Basics Inc*, the US Court of Appeals for the 7th Circuit found that where the arbitrator had been given a discretion in the terms of reference as to what evidence to admit, a refusal to allow a cross-examination on a point (which the tribunal considered to be irrelevant) was not an infringement of due process.[255] The US Court of Appeals for the 2nd Circuit held that an award was enforceable and that due process under Art. V(1)(b) of the New York Convention had been complied with, even though one of the plaintiff's main witnesses had been unable to attend the arbitration hearing. The court found that the 'inability to produce one's witness before an arbitral tribunal was a risk "inherent" in arbitration'. It had not been unreasonable of the tribunal to refuse to reschedule the hearing because the witness could not attend, considering that parties, counsel and arbitrators are frequently 'scattered about the globe' in such arbitrations.[256] It was sufficient for due process that the witness had supplied an affidavit with his evidence in chief.[257]

Hence, in arbitration, restrictions of the traditional, adversarial notion of a fair hearing are common. Arbitrators should merely provide each party with a fair opportunity to present his or her case and answer that of the opponent. Unlike the procedural rules in court, the procedure followed in arbitration need not be proportionate to the risks involved, so that even a factually complex case can proceed without disclosure, without expert witnesses or even without a hearing.

**Party autonomy, flexibility and fair hearing**   When contrasting the procedural requirements for a fair hearing in litigation and arbitration, one fundamental difference becomes immediately apparent: proceedings before an ordinary court are governed by rules on civil procedure with little or no influence by the parties. By contrast, arbitration procedure is largely determined by the parties,[258] the institution (unless it is an ad hoc arbitration) and/or the tribunal. This principle of party autonomy is fundamentally important in arbitration, and allows the parties to decide (if they can agree) how to conduct the arbitration process.

---

[254]   *Generica Ltd* v. *Pharmaceutical Basics Inc* (1998) XXIII *Yearbook Commercial Arbitration* 1076, 1078–9; 125 F3d 1123, 1130 (7th Cir 1997).

[255]   *Ibid.* 1129–30.

[256]   *Parsons & Whittemore Overseas Co Inc* v. *Société Générale de l'Industrie du Papier (RAKTA)*, 508 F2d 969, 975 (2nd Cir 1974).

[257]   *Ibid.* 976.

[258]   Redfern and Hunter, *Law and Practice of International Commercial Arbitration*, 315.

Since there are few predetermined rules and processes (in the case of ad hoc arbitration, none; in the case of institutional arbitration, only some), it is difficult to define a set of minimum standards for a fair hearing in arbitration. As all depends on the parties' agreement and, in the absence of that agreement, on the tribunal's discretion[259] as to how to proceed, the parties have effectively waived many of the procedural protections. The principle of party autonomy means that, if both parties agree, they can renounce procedural protections, such as the ability to adduce expert evidence, even where the case is complex and such evidence would have normally been adduced in equivalent civil proceedings.

Furthermore, in international arbitration, the proceedings may be linked to more than one jurisdiction, which makes the definition of what amounts to a fair hearing in international arbitration even more nebulous, as the concept is subject to variations in different legal systems, and subject to cultural expectations.[260] Plenty of procedural questions arise, to which a clear answer is frequently lacking.[261] In international arbitration, procedural practices that are entirely regular in one legal culture may be regarded as unethical or illegal in another.[262]

**Equal treatment and rationality as the outer boundaries**    The only limitation on the principle of party autonomy is the principle of equal and rational treatment of the parties.[263] Hence, as a bare minimum, an arbitration procedure must treat the parties equally and must use a rational method for fact-finding and applying the law.[264]

If the tribunal or the institution instigated a procedure that seriously limited *one* party's opportunities to present his or her case, then the courts would be likely to set aside the award or refuse enforcement for infringement of the equal treatment principle. Therefore it is important for the tribunal to ensure that procedural rules do not unfairly discriminate against one party. Furthermore, if a tribunal chooses a procedure that is irrational, for example relying on pure chance (such as throwing a dice or drawing a straw), then it could also be said that the procedure is unfair.

---

[259] English Arbitration Act 1996, s. 34.
[260] Jaksic, *Arbitration and Human Rights*, 230 and 235; Park, *Procedural Evolution in Business Arbitration*, 51.
[261] Park, *Procedural Evolution in Business Arbitration*, 45.
[262] Park, *Procedural Evolution in Business Arbitration*, 60–1.
[263] Redfern and Hunter, *Law and Practice of International Commercial Arbitration*, 317–18.
[264] Most writings on this issue emphasise the equal treatment aspect, probably for the reason that rationality is taken for granted.

However, the parties themselves could, in principle, agree procedural rules, even if they were discriminatory or irrational, but only if they were not doing so inadvertently. In other words, the parties could waive their right to equal treatment or rationality, provided that this waiver is given voluntarily, without undue influence and provided each party is fully aware of the consequences.[265]

Since arbitration tribunals have rarely, if ever, applied irrational procedures, the more important question in practice is equal treatment.

By way of example, the equal treatment principle means that any hearing dates should be fixed at a date and place that are roughly equally convenient for each party.[266] Likewise, deadlines or word-limits[267] that are too tight for one party only, or the use of technology[268] that is inaccessible for one party may be a breach of the principle of equal and fair treatment.[269]

Equal treatment here refers to an equal opportunity to present a party's case. It does not necessarily mean that each party should be treated exactly the same[270] (e.g. being able to call exactly the same number of witnesses). The ability to call witnesses should depend on the relevance of the evidence to that party's case. However, the principle of equal treatment would be infringed if, for example, only one party were allowed to call witnesses, or if one party was allowed to cross-examine the other party's witnesses but not the other, or if only one party were able to benefit from disclosure of the other party's documents.

This is exemplified by the ECtHR case of *Dombo Beheer BV* v. *Netherlands*[271] (although this case concerned judicial proceedings before the Dutch courts). A Dutch company brought civil proceedings for breach of an oral contract for an extension of a loan, concluded by the manager of the company and the branch manager of a bank. Because of a rule in Dutch civil procedure, which disallows the parties from appearing as witness on their own behalf, the manager of the company was not allowed to testify as to the content of the contract, whereas the branch manager could as

---

[265] See 6.2.5 and 7.2.     [266] Tackaberry and Marriott, 'General Principles', 161.

[267] *Ibid.*

[268] J. Hörnle, 'Online Dispute Resolution', in J. Tackaberry and A. Marriott, *Bernstein's Handbook of Arbitration and Dispute Resolution Practice*, 4th edn (London: Sweet & Maxwell, 2003), 794.

[269] Jaksic, *Arbitration and Human rights*, 244.

[270] Petrochilos, *Procedural Law in International Arbitration*, 145.

[271] (1994) 18 EHRR 213 (ECtHR).

witness for the bank. The ECtHR found that there had been a breach of the right to a fair hearing, since the equality-of-arms principle had been infringed. The Court held that each party had to be given a reasonable opportunity to present its case, including evidence, under conditions that do not put it at a significant disadvantage *vis-à-vis* its opponent.[272]

The principle of equal treatment also means that both parties must have equal access to all documents and other evidence. Consequently, some opportunity should be given to each party to acquaint itself with, and comment on, the observations as to law and fact made by any other party.[273]

This also means that the arbitrator should not engage in *ex parte* communications. The arbitrator should never discuss the case with only one of the parties or a witness in the absence of the other party. This rule against *ex parte* communications also means that any written communications should always be copied to the other party, even where they concern trivial administrative matters.[274]

Because of the principle of fair and equal opportunity to argue one's case, the adjudicator's decision should only be based on the evidence presented.[275] Arbitrators are frequently chosen for their expertise in a particular field, and hence this requirement raises the issue of the extent to which the arbitrator is entitled to rely on his or her own specific knowledge and experience. For example, the arbitrator may have great experience as to the cost of repairs, and may not believe the expert evidence presented to him or her on this particular issue. In a similar vein, the arbitrator may wish to rely on evidence gathered through the arbitrator's own inspection or tests. Although the prevailing opinion seems to be that arbitrators should be able to rely on their own knowledge and expertise, they should disclose the specific matters to the parties in good time before an award is made, so as to enable the parties to challenge the specific matters relied on.[276]

---

[272] *Ibid.* 229–30.

[273] *Brandstetter* v. *Austria* (1993) 15 EHRR 378 (ECtHR), 413 (in the context of criminal proceedings); *Bricmont* v. *Belgium* (1990) 12 EHRR 217 (ECtHR), 240–1.

[274] E.g. *Norbrook Laboratories* v. *A Tank and Moulson* [2006] WL 1333300 (Comm) – the arbitrator was removed because of bias after contacting a witness directly; see also AAA, *Code of Ethics*, Canon III B; Tackaberry and Marriott, 'General Principles', 160.

[275] Petrochilos, *Procedural Law in International Arbitration*, 146.

[276] *Fox* v. *Wellfair* [1981] 2 Lloyd's Rep 214 (CA), 522 and 528–30; *Checkpoint Ltd* v. *Strathclyde Pension Fund* (2003) 14 EG 124 (CA), para. 41; *Zermalt* v. *Nu-Life Upholstery* (1985) 275 EG 1134, 1138; Tackaberry and Marriott, 'General Principles', 162–7.

## Conclusion

The principle of fair hearing in adjudication at its core requires that each party is allowed to present his or her case as to evidence and law, and to react to the case of the other on an equal footing. However, there is no 'checklist' of fair hearing requirements that each procedure has to comply with, but rather the detailed requirements depend on the nature of the dispute and the issues at stake. While the civil (or even more so, the criminal) procedure rules describe the procedural protections before the courts, in arbitration the procedure is chosen by the parties (by reference to institutional rules or by agreement). Hence it is difficult to define a minimum of procedural protections to which each party is entitled, save for the principle that the arbitrator (and the arbitration institution) must treat the parties equally and rationally. This means that parties may be less well protected in exchange for a (possibly) speedier and more cost-effective procedure. This is not an issue if the parties are aware of the consequences of renouncing procedural protections, and if they have made a well-informed and voluntary waiver of their rights. If arbitration is mandatory, or if the parties are subject to a power imbalance, this may be more problematic.

### 6.5. Duty to give reasons

The duty to give reasons is an important procedural protection in addition to the fair hearing considerations outlined in the preceding section.

Due process requires that the decision-maker does not discriminate against either party (equal treatment) and does not take into account irrelevant considerations (rationality). It is argued here that the giving of reasons aids both these aims.[277]

By giving reasons, the decision-maker explains the basis for the decision and justifies it according to authoritative standards.[278] This leads to better and rational decisions, as the decision-maker will have to explain and defend the decision both in relation to the facts found and the decision he or she comes to,[279] which will result in the parties being treated according to authoritative standards, and, hence, equally and rationally.

---

[277] Fuller, 'The Forms and Limits of Adjudication', 388.

[278] Galligan, *Due Process and Fair Procedures*, 430.

[279] Rau, 'Integrity in Private Judging', 530–1; see also Henry LJ in *Flannery* v. *Halifax Estate Agencies Ltd* [2000] 1 WLR 377 (CA), 381: 'a requirement to give reasons concentrates the mind; if it is fulfilled, the resulting decision is much more likely to be soundly based on the evidence than if it is not'.

The rationalisation of a decision helps to prevent arbitrariness and discrimination in decision-making. Frequently, the instinctive decision of what is right and what is wrong does not accord with the decision reached by proper reasoning according to legal standards. In addition, the reasons form a basis for the review of a decision, enabling others to critically understand and appraise the decision, which is of crucial importance if a party wishes to appeal a decision.[280] Finally, this is a way of providing satisfaction to the parties, as it makes them feel that they have been treated according to authoritative standards, and not arbitrarily.[281]

The detail and nature of reasons clearly depends on the issues to be decided. If they consist merely of statements of facts, they can be brief. As Redfern and Hunter point out, where an arbitrator or other adjudicator merely has to decide whether goods correspond to a sample or not, the answer can be a 'yes' or 'no'.[282]

It seems that, under the common law, there was traditionally no absolute or general duty to give reasons.[283] However, the trend of the law seems to recognise a duty to give reasons for both administrative and judicial bodies, where this is required, as a matter of fairness and openness.[284] Furthermore, under the ECHR,[285] which is now incorporated into UK law under the Human Rights Act 1998, the giving of reasons is required as implicit in the fair hearing principle.[286]

---

[280] Galligan, *Due Process and Fair Procedures*, 432.

[281] Galligan, *Due Process and Fair Procedures*, 433; M. Rutherford, 'Documents-Only Arbitrations in Consumer Disputes', in J. Tackaberry and A. Marriott, *Bernstein's Handbook of Arbitration and Dispute Resolution Practice*, 4th edn (London: Sweet & Maxwell, 2003), 646.

[282] Albeit that the 'no' probably requires a brief explanation of in what way the goods differ from the sample: Redfern and Hunter, *Law and Practice of International Commercial Arbitration*, 453.

[283] Galligan, *Due Process and Fair Procedures*, 435; Flick, *Natural Justice Principles and Practical Application*, 127; *Doody* v. *Secretary of State for the Home Department* [1994] 1 AC 531 (HL), 564; *R (Irvine)* v. *The Royal Burgess Golfing Society of Edinburgh* [2004] LLR 334 (Court of Session), para. 46.

[284] *Flannery* v. *Halifax Estate Agencies Ltd*, 381; *Peter Andrew English* v. *Emery Reimbold & Strick Ltd* [2002] 1 WLR 2409 (CA), paras. 15–16; *R* v. *Secretary of State for the Home Department, ex parte Doody* [1994] 1 AC 531 (HL), 564–656; *Stefan* v. *General Medical Council* [2000] 1 WLR 1293, 1300; *Brabazon-Drenning* [2001] HRLR 6, paras. 24–9; see also Galligan, *Due Process and Fair Procedures*, 435.

[285] *Van de Hurk* v. *Netherlands* [1994] 18 EHRR 481, para. 61; *Hiro Balani* v. *Spain* [1995] 90 EHRR 566, para. 27; *Helle* v. *Finland* [1998] 26 EHRR 159, paras. 59–60; *Garcia Ruiz* v. *Spain* [2001] 31 EHRR 589, para. 23; *Hirvisaari* v. *Finland* [2004] 38 EHHR 7, para. 30.

[286] *North Range Shipping Ltd* v. *Seatrans Shipping Corporation* [2002] 1 WLR 2397 (CA) 2406; *Flannery* v. *Halifax Estate Agencies Ltd*, 381, 383.

In the English case of *Flannery* v. *Halifax Estate Agencies Ltd*,[287] the Court of Appeal stated clearly that the modern judge has a professional obligation to give reasons for a decision.[288] In this case, the Court of Appeal ordered a retrial, as the first-instance judge had preferred the defendants' expert evidence without giving an explanation as to why. In the later Court of Appeal case of *Peter Andrew English* v. *Emery Reimbold & Strick Ltd*,[289] Lord Phillips MR approved of *Flannery* and referred to the cases of the ECtHR but also discussed the problem of applying the principle in practice, due to its elusive nature. In practice, it is difficult to ascertain how detailed the reasons should be. He stated that, as a minimum principle, it should be possible to deduce from a judgment the reasons for the decision.[290] He said that 'justice will not be done if it is not apparent to the parties why one has won and the other has lost'.[291]

In *Hirvisaari* v. *Finland*,[292] the claimant appealed a ruling by a Finnish pension board, who had decided in a brief ruling that the claimant was able to work part-time and hence reduced his pension; this ruling was simply confirmed on appeal by the Finnish Insurance Court. The ECtHR reiterated that Art. 6(1) of the ECHR required that all courts and tribunals should adequately state the reasons on which their judgments are based. The extent of this duty may vary according to the nature of the decision and all the circumstances of the case.[293] The reasons must be in sufficient detail to allow the parties to make effective use of any available right of appeal, but can otherwise be brief.[294]

By contrast, in *Van de Hurk* v. *Netherlands*, the ECtHR held that the court must merely demonstrate that it has addressed the contentions advanced by the parties;[295] in *Helle* v. *Finland*, it found that the court was under a duty to address the essential issues that were submitted to it.[296] Lord Phillips MR in *Peter Andrew English* v. *Emery Reimbold & Strick Ltd* interprets the standard established by the ECtHR as meaning that the reasons must demonstrate that the essential issues raised by the parties have been taken into consideration by the court, and must demonstrate how these issues have been resolved.[297]

---

[287] [2000] 1 WLR 377 (CA).     [288] *Ibid.* 381.     [289] [2002] 1 WLR 2409 (CA).
[290] *Ibid.* para. 2.     [291] *Ibid.* para. 16.
[292] [2004] 38 EHHR 7; see also *Ruiz Torija* v. *Spain* [1994] 19 EHHR 553, para. 29 and *Garcia Ruiz* v. *Spain* [2001] 31 EHHR 589, para. 26.
[293] *Hirvisaari* v. *Finland*, para. 30.     [294] *Ibid.*
[295] *Van de Hurk* v. *Netherlands* [1994] 18 EHRR 481, para. 59.
[296] [1998] 26 EHRR 159, para. 60.
[297] *Peter Andrew English* v. *Emery Reimbold & Strick Ltd*, para. 12.

The implementation of the ECHR by the Human Rights Act 1998 has had the effect in England that, for certain types of decisions where, under the common law, no reasons need be given, now the court is under a duty to give at least minimum reasons. One example of this is a court's refusal to give leave to appeal against an arbitration award under s. 69 of the English Arbitration Act 1996. The Court of Appeal has recently held that in order to comply with Art. 6 of the ECHR, the court has to give at least minimal reasons.[298]

Opinions vary as to whether the giving of reasons should be mandatory in the substantive arbitration award.[299] One view is that reasons should be given as a due process requirement; a person making a binding decision defining the rights and obligations of others should state the reasons for his or her ruling.[300] Another view is that the giving of reasons makes the award vulnerable to being appealed, which conflicts with the principle of finality of arbitration awards.

Some laws[301] and arbitration rules[302] require that awards should always be accompanied by reasons. Other laws, including the English Arbitration Act 1996 and the UNCITRAL Model Law[303] and many arbitration rules,[304] make reasons mandatory, unless the parties have agreed to have an award without reasons, or the award is an agreed award. The English Arbitration Act 1996 provides that if the parties have agreed to an award without reasons, they are deemed to have excluded the right to appeal to the court on a point of law.[305] The parties sometimes agree to have a 'bare' award accompanied by a statement of reasons for the award, which is confidential (i.e. cannot be used in an appeal before a court). This practice has been customary in some kinds of arbitration, such as London maritime arbitrations.[306]

---

[298] *North Range Shipping Ltd* v. *Seatrans Shipping Corporation* [2002] 1 WLR 2397 (CA), para. 27.
[299] Lew, Mistelis and Kröll, *Comparative International Commercial Arbitration*, 647.
[300] Tackaberry and Marriott, 'General Principles', 11–391 and 345.
[301] Belgian Judicial Code, Art. 1701(5); Art. 1704(1)(i) states that an award may be set aside if the reasons are not stated; French Nouveau Code de Procédure Civile, Art. 1471.
[302] ICC Rules, Art. 25(2); ICAC Rules, para. 41(1); ICSID Rules, r. 47(1)(i).
[303] UNCITRAL Model Law, Art. 31(2); English Arbitration Act 1996, s. 52(4); Arbitration Law of the People's Republic of China 1994, Art. 54; German Arbitration Act 1998 (in the Civil Procedure Code), s. 1054(2).
[304] UNCITRAL Rules, Art. 32(3); CIETAC Rules, Art. 55; AAA ICDR Rules, Art. 27(2); LCIA Rules, Art. 26(1); WIPO Rules, Art. 62(c), which also dispense with the reasons if the applicable law states that no reasons need be given.
[305] English Arbitration Act 1996, s. 69(1).
[306] E.g. *The Montan* [1985] Lloyd's Rep 189 (CA); LMAA Rules, r. 22(b), (c) and (d).

However, in exceptional circumstances, even where the parties have agreed to keep the reasons confidential, they may be disclosed to the court if public interest considerations override the parties' intentions. In such cases, the 'confidential award' may be used before the court to correct a logical or clerical error (such as a miscalculation), or to set aside the award for serious irregularity,[307] or bar enforcement for other public policy reasons. However, it may not be used to appeal the award on a point of law.[308]

Finally, some arbitration laws are silent on the point, implying that there is no duty to give reasons.[309] US domestic practice is that no reasons need be given, and the US Supreme Court has expressly held that arbitrators have no obligation to provide reasons for their award.[310]

Hence it seems that many arbitration laws and rules require the giving of reasons, at least unless the parties have agreed otherwise. This is important to ensure the rationality and quality of the award. As has been argued above, the giving of reasons is important for fairness, and this is reflected by those arbitration laws and rules that require the giving of reasons.

## 6.6 Transparency versus confidentiality

In this section, it is argued that the traditional notion of arbitration proceedings being confidential to the parties is problematic from the due process perspective. This traditional notion of arbitration means that the award, any documents and even the fact that arbitration has taken place is classified as confidential.

There is anecdotal evidence that parties frequently choose private arbitration over public litigation for the very reason of confidentiality.[311] In other words, arbitration would lose some of its attractiveness as a dispute resolution process if the principle of confidentiality were undermined. For this reason, arbitration practitioners frequently argue that, as a matter of sound commercial practice, the principle of confidentiality should not

---

[307] English Arbitration Act 1996, s. 68.
[308] Tackaberry and Marriott, 'General Principles', 11–391 and 348; *The Montan*, 192–3; *The Easy Rider* [2004] 2 Lloyd's Rep 626 (Comm), 25–8.
[309] For example the US Federal Arbitration Act 1925.
[310] *United Steelworkers of America* v. *Enterprise Wheel & Car Corp*, 363 US 593, 598 (1960); for the federal jurisdiction, see also *Michael M Pfeifle* v. *Chemoil Corporation*, 73 FedAppx 720, 722 (2003).
[311] Lew, Mistelis and Kröll, *Comparative International Commercial Arbitration*, 660; Redfern and Hunter, *Law and Practice of International Commercial Arbitration*, 32.

be compromised. However, what is good for the business of arbitration practitioners should not necessarily be determining policy.

The extent of confidentiality and the permissibility of disclosure in certain circumstances are highly complex and controversial topics, but there is a developing body of law on the question of when awards can be disclosed. For the model proposed in this book, more transparency in arbitration is desirable. While first movements in this direction have been made by the courts in several jurisdictions, this is an issue that needs much further refinement, particularly in evaluating the *public* interests at stake. This is all the more relevant where the parties are subject to a power imbalance. Interestingly, by way of example, one tentative step in this direction has been made by the Californian Code of Civil Procedure. It requires the publication of statistics about consumer awards, including the name of the business party, type of dispute, the amount of the claim and the amount of the award made.[312]

To this end, it should first be explained why transparency is desirable. The law on confidentiality is then reviewed to show that, at present, the balance between confidentiality and transparency is inadequate.

### 6.6.1 The case for transparency

Needless to say, in relation to the courts, the principle of transparency has been well established. It is usually based on the case of *Scott* v. *Scott*, where Viscount Haldane said that 'courts must, as between parties, administer justice in public'.[313] The principle is also reflected in Civil Procedure Rules 1998 (SI 1998/3132), r. 39.2(1) and ECHR, Art. 6.[314] The Law Commission of New Zealand has also made a clarion call for transparency in arbitration. It has expressly acknowledged that 'public policy concerns about transparency (achieved through disclosure of information) with regard to business enterprises operated in both the public and private sector must be recognised'.[315]

It is possible to distinguish three due process[316] arguments as to why it can be in the public interest to disclose arbitration awards. The first argument is informational equality of the parties. The second argument

---

[312] Californian Code of Civil Procedure, § 1281.96.

[313] *Scott* v. *Scott* [1913] AC 417 (HL), 423, 442.

[314] E.g. *Werner* v. *Austria* (1998) 26 EHRR 310 349.

[315] Law Commission of New Zealand, *Report 83 Improving the Arbitration Act 1996* (February 2003), available from www.lawcom.govt.nz [1 April 2008].

[316] Due process consists of equality and rationality; see 2.2.

presented here is that of scrutiny and quality assurance, which improves rationality and, hence, due process. The third argument is that the law can only develop rationally and consistently if decisions are published.

## Informational equality

The first and foremost reason why transparency is of utmost importance in adjudication generally is informational equality between the parties. Transparency directly counter-balances the inequalities of knowledge between the 'repeat player' and the 'single-shot player'[317] in adjudication.[318]

It is clear that businesses and institutions using a procedure regularly have an advantage over a person using it only once to solve a dispute. Repeat players will have gained superior information about the rulings that have been made on points of law and evidence, about individual adjudicators' propensities and about the procedural tactics to be employed.[319] This differential in information would be compensated if the decisions (awards) and the names of adjudicators were published.

Two US circuit courts, in *Cole* v. *Burns International*,[320] and more recently in *Ting* v. *AT&T*,[321] have explicitly acknowledged that confidentiality provisions for arbitration in adhesion contracts[322] favour companies over individuals if companies continually arbitrate the same claims.[323] However, in *Cole*, in the context of employment arbitration, the court denied that there was any harm to the employees from this 'repeat player' effect in favour of the employer, for the reason that the employees were legally represented and awards were looked at by the appointing institution.[324] By contrast, in *Ting*, concerning a state court and consumer class action against the telecommunications carrier, the court held that a gagging order would reinforce the disadvantage suffered by the consumer plaintiffs, as they were claiming against a very large and powerful institution: 'AT&T has placed itself in a far superior legal posture by ensuring that none of its potential opponents have access to precedent, while, at the

---

[317] Terminology from Galanter, 'Why the "Haves" Come Out Ahead', 97; Rau, 'Integrity in Private Judging', 525–6; Bingham, 'On Repeat Players', 228; discussed further at 3.5.2.

[318] Sternlight, 'Panacea or Corporate Tool?', 686; Reuben, 'Constitutional Gravity', 1085.

[319] Gibbons, 'Private Law, Public "Justice"', 772, 784 and 789; Galanter, 'Why the "Haves" Come Out Ahead', 98–9; for an explicit recognition before the US Court of Appeals for the 9th Circuit, see *Ting* v. *AT&T*, 319 F3d 1126, 1151–2 (9th Cir Cal 2003).

[320] 105 F3d 1465 (DC Cir 1997).     [321] 319 F3d 1126 (9th Cir Cal 2003).

[322] That is, contracts using non-negotiated standard-form terms, such as employment and consumer contracts.

[323] *Cole* v. *Burns International* 105 F3d 1465, 1476 (DC Circuit 1997); *Ting* v. *AT&T*, 1151.

[324] *Cole* v. *Burns International*, 105 F3d 1465, 1486 (DC Circuit 1997).

same time, AT&T accumulates a wealth of knowledge on how to negotiate the terms of its own unilaterally crafted contract.'[325]

It was stated that the confidentiality provisions would hinder potential future claimants from arguing their case against the telecoms giant. For this reason, the court refused to reverse the District Court's decision that the confidentiality clause was unconscionable.[326]

Hence, in summary, the first argument concerns mainly those cases where there is a power imbalance between the parties (e.g. consumer cases[327]), and hence the problem of 'repeat player' advantage arises. In cases where one party uses arbitration repeatedly, whereas the other party only uses arbitration once, there should be a mechanism for publishing the award, as otherwise the 'one-shot' player will suffer considerable disadvantage.

### Scrutiny as quality assurance

The second reason for transparency in decision-making generally is that it is an important form of quality assurance of the decision, to ensure decisions are rational.[328] This is important for due process. It serves to ensure that the decision-maker makes rational findings of fact, properly applies legal standards and does not venture beyond his or her power of authority, since the adjudicator's decision is put to public scrutiny.[329]

Transparency is an essential safeguard against bias and incompetence – to quote Bentham: '[Publicity] is the keenest spur to exertion, and the surest of all guards against improbity. It keeps the judge himself, while trying, under trial.'[330] In addition, transparency has an *indirect* effect in combating power imbalances by exposing potential structural or systemic bias and allowing criticism of possible deficiencies in a process.

This symptom of the 'repeat player' syndrome can only be exposed if awards are published.[331] The publication of rulings under the Uniform Domain Name Dispute Resolution Procedure (UDRP) has led to some

---

[325] *Ting* v. *AT&T*, 1152.    [326] *Ibid.*

[327] M. S. Abdel Wahab, 'Does Technology Emasculate Trust? Confidentiality and Security Concerns in Online Arbitration' [September 2004] (Special Supplement: Using Technology to Resolve Business Disputes) *ICC International Court of Arbitration Bulletin* 43–51, 48.

[328] Park, *Procedural Evolution in Business Arbitration*, 42.    [329] See 6.5.

[330] Works of Jeremy Bentham, quoted by Lord Shaw in *Scott* v. *Scott* [1913] AC 417 (HL), 477.

[331] Gibbons, 'Private Law, Public "Justice"', 783 and 787; Bingham, 'On Repeat Players', 246 and 258. The link between appointment and biased awards is clearly more tenuous in the case of institutions appointing arbitrators than in the case of claimants directly appointing the arbitrators.

criticism of the UDRP on the basis that the institutions offering dispute resolution under the UDRP have to appear friendly to the trademark holders' interests, as the claimant trademark holder chooses the institution. These criticisms have been bolstered by statistics relating to the outcomes of decisions, which would not have been possible without the publication of those decisions.[332] This will be further discussed in the next chapter.

### Development of the law

The third argument for transparency in adjudication is the importance of developing the law through the persuasive force or authority of precedent.[333] This is an important aspect of due process and the rule of law. Under both the common law and the civil law (albeit to a greater extent under the former), important legal standards are established through the interpretation and reinterpretation of existing law.[334]

The development of the law argument has been raised by Colman J to explain that arbitration is not completely confidential: 'If one obliterated from the law reports all those cases where a substantial part of an arbitration award had been published for all to read one would be deprived of a massive part of the development of English commercial law.'[335]

However, to the extent that arbitration is not the mainstream form of dispute resolution, it is hard to see how an individual unpublished award would matter. The function of some awards is merely to solve the dispute in question. Hence, in relation to commercial arbitration, the argument of law development may have limited application. This argument is limited to those cases where an appeal lies on a point of law, and to sectors where arbitration (as opposed to litigation) is the dominant form of dispute resolution. Hence, in sectors where points of law are dealt with by arbitration, and where arbitration constitutes the main form of dispute resolution, the publication of awards should be considered.

A related point is that not all contractual relationships are private, in the sense that they only materially affect the parties to the contract.

---

[332] See, for example, M. Geist, 'Fair.com? An Examination of the Allegations of Systemic Unfairness in the ICANN UDRP' (2002) 27 *Brooklyn Journal of International Law* 903–37; M. Mueller, 'Rough Justice – An Analysis of ICANN's Uniform Dispute Resolution Policy' (research report published by the Convergence Center, Syracuse University School of Information Studies, dated November 2000).

[333] Abdel Wahab, 'Does Technology Emasculate Trust?', 48; Sternlight, 'Panacea of Corporate Tool?', 686; Park, *Procedural Evolution in Business Arbitration*, 11, fn. 51.

[334] In relation to consumer cases, see R. Bamford, 'Shopping Around: Dealing with Cross-Border Complaints' (2004) 14(4) *Consumer Policy Review* 108–12, 110.

[335] *Hassneh Insurance Co of Israel v. Mew* [1993] 2 Lloyd's Rep 243 (Comm), 247.

Standard-form contracts and their interpretation might affect third parties on a large scale. Big players in a given market (be it a large business in their relationships towards consumers, or a large multinational corporation in their business dealings) might impose de facto legal standards by the terms and conditions they trade on, so that the interpretation of these standard terms is a matter of interest to the wider public. While the interpretation of the term in an arbitration award has no precedent value, it may have some persuasive force if future cases came before the same arbitrator, or if there were selective publication. Hence the second category of cases, where awards should be systematically published, is those where the ruling affects other third parties,[336] such as the interpretation of a standard contract term used in a series of transactions by a large corporation.

Having presented three arguments in favour of increased transparency in arbitration, the following section sets out the law on confidentiality in arbitration.

### 6.6.2 Presumption of confidentiality in arbitration

There has been a general assumption in the arbitration community that confidentiality should be an inherent, fundamental principle in arbitration as a *private* dispute resolution process.[337] Unfortunately, the EComHR[338] has also endorsed the notion that arbitration proceedings *a priori* are not public: 'In some respects – in particular as regards publicity – it is clear that arbitral proceedings are often not even intended to be in conformity with Article 6.'

### 6.6.3 What should be kept confidential?

Confidentiality in arbitration proceedings means that no documents, evidence or contents of the award should be disclosed to the outside world, and that all hearings and meetings are conducted in private.[339] In addition,

---

[336] A. Tweedale, 'Confidentiality in Arbitration and the Public Interest Exception' (2005) 21(1) *Arbitration International* 59–70, 69.

[337] Tackaberry and Marriott, 'General Principles', 11–391, 306; Petrochilos, *Procedural Law in International Arbitration*, 150.

[338] *Nordström-Janzen and Nordström-Lehtinen* v. *Netherlands* (EComHR), Admissibility Decision of 27 November 1996, No. 28101/95, available from the HUDOC database.

[339] Tackaberry and Marriott, 'General Principles', 11–391, 310.

confidentiality may encompass the mere fact that there are, or have been, arbitration proceedings between the parties.

### 6.6.4 Who is under a duty of confidentiality?

Another question is 'who is under a duty of confidentiality?', since the obligation of the arbitrators, the administering institution (if any), the parties and any third parties who might have an interest in disclosure should all be assessed differently. The arbitrators and any employees of the arbitral institution may well be bound by a duty of confidentiality, either through professional rules[340] or the rules of the arbitral institution.[341]

Tackaberry and Marriott point out that the obligation of confidentiality inherent in arbitration not only applies to all parties, but to all persons involved in the arbitration, including witnesses.[342] This would mean that if a witness was shown statements by other witnesses, or any other documents prepared in the context of the arbitration, he or she would be under a duty of confidentiality in respect of those documents.[343]

What about the parties themselves, or any third persons who claim to be affected by the award?

### 6.6.5 Contract and institutional rules

Confidentiality obligations between the *parties* to the arbitration can arise from contract law (i.e. where the arbitration agreement or the institutional rules (the latter are a form of implied agreement between the parties) contain an express confidentiality clause). Confidentiality clauses in arbitration agreements are difficult to draft, as the parties might not want absolute confidentiality; therefore the agreement has to provide for

---

[340] See, for example, ICDR, *Code of Ethics*, Canon VI; AAA, *Standards of Ethics and Business Conduct*; or Part 2, r. 2 (correspondence) and r. 4 (relationship of confidentiality) of CIArb, *Code of Professional and Ethical Conduct*, available from the CIArb and on file with the author; see also the declaration arbitrators have to sign under the ICSID Rules, r. 6(2), available from www.worldbank.org/icsid/basicdoc/partF-chap01.htm#r06 [1 April 2008].

[341] See, for example, ICDR Rules of Procedure, 2003, Art. 34; LCIA Rules, Art. 30; ICC Rules, Art. 6; UNCITRAL Rules, Art. 32; DIS Arbitration Rules 1998, s. 43 on confidentiality; WIPO Arbitration Rules, Art. 76.

[342] Cf. Mason CJ in *Esso Australia Resources Ltd* v. *The Right Honourable Sidney James Plowman* (1995) 128 ALR 391 (High Court of Australia), who remarked, obiter, that witnesses were not subject to a general obligation of confidence; see para. 31, fn. 748.

[343] Tackaberry and Marriott, 'General Principles', 11–391, 311.

appropriate contingencies and exceptions.[344] First of all, an arbitration award may need to be enforced by a court, which is, of course, a forum with public access.[345] Furthermore, a party may be under an obligation to make disclosures regarding the arbitration, for example if it is a listed company, or where a party is selling its business and disclosure is required for the purposes of due diligence, or where one party has to make disclosures to an insurance or parent company. Another difficulty in drafting a confidentiality clause may be the question of its validity under the applicable law. Because of these difficulties with confidentiality clauses in arbitration agreements (and the associated costs with specialist legal advice), there has been a call for uniform, general rules for confidentiality. Such uniform rules (including exceptions) could be formulated by the institutional rules. However, institutional rules face the same formidable task of having to define the scope of the duty of confidentiality.

The ICDR Rules 2003 provide a presumption that hearings are private unless the parties agree, or the law requires, to hold them in public.[346] The Rules furthermore establish that any matters relating to the arbitration or the award should not be disclosed by the arbitrator or the administrator unless otherwise agreed by the parties or required by law.[347] The Rules also provide that an award may only be made public with the consent of all the parties or as required by law.[348] However, interestingly, the Rules also say that parts of an award may be made available if edited to conceal the identity of the parties, unless all parties agree not to disclose any part of the award.[349]

The LCIA Rules 1998 provide that all the meetings and hearings should be conducted in private, unless the parties agree otherwise.[350] The parties are under a duty to keep the award, any documents used in the proceedings and any material prepared for the arbitration confidential, unless disclosure is necessary to comply with a legal duty, to pursue a legal right or to enforce or challenge an award before a court.[351]

Under the ICC Rules 1998, the arbitral tribunal has the power to take measures to protect trade secrets and confidential information.[352] Furthermore, Art. 21(3) provides that hearings cannot be attended by third parties unless the tribunal and the parties consent to this. The rules do *not* expressly oblige the parties to keep the award or any associated material

---

[344] Tweedale, 'Confidentiality in Arbitration', 59.
[345] *City of Moscow* v. *Bankers Trust Company*, discussed below, fn. 386.
[346] ICDR Rules, Art. 20(4).    [347] *Ibid.* Art. 34.    [348] *Ibid.* Art. 27(4).
[349] *Ibid.* Art. 27(8); reflecting international practice, see Lew, Mistelis and Kröll, *Comparative International Commercial Arbitration*, 661.
[350] LCIA Rules, Art. 19(4).    [351] *Ibid.* Art. 30(1).    [352] ICC Rules, Art. 20(7).

confidential, but, in practice, the arbitrators recommend that a confidentiality clause is included in the terms of reference agreed by the parties.[353]

The UNCITRAL Arbitration Rules 1976 likewise stipulate that hearings are private[354] and, in addition, that the award may only be made public with the consent of *both* parties.[355] As to maintaining confidentiality of other documents (such as pieces of evidence, written and oral arguments, the identity of the arbitrators and the fact that arbitration is taking place), UNCITRAL recommends that the parties deal with these matters in an agreement on confidentiality.[356]

The WIPO (World Intellectual Property Organization) Arbitration Rules include a duty of the parties and any third party to keep the existence of arbitration a secret.[357] The duty of confidentiality expressly refers to documents and evidence, and expressly includes witnesses (i.e. it is the obligation of each party to ensure that the witnesses called on their behalf maintain confidentiality).[358] Furthermore, there is an express requirement that the award be kept confidential, subject to an exception where disclosure is necessary to comply with the law or for a party to protect their rights *vis-à-vis* another party.[359] Article 76 of the WIPO Arbitration Rules expands these duties of confidentiality to the arbitrator and the WIPO Center.

From this brief qualitative review, it seems that some of the most important sets of arbitral rules provide that the hearing must be private. With the exception of the ICC Rules 1998, it seems that the arbitration rules establish a presumption that the award is maintained confidentially by the parties, i.e. it can only be published with the consent of all parties (subject to exceptions). However, only the LCIA Rules 1998 and the WIPO Rules impose an express duty on the parties to keep other arbitral documents secret. With the exception of the WIPO Rules, the rules seem to put the parties under no obligation to keep confidential the fact that arbitration proceedings are or have been taking place.

### 6.6.6 Arbitration laws

Where there is no contractual arrangement as to confidentiality (whether in the arbitration agreement or in the institutional rules), the question

---

[353] With all the associated difficulties of drafting such a clause; see H. Bagner, 'Confidentiality – A Fundamental Principle in International Commercial Arbitration?' (2001) 18(2) *Journal of International Arbitration* 243–9, 244.
[354] *In camera*; UNCITRAL Arbitration Rules, Art. 25(4).     [355] *Ibid.* Art. 32(5).
[356] UNCITRAL, 'Notes on Organizing Arbitral Proceedings of 1996', paras. 31 and 32.
[357] WIPO Arbitration Rules, Art. 73.     [358] *Ibid.* Art. 74.     [359] *Ibid.* Art. 75.

arises whether there is a duty of non-disclosure under the *general* arbitration law.

There are large variations between different legal systems as to the non-contractual duties of confidentiality in arbitration. Arbitration laws, with the notable exception of New Zealand's,[360] do not expressly provide for arbitral confidentiality.[361] In the United Kingdom, in the case of the English Arbitration Act 1996, this omission was a conscious decision – it was felt that the principle of confidentiality was best developed by the courts, and that a general definition was inappropriate.[362]

The English courts have consistently held that there is an implied duty to maintain confidentiality in arbitration, being a principle intrinsic to arbitration, albeit that this duty may be subject to exceptions.

The first authority on this is the Court of Appeal case of *Dolling-Baker* v. *Merrett*,[363] concerning litigation under a contract for reinsurance. The defendants were the reinsurer and broker of the reinsurance policy. The plaintiff sought to obtain disclosure of arbitral documents (the award, pleadings, evidence, including transcripts) of an earlier arbitration involving the same defendants and under a very similar policy of reinsurance, but with a different claimant. Parker LJ found that there was an implied obligation on both defendants not to disclose or use for any other purpose any document prepared for and used in the arbitration. He based this obligation on the 'essentially private nature of arbitration coupled with the implied obligation of a party who obtains documents on discovery not to use them for any other purpose than the dispute in which they were obtained'.[364] Hence documents used in arbitration proceedings cannot be disclosed in later litigation, except with the consent of both parties or pursuant to a court order. A court order allowing disclosure would only be made if disclosure or inspection of the documents was necessary for the fair disposal of the litigation. Parker LJ set out the relevant criteria for making this assessment, these being: whether the information contained in the arbitral documents to be disclosed was relevant for the litigation before the court, whether there was no other practical means of obtaining this information elsewhere and, most importantly, whether the

---

[360] New Zealand Arbitration Act 1996, s. 14: 'An arbitral agreement, unless otherwise agreed by the parties, is deemed to provide that the parties shall not publish, disclose or communicate any information relating to arbitral proceedings under the agreement or to an award made in those proceedings.'

[361] Lew, Mistelis and Kröll, *Comparative International Commercial Arbitration*, 660.

[362] Tackaberry and Marriott, 'General Principles', 11–391, 315.

[363] [1990] 1 WLR 1205 (CA).  [364] *Ibid.* 1214.

information would be necessary for disposing fairly of the proceedings.[365] The Court of Appeal in *Dolling-Baker* v. *Merrett*, while finding an implied obligation of confidentiality, did not give a comprehensive definition of its extent or exceptions to it.

In another reinsurance case, *Hassneh*,[366] the reinsured was conducting arbitration against the reinsurer and litigation against the broker of the reinsurance. In order to aid settlement with the broker, the reinsured wished to disclose to the broker not only an interim award obtained in his arbitration against the reinsurer, but also other arbitral documents such as pleadings, evidence and the transcript. Colman J confirmed that there was an implied duty of confidentiality in arbitration proceedings, which was implied in the arbitration agreement by business efficacy or custom.[367] He pointed out that arbitration hearings have been held in private for hundreds of years, and that the informality and candour of such private hearings were an essential ingredient to arbitration.[368] He argued further that the private nature of the hearing must, in principle, extend to arbitral documents, as the disclosure of such documents would, in fact, open the doors of the arbitration room to the public.[369] While underlining the importance of confidentiality in arbitration, he also found that a distinction should be made between the reasoned award and other arbitral documents (such as pleadings, evidential documents and transcripts). Since the reasoned award identifies the parties' rights and duties, and since it can be brought into public courts under their supervisory jurisdiction or for the purposes of enforcement, Colman J found that the duty of confidentiality is lower with regard to the award.[370] He pointed out that the award or parts of it may sometimes be published in the context of the court's supervisory and enforcement jurisdiction, and that this is important for the development of English commercial law.[371]

Colman J therefore found that the *award* may be disclosed without leave of the court if this is necessary for the establishment or protection of an arbitrating party's legal rights *vis-à-vis* a third party.[372] By contrast, other arbitral documents can only be disclosed where all parties give consent or with leave or by order of the court. The court should only allow disclosure of other arbitral documents where this is necessary for disposing fairly of the matter or for saving costs.[373]

---

[365] *Ibid.* 1214–15.
[366] *Hassneh Insurance Co of Israel* v. *Mew* [1993] 2 Lloyd's Rep 243 (Comm).
[367] *Ibid.* 246.    [368] *Ibid.* 246–7.    [369] *Ibid.* 247.    [370] *Ibid.*    [371] *Ibid.*
[372] *Ibid.* 248–9.    [373] *Ibid.* 250–51.

The Court of Appeal in *Ali Shipping Corp* v. *Shipyard Trogir*[374] firmly repeated that there was an implied term of confidentiality in arbitration.[375] It also held that this term was not only implied where business efficacy so demanded, but as a matter of law in each and every arbitration, without the need to examine the precise circumstances of the agreement in each case.[376] As to the exceptions, however, the Court of Appeal was not quite as clear about the distinction between the disclosure of awards on the one hand, and that of other arbitral documents on the other. Potter LJ stated four exceptions to the implied duty of confidentiality: (i) consent, (ii) order of the court, (iii) leave of the court and (iv) disclosure necessary for the protection of legitimate interests of an arbitrating party. As to the latter exception, he said: 'although to date this exception has been held applicable only to disclosure of an award, it is clear . . . that the principle covers also pleadings, written submissions and the proofs of witnesses as well as transcripts and notes of evidence given in the arbitration'.[377] Hence it seems that the Court of Appeal found that the overarching principle for exceptions to the implied term of confidentiality was the necessity of disclosure for protecting an arbitrating party's interest.

Interestingly, the Court of Appeal said, albeit obiter, that courts must approach the question of disclosure with a flexible mind, so that in certain cases disclosure could be ordered where this was sought by a third party unconnected to the arbitration, if such disclosure was 'in the interests of justice'.[378] Here, Potter LJ referred to the case of *London and Leeds Estates Ltd* v. *Paribas Ltd (No. 2)*,[379] where Mance J had held that a litigating party was entitled to disclosure of a proof made by an expert witness in an earlier arbitration that seemed to be inconsistent with the views expressed by that expert in the court proceedings.[380]

In yet another reinsurance case, *Associated Electric*,[381] in a reference to the Privy Council from Bermuda, it was found that the award of an earlier

[374] [1998] 1 Lloyd's Rep 643 (CA).
[375] See also *Michael Wilson & Partners Ltd* v. *John Forster Emmott* [2008] 1 Lloyd's Rep 616 (CA), paras. 60–62 (implied obligation of confidence).
[376] *Ibid.* 651.   [377] *Ibid.*
[378] *Ibid.* 651–2; for the latest case on this, see *Michael Wilson & Partners Ltd* v. *John Forster Emmott*, where the Court of Appeal held that disclosure of pleadings to a foreign court can be justified in the interests of justice, in order to prevent that foreign court from being misled.
[379] [1995] 1 EGLR 102 (QB).
[380] *Ibid.* 109; see also *Michael Wilson* [2008] 1 Lloyd's Rep 616 (CA), paras. 103–5, disclosure before foreign court in interests of justice.
[381] *Associated Electric and Gas Insurance Services Ltd* v. *European Reinsurance Company of Zurich* [2003] 1 WLR 1041 (PC).

arbitration *could be used* in a subsequent arbitration involving exactly the same parties, despite an *express* confidentiality clause in the agreement. The respondents in that case sought to use the award, which had decided an important issue in relation to both arbitrations, to support a plea of issue estoppel. Lord Hobhouse treated this use of the earlier award as a question of enforcing the rights conferred by the earlier award – the decision in the earlier award bound the parties, and hence they were estopped from thereafter disputing that decision.[382]

Lord Hobhouse criticised the approach of Potter LJ in *Ali Shipping Corp*, expressing reservations about the desirability or merit of a general, implied duty of confidentiality in arbitration. A general, implied obligation of confidentiality 'runs the risk of failing to distinguish between different types of confidentiality which attach to different types of document...and elides privacy and confidentiality... Generalisations and the formulation of detailed implied terms are not appropriate'.[383] Hence the Privy Council was reluctant to support a broad duty of confidentiality arising from implied terms. Although these statements were, strictly speaking, obiter, as the case concerned an *express* confidentiality clause, it led some authors to conclude that the concept of confidentiality advanced in *Ali Shipping Corp* is now open to doubts.[384] Furthermore, Lord Hobhouse reiterated the distinction first made by Colman J in *Hassneh Insurance Co of Israel* between disclosure of the award itself and other arbitral materials.[385]

A recent case on this issue, *City of Moscow* v. *Bankers Trust Company*,[386] concerned a challenge to an award on the grounds of serious irregularity under s. 68 of the English Arbitration Act 1996. This is the first case on the issue of whether a judgment resulting from the courts' supervisory jurisdiction over arbitration should be published. In particular, the Court of Appeal interpreted the new Civil Procedure Rules 1998 (SI 1998/3132). Rule 62.10(1) states that arbitration claims can be heard either in private or in public. Subject to the court ordering otherwise, r. 62.10(3) effectively states that a determination of a point of law[387]

[382] *Ibid.* 1049–50.   [383] *Ibid.* 1051.
[384] S. Kouris, 'Confidentiality: Is International Arbitration Losing One of Its Major Benefits?' (2005) 22(2) *Journal of International Arbitration* 127–40, 131; Tweedale, 'Confidentiality in Arbitration', 60–1.
[385] *Associated Electric and Gas Insurance Services Ltd* v. *European Reinsurance Company of Zurich*, 1051.
[386] [2005] QB 207 (CA).
[387] Referring to ss. 45 (preliminary point of law) and 69 (appeal on a point of law) of the English Arbitration Act 1996.

under the court's supervisory jurisdiction should be heard in public, whereas all other arbitration matters should be heard in private. Mance LJ said that this distinction should only be the starting point for the analysis.[388] The court should consider hearing the matter in open court, or any party may apply for a public hearing, even where the Rules provide that, prima facie, the hearing should be private.[389] Furthermore, the fact that the hearing is held in private does not necessarily lead to the conclusion than the resulting judgment in the arbitration matter should not be published, as the judgment might incorporate less confidential information than that which would be disclosed during the hearing.[390] He came to the conclusion that the courts should carefully balance considerations of confidentiality in arbitration proceedings with the requirement that all judgments of a public court should be public under Art. 6 of the ECHR and the common law. The court should, in particular, weigh up how much politically or commercially sensitive information would emanate to the public, and whether this information can be protected by anonymising law reports.[391]

Mance LJ clearly stated that there should be a presumption in favour of publicity: 'the desirability of public scrutiny as a means by which confidence in the courts can be maintained and the administration of justice made transparent applies here as in other areas of court activity.'[392] He rejected any suggestion that this would upset the confidence of the business community in English arbitration.[393] However, in the case subject to this appeal, he held that only a summary of the judgment could be published because of the politically and commercially sensitive information contained therein.

Hence, while the English courts recognise an implied principle of confidentiality in arbitration, this principle may be limited where the legitimate interests of the parties so demand and, possibly, where it is in the interests of justice (where disclosure is demanded by a third party).

The English approach contrasts with that taken in the United States, Australia and Sweden, where there is no implied duty of confidentiality, and where confidentiality requires an express agreement of the parties. There are dicta in these jurisdictions that find that confidentiality does not attach to arbitration proceedings, notwithstanding their private nature. Similarly, there have been cases in international arbitration where the disclosure of the award was made in the public interest.

---

[388]  *City of Moscow* v. *Bankers Trust Company* [2005] QB 207 (CA), 209.
[389]  *Ibid.* 231.      [390]  *Ibid.*      [391]  *Ibid.* 231–2.      [392]  *Ibid.* 231.      [393]  *Ibid.* 232.

In the United States, a federal court has refused to recognise a duty of confidentiality in international arbitration. In *United States* v. *Panhandle Eastern Corp*,[394] the US government moved to obtain disclosure of documents relating to an ICC arbitration between Panhandle's subsidiary and an Algerian company, to protect its security interests as guarantor of ship financing bonds. Senior District Judge Latchum, in the District Court, found that there was no general obligation of confidentiality in international arbitration, and granted the US government's request for production of the documents. It seems that the US courts have not recognised a duty of confidentiality applying to arbitration as such,[395] and have even been prepared to overrule an express confidentiality clause in the case of *Ting*, discussed above.[396]

In the infamous case of *Esso Australia Resources Ltd*,[397] the High Court of Australia, on appeal from the Supreme Court of Victoria, categorically denied that there was an implied duty of confidentiality in arbitration, in a majority decision of four out of five judges.[398] All judges agreed that there was a public-interest exception wider than the exception under the English authorities, *viz*, merely allowing an arbitrating party to disclose arbitral documents if necessary, to protect *that party's* legitimate interests.[399]

Mason CJ pointed out that arbitration proceedings had never been completely confidential, since, inter alia, the supervisory and enforcement jurisdiction of the courts was of a public nature.[400] He expressly rejected the English rulings finding an implied term of confidentiality (such as

---

[394]  118 FRD 346 (DDel 1988).

[395]  *Ibid.*; *Industrotech Constructors Inc* v. *Duke University*, 314 SE2d 272, 274 (1984); *Giacobazzi Grandi Vini SpA* v. *Renfield Corp*, not reported in FSupp; WL 7938 (SDNY 1987); contrast this with the position in mediation, where confidentiality was held to prohibit disclosure of all statements, documents and discussions: *In re Anonymous*, 283 F3d 627 (CA 4th 2002).

[396]  See 6.6.1, fn. 319.

[397]  *Esso Australia Resources Ltd* v. *The Right Honourable Sidney James Plowman* (1995) 128 ALR 391 (High Court of Australia).

[398]  Mason CJ, Brennan J, McHugh J and Dawson J agreeing, and Toohey J dissenting.

[399]  *Esso Australia Resources Ltd* v. *The Right Honourable Sidney James Plowman*, para. 38 (Mason CJ); para. 8 (Brennan J); para. 26 (Toohey J). The Australian High Court referred to the English decisions of *Dolling-Baker* and *Hassneh Insurance Co of Israel*; however, compare the English case of *London and Leeds Estates Ltd*, where the court allowed disclosure of arbitral documents (an expert proof) on the application of a third party, unconnected to the arbitration, since this was in the interests of justice. See also the dicta by Potter LJ in *Ali Shipping Corp*, discussed above.

[400]  *Esso Australia Resources Ltd* v. *The Right Honourable Sidney James Plowman*, para. 31; however, compare the English approach as exemplified by the decision in *City of Moscow* v. *Bankers Trust Company* (discussed above), where the court decided that the full judgment of a challenge to an award could not be published, precisely because of confidentiality reasons.

*Dolling-Baker* and *Hassneh Insurance Co of Israel*). Mason CJ held that there was no implied term of confidentiality, and confidentiality could only be based on an express term in the arbitration agreement (and such a term would not bind third parties in any case).[401]

### 6.6.7 Conclusion: an inadequate balance under English law

The English cases (*Dolling-Baker, Hassneh Insurance Co of Israel* and *Ali Shipping Corp*) described above do not make clear as to whether the implied obligation of confidentiality in arbitration is based on the long-established equitable principles relating to confidentiality.

The legal (or, more accurately, equitable) principles relating to breach of confidence allow a claimant to obtain an injunction to prevent disclosure of confidential or private information, and, where such information has already been disclosed, damages and other remedies such as delivery up. The requirements for an action of breach of confidence are that the information must be of a confidential or private nature, and it must have been imparted in a situation of confidence and therefore must have been an unauthorised disclosure (or threat of such disclosure) to the disadvantage of the person who communicated it.[402] A situation of confidence can arise even without express contractual provisions to this effect, where it should have been clear to the recipient of the information, from all the circumstances, that the information was to be kept confidential, taking into account the harmfulness of the disclosure (which must not necessarily lead to financial detriment), the relationship of the parties and the parties' expectation of privacy.[403]

However, the equitable principles relating to confidence provide for a public-interest exception, and if the duty of confidence in arbitration is based on these principles, a public-interest exception would *clearly* be available.[404] In *Ali Shipping Corp*, Potter LJ gave a clear indication to the business community that there was no wide, general public-interest defence lurking under English law.[405] He expressly referred to the *Esso*

---

[401] *Esso Australia Resources Ltd* v. *The Right Honourable Sidney James Plowman*, paras. 35–7.

[402] *Malone* v. *Commissioner of Police of the Metropolis (No. 2)* [1979] Ch 344 (ChD), 375; *Coco* v. *AN Clark (Engineers) Ltd* [1969] RPC 41 (ChD), 47; *Faccenda Chicken Ltd* v. *Fowler* [1987] Ch 117 (CA), 121.

[403] *Attorney General* v. *Guardian Newspapers (No. 2)* [1990] 1 AC 109 (HL), 281 (Lord Goff); *Campbell* v. *MGN Ltd.* [2004] 2 AC 457 (HL), paras. 13–14, 21 (Lord Nicholls); 47–8 (Lord Hoffmann); 85 (Lord Hope); 134–5 (Lady Hale).

[404] Tweedale, 'Confidentiality in Arbitration', 61.

[405] *Ali Shipping Corp* v. *Shipyard Trogir* [1998] 1 Lloyd's Rep 643 (CA), 652.

*Australia Resources Ltd* case, discussed above, where the public-interest exception had been expressed in the widest terms. This indication notwithstanding, he left the door ajar by saying that there might be further exceptions to the general rule of confidentiality: 'while it may well fall to the English court at a future time to consider some further exception to the general rule of confidentiality based on wider considerations of public interest, it is not necessary to do so in this case'.[406] At this time, it seems that the English courts have had no opportunity to rule on the question of whether disclosure of an arbitration award could be in the public interest under certain circumstances. Hence it is open to some speculation under what circumstances such disclosure would be in the public interest. It is, however, unlikely that such a public-interest exception would go as widely as the point made at the beginning of this section (i.e. that publication is necessary for the interests of justice and transparency).

As has been discussed above, it seems that the English courts have assumed that there is a duty of confidentiality in arbitration. English courts have defined the exceptions narrowly, limiting them to the legitimate interests of the parties or the interests of justice rather than the wider public interest. The courts have refused to acknowledge the wider implications of confidentiality, and hence no adequate balance between confidentiality and transparency has been established under English law. This can also be contrasted with the position in other jurisdictions, where the courts have found in favour of transparency in arbitration by rejecting an implied duty of confidentiality. A clearer definition of the public interest in line with the arguments presented above[407] is required here.

## 6.7 Right of appeal / judicial review of arbitration awards

The relevance of a right to appeal in the due process discussion is that, in addition to the duty to give reasons and transparency discussed above, an appeal helps to eliminate bad judgments and mistakes occurring at first instance, and thereby contributes to a fair outcome (in terms of finding the true facts and applying the law to the facts correctly).[408] It thus contributes to equal treatment and rationality.[409]

This function of appeals has two implications: one in the private interest and one in the general public interest. Firstly, a right of appeal increases

---

[406] *Ibid.*     [407] See 6.6.1.     [408] Sternlight, 'Panacea or Corporate Tool?', 686.
[409] See elements of due process at 2.2.

the chance of justice for the particular party appealing. Secondly, however, and more importantly, there is also a public-interest element. The availability of an appeal ensures that there is a body of decisions interpreting the law in a more authoritative manner, leading to greater consistency of the law overall. In courts, a hierarchical appeal system, providing for appeals on points of law, has the important function of ensuring an intelligent and authoritative interpretation of the law, thus contributing to the quality and predictability of the law. For an individual, it is equally tragic whether he or she loses on the facts or on the law. However, the law usually restricts appeals to points of law, which shows that the public interest is more important than the private interest.

Thirdly, appeals are also necessary to guarantee the application of mandatory public norms, such as consumer protection. If there is no review of awards on the merits, and if the parties cannot appeal on the basis that the arbitrator has not applied the law, this means that the strict law may well not be applied.[410] For this reason, it can be argued that arbitration not only leads to privatisation of procedure but also to privatisation of substantive law.[411] An appeal should therefore be considered as part of the procedure for fair adjudication.[412]

However, appeals increase costs and add further significant delay. If the right to an appeal were not restricted in any way, the dissatisfied party losing a case would always seek to reverse the result. Hence the right to appeal has to be limited to the most deserving cases for any system of justice not to collapse. The question arises as to what extent these considerations apply to the review of arbitration awards by the courts.

First of all, there is agreement that courts cannot review matters of fact, unless there are obvious and objectively ascertainable mistakes (such as a calculation error) to be corrected. Provided the parties have selected the arbitrator according to the agreed procedure, and the award has been issued by an impartial arbitrator after having allowed each party a fair opportunity to argue their case, the parties should be bound by the arbitrator's evaluation of all *factual* matters. Another question is

---

[410] Park, *Procedural Evolution in Business Arbitration*, 11, fn. 51.

[411] Ware, 'Default Rules from Mandatory Rules', 719–20 and 725.

[412] Ware, 'Default Rules from Mandatory Rules'; Ware argues that, without an appeal, mandatory laws are not applied to arbitration; however, he prefers the non-arbitrability of certain disputes to the creation of an appeal system: 751 and 754. This would not be an option for Internet disputes; hence an appeal system is necessary: Philippe, 'Where is Everyone Going with Online Dispute Resolution?', 188; Schultz, 'Does Online Resolution Need Governmental Intervention', 100.

whether the parties are also bound by the arbitrator's interpretation of the law.

Different considerations apply here for domestic and international arbitration. In international arbitration, a distinction has to be made between the courts of the seat of the arbitration (which the parties select to reflect their preference about which law should govern the arbitration procedure) and the enforcement courts.

Firstly, review by the courts at the seat is considered. Under English arbitration law, both for domestic arbitrations and in arbitrations where England is the *seat*, there are three distinct grounds for challenging an award before the courts: (i) lack of substantive jurisdiction,[413] (ii) serious irregularity[414] and (iii) appeal on a point of law.[415]

These grounds for review are subject to a requirement of exhausting the arbitral tribunal's own powers to correct any clerical errors or accidental slips or oversights,[416] and are also subject to any arbitral appeal or review processes provided in the arbitration procedure itself. Furthermore, there is a time limit of twenty-eight days for bringing any appeals.[417] Neither of these requirements is particularly problematic from a due process perspective.

A party therefore has a right to challenge an award for lack of substantive jurisdiction, on the basis that it did not agree to arbitration or on the basis that it objects to the appointment or constitution of the arbitral tribunal. Furthermore, if the tribunal has infringed on its obligations to act impartially and to give each party a fair hearing, the award can be challenged under the grounds of serious irregularity.[418] This right of appeal also applies to the other eight forms of irregularity or misconduct listed in s. 68 (such as the tribunal exceeding its powers,[419] or failure by the tribunal to conduct the arbitration according to the procedure agreed by the parties[420]), which are wide enough to encompass all forms of serious irregularity of procedure. However, irregularity, again, is interpreted narrowly, and is only available in extreme cases where the tribunal has gone so wrong as to cause substantial injustice.[421] A party may have lost

---

[413] English Arbitration Act 1996, s. 67.    [414] English Arbitration Act 1996, s. 68.
[415] English Arbitration Act 1996, s. 69.    [416] English Arbitration Act 1996, ss. 57 and 70(2).
[417] English Arbitration Act 1996, s. 70(3).    [418] English Arbitration Act 1996, s. 68(2)(a).
[419] English Arbitration Act 1996, s. 68(2)(b).
[420] English Arbitration Act 1996, s. 68(2)(c).
[421] *Egmatra AG* v. *Marco Trading Corporation* [1999] 1 Lloyd's Rep 862 (Comm), 865; *Cameroon Airlines* v. *Transnet Ltd* [2004] EWHC 1829 (Comm), para. 102; for example, where a party is not given a fair opportunity to address a *key* issue.

the right to challenge the award on the grounds of lack of substantive jurisdiction or serious irregularity if they knew (or could have known) about the grounds for challenge but failed to raise objections in a timely manner.[422]

If England is the seat, or if the proceedings are domestic English arbitration, a party can also appeal on a point of (English[423]) law,[424] but only if the parties have not agreed to exclude this ground of appeal,[425] and there is a presumption that if the parties have agreed to dispense with reasons for the award, that they have also excluded the right to an appeal on a point of law. An exclusion of the right to appeal on a point of law may be incorporated into the arbitration agreement by way of reference to arbitration rules, and need not be set out explicitly in the arbitration clause,[426] such as the rules of institutions such as the ICC, which incorporate an automatic exclusion of appeal.[427]

In any case, under s. 69, an appeal under this ground can only be brought with leave of the court.[428] The court must give reasons for the decision on whether to allow an appeal,[429] but will usually consider an application for leave to appeal without an oral hearing.[430]

Section 69(3) essentially severely limits appeals on a point of law to the most deserving cases, taking into account the perspective of the parties' rights and the importance of the point of law for the public interest.[431]

---

[422] English Arbitration Act 1996, s. 73; *ASM Shipping Ltd of India* v. *TTMI Ltd of England* [2006] EWCA Civ 1341, Judgment of 16 October 2006, paras. 9, 11 and 13.

[423] Other laws are facts.

[424] Limited rights of appeal are also possible under some other laws, for example Australia's New South Wales Commercial Arbitration Act 1984, s. 38.

[425] Cf. English Arbitration Act 1996, s. 87(1)(b).

[426] *Sukuman Ltd* v. *Commonwealth Secretariat* [2006] EWHC 304 (Comm), para. 21.

[427] ICC Arbitration Rules, Art. 28.     [428] English Arbitration Act 1996, s. 69(2).

[429] *North Range Shipping Ltd* v. *Seatrans Shipping Corporation* [2002] 1 WLR 2397 (CA), para. 27.

[430] English Arbitration Act 1996, s. 69(5); *BLCT Ltd* v. *J Sainsbury Plc* [2004] 2 P&CR 3 (CA), para. 36.

[431] English Arbitration Act 1996, s. 69(3) provides that: (a) the determination must affect the *rights* of at least one party; (b) it was a question that the tribunal was asked to determine; (c) the decision of the tribunal is either obviously wrong or it concerns a question of general public importance, and the decision is at least open to serious doubt; and (d) it is just and proper for the court to determine the question; the English courts have also made clear that an error of law cannot be disguised as a serious irregularity, such as the tribunal exceeding its powers. This is important, as the courts' power to review cases on points of law can be excluded, whereas the courts' power to review cases of serious irregularity cannot be excluded. So, for example, a mistake as to currency was not a serious irregularity; see *Lesotho Highlands* v. *Impreglio SpA* [2005] UKHL 43 (HL).

If the legal point that is appealed is not of general public importance, then the test is that the arbitrators must have been obviously wrong on a question of law. This test imposes a high standard: 'it is not enough to say maybe they were wrong or even that there is only a possibility that they were right. The Court has to be satisfied that the arbitrators were obviously wrong on a question of law.'[432]

In *BLCT Ltd* v. *J Sainsbury Plc*, the Court of Appeal said expressly that the limitations on the right of appeal in s. 69 of the English Arbitration Act 1996 are in accordance with Art. 6 of the ECHR.[433]

While English law still allows for some vestiges of review on the merits, there is a clear tendency to interpret the parameters for review narrowly.

In other common-law jurisdictions, there are also relics of a right to have a review on the merits. As to procedure, under US federal law, an award can be challenged in certain instances of fraud or corruption, arbitrator misconduct or where the arbitrators exceeded their power.[434] As to the merits, there is a ground for review created by case law: an award can only be set aside on the merits if it is in manifest disregard of the law.[435] This is a much stricter standard than merely applying the law erroneously; it must amount to the arbitrators wilfully disregarding the law.[436]

By contrast, in many civil-law countries, courts have no control of the merits of the award where the appeal is on a question of law (as opposed to due process).[437] Likewise, the UNCITRAL Model Law provides for recourse to a court for setting aside the award on due process grounds, but does not provide for any appeal on a point of law.[438] However, some civil-law[439] jurisdictions and the UNCITRAL Model Law[440] contain a public-policy gloss on this – they include public policy as a ground for judicial review. The public-policy ground (even if interpreted as the more limited notion of public international policy) may well contain substantive aspects. As Park points out: 'Public policy . . . implicates a cluster of

---

[432] Mr Justice Tuckey in *Egmatra AG* v. *Marco Trading Corporation* [1999] 1 Lloyd's Rep 862 (Comm), 864.

[433] [2004] 2 P&CR 3 (CA), para. 33; *Sukuman Ltd* v. *Commonwealth Secretariat* [2006] EWHC 304 (Comm), para. 26.

[434] 9 USC, §10.

[435] For example, *Bowen* v. *Amoco Pipeline Co*, 254 F3d 925, 932 (10th Cir 2001).

[436] *Ibid.*

[437] Lew, Mistelis and Kröll, *Comparative International Commercial Arbitration*, 677–8; Park, *Procedural Evolution in Business Arbitration*, 11.

[438] UNCITRAL Model Law, Art. 34, essentially the same list as that in New York Convention, Art. V.

[439] See, for example, French Nouveau Code de Procédure Civile, Art. 1502(c).

[440] UNCITRAL Model Law, Art. 34(2)(b)(ii).

chameleon-like notions whose unifying essence lies in overriding societal interests that constrain how arbitrators decide cases.'[441]

This public-policy gloss notwithstanding, Park claims that this *laissez-faire* model of judicial review represents the predominant trend for international commercial arbitration for review at the seat of arbitration.[442] He states that international arbitration has been driven in recent years by a tendency to give arbitration tribunals greater autonomy from supervision by national courts at the seat of the arbitration.[443] Some commentators even argue for the complete abolition of review by the courts at the seat of arbitration, foreclosing any review there on procedural or substantive grounds.[444]

The reason for this growing tendency to restrict control of awards at the seat is that, for international arbitration, a multitude of different national courts may, in certain scenarios, be competent to review an award, and this causes obvious conflicts and inefficiencies, for example the court at the seat may set aside the award, and a party may nevertheless attempt to enforce the award in a different country.[445]

Up until this point, the discussion has been limited to the position at the seat of the arbitration or domestic arbitration. Looking at the position of the enforcing courts, this is governed by the 1958 New York Convention[446] for signatory states. Their courts can only refuse to recognise and enforce an award in the limited circumstances set out in Art. V of that Convention, and these are reflected in s. 103 of the English Arbitration Act 1996 (for New York Convention awards). While these grounds have been briefly

---

[441] Park, *Procedural Evolution in Business Arbitration*, 15.

[442] Park, *Procedural Evolution in Business Arbitration*, 12.      [443] *Ibid.*

[444] P. Fouchard, 'La Porteé Internationale de l'Annulation de la Sentence Arbitrale dans son Pays d'Origine' (1997) 3 *Revue de l'Arbitrage* 327–52, 349: 'On le voit, la primauté reconnue au juge du siege de l'arbitrage aux fins de coordination du contrôle de la sentence présente bien des dangers. Il n'est donc pas illégitime de limiter ses inconvénients.' [One can see that the primacy that is accorded to the judge at the seat of arbitration leads to problems as far as the co-ordination of the control of the award is concerned. It is therefore not wrong to limit its negative effects.] He concludes: 'Le seul contrôle judiciare dont elles seraient l'objet aurait lieu lors d'une demande de reconnaissance ou d'exécution dans un pays determine . . . sa justification ultime est d'ordre logique: pourquoi annuler une sentence si elle n'a pas à être execute dans ce pays?' (at 352). [The only judicial control to which they should be subjected would take place at the time of a request for recognition or enforcement in a particular country . . . its ultimate justification is of a logical nature: why revoke an award if it is not enforced in this country?].

[445] See Fouchard, 'La Porteé Internationale de l'Annulation de la Sentence Arbitrale dans son Pays d'Origine'.

[446] 330 UNTS 3, adopted on 10 June 1958, entered into force on 7 June 1959.

discussed above[447], it suffices to say here that these grounds do not directly include a review on substantive points of law. They do include public policy as a ground,[448] the malleability of which has been pointed out above. However, as has been discussed above,[449] courts, in general, have been slow to enforce foreign awards on public-policy grounds in order to encourage arbitration as a dispute resolution mechanism in international trade. For example, in the case of *OTV SA* v. *Hilmarton Ltd*,[450] the English courts enforced an award, even though the contract underlying the claim was illegal in the place where the contract was to be performed. The case concerned the payment of a fee to an intermediary, and the court pointed out that there had been no bribery and the contract had not been illegal under Swiss law, which was the law applying to the contract.

Therefore, for English courts there are wider grounds for the courts to annul an award when acting under the supervisory jurisdiction of the seat than there are if the English courts are enforcing a foreign New York Convention award.

If the system were changed to disallow any setting aside of awards at the seat, this would mean that, for most international arbitrations, the grounds would be limited to those contained in the New York Convention, disallowing all reviews on the merits on points of law.

In conclusion, there is an observable trend to restrict the review of arbitration awards on the substantive merits. This is particularly true for international arbitration, to avoid conflicts between courts and forum shopping. This restriction of the review of the merits is an expression of a preference for efficiency and speed, even at the cost of allowing the occasional false interpretation of law. This means that the public general interest in appeals (i.e. the development of the law through precedent) is definitively and increasingly taking a backseat.

The right of appeal has been severely curtailed in arbitration for the sake of finality and to prevent delay and reduce costs, and because it is in line with commercial expectations.[451] It makes sense for traditional commercial arbitration if the parties are aware that, by choosing arbitration, they may limit the availability of an appeal, so that it can be said that they have waived recourse to the courts and appeal.

However, the limitations on appeals may be more problematic in cases where the parties have not made a voluntary choice in bringing their case

---

[447] See 6.2.6.     [448] English Arbitration Act 1996, s. 103(3).
[449] See 6.2.6.     [450] [1999] 2 Lloyd's Rep 222 (Comm).
[451] As pointed out by Park, *Procedural Evolution in Business Arbitration*, 11.

to arbitration. The limitation on appeals is also problematic if arbitration is becoming the predominant model of dispute resolution, as it hinders the development of the law through the creation of precedent.

## 6.8 Conclusion

Despite the rhetoric of due process rights, arbitrators effectively apply lower standards of due process than those applied by judges in litigation, due to the party autonomy and waiver principles. On the one hand, lawyers express a concern for due process in arbitration as a general principle; on the other hand, there is a need for procedural efficiency and flexibility, which is expressed in the twin tenets of party autonomy and waiver of due process rights. This chapter has attempted to expose this conflict between the twin principles of party autonomy and waiver on the one hand, and due process on the other.

The chapter has identified the main due process principles and examined to what extent they apply to arbitration and how they are implemented in the arbitration process. For this purpose, the two classic elements of due process have been discussed: independence and impartiality of the arbitrators and the fair hearing principle. The overall conclusion is that lesser standards in arbitration proceedings than in litigation are observed with respect to these two principles.

In relation to the first of the two core principles of due process (i.e. independence and impartiality), the courts have frequently asserted that the same standards apply as in litigation. As shown in this discussion, this is only rhetoric, as arbitration is in its very nature different from litigation before the courts. It has been explained that arbitrators in commercial arbitration cannot be independent in the same way as judges. This is a factor that is rarely (if ever) acknowledged by the English courts.

In relation to the second of the two core principles of due process (i.e. fair hearing), it has been difficult to define *any* minimum standards that arbitration is required to meet. It *should be* acknowledged more openly that there exists a trade-off between fairness of procedure and costs and delay. Since one of the declared goals of arbitration is to cut costs and delay, a curtailment of fairness in hearings standards is inevitable.

In addition, three aspects of what may be loosely called 'principles of accountability and transparency' in political terminology have been examined: (i) the duty to give reasons, (ii) privacy and confidentiality and (iii) the right to an appeal. These three requirements are also important for due process, as they provide the checks and balances to ensure due process is complied with.

In relation to these three aspects of accountability and transparency, the courts not only openly acknowledge that there is a lesser duty in arbitration; on the contrary, it is frequently stated by the courts that it is in the very nature of arbitration that it is confidential, or that there is only a limited right to judicial review, and since these restrictions are immanent to arbitration it is assumed that the parties have waived their rights by agreeing to arbitration as a form of dispute resolution. The courts rarely discuss the procedural values, but tend to make an assumption that, in arbitration, there is no need for either accountability or transparency.

To the extent that the courts admit that lesser due process rights apply, this is usually justified by the parties' choice of arbitration (waiver doctrine) and their control over the procedure (party autonomy). Hence an important justification for the application of fewer and lesser due process rights is the fact that the parties have chosen arbitration. As has been explained, under the jurisprudence relating to the ECHR, such a waiver is only effective if it is given voluntarily and the parties are well informed. This will indeed be the case for most cases of commercial arbitration between business parties. However, as arbitration expands as a form of dispute resolution into other sectors, waivers may not always be effective. In particular, where there is no recourse to the courts (because of lack of enforcement or because of costs) or in the case of non-negotiated, standard consumer contracts, the waiver doctrine *should not* apply. This will be discussed in Chapter 7.[452] The intention of this chapter is not to criticise traditional commercial arbitration, but to explore how arbitration as a process needs to be adapted to comply with the higher standards of due process for the model of dispute resolution for Internet disputes found in Chapter 8.

---

[452] See 7.2.

# Internet disputes and fair arbitration

Generally, nobody behaves decently when they have power.

(Kingsley Amis, 1922–1995)

## 7.1 Introduction

As has been seen in Chapter 3,[1] the Internet as a communications medium harbours a great potential for an increase in cross-border disputes. These disputes may involve individuals (consumers and sole traders) who, before the arrival of the Internet, were unlikely to be involved in cross-border disputes. It has been suggested in Chapter 4[2] that online arbitration could provide a suitable (binding) method of dispute resolution for many Internet disputes. This raises the question of under what circumstances such arbitration is fair.

The original remit of arbitration was to provide a method of dispute resolution for members of the same industry or trade. Traditionally, the parties were all business members of the same trading community, with shared sets of values.[3] The original type of disputants can be contrasted with the nature of many Internet disputants, who may not share a common background and may well be very diverse indeed.[4]

In traditional commercial arbitration, parties have been allowed to value factors such as efficiency and speed over due process. The preceding chapter has shown that less stringent due process standards have been applied in commercial arbitration (compared to litigation) because of the twin tenets of party autonomy and the waiver doctrine.

---

[1] See 3.2.  [2] See 4.2.
[3] M. Budnitz, 'Arbitration of Disputes between Consumers and Financial Institutions: A Serious Threat to Consumer Protection' (1995) 10 *Ohio State Journal on Dispute Resolution* 267–342, 318–19.
[4] See 3.2.

It is argued in this chapter that if Internet disputants have no other realistic option but to choose online arbitration, it cannot be said that they freely choose arbitration or that they have opted out of the state court system; hence, the waiver doctrine should not apply in the model espoused here. Furthermore, if there is a power imbalance between the parties, and the 'stronger' party imposes its terms on the 'weaker' party, it is also difficult to argue that *both* parties have voluntarily chosen arbitration and opted out of litigation. In these cases, although arbitration is based on contract, it is not fully consensual.[5] In such a situation of power imbalance, the doctrine of party autonomy is also deprived of its meaning, as only the stronger party is truly autonomous.

To support this argument, this chapter examines two examples of arbitration in constellations where it cannot be said that both parties have freely chosen arbitration: where the procedure is mandatory (UDRP) and where they are of unequal bargaining power, with one party imposing terms on the other (B2C arbitration). Although the relevant Internet disputes in this book have been defined more widely than the B2C paradigm, and although the consumer arbitration cases examined here do not exclusively arise from Internet transactions, they serve as a useful example for arbitration between unequal parties.

The argument of this chapter is that the principles of party autonomy and the waiver doctrine should have limited application to the relevant Internet disputes. For the model of dispute resolution espoused here (see Chapter 8), traditional arbitration must be adapted.

This chapter also examines the restrictions placed on B2C arbitration by law to compensate for the fewer due process protections found in arbitration. It argues that a new paradigm has to be found. The traditional paradigm, which applies lesser due process rights and at the same time restricts arbitration for certain relationships (such as B2C cases), has to be changed. The solution is not to restrict access to arbitration for such Internet disputes, as access to *binding* dispute resolution is required, but to ensure that due process applies. Therefore this section advances the argument that stricter due process standards should be applied to online arbitration of Internet disputes (as defined in Chapter 3[6]) than

---

[5] D. Beyleveld and R. Brownsword, *Consent in the Law* (Oxford and Portland, Oreg.: Hart Publishing, 2007): 'it is implicit in the idea of consent that it should be given on a free and informed basis' (130).

[6] Parties subject to a power imbalance, as crystallised in the corporate entity–individual paradigm; see 3.6.3.

have hitherto been applied to offline commercial arbitration between businesses.

The first example to support this contention is the use of arbitration clauses in consumer contracts.

## 7.2 Legal controls on the use of arbitration clauses in consumer contracts

An arbitration contract or clause involves a waiver of the right to go to court[7] (which, as a waiver of a right, requires consent) and an agreement by which the parties undertake an obligation to take part in the arbitration procedure (which also requires consent). This consent should be voluntary and fully informed.[8] However, it is questionable whether, in the B2C context, consent to arbitration complies with these requirements, as there may be a lack of choice of options due to market failures caused by the imposition of standard contract terms by the more powerful (business) party.

In B2C E-commerce, where the supplier includes an arbitration clause in the standard form contract, the consumer is in a far inferior bargaining position. In fact, it can be said that the consumer is in no bargaining position at all, as the contract is offered on a 'take it or leave it' basis. It is also likely that the consumer has not read the standard terms and conditions (even if there was a clear link from the ordering webpage) and thus that the consumer is not even aware that there is an arbitration clause in the contract.[9] Another reason consumers are likely to be unaware of the arbitration clause in the contract is that they do not make their choices according to whether or not there is an arbitration clause in the contract, since, at the stage of contract conclusion, consumers are unlikely to give any thought to the issue of later disputes. Finally, even if the consumer has seen the clause, he or she may not appreciate its significance.

Consumers frequently have no real choice about the terms on which they contract, as different businesses use similar terms, or a particular supplier may have a very strong market position. Consumer choice and market competition will therefore not solve the problem of the consumer's inferior bargaining position. For these reasons, it is a fallacy to say that the consumer has *chosen* arbitration.[10]

---

[7] See 6.2.5.    [8] See fn. 5.
[9] See also Case C-168/05, *Mostaza Claro* v. *Centro Movil* [2007] 1 CMLR 22 (ECJ), para. 25.
[10] Sternlight, 'Panacea or Corporate Tool?', 688; Bundnitz, 'Arbitration of Disputes between Consumers and Financial Institutions', 321.

A second imbalance in the relationship between consumer and supplier arises because the supplier chooses the arbitrator or, at least, the arbitration institution. Most likely, the business is a 'repeat player', conducting numerous arbitrations each year and being familiar with the arbitration institution and the procedure. By contrast, the consumer is the 'single-shot' player who, in most cases, arbitrates only one case against a particular E-commerce supplier. This disadvantages the consumer substantially.[11] In extreme cases, the arbitration institution might even (consciously or not) regard the supplier as a repeat customer for referral, and hence this might mean that there is some degree of (unconscious) systemic bias.[12]

Because of this lack of free choice and the 'repeat player' effect, the law in some jurisdictions restricts the enforceability of pre-dispute arbitration clauses. Furthermore, consumer groups have long argued that consumers should not be bound by pre-dispute arbitration clauses.[13]

The law makes an important distinction between pre- and post-dispute arbitration agreements. A B2C arbitration agreement entered into before the dispute has arisen is potentially unfair, as at that point the consumer is likely to be unaware of its significance. The consumer is not likely to think of a possible dispute at this stage, nor to envisage that he or she may need an avenue of redress later on. By contrast, after a dispute has arisen, the consumer is likely to think about different dispute resolution options, and if at that point he or she chooses not to go to court but to try arbitration instead, then there is no reason why the law should not accept such a

---

[11] This has been recognised explicitly in the recent US Court of Appeals decision of *Ting v. AT&T*, 319 F3d 1126, 1151–2 (9th Cir Cal 2003). Because of this disadvantage to the consumer, the court found an arbitration clause in an adhesion contract unenforceable. See also the discussion of repeat players at 3.5.2.

[12] See further at 3.5.2; see the discussion of independence at 6.3.

[13] M. Doyle, K. Ritters and S. Brooker, *Seeking Resolution* (research report published by the DTI and the National Consumer Council, January 2004, URN 03/1616), 78; see also Consumers International, 'Disputes in Cyberspace' (December 2000), ISBN 19023913162, 29–30 (Recommendations) (available at www.consumersinternational.org [1 August 2008]) and EC Recommendation 98/257/EC, Principle VI, second sentence; see also AAA, *Consumer-Related Disputes Supplementary: Procedures* of 15 September 2005, available from www.adr.org/sp.asp?id=22014 [1 April 2008] and AAA, *Due Process Protocol for Consumers*, Principle 5; BEUC position paper, 'Alternative Dispute Resolution' of 21 November 2002, BEUC/X/048/2002, 5–6; TACD (Transatlantic Consumer Dialogue), 'Alternative Dispute Resolution in the Context of E-Commerce', position statement of February 2000, Ecomm 12–00, Resolution No. 4, available from www.tacd.org/cgi-bin/db.cgi?page=view&config=admin/docs.cfg&id=41 [1 April 2008]; Bamford, 'Shopping Around', 110, OECD Report, *Consumer Dispute Resolution and Redress in the Global Marketplace* (2006), 20.

choice. Hence, generally speaking, most laws restrict (in some way) the enforceability of pre-dispute arbitration clauses against a consumer, but only very few (if any) jurisdictions disallow a B2C arbitration agreement *after* the dispute has arisen.[14]

The question of whether a pre-dispute, B2C arbitration agreement is enforceable against a consumer can arise in different contexts, and this raises the question of which law will determine the enforceability of the arbitration agreement.[15] It may arise when the consumer starts litigation before his or her national court, and the defendant business claims that the court has no jurisdiction because of the arbitration agreement. In this situation, the court may apply the law of the forum (i.e. its national law) on the basis of mandatory consumer-protection law overriding the law of the arbitration agreement.[16] The question may also arise before the courts at the seat of the arbitration if the consumer challenges the jurisdiction of the arbitration tribunal under the law chosen by the parties or the law of the seat.[17] Finally, once an award (or a judgment) has been rendered, the issue may again arise in enforcement proceedings at the place where the defendant has assets. The enforcement court is likely to apply the law chosen by the parties[18] and/or the provisions of the New York Convention.[19]

### 7.2.1 Subject-matter arbitrability

Arbitrability refers to the question of whether a particular type of dispute may be submitted to arbitration. States may reserve certain types of disputes to the exclusive domain of the courts, for reasons of public policy or the public interest.[20] If a particular category of disputes is not

---

[14] Kaufmann-Kohler and Schultz, *Online Dispute Resolution*, 173; French Civil Code, Art. 2061 states that domestic pre-dispute arbitration agreements with consumers are invalid; see below for the position in the United Kingdom and the United States.

[15] Applicable law is discussed at 4.3.

[16] *Richard Zellner v. Phillip Alexander Securities and Futures Ltd* [1997] ILPr 730 (QB), 724; see also s. 89(3) of the English Arbitration Act 1996: 'whatever the law applicable to the arbitration agreement'.

[17] Redfern and Hunter, *Law and Practice of International Commercial Arbitration*, 148–51; Kaufmann-Kohler and Schultz, *Online Dispute Resolution*, 174.

[18] *Ibid.* and *Richard Zellner v. Phillip Alexander Securities and Futures Ltd* [1997] ILPr 730 (QB), 736–8.

[19] New York Convention, Arts. V(1)(a), V(2)(a) or V(2)(b).

[20] Redfern and Hunter, *Law and Practice of International Commercial Arbitration*, 163; Kaufmann-Kohler and Schultz, *Online Dispute Resolution*, 170.

arbitrable, then a dispute falling into that category can never be submitted to arbitration, regardless of the consent of the parties. It seems that consumer disputes can be submitted to arbitration in principle, subject to conditions. In other words, the laws of most jurisdictions impose conditions on the giving of consent, but do not exclude consumer arbitration agreements from arbitration altogether.[21] In jurisdictions allowing the enforcement of post-dispute arbitration agreements, it also cannot be said that consumer disputes are not arbitrable.[22]

### 7.2.2 Control of consumer arbitration under English law

#### Small-claims disputes

In England and Wales, an arbitration agreement concluded with a consumer (whether pre- or post-dispute)[23] is considered to be unfair, and hence unenforceable,[24] if the claim does not exceed £5,000.[25]

Furthermore, under English law, s. 90 of the Arbitration Act 1996 stipulates that the consumer provisions apply to natural *and* legal persons – such as a company – that obtains goods and services for purposes outside its trade, business or profession.[26]

---

[21] Kaufmann-Kohler and Schultz, *Online Dispute Resolution*, 170–2; for example, the German Civil Procedure Code (ZPO) imposes specific form requirements on consumer arbitration agreements in § 1031(5) (the consumer arbitration clause must be contained in a separate signed document or have certification by a notary public); as to the position in England and the United States, see the next section. V. Heiskanen puts forward the view that consumer disputes are not arbitrable (quoting Finland as an example; Heiskanen, 'Dispute Resolution in International Electronic Commerce', 31).

[22] For example, in France, the law distinguishes between a pre-dispute arbitration clause ('clause *compromissoire*') and a post-dispute arbitration agreement ('*compromis*'). The pre-dispute arbitration clause is only valid between merchants and professionals: French Code Civile, Art. 2061; French Code Commercial, Art. 631.

[23] English Arbitration Act 1996, s. 89(1): 'present or future disputes or differences (whether or not contractual)'.

[24] Such a clause would not be binding on the consumer but binding on the business supplier; Unfair Terms in Consumer Contracts Regulations 1999 (SI 1999/2083), reg. 8(1).

[25] English Arbitration Act 1996, s. 91(1) and Unfair Arbitration Agreements (Specified Amounts) Order 1999 (SI 1999/2167) reg. 1. Consumer Arbitration Agreements Act 1988, s. 1(1) used to contain a complete prohibition of all domestic, pre-dispute arbitration clauses in consumer contracts, but this has been repealed by the 1996 Act.

[26] See, for example, the case of *Heifer International Inc* v. *Christiansen (and Others)* [2007] EWHC 3015 (TCC), paras. 226 and 250, where a Russian individual entered into an agreement for the restoration of the family home through a British Virgin Islands company (who also owned the house for capital gains tax avoidance). The court concluded that the agreement was within the scope of the consumer regulations.

Under English law, if the amount in dispute is no more than £5,000,[27] an arbitration clause is automatically not binding on consumers, so there is no need to apply any of the tests set out in Directive 93/13/EEC on Unfair Terms in Consumer Contracts ('the Directive'), implemented in the United Kingdom by the Unfair Terms in Consumer Contracts Regulations 1999 (SI 1999/2083) ('the Regulations').

## Regulation of unfair contract terms

If the amount in dispute exceeds £5,000, the tests in the Directive and the Regulations apply to assess whether the arbitration clause is binding on the consumer.[28] If the arbitration clause is considered unfair, it is not binding on the consumer but may still be binding on the business.[29]

**Example in the Annex to the Directive**   Example (q) in the Annex to the Directive and the Regulations is the most relevant example of an unfair term: 'excluding or hindering the consumer's right to take legal action or exercise any other legal remedy, particularly by requiring the consumer to take disputes exclusively to arbitration not covered by legal provisions'. The meaning of the phrase 'arbitration not covered by legal provisions' is not entirely clear; several interpretations are possible. One interpretation could be that this phrase distinguishes private arbitration from public forms of 'arbitration', such as the small-claims procedure or a statutory ombudsman scheme. Another interpretation is that it refers to a distinction between arbitration based on the applicable law and arbitration where the arbitrator does not base his or her decision on strict law. It seems that the courts have interpreted the clause to mean the former.[30]

---

[27] This amount can be changed by statutory instrument. It seems that this amount tallies with the upper limit for the small-claims procedure. The policy behind this is that, up to this amount, it may be better for the consumer to choose the statutory small-claims procedure, whereas for larger amounts in dispute, arbitration may, under certain circumstances, actually be in the consumer's interest.

[28] C. Drahozal and R. Friel, 'A Comparative View of Consumer Arbitration' (2005) 71 *Arbitration* 131–39, 134; OFT, *Unfair Contract Terms Guidance* (February 2001), paras. 17.2 and 17.3.

[29] Directive 93/13/EEC, Art. 6(1); Unfair Terms in Consumer Contracts Regulations 1999 (SI 1999/2083), reg. 8(1).

[30] By implication: Landgericht Krefeld Case 6 O 186/95, Judgment of 29 April 1996 [1997] ILPr 716; *Picardi* v. *Cuniberti* [2002] EWHC 2923 (QB), para. 102; *Heifer International Inc* v. *Christiansen (and Others)*, paras. 231–2. Explicit: *Mylcrist Builders Ltd* v. *Mrs G. Buck*, Decision of 19 September 2008 (TCC) [2008] EWHC 2172, para. 54.

In a recent case, the European Court of Justice (ECJ) held that if a pre-dispute arbitration clause is held to be unfair by the national court, the award has to be annulled, even if the consumer has failed to raise the unfair nature of the term during the arbitration proceedings, the reason for which may be that the consumer is unaware of his or her rights, or that the consumer is deterred from enforcing them on account of the costs that judicial proceedings would involve.[31]

It is also interesting to note that Recommendation 98/257/EC also provides, in Art. 4, that consumers should not be bound by a pre-dispute arbitration clause.[32]

**The fairness test** In any case, Art. 3(3) of the Directive makes it clear that the examples in the Annex are only indicative, and hence a case-by-case assessment has to be made in order to see whether the arbitration clause: (1) has been individually negotiated, (2) is contrary to the requirement of good faith, and (3) causes an imbalance in the parties' rights and obligations to the detriment of the consumer.[33] The courts must also take into account the nature of the goods and services for which the contract was concluded, the other terms of the contract and also all circumstances occurring at the point the contract was concluded.[34]

A mere explanation or the pointing out of an onerous clause in the consumer contract may be necessary to ensure incorporation under the common law, but will *not* be sufficient to render the clause fair or, for that matter, 'individually negotiated'. Pre-formulated terms, which the consumer has not been able to influence, are never 'individually negotiated'.[35]

The two core elements of the assessment used to see whether a term is fair or unfair are the imbalance and the 'contrary to good faith' requirements. These elements have been interpreted by the House of Lords in the case *Director-General of Fair Trading* v. *First National Bank Plc.*[36] Lord Bingham described the imbalance test by the question: is the term

---

[31] Case C-168/05, *Mostaza Claro* v. *Centro Movil* [2007] 1 CMLR 22 (ECJ), paras. 29–30.
[32] Recommendations have no binding force.
[33] Directive 93/13/EEC, Art. 3(1); Unfair Terms in Consumer Contracts Regulations 1999 (SI 1999/2083), reg. 5(1).
[34] Directive 93/13/EEC, Art. 4(1); Unfair Terms in Consumer Contracts Regulations 1999 (1999/2083), reg. 6(1).
[35] Directive 93/13/EEC, Art. 3(2); Unfair Terms in Consumer Contracts Regulations 1999 (1999/2083), reg. 5(2).
[36] [2002] 1 AC 481 (HL).

weighted in favour of the supplier so as to tilt the parties' rights and obligations under the contract?[37] Lord Millett, in the same case, approached the assessment from a practical standpoint by asking whether the parties would have accepted the term if their attention had been drawn to it.[38] The assessment has both a procedural and a substantive element, and is not limited to an inquiry of whether the term has been brought to the consumer's attention, but, in addition, whether it is substantially fair.[39] What does this mean in the context of pre-dispute, consumer arbitration clauses?

**Substantial fairness in the context of pre-dispute arbitration clauses**
In the context of construction adjudication, *pre-dispute* adjudication clauses have been upheld where the consumer had received competent and independent professional advice, for example from the surveyor.[40] In these cases, the courts seem to have equated the requirement of good faith with the requirement that the consumer is fully informed of the consequences of adjudication.[41]

In *Heifer International Inc* v. *Christiansen* v. *Others*[42] Mr Justice Tulmin QC referred,[43] with approval, to Mr Justice Riner's description of unfairness in *Bryen & Langley* v. *Boston* as being 'loaded unfairly in favour of the supplier',[44] and to Mr Justice Riner's dictum that there is no unfairness if the standard terms are introduced by the consumer's professional adviser.[45] In *Heifer International Inc*, the claimant was a wealthy Russian consumer who wished to have his family home renovated by an architect and workmen from Denmark, believing Danish construction standards to be better than English standards. He obtained legal advice for the construction project from a Danish law firm who prepared the agreement, incorporating an arbitration agreement. In these circumstances, Mr Justice Tulmin held that the claimant had been able to influence the substance of the term, and it could not be said that it was contrary to good faith or inherently unfair.[46] He applied Lord Millet's test and said it was not clear that the claimant would have opposed the arbitration clause if it had been pointed out to him at the point when the agreement was negotiated,

---

[37] *Ibid.* para. 17.    [38] *Ibid.* para. 54.
[39] *Ibid.* paras. 17 (Lord Bingham) and 36–7 (Lord Steyn).
[40] *Allen Wilson Shopfitters and Builders* v. *Buckingham* [2005] EWHC 1165 (TCC), para. 43; *Westminster Building Company Ltd* v. *Beckingham* [2004] BLR 163 (TCC), para. 31.
[41] *Ibid.*    [42] [2007] EWHC 3015 (TCC), Judgment of 18 December 2007.
[43] *Ibid.* paras. 240–1.    [44] [2005] BLR 508 (QB), para. 45.    [45] *Ibid.* para. 46.
[46] [2007] EWHC 3015 (TCC), para. 304.

as he had insisted on using a Danish architect who would apply Danish building standards.[47]

In *Picardi* v. *Cuniberti*, the court held that an arbitration clause in a contract between an architect and a consumer is an onerous term that must be drawn to the specific attention of the consumer, and that the term had therefore not been validly incorporated.[48] The court also held (obiter) that the arbitration clause was an unfair term, and that it was an example of a significant imbalance to the detriment of the consumer,[49] as it may hinder the consumer's right to take legal action.[50] In that case, the consumers had not been professionally advised.

The litigation in the case of *Richard Zellner* v. *Phillip Alexander Securities and Futures Ltd*, before the German Landgericht (District Court) Krefeld and the English High Court, is another example where an arbitration clause in an agreement with a consumer has been held an unfair, and hence unenforceable, term. The claimant, a German consumer, had been solicited by cold-calling into entering a 'futures and options' agreement, under which he lost a substantial sum of money. One of the clauses in the agreement provided for arbitration in London before the LCIA under English law. The German court applied German mandatory consumer-protection law, and held that the term was unfair as it deprived the consumer of access to his local court, and since the term was hidden in small print extending over several pages, it had the effect of 'duping' the consumer.[51] The claimant won the case and moved to enforce the judgment in England by registering it with the English High Court. The defendant appealed against the Master's Order for registration, again arguing that the German Court had no jurisdiction because of the arbitration agreement. On appeal, the English High Court had to assess the validity of the arbitration agreement, this time under English law. It also came to the conclusion that the arbitration agreement was invalid.[52]

---

[47] *Ibid.* para. 306.    [48] [2002] EWHC 2923 (QB), para. 127.

[49] *Ibid.* para. 128; also: *Mylcrist Builders Ltd* v. *Mrs G. Buck*, Decision of 19 September 2008 (TCC) [2008] EWHC 2172, para. 53.

[50] *Ibid.*

[51] Landgericht Krefeld Case 6 O 186/95, Judgment of 29 April 1996; *Richard Zellner* v. *Phillip Alexander Securities and Futures Ltd* [1997] ILPr 716, 724; the court applied the German law and referred to Directive 93/13/EEC on Unfair Terms in Consumer Contracts, which at that point only had indirect application as it had not yet been implemented into German law.

[52] [1997] ILPr 730 (QB), 736–8; the English court did not refer to Directive 93/13/EEC on Unfair Contract Terms, which at that point had not been implemented in the United Kingdom. Instead, it based its findings that the arbitration agreement was invalid

## Conclusion: English law

It is clear from this discussion that an arbitration clause can be an unfair term, depending on the circumstances, as it may deprive the consumer of access to national courts and application of mandatory consumer-protection norms.

Some English cases have made a distinction between a professionally advised consumer, who would be bound by the arbitration clause, and a consumer who is not advised and, hence, would not be bound. It will depend on the circumstances whether professional advice obtained by the consumer re-tilts the power imbalance in favour of the consumer.

However, it is important not to make too much of the case law based on construction cases, as the interpretation of what amounts to an unfair term depends on the context,[53] and the answer may well be different for Internet and, in particular, E-commerce disputes.[54] For claims above the £5,000 threshold, it is ultimately not clear whether a pre-dispute arbitration clause, for example contained in standard terms on a website, would be binding on the consumer or not. It is argued here that the courts will interpret the Regulations to see whether the consumer has not only understood the arbitration clause but also whether the clause deprives the consumer of mandatory consumer-protection law[55] or due process on a case-by-case analysis.

Therefore, English law restricts the use of pre-dispute arbitration clauses considerably, thus acknowledging that consumers must be 'protected' from the lesser due process standards of arbitration, and must be given the choice to go to court.

In a similar vein, it is likely that an English court would, for public-policy reasons, refuse enforcement of an arbitration award that had been based on an unfair arbitration agreement in a standard-term contract.

---

on s. 1(1) of the Consumer Arbitration Agreements Act 1988, which provided that pre-dispute consumer-arbitration agreements were unenforceable. Section 2(a) of the same Act limited this to domestic agreements; however, the court found that s. 2(a) was discriminatory against EU citizens, and hence should not be applied. The Consumer Arbitration Agreements Act 1988 and its blanket prohibition on pre-dispute consumer-arbitration agreements has been repealed by the English Arbitration Act 1996.

[53] Directive 93/13/EEC, Art. 4(1); Unfair Terms in Consumer Contracts Regulations 1999 (SI 1999/2038), reg. 6(1).

[54] The argument advanced here is that arbitration clauses should not be regarded as unfair if, and only if, arbitration respects due process. This could be achieved by interpreting the unfair contract term provisions accordingly.

[55] See 4.3.5.

## 7.2.3 Control of adhesion contracts under US state law

By contrast to England/the European Union, in the United States, arbitration clauses in a written contract with a consumer are usually enforceable.[56] There is a strong presumption in favour of arbitration under the Federal Arbitration Act 1925.[57] This has been shown in cases concerning specific *state* consumer-protection legislation[58] (providing for mandatory, non-waivable consumer rights), where the courts have validated the arbitration clause, even if it had the effect of depriving the consumer of these rights.[59]

However, an arbitration clause in a consumer contract must have been brought to the consumer's attention. In *Specht* v. *Netscape Communications Corpn*,[60] the courts have made a distinction between 'browse wrap' contracts and 'click wrap' contracts. The court found that the arbitration clause was not incorporated in a 'browse wrap' contract, as the consumer may have not followed the link to the terms and conditions.[61]

Furthermore, under general, state contract law, any term in a consumer contract can be unenforceable if it is procedurally and substantially unconscionable, and this doctrine of unconscionability equally applies to arbitration agreements, notwithstanding the Federal Arbitration Act's pro-arbitration stance.[62] A term is procedurally unconscionable if it is in a contract of adhesion, which is a standard-term contract drafted by a party with a superior bargaining position.[63] However, the mere fact that an arbitration clause is contained in a standard contract does *not*

---

[56] Carbonneau, 'Arbitral Justice', 19; *Allied-Bruce Terminix Cos* v. *Dobson*, 513 US 265; 115 SCt 834, 281–2 (1995).

[57] 9 USC, § 2: an arbitration agreement 'shall be valid, irrevocable, and enforceable, save upon such grounds as exist at law or in equity for the revocation of *any* contract'. However, Jean Sternlight has found that this preference for arbitration was not part of the original intent of Congress but was a myth developed by later courts out of a misguided policy to deal with overburdened courts: Sternlight, 'Panacea or Corporate Tool?', 644–56, 660–74; see similar, Budnitz, 'Arbitration of Disputes between Consumers and Financial Institutions', 289–90.

[58] Because of the supremacy of federal law, see also Carbonneau, 'Arbitral Justice', 27.

[59] *Commerce Park at DFW Freeport* v. *Mardian Constr Co*, 729 F2d 334, 338–9; 39 FedRServ2d 134 (5th Cir 1984); *Marley* v. *Drexel Burnham Lambert Inc*, 566 FSupp 333, 335 (1983 ND Texas); *Ting* v. *AT&T*, 319 F3d 1126, 1147–48 (9th Cir Cal 2003) (arbitration clause held unenforceable for other reason).

[60] 306 F3d 17; 48 UCCRepServ2d 761 (2nd Cir 2002).     [61] 306 F3d 17, 30–3, 35.

[62] Court decisions finding arbitration agreements unconscionable and unenforceable have been relatively common in the state and federal courts in California; see Carbonneau, 'Arbitral Justice', 27.

[63] For example *Ting* v. *AT&T*, 319 F3d 1126, 1148 (9th Cir Cal 2003).

make the arbitration agreement unenforceable against the consumer. An additional factor is required in that the term must also be substantively unconscionable.[64] Substantive unconscionability is concerned with the one-sided nature of the contract and its oppressiveness, looking at the actual effects of the challenged provision.[65] Such one-sidedness can stem from the fact that the consumer has to bear an excessive filing-fee, the fact that the consumers cannot resort to class action or that the process is confidential, hence enhancing the 'repeat player' effect.[66] A clause restricting the consumer's avenue of redress to arbitration, while allowing the company the choice to litigate, would also be invalid for the same reason.[67]

The courts have held in several decisions[68] that an arbitration agreement in a consumer contract that forces the consumer to incur *excessive* arbitration fees is unconscionable. For example, in the much-cited case of *Brower* v. *Gateway Inc*,[69] involving the purchase of a personal computer and related software products,[70] the arbitration agreement stipulated arbitration before the ICC Court of Arbitration. The ICC advance fee for the claim was US $4,000, half of which was non-refundable. The New York Appellate Court held that the arbitration agreement was unenforceable, and remanded the case back to a lower court to encourage the parties to find an appropriate arbitration procedure for their small-claims dispute.

In another line of cases, the courts have held an arbitration clause to be unenforceable against a consumer if it prevented consumers resorting to class action, which existed as a right under state law.[71]

---

[64] *Iberia Credit Bureau* v. *Cingular Wireless LLC, Sprint Spectrum Company, Centennial Wireless*, 379 F3d 159, 167–8 (5th Cir 2004).

[65] *Ting* v. *AT&T*, 319 F3d 1126, 1149 (9th Cir Cal 2003).

[66] *Ibid.* 1151–2 (9th Cir Cal 2003), but different in *Iberia Credit Bureau* v. *Cingular Wireless LLC, Sprint Spectrum Company, Centennial Wireless*, 379 F3d 159, 175–6 (5th Cir 2004).

[67] *Iberia Credit Bureau* v. *Cingular Wireless LLC, Sprint Spectrum Company, Centennial Wireless*, 168–9.

[68] *Brower* v. *Gateway2000 Inc*, 676 NYS2d 569, 572 (1998); *Green Tree Financial* v. *Randolph*, 531 US 79, 81; 121 SCt 513, 517 (2000) (in this case the US Supreme Court accepted that prohibitive costs may invalidate an arbitration agreement against a consumer, but the court was not convinced that the petitioner would in fact incur such costs); *Knepp* v. *Credit Acceptance Corp*, 229 BR 821, 838 (1999); *Patterson* v. *ITT Consumer Fin Corp*, 18 CalRptr2d 563, 565–7 (1993); *Gutierrez* v. *Autowest Inc*, 114 CalApp4th 77, 86 (CalApp 2003); *Ting* v. *AT&T*, 319 F3d 1126, 1151 (9th Cir Cal 2003).

[69] 676 NYS2d 569, 572 (1998).

[70] Value of the claim was, on average, about US $1,000.

[71] *Ting* v. *AT&T*, 319 F3d 1126, 1150 (9th Cir Cal 2003); *Ingle* v. *Circuit City Stores*, 328 F3d 1165, 1175–6 (9th Cir 2003); *Szetela* v. *Discover Bank*, 118 CalRptr2d 862, 867–8 (CtApp

In summary, it can be said that if the arbitration agreement provides
for an accessible and affordable forum, it will be enforced against a consumer.[72] The underlying approach in the United States is that arbitration
is as effective as court proceedings in adjudicating disputes, and that
arbitration may be in the parties' and society's interest.[73]

Nevertheless, where an arbitration agreement in an adhesion contract
deprives the consumer of access to a forum to vindicate his or her rights, an
arbitration clause may be struck out. Hence some restrictions against consumer arbitration agreements also exist under the US approach. However,
these restrictions are insufficient to guard consumers from unfairness,[74]
as will be explained in the next section.

### 7.2.4 A critique of consumer arbitration

As explained in the preceding section, although there are some restrictions
on arbitration clauses in adhesion contracts, on the whole there has been
a presumption that arbitration agreements in such contracts are valid.
This approach has been heavily criticised in legal literature.[75]

2002); *Discover Bank* v. *Superior Court*, 36 Cal4th 148, 162 (2005); *Dana Klussman* v. *Cross Country Bank*, 134 CalApp4th 1283, 1291; 36 CalRptr3d 728, 733–4 (CalApp 2005); *Aral* v. *Earthlink*, 134 CalApp4th 544, 564; 36 CalRptr3d 229 (CalApp2Dist 2005), but different in *Charles Provencher* v. *Dell Inc*, 409 FSupp2d 1196 (US District Court CD California 2006). In the *Discover Bank* v. *Superior Court* case, the court said that an arbitration clause is unenforceable if found 'in a setting in which disputes between the contracting parties predictably involve small amounts of damages, and when it is alleged that the party with the superior bargaining power has carried out a scheme to deliberately cheat large numbers of consumers'. The judge in the *Charles Provencher* case distinguished this case on its facts, by finding that there was no blanket policy in California against class-action waivers in the consumer context: *Charles Provercher* v. *Dell Inc*, 409 FSupp2d 1196, 1201 (US District Court CD California 2006). The court in the *Charles Provencher* case found on the facts that the arbitration clause and class-action waiver did not deprive the consumer of effective redress and did not exempt Dell from the consequences of any alleged wrongdoing: *ibid.* 1202–3. The court upheld the validity of the clause: *ibid.* 1203–4; similarly, in *Iberia Credit Bureau* v. *Cingular Wireless LLC, Sprint Spectrum Company, Centennial Wireless*, 379 F3d 159, 174–5 (5th Cir 2004), the court also found that the bar on class actions is also insufficient to render an arbitration clause automatically unconscionable.
[72] *Charles Provencher* v. *Dell Inc*, 1202–3.    [73] Carbonneau, 'Arbitral Justice', 19.
[74] Park, *Procedural Evolution in Business Arbitration*, 22–3.
[75] R. Alderman, 'Pre-Dispute Mandatory Arbitration in Consumer Contracts: A Call for Reform' (Winter 2001) 38 *Houston Law Review* 1237–68, 1240–2; P. Carrington, 'Regulating Dispute Resolution Provisions in Adhesion Contracts' (1998) 35 (Winter) *Harvard Journal on Legislation* 225–31, 225–6; Sternlight, 'Panacea or Corporate Tool?', 704–5; Budnitz, 'Arbitration of Disputes between Consumers and Financial Institutions', 287; Reuben, 'Constitutional Gravity', 1032; Park, *Procedural Evolution in Business Arbitration*, 21.

For example, Jean Sternlight writes:[76] 'In case after case since . . . 1983, the Supreme Court has reiterated that arbitration should be preferred over litigation. However, when the parties have not knowingly and voluntarily agreed to arbitration, this preference has no justification as a matter of legislative history, nor can it be defended as a matter of policy.' Therefore, calls have been made that pre-dispute arbitration agreements should be unenforceable unless there is a *voluntary and fully informed waiver.*[77] The main problem with consumer arbitration agreements is that consumers have no real choice, as the arbitration clause is usually imposed on them.[78]

There are six factors that may potentially render arbitration as a process unfair to consumers. This does *not* mean that arbitration is *always* unfair to consumers; how these factors weigh against the efficiency gains described in Chapter 5[79] depends on the circumstances of each case. Most of these factors have already been discussed in the general discussion of due process in Chapter 6. However, they will briefly be listed again here in the specific context of consumer arbitration as an example of a power imbalance situation, and it will be explained how they disadvantage consumers more than businesses.[80]

### The risk of systemic bias against consumer complainants

The root cause for such systemic bias in the consumer context is the 'repeat player' effect[81] explained in Chapter 3.[82]

It has been explained in Chapter 6 that the concept of a fair hearing is a flexible one, and that in arbitration particularly it is common practice to

---

[76] Sternlight, 'Panacea or Corporate Tool?', 711.

[77] Alderman, 'Pre-dispute Mandatory Arbitration in Consumer Contracts', 1264–5; Carrington, 'Regulating Dispute Resolution Provisions in Adhesion Contracts', 230–1; Sternlight, 'Panacea or Corporate Tool?', 705; Budnitz, 'Arbitration of Disputes between Consumers and Financial Institutions', 333–5; Reuben, 'Constitutional Gravity', 1032.

[78] Alderman, 'Pre-dispute Mandatory Arbitration in Consumer Contracts', 1240, 1246ff.; Carrington, 'Regulating Dispute Resolution Provisions in Adhesion Contracts', 226; Sternlight, 'Panacea or Corporate Tool?', 676–7.

[79] See 5.5.2.

[80] In this discussion, I rely mainly on US sources and literature, as in the UK, mandatory, pre-dispute arbitration clauses are frequently not binding (see the last section). In the United States, consumers are also disadvantaged, as arbitration deprives them of the benefits of class action, and in some areas, also of the benefit of punitive damages; see, for a discussion of this, Budnitz, 'Arbitration of Disputes between Consumers and Financial Institutions', 285–6. Since these are features specific to the US litigation systems, they will not be further discussed here.

[81] Sternlight, 'Panacea or Corporate Tool?', 678–9, 684–5; Budnitz, 'Arbitration of Disputes between Consumers and Financial Institutions', 294.

[82] See 3.5.2.

take shortcuts in the quantity and quality of evidence adduced.[83] This sets the consumer in a B2C E-commerce dispute at a particular disadvantage, as usually the consumer has to prepay for any goods or services, so that if a dispute arises, the consumer will be the claimant who has to prove the facts to substantiate the claim.[84]

## Transaction costs

Arbitration may or may not be cheaper than litigation. For consumer disputes, it may well be that small-claims proceedings are cheaper. The point here is that court judges need not be paid, whereas arbitrators must be paid (unless the business bears all the cost). If the arbitration agreement applies a law foreign to the consumer, he or she may incur additional cost in obtaining foreign legal advice.[85]

## Confidentiality

Chapter 6 discusses the implications of confidentiality for due process.[86] The first main point is that confidentiality exacerbates the informational inequality between the parties.[87] Secondly, confidentiality deprives the law of a precedent. If there is no precedent, the law cannot develop in a coherent fashion.[88] If there are no cases interpreting consumer-protection legislation, it can be argued that this disadvantages consumers generally, as it makes consumer-protection legislation less effective.[89] Thirdly, the non-publication of arbitration awards means that there is not the same scrutiny and criticism of awards as there is with public judgments.[90]

## No reasons and no appeal

The arbitration agreement a business imposes on a consumer may well provide that no reasons should be given and that the award is final. The

---

[83] See 6.4.

[84] Sternlight, 'Panacea or Corporate Tool?', 678–9, 683–4; Budnitz, 'Arbitration of Disputes between Consumers and Financial Institutions', 311, 314; Thornburg, 'Going Private', 206–7.

[85] Alderman, 'Pre-dispute Mandatory Arbitration in Consumer Contracts', 1241–2, 1249ff.; Sternlight, 'Panacea or Corporate Tool?', 678–9, 682–3.

[86] See 6.6.

[87] Budnitz, 'Arbitration of Disputes between Consumers and Financial Institutions', 285, 287.

[88] See 6.6.1.

[89] Alderman, 'Pre-dispute Mandatory Arbitration in Consumer Contracts', 1242, 1258 and 1262ff.; Carrington, 'Regulating Dispute Resolution Provisions in Adhesion Contracts', 229.

[90] Mentioned by Sternlight, 'Panacea or Corporate Tool?', 678–9, 686; Budnitz, 'Arbitration of Disputes between Consumers and Financial Institutions', 327–8; Thornburg, 'Going Private', 210–11; Perritt, 'Dispute Resolution in Cyberspace, 675–703, 681.

implications of this have been discussed in Chapter 6.[91] This is problematic, since this renunciation of rights has been imposed by one side and
may disadvantage the consumer, as claimant, disproportionately because
of the 'repeat player' effect.[92]

## Applicable law

The business may state in an arbitration agreement which law is to apply
to the dispute, thereby defeating or curtailing mandatory consumer-
protection provisions that may otherwise apply.[93] Also, since the judicial
review of arbitration awards on the merits is limited, arbitrators may
not properly apply the law,[94] and, in particular, they may not apply (foreign) mandatory consumer-protection laws.[95] These two factors mean
that consumer-protection law is less effective than it otherwise would
be.[96]

## One-sided procedure

Finally, since the business acts as an experienced repeat player by selecting
the arbitration institution and shaping the procedure to its own advantage,
this further disadvantages the 'one-shot' player, the consumer.[97] This puts
the principle of party autonomy on its head, as, in fact, only *one* of the
parties is autonomous.

### 7.2.5 Conclusion

As the example of consumer disputes has shown, *commercial* arbitration
may not be the suitable paradigm for solving all disputes arising on the
Internet. In a situation of considerable power imbalance, such as consumer
E-commerce disputes, there is no voluntary and informed waiver of due
process. For Internet disputes, it is no solution to provide that pre-dispute
arbitration clauses should not be binding, as this would deprive the weaker
party of all access to redress, as the courts are not a viable or affordable
option. This is even more the case where the parties are located at a
distance or even in two different jurisdictions. Hence this is a Catch-22

---

[91] See 6.5 and 6.7.     [92] See 6.6.1; Sternlight, 'Panacea or Corporate Tool?', 678–9, 686.
[93] See 4.3.5.     [94] Ware, 'Default Rules from Mandatory Rules', 719–20.
[95] Thornburg, 'Going Private', 216.
[96] Sternlight, 'Panacea or Corporate Tool?', 678–9, 685; cf. Budnitz, 'Arbitration of Disputes
between Consumers and Financial Institutions', 285, who doubts whether the fact that
arbitrators do not have to apply strict law necessarily disadvantages consumers.
[97] Alderman, 'Pre-dispute Mandatory Arbitration in Consumer Contracts', 1242, 1253ff.;
Carrington, 'Regulating Dispute Resolution Provisions in Adhesion Contracts', 226; Sternlight, 'Panacea or Corporate Tool?', 685; Budnitz, 'Arbitration of Disputes between Consumers and Financial Institutions', 293.

situation for Internet disputes: on the one hand, traditional arbitration is not working to provide fair dispute resolution in a situation where there is a considerable power imbalance between the parties, such as consumer E-commerce disputes. On the other hand, it is no good to simply limit the availability of arbitration in the online environment, as it is the only viable form of binding dispute resolution. Hence the controls on arbitration clauses provided by the law on unfair contract terms (in the United Kingdom and the European Union) or adhesion contracts (in the United States) are not effective to ensure the fairness of arbitration, and are not sufficient to protect consumers. The outcome of this is that arbitration has to change for Internet disputes – it has to reinvent itself to cater for a wider range of Internet disputes and disputants. Arbitration has to comply with stricter due process standards when employed for the solution of Internet disputes, at least where there is a power imbalance between the parties. If online arbitration is the only viable binding dispute resolution procedure in many cases (and not only an alternative to litigation), it is crucial that due process standards are incorporated into online arbitration of Internet disputes.

The second example of due process and arbitration of Internet disputes is the UDRP, which will be discussed in the next section.

### 7.3 UDRP as a model for ODR

This section describes the UDRP, analyses its procedural fairness and discusses to what extent this procedure could serve as a model for the resolution of Internet disputes.

#### 7.3.1 Brief description of the UDRP

The Internet Corporation for Assigned Names and Numbers (ICANN), the body tasked with governing the Internet domain-name system by the US government, adopted the UDRP on 26 August 1999. The UDRP is designed to solve disputes between a trademark owner and a domain-name registrant[98] where the registrant has registered a domain name identical or confusingly similar to the trademark, the registrant has no rights or legitimate interests in the name, and the registrant has registered and used the domain name in bad faith.[99] The UDRP cannot be used to deal with conflicts between two trademark holders or between

---

[98] For generic top-level domains such as .com and .biz.
[99] UDRP Policy, para. 4(a), as approved by ICANN on 24 October 1999, available at www.icann.org/en/dndr/udrp/policy.htm [1 April 2008].

a trademark holder and a registrant who has rights or legitimate interests. In particular, the UDRP does not apply if the registrant has been known by the name or used it in connection with a bona fide offering of goods or services or for a legitimate non-commercial purpose.[100]

The UDRP has been drafted narrowly to combat the Internet phenomenon of cybersquatting, i.e. the registration of a domain name similar to a trademark for an illegitimate purpose, such as selling the domain name to the trademark owner or to a competitor of the trademark owner, preventing the trademark owner from reflecting the name in the corresponding domain, vexing the trademark owner or in order to deflect traffic from the (famous) trademark owner onto the registrant's own site, who may, by this last tactic, increase traffic and advertising revenue.[101]

A further discussion of the substantive issues of the UDRP is outside the scope of this book. Suffice to say here that the UDRP (and its associated rules) do not merely lay down the procedure for the dispute resolution; it also forms the applicable substantive law for the resolution of disputes within its scope. The main consideration in the design of the UDRP was to create a convenient, cost-effective and fast procedure to combat cybersquatting.[102]

The UDRP as a procedure[103] is similar to arbitration in that a private adjudicator (a one- or three-member panel) produces a decision that is binding on the parties. However, the procedure is not, strictly speaking, arbitration, as the decisions are not final and do not have *res judicata* effect between the parties.[104] Either party can start

---

[100] *Ibid.* para. 4(c), as approved by ICANN on 24 October 1999, available at www.icann.org/en/dndr/udrp/policy.htm [1 April 2008].

[101] *Ibid.* para. 4(b), as approved by ICANN on 24 October 1999, available at www.icann.org/en/dndr/udrp/policy.htm [1 April 2008]; WIPO Case No. D2006–0882, *Geoffrey Inc* v. *NOT THE USUAL.*

[102] *WIPO Report: New Generic Top Level Domains – Intellectual Property Considerations*, para. 38.

[103] The UDRP calls the procedure the 'Mandatory Administrative Procedure'.

[104] For arbitration, the award disposes of the dispute between the parties; Redfern and Hunter, *Law and Practice of International Commercial Arbitration*, 459; cf. for the position under the UDRP, *Stenzel* v. *Pifer*, WL 1419016 (District Court WDWash 2006), Decision of 22 May 2006; *Storey* v. *Cello Holdings LLC*, 347 3Fd 370, 373–4, 381 (2nd Cir NY 2003); *Parisi* v. *Netlearning Inc*, 139 FSupp2d 745, 752 (District Court ED Va 2001); *Sallen* v. *Corinthians Licenciamentos LTDA*, 273 F3d 14, 26–7 (1st Circuit 2001); see also N. Chatterjee, 'Arbitration Proceedings under ICANN's Uniform Domain Name Dispute Resolution Policy – Myth or Reality?' (2006) 10 *Vindobona Journal of International Commercial Law & Arbitration* 67–90, 86–7; C. Emerson, 'Wasting Time in Cyberspace: The UDRP's Inefficient Approach toward Arbitrating Internet Domain Name Disputes' (2004) 34 *University of Baltimore Law Review* 161–97, 177.

proceedings before a competent court after the panel has produced a decision.[105]

Like arbitration, the UDRP is based on a contractual regime. The UDRP has been described as a 'contractually-mandated private system for the benefit of non-contracting parties'.[106] This works as follows: the domain-name registrant has agreed to submit disputes to the UDRP regime under the terms of the contract between the domain-name registrar and the domain-name registrant. However, this agreement is in no sense voluntary. ICANN, as the ultimate regulator of the domain-name system, has imposed a requirement on each domain-name registrar to incorporate the UDRP into their contracts with their customers. The UDRP is a regulatory dispute resolution scheme implemented by a chain of contracts.[107]

Furthermore, the decisions are also binding, since they are enforced by action of the registrar if neither party commences litigation before the courts.[108] The registrars are contractually obliged (as part of their licence from ICANN) to comply with an order by a panel to cancel or transfer a domain name. Since the only remedy a panel can award is to cancel or transfer a domain name[109] (panels cannot order any other remedy such as damages), the order of a panel can be directly implemented by the registrar, who has the de facto power to cancel or transfer domain names. This means that the UDRP is self-enforcing.[110] While this is effective, it creates the risk that the process is not seen as legitimate if it does not comply with due process.[111]

To the extent that the UDRP lowers the hurdle for complainants by cutting the cost, time and effort to seek redress, it can be said that it shifts

---

[105] UDRP Policy, para. 4(k); however, the party has to rely on an independent cause of action: *Pankajkumar Patel* v. *Allos Therapeutics Inc*, Decision of 13 June 2008 (ChD) WL 2442985, para. 15.

[106] E. Thornburg, 'Fast, Cheap and Out of Control: Lessons from the ICANN Dispute Resolution Process' (Spring 2002) 6 *Journal of Small and Emerging Business Law* 191–233, 197.

[107] *Parisi* v. *Netlearning Inc*, 139 FSupp2d 745, 751 (District Court ED Va 2001); *Storey* v. *Cello Holdings LLC*, 347 3Fd 370, 381 (2nd Cir NY 2003).

[108] The UDRP states that the registrar must wait ten days before implementing a decision to transfer or cancel the domain name, in order to see whether the registrant commences court proceedings: para. 4(k).

[109] UDRP Policy, para. 4(i).

[110] In fact, some courts have held that a UDRP decision cannot be enforced as an arbitration award; see, for example, in relation to Federal Arbitration Act 1925, § 10, *Parisi* v. *Netlearning Inc*, 139 FSupp2d 745, 752 (District Court ED Va 2001); *Dluhos* v. *Strasberg*, 321 F3d 365, 372–3 (3rd Cir 2003).

[111] L. Helfer, 'Whither the UDRP: Autonomous, Americanized or Cosmopolitan?' (2004) 12 *Cardozo Journal of International and Comparative Law* 493–505, 496.

the burden to litigate before the courts from the trademark holder to the domain-name registrant, who has to go to court to prevent or remedy a transfer or cancellation of the name. However, the mere fact that the UDRP shifts the burden to litigate from the trademark holder to the domain-name registrant within its (narrow) scope does not render the UDRP automatically unfair.[112]

Five[113] dispute-resolution service providers have received ICANN approval. At present, only three are deciding cases under the UDRP: (i) the WIPO Arbitration and Mediation Center (WIPO Center),[114] (ii) the National Arbitration Forum (NAF)[115] and (iii) the Asian Domain Name Dispute Resolution Centre (ADNDRC).[116] The complainant trademark owner selects which of the dispute-resolution service providers should hear the case.[117]

For .eu domain names, the European Commission has set up, in conjunction with the .eu registry (EURID), a dispute resolution procedure clearly modelled on, and almost identical to, the UDRP.[118] The first (and to date only) dispute-resolution service provider accredited to resolve disputes under this .eu ADR policy[119] is the Czech Court of Arbitration.[120] In the next section, procedural variations will be pointed out, as they are relevant and significant for the due process discussion.

---

[112] Suggested in Thornburg, 'Going Private', 193 and 'Fast, Cheap and Out of Control', 215–16.

[113] ICANN has approved a total of five dispute-resolution service providers; however, two of these have ceased to accept cases. E-Resolution ceased operations on 30 November 2001. Recently (1 January 2007), CPR has also ceased to accept UDRP cases. This section refers to the CPR Rules, where they contained interesting points, but it should be noted that the scheme is not operative. CPR had registered 141 cases (including pending cases) until 11 July 2006.

[114] WIPO has 8,925 cases on its files (including pending cases) up to 11 July 2006; see www.wipo.int/amc/en/domains/statistics [11 July 2006].

[115] NAF has registered 6,694 cases (including pending cases) up to 11 July 2006; see http://domains.adrforum.com/decision.aspx [11 July 2006].

[116] The Beijing office has had about 88 cases (including pending cases) up to July 2006, the Hong Kong office about 84 (including pending cases); see www.adndrc.org/adndrc/index.html [11 July 2006].

[117] UDRP Policy, para. 4(d).

[118] See Arts. 21–23 of Commission Regulation 874/2004/EC of 28 April 2004, Laying Down Public-Policy Rules Concerning the Implementation and Functions of the .eu Top Level Domain; see OJ L162 of 30 April 2004, 40.

[119] Like the UDRP, this does not compromise any mediation (unlike the Nominet procedure – Nominet claims to settle 60 per cent of all its cases by mediation; see http://www.nominet.org.uk/disputes/drs [1 April 2008]).

[120] Appointed by EURID on 12 April 2005.

This subsection has given a brief outline of the purpose and structure of the UDRP. The task of the next section is to provide a critique of the procedure from the viewpoint of due process.

### 7.3.2 A critique of the UDRP

This section analyses the due process issues arising from the UDRP.

#### Independence and impartiality

**Complainant win rates**   Various studies have examined the statistical outcomes of UDRP decisions. Milton Mueller found, in his study conducted in 2000, that trademark owners succeed in obtaining the disputed domain name in about 80 per cent of cases, on average, across all dispute-resolution service providers.[121] Some six years later, this figure of the average percentage of complainants winning across all dispute-resolution service providers has increased to around 84 per cent.[122] While these figures in themselves seem high, they do not, by themselves, evidence any unfairness in the procedure, as it is impossible to know what percentage of cases are 'true' cybersquatting cases.

A comparison between the complainant win rate of each dispute-resolution service provider with that provider's market share is more fruitful. Milton Mueller found, in 2000,[123] that the complainant win rate between the different providers varies considerably, and that the two providers with the overwhelming market share each have much higher complainant win rates[124] than the provider with the lowest market share.[125] Ignoring any pending cases, this analysis counts the number of decisions in which the domain name(s) was (were all) transferred or

---

[121]  M. Mueller, 'Rough Justice', 10, Table 3 (this does not take into account the cases settled or withdrawn).

[122]  The group of UDRP dispute-resolution service providers has changed since then, as ADNDRC started to operate in April 2002, and e-Resolution has gone out of business. However, the lion's share of the cases is still heard by WIPO and NAF; see fn. 124. The author has examined the statistics of each provider as shown on the respective websites on 12 July 2006. This figure ignores not only pending cases but also any withdrawn cases or split decisions, and is therefore higher than the figures detailed below. This method has resulted in 10,680 'claimant win' cases out of a total of 12,675 cases (not counting withdrawn cases), equalling 84.3%.

[123]  Mueller, 'Rough Justice', 14–16.

[124]  WIPO: 67.5% and NAF: 71.5% 'complainant win' rate (these figures include the withdrawn/settled cases); 11, Table 4; WIPO: 61% and NAF: 31% market share; *Ibid.* 14, Chart 4.

[125]  e-Resolution complainants won in 44.2% of cases (this includes the withdrawn/settled cases); *ibid.* 11, Table 4; e-Resolution: 7% market share; *ibid.* 14, Chart 4.

cancelled (claimant win) and the cases where the claim was denied (respondent win), as well as those cases that were withdrawn or where the panel returned a split verdict, i.e. where there are several domain names and only some are transferred (neither claimant nor respondent wins). The analysis of the website data of 12 July 2006[126] has produced the following figures:

Table 1. *Market shares and complainant win percentages of the UDRP providers*

|  | WIPO | NAF | CPR | ADNDRC |
|---|---|---|---|---|
| Complainant win | 66.3% | 74.5% | 54.2% | 54.1% |
| Market share | 55.9% | 42.5% | 0.9% | 0.7% |

This would tally with Milton Mueller's figures; however, this does *not* examine other factors such as price or country of origin of complainants. He poses the question of whether these figures are an indication for systemic bias, as the complainant selects the dispute-resolution service provider who, as a consequence, has an incentive to appear to be 'complainant-friendly' in order to increase its market share.[127] In order to avoid such systemic problems, he recommends that the registrar of the domain name concerned, rather than the complainant, should choose which dispute-resolution service provider hears the case.[128]

The claim that forum shopping according to outcome leads to bias, while striking, should at least be questioned. It is difficult to demonstrate a clear and persuasive causal link between the forum shopping and the

---

[126] See fn. 124.

[127] See Mueller, 'Rough Justice', 18: 'it proves that forum-shopping exists to some degree'. He also examined other factors such as price, which he concludes is not a strong explanatory factor (at 15), the complainant's country of origin, which he found significant (NAF for US complainants; WIPO for complainants outside the US; at 17), and speed of decision (at 18). He nevertheless concludes that decision outcome is the strongest factor (at 18). See also M. Halpern and A. Mehrotra, 'Exploring Legal Boundaries within Cyberspace: What Law Controls in a Global Marketplace?' (2000) 21 *University of Pennsylvania Journal of International Economic Law* 523–61, 558 and Geist, 'Fair.com?', 906; A. M. Froomkin and D. Post, 'Froomkin and Post Send Letter to ICANN Board', Letter of 26 January 2000, available from www.icannwatch.org/archive/post_froomkin_udrp_letter.htm [1 April 2008]; and M. Froomkin, 'ICANN's Uniform Dispute Resolution Policy – Causes and (Partial) Cures' (2002) 67 *Brooklyn Law* Review 608–718, 672–3.

[128] See Mueller, 'Rough Justice', 19–20; Froomkin, 'ICANN'S Uniform Dispute Resolution Policy', 673; this, however, may lead to the reverse problem, that service providers have to appear to be registrant-friendly.

actual decision-making. This does not mean that such a link does not exist. Providers have an incentive to create the right perception about dispute outcomes in the minds of the complainants' advisers.[129] The incentive for providers to appear complainant-friendly *may furthermore indirectly* impact on the independence and impartiality of the panellists themselves, but this is extremely difficult to show.[130] The provider's role is limited to providing administrative support.[131] The following discussion will therefore mainly focus on the impartiality and independence of the panellists.

**Impartiality and independence of the panellists**   It should be pointed out that the individual panellists are subject to an express obligation of independence and impartiality, and they have to declare any conflicts of interest.[132]

The panels have held that a panel must only recuse itself if there are grounds on the basis of which a reasonable, objective person would doubt the panellist's impartiality. This would be the case if the panellist had a conflict of interest, such as a financial interest, or had represented a party or a third party in a dispute against one of the parties, or where the panellist had demonstrated personal bias. The evidence relating to bias must establish more than just a hint or insinuation; it must establish serious doubt.[133] This is roughly in line with the traditional jurisprudence on independence and impartiality outlined in Chapter 6.[134]

However, the UDRP Rules do *not* expressly provide for a *challenge* of the panel by one of the parties before an independent third party on the grounds of lack of independence or partiality.[135] Clearly a provision allowing either party to challenge the appointment of a panellist before an independent third-party body, even after a decision has been

---

[129]  Froomkin, 'ICANN's Uniform Dispute Resolution Policy', 690; Thornburg, 'Fast, Cheap and Out of Control', 220.

[130]  In the WIPO Case No. D2001–0558, *AFMA Inc* v. *Globemedia*, the panel pointed out that the provider's role is limited to the administration of cases, and refused to accept that the provider can be biased.

[131]  See also the discussion of bias and the difficulty of proving actual bias at 6.3.1.

[132]  UDRP Rules, r. 7; supplemental rules, ADNDRC Rules, Art. 9; CPR Rules, Art. 7; NAF Rules, Art. 10; and WIPO Rules, Art. 8.

[133]  WIPO Case No. D2001–0505, *Britannia Building Society* v. *Britannia Fraud Prevention*.

[134]  See 6.3.

[135]  Only the .eu ADR Rules and the NAF Rules expressly provide for a challenge of a panellist on the basis of lack of impartiality, independence or integrity, but then only before the institution itself and not an independent third party; see .eu ADR Rules, r. 5(c)–(e) and NAF Rules, r. 10(c)–(e), available from http://domains.adrforum.com/main.aspx?itemID=631&hideBar=False&navID=237&news=26 [1 April 2008].

made, is necessary to render these provisions effective in preventing the appointment of biased panellists.[136] This independent body could be an appeals body.[137]

Also, the providers can influence the outcome of decisions through the selection and allocation of panellists.[138] For this reason, it is necessary to examine in more detail *who* the panellists are and *how* panellists are allocated to a particular case.

**Selection of panellists**    In connection with the question *who* the panellists are, it is important to address questions of *systemic* bias.[139] For example, if *all* panellists were practising trademark lawyers representing trademark owners' interests in their professional capacity, carrying out their 'day' job, it could be concluded that such panel composition is indicative for systemic bias, even if the individual panellist cannot be shown to be biased. Unsurprisingly, the panels themselves have not accepted any arguments that trademark lawyers should not sit on panels on the grounds of bias, since there was no sign of the *individual* panellist's bias.[140]

While in commercial arbitration it has been widely accepted that arbitrators are appointed who are active in the relevant sector,[141] the same should not be automatically assumed for the UDRP procedure, which is mandatory and public. M. Scott Donahey also suggests that the requirements for appearance of impartiality have to be more stringent under the UDRP than in commercial arbitration.[142]

He argues, while asserting the actual integrity and impartiality of the panels, that it would be better if panellists were not representing clients in (other) UDRP procedures, to avoid allegations of systemic bias. However, he also argues that this is unrealistic, as it would effectively bar practitioners from serving as panellists.[143]

By way of example, looking at the CVs of the panellists on the WIPO panel, it appears that the majority of them are, indeed, trademark lawyers,

---

[136] Froomkin, 'ICANN's Uniform Dispute Resolution Policy', 689; see the discussion about appeals, below, at 7.3.2.

[137] See the discussion below.

[138] As Milton Mueller points out himself; 'Rough Justice', 11.

[139] See discussion of systemic bias at 6.3.2.

[140] WIPO Case No. D2001–0505, *Britannia Building Society* v. *Britannia Fraud Prevention*; WIPO Case No. D2004–0535, *United Services Automobile Association* v. *Ang Wa Assoc.*

[141] See 6.3.2.

[142] M. Scott Donahey, 'The Uniform Domain Name Dispute Resolution Process and the Appearance of Partiality – Panelists Impaled on the Horns of a Dilemma' (2002) 19(1) *Journal of International Arbitration* 33–8, 35.

[143] Donahey, 'The Uniform Domain Name Dispute Resolution Process and the Appearance of Partiality', 38.

but a significant proportion of panellists have a different background. For example, forty-eight panellists out of 391 are academics. This figure amounts to 12.3 per cent.[144] The bulk of panellists are trademark lawyers. A more balanced composition of the panellists would be desirable.[145]

**Allocation of panellists**   As to the question of *how* panellists are allocated to individual cases, Michael Geist found that this is an important and troubling aspect of the UDRP in this context.[146] This raises the question of whether, if appointment is left to the provider, providers are apt to appoint panellists who have shown pro-complainant leanings. This problem is mitigated if the parties influence the appointment of panellists.

At a minimum, the parties can decide whether the case should be heard by a one-member or three-member panel.[147] However, the parties do not choose who 'sits' on the single-member panel – panellists are appointed by the dispute-resolution service provider.[148] If the complainant or the respondent decides that the case should be heard by a three-member panel, each party should provide a list nominating three candidates for appointment; the provider then selects one member from each list. The third member of the panel is determined from a list of five possible candidates drawn up by the provider, usually by each party deleting two names from that list.[149] So, for *three-member panels*, the parties cannot appoint the panellists, but they at least have some degree of influence over panel composition.[150]

Therefore, non-transparent or even biased panel allocation is more of an issue for single-member panels. Michael Geist examined the difference in the 'complainant win' rates for single-member panels (with

---

[144] Looking at the list of WIPO panellists on the relevant website on 15 July 2006, and counting the panellists on the lists whose CV indicated that their main occupation was academic. It is the author's assumption that there is a lower likelihood of systemic pro-trademark-holder bias among academics than there is among trademark lawyers.

[145] Froomkin, 'ICANN's Uniform Dispute Resolution Policy', 693; Ware, 'Default Rules from Mandatory Rules', 163; looking at the CVs of the panellists used for the .eu domain name ADR, it also seems the case that the majority of panellists are IP attorneys; see www.adr.eu/adr/panelists/index.php [1 April 2008].

[146] Geist, 'Fair.com?', 911: 'The study finds that influence over panel composition is likely the most important controlling factor in determining case outcomes.'

[147] UDRP Rules, r. 3(b)(iv) and 5(b)(iv), available from www.icann.org/dndr/udrp/uniform-rules.htm#3bxiii [1 April 2008].

[148] UDRP Rules, r. 6(b) provides that a single panellist is appointed by the dispute-resolution service provider. This is the same under the .eu domain-name procedure; .eu ADR Rules, r. 4(b).

[149] UDRP Rules, r. 6(e).      [150] At least where the respondent takes part in the procedure.

panel allocation being solely controlled by the provider) and for three-member panels (where the parties have some degree of control over who is appointed). This produced an astonishing result: for cases decided by sole panellists, complainants win in 83 per cent of cases, whereas for three-member panels, that rate drops considerably to 58 per cent.[151]

He posits that the reason for this remarkable difference is that respondents have an input to who sits on the panel, and that deliberation between the panellists results in more balanced decision-making.[152] For this reason, he recommends that all UDRP cases should be heard by three-member panels.[153]

The process for the appointment of single panellists is, indeed, not transparent. The UDRP Rules merely provide that if no three-member panel is requested, the dispute-resolution service provider selects the single panellist to decide the case.[154] The WIPO Rules[155] and the NAF Rules[156] do not contain any supplemental provisions on the criteria to shed any light on the question of how single-panel members are selected. The .eu ADR procedure also does not explain how panellists are appointed.[157]

Interestingly, the ADNDRC Rules make an exception, stating that panellists shall be appointed according to the following benchmarks:[158]

  (i)   the nature of the dispute
 (ii)   the availability of the panellist
(iii)   the identity of the parties
 (iv)   the independence and impartiality of the panellist
  (v)   any stipulation in the registration agreement and
 (vi)   any suggestions made by the parties themselves.

---

[151] Geist, 'Fair.com?', 912, 922.

[152] He excluded other factors, such as the possibility that in three-member-panel cases, the respondent has a better case, and hence elects a three-member panel. He found that a significant number of three-member panels are requested by complainants, and that in some cases where a three-member panel is requested by the complainant, the respondent defaults (which might indicate, on the contrary, that the respondent has a 'bad' case): Geist, 'Fair.com?', 923–6.

[153] Geist, 'Fair.com?', 930–1.       [154] UDRP Rules, r. 6(b).

[155] WIPO Rules, available from http://arbiter.wipo.int/domains/rules/supplemental/index.html#7 [1 April 2008].

[156] NAF Rules (Version 1 January 2006), available from http://domains.adrforum.com/main.aspx?itemID=631&hideBar=False&navID=237&news=26 [1 April 2008].

[157] .eu ADR Rules, r. 4(a) merely states that 'the panelists shall be selected in accordance to the internal procedures of the Providers'.

[158] ADNDRC Rules, Art. 8(1), available from www.icann.org/en/dndr/udrp/uniform-rules.htm [1 April 2008].

While it is laudable that the ADNDRC has attempted to formulate criteria for the selection of panellists in order to make the process more transparent, looking at the criteria more closely, it is questionable how useful they are, due to their vagueness. It is unclear how criterion (i), the nature of the dispute, should influence the selection. Furthermore, the question must be asked how the identity of the parties should be relevant for choosing a panellist. It would be sensible to choose a panellist of the same nationality as the parties if the parties are both nationals of the same country,[159] or to choose a panellist of a nationality different from each party where the parties are nationals of different countries.[160] Furthermore, language capability[161] and availability of the panellist are other important, practical criteria. These factors apart, a completely random selection of panellists would be fairer.

It is even more significant that the ADNDRC Rules allow the parties some influence over the selection, even where only a single panellist is appointed. This occurs in two ways. Firstly, one of the selection benchmarks is a stipulation in the registration agreement, which gives the registrant some influence.[162] Secondly, the Rules provide that if the parties do not elect a three-member panel for the dispute, and if the respondent files a defence, the ADNDRC sends the parties a list of five panellists, and the panellist ranking highest with both parties is appointed.[163]

The aim of this book is not to prove whether or not panellist allocation under the UDRP is in fact biased or not,[164] but merely to point out that non-transparent allocation of arbitrators to a case is problematic.

---

[159] WIPO Case No. D2005–0597, *Tvist Giyim Sanayi Pazarlama Ve Ticaret A. S. v. Machka Company.*

[160] WIPO Case No. D2000–0827, *William Hill Organization Limited v. Lisa Jane Statton.* This may be a problem where the panellist needs to speak the language of one of the parties; see the discussion on language at 7.3.2. Also, WIPO Case No. D2004–0643, *Tatra banka v. US WARE INC,* where the appointment of the panellist was challenged on the basis that he was Czech and one of the parties was Slovak; this challenge rightly failed, as it would have been impossible to find a panellist who spoke the relevant language, as there are few, if any, e.g. Korean panellists who speak Czech.

[161] UDRP Rules, r. 11(a); the language of the proceedings should generally be the language of the registration agreement – this provision, of course, has an impact on panellist selection.

[162] If only by choosing the registrar in the first place.

[163] If the case is a default case, then the ADNDRC appoints a single panellist without reference to a list. ADNDRC Rules, Art. 8(4) and (5), available from www.adndrc.org/adndrc/bj_supplemental_rules.html [1 April 2008]. This footnote refers to the rules of the Beijing Office, but Art. 8 is the same in the supplemental rules for the Hong Kong and the Seoul Offices.

[164] Merely working out how many cases each panellist has heard, and in how many cases he or she has ruled in favour of the complainant, is probably not sufficient, as this would not take account of other factors. However, it would be interesting to compile these figures,

There are two possible solutions to avoid *any appearance* of bias. One solution would be to allow the parties some control over the choice of arbitrator.[165] The other is random selection, after practical criteria such as availability, nationality and language capability have been satisfied.[166] In the context of the UDRP, it may, indeed, be advisable to have all cases decided by a three-member panel, as this would be likely to improve the quality of the decision-making.[167]

**Conclusion** From discussing the independence and impartiality of the UDRP, a distinction has to be made between the role of the dispute-resolution service provider and the panellists. The independence and impartiality of the provider can only be guaranteed if providers are allocated randomly to cases. However, the independence and impartiality of the panellists is more important for the outcome, and should hence be the focus of this discussion. It is recommended here that there should be an independent third-party ruling on any challenge brought by a party alleging a conflict of interest or bias of a panellist. In addition, the composition of the panels should be more balanced, with fewer trademark attorneys and more non-trademark interests, such as academics, being represented on the lists. The parties should have more control over the allocation of the panellists to a case, or such allocation should be random. Furthermore, the introduction of three-member panels for all UDRP cases should be considered in order to improve the quality of decision-making.

### Notice and service to the respondent

Tracing a respondent and effecting actual notice can be difficult to achieve for any complainant in an international dispute. In order to overcome this issue, the UDRP Rules state that the complainant need not necessarily achieve actual notice, and service is effected by the dispute-resolution service provider sending the notification and complaint to the contact points

---

as Michael Geist's study is now five years old and there are many more decided cases to gain data from.

[165] For example by giving the parties a list of nine arbitrators from which they can each delete four.

[166] Froomkin, 'ICANN's Uniform Dispute Resolution Policy', 691 – discussing all options and stating that registrar selection would be best. However, the problem there is that registrars themselves have an incentive to be 'registrant-friendly' – hence such a system might create systemic bias poled the reverse way.

[167] And would still be cheaper than court proceedings: the current fees are $4,000 (WIPO for one to five domain names), $2,600–2,900 (NAF for one to five domain names), $4,500–6,000 (CPR for one to five domain names) and $2,500–3,000 (ADNDRC for one to five domain names).

listed in the UDRP Rules. These are: (i) all contacts in the registrar's Whois and billing database (by post, fax, email); (ii) an email to 'postmaster@' at the disputed domain name; (iii) an email address on the website to which the domain name resolves; and (iv) any contact details provided by the respondent or the complainant. The provider must send the notification and the complaint to all these various contact points.[168] Since it is in the respondent's sphere of control to keep his or her contact details with the registrar up to date, these provisions on notice and service are fair.

## Fair hearing: minimum standards and equality

As has been shown in Chapter 6 of this book, the principle of fair hearing means that the parties should have a fair and equal opportunity to argue their case as to law and fact.[169] The principle raises two distinct but frequently confounded issues, namely: minimum standards of quality and rationality, and equality.[170]

In commercial arbitration, it is difficult to draw a bottom line of minimum requirements as to procedural fairness because of the principle of party autonomy, with the consequence that a discussion of 'fair hearing' is usually limited to the issue of equality. However, the UDRP is fundamentally different from commercial arbitration in that it is not a voluntary but a mandatory procedure, and hence fairness should have a separate meaning in addition to equality.[171] The reason for this is that the UDRP is not an entirely private procedure, but has public law elements.[172]

An examination of whether the UDRP provides for a fair hearing therefore raises the two questions of whether the UDRP complies with

---

[168] UDRP Rules, r. 2(a).    [169] See 6.4.2.    [170] See 2.2.1 and 2.2.2.

[171] Thornburg, 'Fast, Cheap and Out of Control', 215; Donahey, 'The Uniform Domain Name Dispute Resolution Process and the Appearance of Partiality', 34–5; see also *Parisi v. Netlearning Inc*, 139 FSupp2d 745, 751 (District Court ED Va 2001): 'the UDRP's unique contractual arrangements renders the FAA's provisions for judicial review of arbitration awards inapplicable'. This is a similar argument to the one advanced in relation to consumer arbitration above; see 7.2; S. Ware, 'Domain Name Arbitration in the Arbitration-Law Context: Consent to, and Fairness in the UDRP' (2002) 6 *Journal of Small and Emerging Business Law* 129–65, 150. He argues that fairness is secondary to consent, and since domain-name registrants consent to participate in the UDRP when registering a domain name, this provides sufficient legitimacy; see 153–4.

[172] This has been recognised by the US courts. For example, in *Eurotech Inc v. Cosmos European Travels AG*, 189 FSupp2d 385, 392 (District Court ED Va 2002), the Court held that 'arbitration' under WIPO auspices was not an entirely private matter, as WIPO was a quasi-public organisation.

minimum standards of fairness *and* whether the UDRP treats both parties equally. With these two questions in mind, the procedural rules are examined.

These two principles are contained in r. 10(b) of the UDRP Rules, which provides that 'in all cases, the Panel shall ensure that the Parties are treated with equality and that each Party is given a fair opportunity to present its case'.

This statement of principle notwithstanding, each party's opportunity to present its respective case is severely and stringently curtailed in five ways.

**No (online) hearings**    Firstly, both parties are affected by the rule that there will be no hearings unless exceptional circumstances are present.[173] The UDRP Rules make clear that this includes any form of tele-, Web- or video-conferencing.[174] In practice, this means that any form of hearing will be extremely rare.[175]

The same applies for the .eu domain-name procedure.[176] Interestingly, the only dispute-resolution service provider accredited to date, the Czech Arbitration Court, *does* envisage the use of ICT and online hearings. In its Supplemental .eu ADR Rules, it provides:[177] 'In case the Panel determines, in its sole discretion, that an in-person hearing is necessary, the hearing will be carried out by teleconference, videoconference, or webconference at the CHAT address of the Provider if both Parties agree with the use of such technology.'

In the ordinary procedure, the parties' submissions are limited to two documents – a complaint and a response – in the vast majority of cases.[178] The issue here is the credibility and accuracy of these documents, there being no opportunity to probe this information in the examination of witnesses, and the UDRP not providing any penalties for making false statements in the complaint or the response.[179]

---

[173] UDRP Rules, r. 13.       [174] *Ibid.*
[175] WIPO Case No. D2001–0830, *AT&T Corp* v. *Randy Thompson*; WIPO Case No. D2001–1369, *Nintendo of America Inc* v. *Enic. Net*; WIPO Case No. D2004–1042, *Jenna Massoli p/k/a Jenna Jameson* v. *Linq Entertainment Inc*; and in NAF Case No. 95752, *Millennium Broadcasting Corporation* v. *Publication France Monde*, the panels refused to allow a request for an oral hearing by stating that no such hearing was necessary.
[176] See .eu ADR Rules, r. 9.       [177] At r. 7.
[178] See the UDRP Rules, rr. 3 and 5, and see the discussion on further submissions in the next section.
[179] Thornburg, 'Fast, Cheap and Out of Control', 217–18.

**Further submissions**    Secondly, considering this limitation of the material on which the decision is based, the question arises whether the panel has the power to probe further if there are any gaps in the evidence. To what extent can panels ask for further submissions or ask for clarification of specific points?

The UDRP Rules provide that a panel may request further statements or documents.[180] However, this power is rarely exercised. According to the Legal Index of all WIPO UDRP decisions, panels have availed themselves of this power only in 0.42 per cent of all cases.[181] Panels may well find it difficult to find the time to request and consider additional evidence, as the panel has only fourteen days from its appointment to make a decision.[182] However, in exceptional circumstances, the panel can extend the time for reaching its decisions; in some of the few cases where the panels have asked for further evidence, this has been done.[183]

**Complainant has no right of reply**    The third point to make here is that the complainant has no regular right to a reply. The UDRP Rules do not expressly allow the parties to submit further statements or documents on their own initiative.[184] The Rules merely provide that the panel decides the admissibility of evidence, and this includes any supplemental filings.[185]

The WIPO and ADNDRC Rules do not add anything to the UDRP Rules on this point. By contrast, the NAF Rules allow either party to file additional written statements or documents[186] within five days after the deadline for the response, for the additional substantial sum of $400.[187] If one party files such an additional statement or document, the other party is entitled to respond to it within five days.[188] The CPR (International Institute for Conflict Prevention & Resolution) Rules allowed parties to submit further statements and documents, but left it to the discretion of each individual panel whether or not it admitted such further statements and documents.[189]

---

[180] UDRP Rules, r. 12; likewise the .eu ADR Rules, r. 8: the panel may request or admit, in its sole discretion, further statements or documents from either of the parties.

[181] Thirty-eight cases out of 9,008 as of 31 July 2006.     [182] UDRP Rules, r. 15(b).

[183] WIPO Case No. 2000–0017, *Draw-Tite Inc* v. *Plattsburgh Spring Inc*; WIPO Case No. 2003–0043, *Fiji Rugby Union* v. *Webmasters Limited*.

[184] Pointed out by the panel in WIPO Case No. D2002–0635, *Classmates Online Inc* v. *John Zuccarini*.

[185] UDRP Rules, r. 10 (d); WIPO Case No. D2005–1246, *Admerex Limited* v. *Metyor Inc.*

[186] But no amendments to the original 'pleadings'.

[187] NAF Rules, r. 7(a) and (b).     [188] *Ibid.* r. 7(c).     [189] CPR Rules, r. 10.

While the respondent is able to react to and answer to the allega-tions made by the complainant, the complainant cannot, as a matter of course, respond to the points raised in the response, and therefore has to anticipate and second-guess the respondent's case. This disadvantages the complainant and is contrary to the principle that each party should have an opportunity to respond to the submissions of the other. For this reason, some WIPO panels have allowed complainants to submit an additional statement to deal with unanticipated defences.[190] However, in most cases, the panels have disallowed a reply in the interest of expedition.[191]

**Narrow word or page limit**   Fourthly, most dispute-resolution service providers provide a narrow word or page limit for the complaint and the response.[192] Considering that the complaint and the response contain all legal arguments forming the basis for the decision, this is restrictive. The word and page limits have, in fact, been insisted upon by providers in some cases;[193] however, in other cases, panels have generally taken into account the full submissions, even though they exceeded the word or page limit.[194]

[190] The WIPO Legal Index of Decisions indicates that there have been ninety-nine deci-sions in which a supplemental filing was requested, and forty of these have been granted; see http://arbiter.wipo.int/cgi-bin/domains/search/legalindex?lang=eng#12300 [13 August 2006]. For example, WIPO Case No. D2000–0853, *Investissement Marius Saradar S. A. L.* v. *John Naffah*; WIPO Case No. D2004–0023, *Custom Bilt Metals* v. *Con-quest Consulting*; WIPO Case No. D2005–0410, *Southwest Airlines Co* v. *Cattitude a/k/a LJ Gehman*; WIPO Case No. D2005–0508, *Microsoft Corporation* v. *Source One Management Services Inc.* In WIPO Case No. D2000–1648, *Benzer* v. *FutureSoft Consulting Inc and Sunil Bhatia*, the panel even went so far as saying that the complainant had a right to reply.
[191] In fifty-nine out of ninety-nine decisions, the panels refused to consider supplemental fil-ings; see http://arbiter.wipo.int/cgi-bin/domains/search/legalindex?lang=eng#12300 [13 August 2006]. For example, WIPO Case No. D2000–0166, *Plaza Operating Partners Ltd* v. *Pop Data Technologies Inc*; WIPO Case No. D2000–0938, *Parfums Christian Dior SA* v. *Jadore*; WIPO Case No. D2003–0447, *The EW Scripps Company* v. *Sinologic Industries*; WIPO Case No. D2003–0780, *DK Bellevue Inc d/b/a Digital Kitchen* v. *Sam Landers*.
[192] WIPO provides a word limit of 5,000 words each for the complaint and the response, but no word limit for the panel decision: WIPO Rules, r. 10; NAF provides that the complaint and the response must not exceed ten pages: NAF Rules, rr. 4(a) and 5(a); CPR Rules provided the same as NAF: see CPR Rules, rr. 4 and 5; and ADNDRC Rules provide for an even tighter word limit of only 3,000 words for the complaint and the response, but no word limit for the panel decision: ADNDRC Rules, r. 13; the Czech Arbitration Court provides a word limit of 5,000 words for the complaint, response and panel decision: see .eu ADR Rules, r. 11.
[193] See WIPO Case No. D2005–0976, *Giga Pty Limited* v. *Elena Sadkovaya*, where the com-plainant was asked to submit a shorter complaint complying with the word limit.
[194] See WIPO Case No. D2001–0581, *Valero Energy Corporation* v. *American Distribution Systems*; NAF Case No. 97031, *Dykema Gossett PLLC* v. *DefaultData.com*; in NAF Case

Furthermore, the word or page limits only apply to the legal argument, not to the evidence adduced in any annexes.[195] Hence, in practice, this limit does not unduly restrict the parties' opportunity to present their respective cases.

**Short time limit for filing the response**    Fifthly, the main restriction is the short time limit for the filing of the response. This is a significant restriction that affects respondents only.

The respondent has twenty days from the day on which the dispute-resolution service provider has forwarded the complaint[196] to file a response – this time period is less than three weeks.[197] This is a short time period in itself if the respondent has to find a lawyer, prepare his or her case and gather evidence, for example in respect of showing a legitimate use of the domain name.[198] Moreover, the period for preparing the response is even shorter if the respondent cannot be reached by (more or less) instantaneous forms of communication such as fax and email and the communication is delayed in the post, or where the respondent is an individual who is temporarily absent. In addition, this extremely short time limit for serving a response is determinative for the outcome in a case, as there are usually no other opportunities to submit legal argument or evidence. Therefore this time limit is likely to hamper the respondent's defence significantly.

> No. 122224, *The Trustees of the Trust Number SR-1* v. *Turnberry, Scotland Golf and Leisure*, the panel found that the respondent complied with the ten-page limit, even though the response was 11,000 words (which in font size 12 of Times New Roman would be about twenty-two to twenty-five pages). By contrast, in NAF Case No. 318079, *Advanced Research & Technology Institute, Inc* v. *Eric LeVin*, the panel refused to consider the respondent's 102-page (sic) response, which mainly consisted of diatribe irrelevant to the case at issue, and the panel rightly pointed out that it was not its function to 'search through Respondent's venomous attacks on others to find substance somewhere within the many pages of offensive, boorish, racist and anti-Semitic statements'.

[195] The word limit only applies to the description of the grounds set out in the policy, and so does not cover evidence, which may be submitted in the annexes; see WIPO Case No. D2001–0558, *AFMA Inc* v. *Globemedia*.

[196] UDRP Rules, rr. 4(c) and 5(a).

[197] Under the .eu domain-name procedure, the respondent has thirty *working* days, which is about six weeks; see EC Regulation 874/2004, Art. 22(8). It seems that a lesson has been learnt from the tightness of the deadline under the UDRP.

[198] Such as showing demonstrable preparations to use the domain name in connection with a bona fide offering of goods or services: UDRP Policy, para. 4(c)(i); or a showing that he or she was known under that name: *ibid.* para. 4(c)(ii); or demonstrating legitimate non-commercial fair use: *ibid.* para. 4(c)(iii).

The UDRP Rules provide that in *exceptional circumstances*, the dispute-resolution service provider may extend the deadline for filing the response.[199] This wording suggests that an extension is not to be granted as a matter of course, and that the dispute-resolution service provider or the panel have discretion as to whether or not to grant such an extension.

The WIPO and ADNDRC Rules do not elaborate further on the question of under what precise circumstances and how the deadline for filing a response can be extended.

The NAF Rules stipulate[200] a procedure that must be complied with. The respondent must ask the complainant whether he or she agrees to the extension, and must submit the request in writing before the deadline for filing the response, stating the exceptional circumstances for the request and how much additional time is needed. The maximum extension granted is an additional twenty days, and the respondent must accompany the request with a filing fee of $100.[201]

This raises the question of whether and in what circumstances extra time has, in fact, been allowed, and how restrictive the criterion of 'exceptional circumstances' is.[202]

Looking at some of the relevant WIPO decisions,[203] it seems that the WIPO Center (WIPO Arbitration and Mediation Center) obtains the complainant's comments before deciding whether or not to grant an extension of time for filing the response.[204] In some cases, short

---

[199] UDRP Rules, r. 5(d).       [200] NAF Rules, r. 6(a)(i).

[201] Presumably this fee is to cover additional administrative costs, but also to deter respondents.

[202] Based on an examination of WIPO and NAF panel decisions, as these two cover the lion's share of all cases.

[203] No quantitative research has been undertaken that analyses all the decisions in which the issue of an extension of time for filing the response, or the issue of a late filing of a response, has arisen – a keyword search of all WIPO domain-name decisions for 'extension of time' in the same phrase as 'response' indicates that there are 6,767 decisions (as of 31 July 2006); see the search engine provided on the WIPO Center website www.wipo.int/amc/en/domains/search [31 July 2006]. A random sample of twenty WIPO cases have been examined in closer detail.

[204] UDRP Rules, r. 5(d) also provides that the parties may extend the time by written agreement with the approval of the dispute-resolution service provider. If the complainant agrees to the extension of time, the WIPO Center will usually grant such an extension; see, for example, WIPO Case No. D2002–1129, *Puerto Rico Tourism Co* v. *Virtual Countries Inc*, where the due date for the response fell on 2 January 2003, and the complainant agreed that the deadline should be extended by twenty days because of the Christmas holiday period.

extensions of time of two to twelve days have been allowed.[205] However, the WIPO Center has been reluctant to grant an extension of fourteen days or more in cases where the complainant did not consent to such an extension.[206]

In reviewing the question of an extension of time, panels emphasise the duty of the panel to ensure that proceedings are conducted in an expeditious manner.[207] Most panels have interpreted the 'exceptional circumstances' for extension narrowly, and, likewise, several panels have held that late responses should be disregarded where real, exceptional circumstances are absent.[208]

In sharp contrast, the NAF more readily allows extensions of time, provided a formal request for extension, accompanied by the fee of $100, is filed in a timely manner, and the procedure set out in r. 6(a)(i) of the NAF Rules has been complied with.[209]

---

[205] WIPO Case No. D2004–1030, *Allee Willis* v. *NetHollywood*: the respondent asked for an extension of sixty days; the WIPO Center permitted seven days; WIPO Case No. D2000–1648, *Benzer* v. *FutureSoft Consulting Inc and Sunil Bhatia*: the panel allowed twenty days because one of the respondents was out of his country of residence.

[206] WIPO Case No. D2003–0091, *International Health Insurance Danmark Forsikringsaktiesel-skab* v. *Cortes jr. Fernando*; WIPO Case No. D2004–1030, *Allee Willis* v. *NetHollywood*; WIPO Case No. D2002–0241, *The Leading Hotels of the World Ltd* v. *Online Travel Group*.

[207] UDRP Rules, r. 10(c); WIPO Case No. D2004–1030, *Allee Willis* v. *NetHollywood*; WIPO Case No. D2004–0614, *Museum of Science* v. *Jason Date*: 'otherwise parties will feel free to disregard deadlines and respondents will regularly submit late responses'.

[208] In WIPO Case No. D2003–0033, *1099Pro Inc* v. *Convey Compliance Systems Inc*, the majority of the panel refused to accept a response filed ten days late, even though the respondent was not legally represented or advised. The reason that the period concerned was the 'busiest time of our season' was not regarded as sufficient cause for an extension. In WIPO Case No. D2005–1304, *Mobile Communication Service Inc* v. *WebReg*, the panel refused to accept a response eight days late. It considered that the respondent's clerical error in entering the wrong date in its calendar was not a valid ground to accept a late submission, nor that the respondent's legal representative was busy on another case. In WIPO Case No. D2005–0994, *Fashiontv.com GmbH* v. *Chris Olic*, a response filed two days late was disregarded; the reason given was that the respondents had difficulties in obtaining evidence. Again, this was not regarded as exceptional circumstances. Finally, the mislaying of files in the respondent's archive was also not considered a sufficient ground for an extension of time in WIPO Case No. DRO2005–0005, *OMV AG* v. *SC Mondokommerz SRL*.

[209] A search for the phrase 'extension of time' in the search engine for the NAF decisions at http://domains.adrforum.com/decision.aspx [26 July 2006] flushed out fifty-five records. Out of these, the NAF did not accept a request for an extension of time in two cases, and in another four cases it did not allow a late response. Many decisions simply state that the respondent applied for an extension of time in accordance with the procedure, and that it was granted, without detailing the exceptional circumstances relied on. In some cases, the reasons are stated, for example NAF has allowed an extension of time of

Most NAF panel decisions do not state whether or not the complainant has agreed to the extension, but the respondent must have conferred with the complainant as part of the procedure. In the few cases where the panel did not allow an extension of time, the respondent had not complied with the procedure for the request under NAF Rules, r. 6(a)(i).[210] Where the response was simply late, most panels have refused to take it into account,[211] whereas a few other panels have still considered it.[212]

The conclusion from the foregoing is that although there is a possibility to extend the extremely short time limit for serving the response in exceptional circumstances, this does not alleviate the problem that this time limit is too short, as an extension will only be granted in really exceptional circumstances (WIPO) or is restricted to an additional twenty days (NAF). Furthermore, the panel decisions on whether a late response is permissible are inconsistent.

The mere fact that the keyword search used to find WIPO cases[213] – in which there was an issue about the extension of time for filing a response – flushed up 6,767 cases (out of a total of 9,008[214]) shows that the tightness of the twenty-day deadline causes problems for many respondents preparing their case. Milton Mueller explains the high default rate partly by the fact

---

fifteen days where the respondent had problems in finding an available lawyer: NAF Case No. 94243, *Youtv Inc* v. *Erkan Alemdar*, or NAF Case No. 692150, *Charles Letts & Co Ltd* v. *Citipublications*, where the respondent was given an additional twenty days with the agreement of the complainant, as he was out of his country of residence.

[210] NAF Case No. 545232, *Tata Sons Ltd* v. *US Citizen aka Sojan Pulickal*; NAF Case No. 96694, *Victoria's Secret et al* v. *Sherry Hardin*.

[211] NAF Case No. 114758, *Foley & Lardner* v. *Brian G Wick*: the panellist refused to accept the response, even though the electronic copy was filed on time, as the hardcopy form and annexes were four days late; NAF Case No. 545232, *Tata Sons Ltd* v. *US Citizen aka Sojan Pulickal*, where the response was a couple of days late; see also NAF Case No. 95823, *Wombat Enterprises Inc d/b/a Domain-It!* v. *Advanced Network Technologies* and NAF Case No. 94941, *Gorstew Limited* v. *Shop A-Z.com Inc*.

[212] For example, in NAF Case No. 94346, *Tall Oaks Publishing Inc* v. *National Trade Publications Inc*, the panel took into consideration a response that was eleven days overdue, without having been given any reason for the late filing; see also NAF Case No. 112469, *Gaiam Inc* v. *Nielsen*, where the panel accepted a response twenty-two days after the deadline, as the respondent asserted that he had not received the complaint until after the deadline had expired.

[213] A similar search was not possible for the NAF cases, as the search engine on the NAF decision site does not allow the use of the Boolean connector 'within', which makes it impossible to search for a phrase.

[214] As of 31 July 2006.

that the UDRP procedure moves so fast that ordinary domain-name registrants may be prevented from defending themselves.[215]

It can also be argued that there is an imbalance between the complainant and the respondent: the complainant has no time limit for preparing the complaint, which contrasts with the extremely tight deadline for respondents.[216] Admittedly, this is a prejudice inherent in all forms of adjudication. The party commencing the proceedings is always at a tactical advantage, as they may choose the right moment to do so. However, under the UDRP, the trademark owner always starts the proceedings, and the registrant is always in the position of respondent, as the UDRP does not allow the registrant to ask for a declaration that it had legitimate rights and that the registration was not abusive. In that sense, it could be argued that the UDRP is severely discriminating against the domain-name registrant, who is handicapped in the preparation of a defence.

**Conclusion**    This section has discussed the procedural restrictions that the UDRP and the supplemental rules impose on the parties in proving their case. The question that has to be answered is whether these strictures make the procedure unfair. For this, it is important to decide which yardstick the procedure should be measured against. As has been said at the outset of this section, the procedural standards of traditional commercial arbitration should not be applied, the UDRP being a mandatory procedure. If the purpose of a procedure is to establish the facts and to apply the law, sufficient legal argument and evidence must be allowed to make the procedure rational and fair.[217] Decision outcomes, based on partial argument and facts, become irrational. However, too much procedure will lead to delay and expense, making the procedure inaccessible and slow. Hence the amount of procedural protection has to be proportionate to the issues at stake.

A domain name can be extremely valuable to the parties, and the application of the UDRP involves many fact-intensive issues, on which evidence must be led.[218] Such fact-intensive issues include, for example, proving the existence of an unregistered trademark, the respondent's legitimate interest in the domain name or the question of bad faith. As discussed above, the parties' opportunity to present their case has been severely

---

[215] Mueller, 'Rough Justice', 12.
[216] Thornburg, 'Fast, Cheap and Out of Control', 216.
[217] See Chapter 2 for a discussion of the relationship between rationality and fairness.
[218] Thornburg, 'Fast, Cheap and Out of Control', 198–9.

curtailed. Many authors have stated that the UDRP is not suitable to decide such complex and important issues.[219]

The main procedural defects identified are: the rule that there are no (online) hearings; that there is no right to a reply; the restrictions on further submissions of material; and, most significantly, the short time limit for filing the response. These defects mean that the UDRP has too stringently curtailed legal argument and factual evidence, and this restricts the amount of material the panels can consider, leading to irrational and inconsistent decisions. In addition, there is also a violation of the principle of equality. The procedure does not treat the parties equally, as complainants have the unequal burden of anticipating the respondents' case, and respondents are crippled by the short timeframe set for the response. It is therefore submitted that the procedure is unfair.

A longer time period for filing the response, such as eight rather than three weeks would not prejudice the complainant disproportion-ately. Likewise, the use of ICT to allow for distance hearings (by tele-conferencing, Web- or video-conferencing) may make the procedure fairer by allowing more argument and evidence to be admitted, and by allow-ing further questions be put to the parties to clarify issues and some limited cross-examination, without adding too much in terms of cost and delay. The rules governing further submissions should be relaxed, and a right of reply introduced. These procedural issues will be taken into account for the due process standards established in the model in Chapter 8.[220]

## Language

In many UDRP proceedings, the complainant trademark holder and the respondent domain-name registrant will be located in different countries and will be speaking different languages. The language issue is a tricky one. Proceedings conducted in a language foreign to one party may well deprive that party from having meaningful access to the proceedings or a fair and equal opportunity to present his or her case. Also, translation may add significant cost.[221]

In this context, it should be pointed out that an official version of the UDRP only exists in English.

---

[219] Froomkin, 'ICANN's Uniform Dispute Resolution Policy', 698.
[220] See 8.3.
[221] Discussed in WIPO Case No. D2000–1759, *Beiersdorf AG* v. *Good Deal Communications.*

Rule 11(a) of the UDRP Rules states that the proceedings shall be held in the language of the registration agreement.[222] The panel may direct that documents be translated into that language.[223] The purpose of this rule is to protect the respondent, who, of course, chooses the registrar and hence has some influence on the language of the registration agreement and, indirectly, the proceedings.

However, r. 11(a) of the UDRP Rules also states that the panel has discretion to direct that the proceedings may be conducted in another language. A rigid rule that proceedings should always be conducted in the language of the registration agreement clearly does not make sense, for example, where both parties are proficient and comfortable to communicate in the same language[224] and the registration agreement is in a language different from that, or where the respondent, despite being notified in the language of the registration agreement, does not file a response.[225]

WIPO panels have made clear that the notification of the complaint to the respondent should always be in the language of the registration agreement, to give the respondent an opportunity to appreciate the true nature of the proceedings and a chance to object to the proceedings being held in English.[226]

An issue may arise from the way panels have exercised their discretion under r. 11(a) of the UDRP Rules. In particular, here the question arises as to whether panels are able to assess the respondent's language proficiency merely on the basis of a one-off communication such as a letter written to the dispute-resolution service provider or to the complainant. In many cases, panels have allowed proceedings in English on a vague assessment that the respondent would be proficient in that language.[227] For example,

---

[222] The same applies to the .eu ADR proceedings; see EC Regulation 874/2004, Art. 22(4) – most panel proceedings are conducted in English; see www.adr.eu/adr/decisions/index.php [1 April 2008].

[223] UDRP Rules, r. 11(b).

[224] See, for example, WIPO Case No. D2003–0679, *Deutsche Messe AG* v. *Kim Hyungho*; WIPO Case No. D2003–0989, *Dassault Aviation* v. *Mr Minwoo Park*; in both cases the panel determined that the Korean respondent was able to communicate in English without difficulty.

[225] See, for example, WIPO Case No. D2003–0774, *Amazon.com Inc* v. *Kim Yoon-Jo* or WIPO Case No. D2005–0407, *Auchan* v. *Oushang Chaoshi*.

[226] Expressly stated in the WIPO Rules, r. 4(a); see also WIPO Case No. D2000–1759, *Beiersdorf AG* v. *Good Deal Communications*; WIPO Case No. D2005–0407, *Auchan* v. *Oushang Chaoshi*.

[227] For example, WIPO Case No. D2000–1759, *Beiersdorf AG* v. *Good Deal Communications*; WIPO Case No. D2003–0679, *Deutsche Messe AG* v. *Kim Hyungho*; WIPO Case

in one case,[228] the domain name was registered with Neptia, a Korean registrar, and the respondent requested in a letter, written in English, that the proceedings be held in Korean, pointing out that the registration agreement was in Korean and that he did not speak English well. The panel simply took this letter itself as proof that the registrant was able to communicate in English, and for this reason declined to conduct the proceedings in Korean and reached a default decision when the complainant did not file a response.

In conclusion, it should be pointed out that to comply with rr. 10(b) and 11(a) of the UDRP Rules, the notification at least should be translated into the language of the registration agreement; panels should be slow to infer that respondents are proficient in English, and respondents should be allowed to file documents in the language of the registration agreement.

## Use of online technology

As has been discussed in Chapter 5, the use of online technology is important, as it renders dispute resolution more efficient and, hence, fairer.[229]

The use of online technology in the UDRP procedure varies slightly between the different dispute-resolution service providers. Two types of online technology are currently in use: WIPO, NAF and ADNDRC allow the parties to submit the complaint and the response as an attachment to an email and to communicate by email; alternatively, WIPO, NAF, ADNDRC and the Czech Court of Arbitration have set up an online case-filing system, which enables both parties to file their submissions by uploading documents via the Internet. In addition, the WIPO, NAF and ADNDRC have made available electronic templates of forms to facilitate filing.[230]

As has been discussed above, the UDRP does not envisage the use of innovative communications for online hearings.[231] The imaginative use of technology for real-time interaction, such as Web- and

---

No. D2003–0989, *Dassault Aviation* v. *Mr Minwoo Park*; WIPO Case No. D2005–0407, *Auchan* v. *Oushang Chaoshi*; NFA Case No. 110843, *BEA Systems* v. *Park Sung Jo*.

[228] NFA Case No. 110843, *BEA Systems* v. *Park Sung Jo*.          [229] See 5.5.

[230] WIPO Rules, r. 3(a)(ii) and (iii): see www.wipo.int/amc/en/domains/filing/udrp/index. html; NAF website at http://domains.adrforum.com/main.aspx?itemID=276&hideBar= False&navID=202&news=26 and ADNDRC, NAF Rules, r. 3(1) and website at www.adndrc.org/adndrc/bj_download.html [1 April 2008].

[231] Contrast this with the provisions in the Czech Court of Arbitration's Supplemental .eu ADR Rules, discussed above.

video-conferencing and chat, should be explored[232] to improve communication and the decision process.

## Lack of appeal and inconsistency of decisions

The significance of the right to appeal for due process has been explored in Chapter 6.[233] One defect of the UDRP procedure in this respect is that it does not provide for any appeal process whatsoever. This is the case for both challenges to procedural matters and appeals of substantive matters.[234]

**Challenge on procedural matters**      Important in this discussion of due process is whether a party can challenge aspects of the *procedure*, either before or after a decision has been reached. One party may assert a serious irregularity of procedure, preventing it from having an opportunity to present its case. An example for this may be where the panel disregards a response, or where a panel may, on occasion, breach a procedural rule (e.g. by inadvertently allowing *ex parte* communications), or a party may challenge the appointment of a panellist on the basis of a conflict of interests. In these scenarios, the question arises as to whether and how the aggrieved party can challenge the procedure, or, if a decision has already been reached, the decision.

While the UDRP Rules contain various procedural protections for the parties, including a stipulation about fair hearing[235] and independence and impartiality of the panels,[236] there is no procedure for the parties to challenge a panel decision if these rules have been breached,[237] and this puts their effectiveness into doubt.[238]

Since there is no appeal body or procedure, the only institutions apt to hear such a challenge are the panel itself or the dispute-resolution service

---

[232] Froomkin, 'ICANN's Uniform Dispute Resolution Policy', 705; Thornburg, 'Fast, Cheap and Out of Control', 219.

[233] See 6.7.

[234] The same is true for the .eu procedure; see .eu ADR Rules, r. 12(a); unlike the procedure established by Nominet for .uk country-code domain names, which provides for an appeal to a panel of three experts; see www.nominet.org.uk/disputes/drs/appeals [1 April 2008].

[235] UDRP Rules, r. 10(b).      [236] *Ibid.* r. 7.

[237] In WIPO Case No. D2001–0505, *Britannia Building Society* v. *Britannia Fraud Prevention*, the panel was concerned about this issue: 'Neither the Policy nor the Rules explicitly create a procedure by which a party can raise concerns about the suitability of a designated Panellist. However it is critical that a mechanism be provided to ensure compliance with Rule 7 and Rule 10 (b).'

[238] Froomkin, 'ICANN's Uniform Dispute Resolution Policy', 689: 'Current procedures rely on arbitrators to disclose potential conflicts, but this is clearly insufficient, since the truly biased person will tend to downplay the extent of conflicts.'

provider.[239] There is no 'higher' appeal body or third party considering procedural challenges, unlike traditional arbitration where the ordinary courts can hear procedural challenges under their supervisory and/or enforcement jurisdiction.[240]

The procedural rules of the providers are mostly silent on this point. The NAF Rules state expressly that a party can challenge the appointment of a panellist on the grounds of lack of independence or impartiality, before a decision has been reached, by filing a request with the NAF.[241]

Procedural challenges are usually considered by the panels when reaching a decision.[242] However, no procedural challenges are possible after the panel has reached its decision.

Panel decisions have found that in very exceptional cases, a panel may allow a case to be reheard on the application of the complainant, where in the first proceedings the complainant was deprived of justice: because of a serious misconduct on the part of a panellist, witness or lawyer; because of perjured evidence; or, more generally, where there has been another serious breach of due process. However, these decisions have held that such a refiling of the complaint is only permissible if the breach is so serious that it amounts to a miscarriage of justice. This establishes a high burden of proof.[243]

In any case, these rulings on rehearing the same case again only benefit the *complainant*, not the respondent.[244] This is unfair, as it infringes the principle of equality between the parties, giving the complainant a second bite of the apple to rectify infringements of due process, but not the respondent.[245]

For these reasons, it is argued here that the UDRP Rules should provide for a procedure to allow either party to challenge a decision if there has

[239] WIPO Case No. D2001–0505, *Britannia Building Society* v. *Britannia Fraud Prevention*.
[240] See 6.7.    [241] NAF Rules, r. 10(c), (d) and (e).
[242] WIPO Case No. D2004–0643, *Tatra Banka* v. *US WARE INC*; WIPO Case No. D2004–0535, *United Services Automobile Association* v. *Ang Wa Assoc*; WIPO Case No. D2000–0629, *Consorzio del Prosciutto di Parma* v. *Domain Name Clearing Company*; NAF Case No. 139595, *CV Ranch* v. *Default Data.com*.
[243] WIPO Case No. D2000–0703, *Grove Broadcasting Co Ltd* v. *Telesystems Communications Limited*; WIPO Case No. D2000–1490, *Creo Products Inc* v. *Website In Development*; WIPO Case No. DWS2002–0001, *Philips* v. *Relson Ltd*; NAF Case No. 721968, *AOL LLC* v. *Robert Farris*.
[244] A respondent cannot counter-claim or seek a free-standing declaration of reverse domain-name hijacking; see, by way of illustration, NAF Case No. 098010, *Glimcher University Mall* v. *GNO*.
[245] Froomkin, 'ICANN's Uniform Dispute Resolution Policy', 699.

been a breach of the requirement for a fair hearing or the requirement for an independent and impartial panel. This could be done by way of a rehearing by a different panel, or by appeal to a 'superior' body.[246] Successful challenges are probably rare, so, overall, allowing such challenges will not lead to a significant increase in costs or delay.

**Substantive appeals**    As to substantive appeals, the UDRP does not provide for an appeal in matters of substance. There is no procedure to review the decision on the factual findings, and no appeal on points of law. As has been discussed in Chapter 6,[247] the lack of an appeal procedure for a substantive review lowers standards for individual justice, as the losing party has no opportunity to correct mistakes in the application of the law, but it also leads to a lower quality of justice overall, as there are no authoritative rulings on points of law, streamlining reams of inconsistent decisions.

The lack of appeal and the discrepancies of UDRP decisions have been criticised.[248] The UDRP has established a novel substantive law combating cybersquatting on a global basis, and the panels are staffed by lawyers from many different legal cultures and traditions. Furthermore, panellists are free to take into account any law that they deem applicable.[249] Given this diverse and cosmopolitan nature of panels and the murky choice-of-law clause,[250] it is perhaps not surprising that there are many inconsistent interpretations of the UDRP.[251]

An appeal process would help to generate coherence and a greater degree of legal certainty.[252] Appeals could be heard by special, more senior, appeal panels, composed of three or five special-appeal panellists. These appeal panellists should be senior lawyers with long-standing experience in hearing UDRP cases.

---

[246] The establishment of an appeal body is discussed below.    [247] See 6.7.

[248] Thornburg, 'Fast, Cheap and Out of Control', 224; M. Scott Donahey, 'A Proposal for an Appellate Panel for the Uniform Domain Name Dispute Resolution Policy' (2001) 18(1) *Journal of International Arbitration* 131–4, 131–2.

[249] UDRP Rules, r. 15(a).

[250] Thornburg, 'Fast, Cheap and Out of Control', 215: this has 'resulted in eclectic and unprincipled choice of law decisions, creating uncertainty about applicable law'; see also Helfer, 'Whither the UDRP', 495.

[251] Panels tend to refer to other panel decisions, but there is a huge body of decisions, and a systematic search through all decisions is next to impossible.

[252] Helfer, 'Whither the UDRP', 495.

However, an appeal procedure is obviously apt to lead to delay and an increase of costs.[253] This could be remedied by appeals being subject to a leave requirement, and leave should only be given where the outcome of a case depends on the interpretation of the UDRP and where the case raises new issues that are important for the development of a consistent UDRP law.[254] The appeal process should also contain strict time limits.[255] The leave requirement and the time limits would ensure that the appeal process does not introduce excessive costs and delay.

One way to spread the costs of appeals would be to finance the appeal by a combination of a special fee paid by the party lodging the appeal, and a small, additional fee imposed either on each domain-name registration or an appeal fee added to each UDRP case.[256]

**Conclusion as to appeals**   The UDRP should provide for an appeal system that allows an aggrieved party to challenge a procedural mischief or a decision based upon a procedural mishap and appeals on points of law. Such appeals could be heard by special appeal panels composed of three to five senior panellists (such panels being established across all service providers).

The lack of an appeal system notwithstanding, the losing party can, however, go to court.[257] However, the defects in the UDRP are not cured by the rule that the parties can go to court to rectify a bad panel decision, as the courts frequently are not accessible because of the costs and the jurisdictional quagmire associated with international disputes, a quagmire that the UDRP was supposed to overcome in the first place.

## Transparency

Unlike arbitration awards, the reasoned UDRP decisions are publicly available from the dispute-resolution service providers' websites.[258] Two providers, WIPO and NAF, even provide some limited keyword search facilities for their databases of decisions. Thus, it seems fair to say that the UDRP process is more transparent than commercial arbitration. The fact

---

[253]  For this reason, Milton Mueller argues against an appeal system for the UDRP; see Mueller, 'Rough Justice', 12.

[254]  Donahey, 'A Proposal for an Appellate Panel', 133.      [255]  *Ibid.*      [256]  *Ibid.*

[257]  UDRP Policy, para. 4(k).

[258]  *Ibid.* para. 4(j) and UDRP Rules, rr. 15(d) (providing for reasons) and 16(b); see www.wipo.int/amc/en/domains/search/index.html, http://domains.adrforum.com/ decision.aspx, and www.adndrc.org/adndrc/index.html [1 April 2008].

that decisions are published has undoubtedly enabled academic criticism and awareness of the shortcomings of the UDRP.

### 7.3.3 Conclusion

In conclusion, the UDRP has several serious procedural deficiencies that impinge on the due process granted to the parties. The UDRP should be improved by ensuring that the panel list is not composed of a majority of trademark attorneys, and by ensuring that panellists are allocated randomly, or preferably, that all cases are heard by panels chosen by the parties. There should be an internal appeal system to a different body of panellists, allowing the parties to challenge decisions on both procedural and substantive grounds. Furthermore, the time limit for filing the response should be extended significantly, and provision should be made for additional filings and online hearings. It should be ensured that the procedure is held in a language that both parties can understand. Finally, the UDRP should be binding on corporate entities, to avoid tactical litigation.[259]

This section has shown that the UDRP is not, as such, a model procedure for online arbitration of Internet disputes. The UDRP was drafted with the model of commercial arbitration in mind. However, as has been shown, this is inappropriate for a procedure that is mandatory and coercive and which therefore is more in the nature of an international, public dispute resolution procedure.

This chapter has found that both B2C arbitration and the procedure under the UDRP are unfair because they have been modelled on traditional arbitration. Having examined two paradigms for Internet disputes, namely consumer disputes and domain-name disputes, this chapter will conclude by reflecting on a different model, which should be termed the 'proportionate model of dispute resolution'.

## 7.4 Proportionate model of dispute resolution

This chapter argues that due process should apply to Internet disputes.[260] This means that such disputes should not be entirely relegated to the private dispute-resolution field, with the consequence that no due process protections apply.

---

[259] See example 3 discussed at 3.3 and at 8.2.1.
[260] For the definition of relevant Internet disputes, see Chapter 3.

## 7.4.1 Two spheres: one public and one private

The current model of dispute resolution is dichotomous, consisting of two conceptually[261] separate spheres: one public (traditional court litigation), the other private (ADR processes, including arbitration). In traditional court litigation, high standards of due process are applied, whereas in arbitration, the parties are deemed to have waived some important due process standards simply by agreeing to this form of dispute resolution, which is deemed private. As explained in Chapter 6, much less stringent standards of due process have, in practice, been applied to traditional commercial arbitration.

This dichotomy of our current perception of dispute resolution stems from the fundamental distinction between private and public law in Western law systems. The reason for this distinction is that the law protects two, potentially conflicting, fundamental principles, i.e. individual autonomy and contractual freedom on the one hand, and the supremacy and pervasiveness of fundamental values and human rights on the other.

The potential conflict between these two principles is solved by dividing the law between a public (pertaining to the state) and a private (pertaining to the individual) sphere.[262] Human rights and due process apply in the former, whereas they do not apply in the latter.

## 7.4.2 The waiver doctrine – fully informed and voluntary approach

At present, the waiver doctrine discussed in Chapter 6,[263] is the tool for this demarcation in the context of traditional commercial arbitration. According to this doctrine, arbitration is truly private, since the parties have opted out of public dispute resolution and have thereby waived some or all of their rights to a fair trial.

---

[261] These spheres are linked by court-mandated forms of ADR and the involvement of courts in arbitration.

[262] Albeit that the public–private dichotomy has recently come under attack: see, for example, from an administrative law point of view, J. Freeman, 'The Private Role in Public Governance' (2000) 75 *New York University Law Review* 543–675, 547–8. She regards governance as a series of negotiated relationships (at 571). She admits, however, that the constraint of private law on private discretion is not sufficient (at 591) and she suggests additional checks on private actors (at 593). See also the article by R. H. Mnookin, 'The Public/Private Dichotomy: Political Disagreement and Academic Reputation' (1982) 130 *University of Pennsylvania Law Review* 1429–40, 1430ff., where it is argued that the line between private and public may be impossible to define generally.

[263] See 6.2.5.

Just to recap what has been explained in Chapter 6,[264] in the United States, the parties are, indeed, regarded as having absolutely waived their due process rights guaranteed under the Constitution. The US approach is clear-cut: the state-action doctrine does not apply to arbitration, as arbitration is regarded to be a *private* form of dispute resolution, outside the constitutional reach.

By contrast, under the ECHR, the question of whether or not the right to a fair trial applies to arbitration is contentious and opaque. My conclusion in Chapter 6 was that under the ECHR, although due process is not completely inapplicable, some due process rights are automatically and implicitly waived by the parties resorting to arbitration as a process of dispute resolution.[265] The European doctrine is that some elements of due process – such as transparency, the right to an appeal or some aspects of fair hearing (such as extensive disclosure under English litigation) or the complete independence of arbitrators – are not applicable to arbitration *because of* the very nature of arbitration.[266] The logic is that if the parties have chosen arbitration as a process, then they have accepted these characteristics of arbitration and have thereby waived these aspects of their right to a fair trial. Furthermore, other aspects of due process can be specifically waived, for example where the arbitrator discloses a relevant conflict of interest and the parties omit to challenge the appointment.[267]

The waiver doctrine under European and US law allows parties to opt out of the state court system and to choose a form of dispute resolution that allows for flexibility of procedure, speed, efficiency and possibly lower costs. Therefore, this doctrine makes sense for traditional commercial arbitration, where the parties are roughly of equal bargaining power and, as business parties, are aware of the implications of arbitration, or have, at least, access to professional advice.

### 7.4.3 Internet disputes and the waiver doctrine

In relation to Internet disputes, if the parties are subject to a power imbalance, the waiver doctrine does not make sense, as here arbitration is not entered into voluntarily. Arbitration is not voluntary, since the more powerful party makes the weaker party contract on the more powerful party's terms (as in B2C cases), or since arbitration is mandatory through a contractual regulatory regime (as in the UDRP). Arbitration is also not

---

[264] See 6.2.5.    [265] See 6.2.5.    [266] See 6.2.5.    [267] See 6.2.5.

voluntary because in many cases it will be the only available and affordable means of redress.

Hence the 'fully informed and voluntary waiver approach' is no real solution to the problem of finding a fair dispute resolution mechanism for Internet disputes. Where the parties are located at a distance, and particularly where there is a considerable power imbalance between the parties, the parties should not be deemed to have waived their due process rights as there are serious doubts as to whether this waiver is voluntary.

The rationale for the use of arbitration for Internet disputes is not to opt out of the state court system but to provide an affordable and fair means of redress. If online arbitration complies with due process, there is no requirement for a waiver.

### 7.4.4 The proportionate model explained

A new paradigm is required for these kinds of disputes, and this should be termed 'the proportionate model of dispute resolution for Internet disputes'. Proportionate due process protections should be introduced to deal with power imbalances and distance disputes. This model takes an all-encompassing approach to dispute resolution, and bridges the current dichotomy between private and public dispute resolution. The idea here is that all dispute resolution is, to an extent, public as it involves the carrying out of a public function, and it is for this reason that due process should apply to all forms of dispute resolution, but on a proportionate basis.

Fairness requires different standards of due process, depending on the nature of the dispute and the parties involved.[268] However, this does not alter the thesis that a minimum of fairness and due process standards should apply to online arbitration of Internet disputes.[269]

Richard Reuben, writing about arbitration in general, has described this approach in his unitary theory of dispute resolution. He uses the metaphor of a planetary system. The closeness of each planet to its sun determines the gravitational pull. In the same manner, so he argues, the closer a form of dispute resolution is to the power of the state, the higher the standards of due process that apply to that dispute resolution. Therefore the gravitational pull is the highest for litigation, less so for arbitration and the least for mediation.[270]

---

[268] Richardson and Genn, 'Tribunals in Transition', 122; see also 6.4.2.
[269] For the discussion of the relevant disputes, see Chapter 3.
[270] Reuben, 'Constitutional Gravity', 1047–8.

His theory should be adapted to the model of dispute resolution for Internet disputes espoused in this book. Since online arbitration used for Internet disputes will encounter a great variety of disputes, a distinction should be made between different types of arbitration. Commercial arbitration between business parties would orbit further away from the due process centre than arbitration involving parties with power imbalances and those where arbitration is mandatory (such as the UDRP). Hence the model of resolution for Internet disputes outlined in Chapter 8 is an intermediate form of dispute resolution positioned between litigation and commercial arbitration, providing for a minimum of due process. This intermediate model would also be a solution to the conflict between due process and access that has been described in Chapter 2.[271] It would reduce the formality of dispute resolution, allowing for more flexible procedures and, hence, increasing access without waiving due process completely.

In conclusion, this means that there is a requirement to design private dispute-resolution systems that have public due-process safeguards incorporated.

## 7.5 Conclusion

This chapter has looked in depth at consumer arbitration and found that certain pre-dispute arbitration clauses in B2C contracts are invalid in the United Kingdom, whereas in the United States, such clauses are frequently enforceable. The chapter has also examined the UDRP as a dispute resolution procedure, modelled on commercial arbitration, which is mandatory and coercive. This chapter has shown that neither the US model of consumer arbitration nor the model of the UDRP administrative procedure is fully respecting of due process, the result being that they are unfair.

This chapter has argued that the traditional model of commercial arbitration using only abbreviated due process protections is not suitable for Internet disputes, and it has explained that online arbitration of Internet disputes is fundamentally different from the traditional arbitration model, since arbitration may not be an alternative to court litigation but is the only process that can provide a remedy for an aggrieved party. Furthermore, under the traditional paradigm, there is an implicit acceptance (despite some rhetoric to the contrary) that arbitration provides lower

---

[271] See 2.6.

standards of due process, but that the parties have freely waived their rights and are therefore autonomous to fashion the procedure according to their needs. This does not make sense where one party imposes arbitration on the other, or where arbitration is mandatory and/or there is no other viable redress.

Furthermore, the traditional paradigm accepts that lower due process rights can be against public policy in certain types of disputes where there are strong power imbalances, such as B2C disputes. However, in order to protect the weaker party, arbitration has been restricted for these types of disputes (at least in the form of pre-dispute arbitration clauses), or, as in the UDRP, the dispute resolution mechanism is not final.

This paradigm needs to be changed. Online arbitration is a necessary dispute resolution mechanism for Internet disputes and, in particular, for those disputes where there is a strong power imbalance between the parties. Therefore, rather than excluding these disputes from arbitration or making the process not final, higher due process guarantees should ensure that the process is fair. The new model proposed would be to allow pre-dispute arbitration clauses for all disputes but impose stricter due process standards for Internet disputes. The final chapter of this book will explore what the minimum due process standards should be and how they should be implemented for a fair model of dispute resolution.

# 8

# A model of dispute resolution for the Internet

Reform? Reform? Are things not bad enough already?

(Sir John Astbury, 1926)

## 8.1 Introduction

Given the limitations of existing court procedures and other dispute resolution mechanisms, Chapters 3 and 5 have demonstrated a need for binding online-arbitration mechanisms to solve Internet disputes. Online arbitration as a mechanism is likely to capture a whole range of Internet disputes that cannot be solved by any other means.

Chapter 6 has shown that, by comparison to the safeguards adopted in common law and human rights doctrine, due process is a low priority in commercial arbitration. This has traditionally been justified by the principle that the parties should be able to fashion their own procedure (principle of party autonomy) and that the parties have waived some of their due process rights (waiver principle).

However, if the same principles are applied to arbitration in situations where the parties are subject to a significant power imbalance, where the parties have no access to litigation and/or where arbitration is mandatory, this renders the procedure potentially unfair. In Chapter 7, the discussion of consumer arbitration and the analysis of the UDRP have flagged unfairness problems, caused by the fact that these procedures are modelled on traditional, commercial arbitration. For this reason, it has been argued in Chapter 7 that private commercial arbitration, without any adaption, does not provide a suitable model for the resolution of Internet disputes. Chapter 7 has concluded that an intermediate form of dispute resolution has to be found, providing for due process but without the formality and complexity of litigation. The conclusion from this is that online arbitration that complies with minimum due process standards can be used to fill this void.

Fairness has three constituent elements, which have been explained in Chapter 2: (i) due process, (ii) access and (iii) the counterpoise. Hence, in addition to due process, dispute resolution for Internet disputes must be accessible and must rebalance (to an extent) pre-existing power imbalances. It has been discussed in Chapter 5 that online arbitration provides for greater access.

The main task of this chapter is to outline the parameters for a workable model of fair dispute resolution for Internet disputes, drawing on the conclusions from previous chapters. This model applies to Internet disputes where one party is a corporate entity and the other an individual, or where both parties are individuals.[1] In order to accomplish this task, themes are discussed that can be best circumscribed by the following four questions: (i) how do you bring the parties to online arbitration? (ii) what are the minimum standards that should apply to the resolution of Internet disputes? (iii) how do you implement the due process standards? and (iv) what are the costs, and who should bear these?

## 8.2 Bringing the parties to arbitration

The first issue a model for the resolution of Internet disputes has to address is how to bring the parties before the (online) arbitrator. Traditional commercial arbitration is based on an agreement between the parties to arbitrate.[2] Such an agreement can be concluded at the outset, before the dispute has arisen, and provided it is in writing, this agreement is binding and enforceable.

In Chapter 7,[3] it has been explained that exceptions to the binding nature of arbitration are (most) pre-dispute consumer-arbitration agreements in the European Union / European Economic Area, which may not be binding on or enforceable against the consumer. More generally, it is questionable whether it is fair if the more powerful party effectively imposes arbitration on the 'weaker' party.[4] However, even if the use of pre-dispute consumer-arbitration clauses raised no fairness issues, it would be unlikely that they would be adopted by companies in the European

---

[1] See 3.6.    [2] See discussion at 4.2.2.    [3] See 7.2.
[4] See discussion at 7.2, which, by way of example, has illustrated this in the context of consumer arbitration.

Union / European Economic Area to the same extent as they are in use in the United States. The reason for this preponderance of arbitration clauses in contracts used by US corporations is that specific features of US litigation – such as the availability of class actions, jury trial and punitive damages – provide incentives for the more powerful party to avoid litigation in favour of arbitration.[5] The same incentives do not exist in the European Union.

Hence it could be said that it is necessary that the arbitration agreement is concluded after the dispute has arisen. This immediately raises the question of whether the respondent will agree to arbitration at this stage.[6] Such agreement is unlikely if the claimant is the 'weaker' party in an Internet dispute, who is without effective access to dispute resolution in the courts.[7] If the 'weaker' party (such as an individual in state A) has no access to the courts, why would the 'stronger' party (such as a multinational company involved in E-commerce established in state B) agree to arbitration?

This Catch-22 situation is a serious obstacle to the availability and feasibility of online arbitration for Internet disputes.

The concern of this book is access, and this includes the availability of fair and proportionate dispute resolution for Internet disputes. The availability of online arbitration as a form of redress can only be secured by some form of encouragement or compulsion to take part in arbitration.

In order to make such an obligation to arbitrate fair in a situation of power imbalance in respect of Internet disputes, it *should* only be imposed on the more powerful party (in this book, corporate entities) and not on the weaker party (in my argument, individuals, including consumers).[8] There seems to be consensus among consumer organisations and policy

---

[5] For further details of this argument, see Drahozal and Friel, 'A Comparative View of Arbitration', 131.

[6] G.-P. Calliess, 'Transnational Consumer Law: Co-Regulation of B2C E-Commerce' (2007) 3(3) *Comparative Research in Law & Political Economy* 2.54, 19.

[7] Bamford, 'Shopping Around', 109; ECC-Net, *The European Online Marketplace: Consumer Complaints 2005* (Stockholm, 2006), para. 6.3 (Enforcement).

[8] See, for example, ombudsman schemes discussed below at 8.2.2; this raises the question of whether, in a dispute between two individuals (raising no power imbalances), the parties should be bound by the online arbitration clause. The argument in favour of this is that the second-generation Internet is much more interactive than the early Internet, and that hence there is a greater likelihood of individual-to-individual disputes.

makers that consumers, for example, should not be bound by a pre-dispute arbitration clause.[9]

Such an asymmetric obligation on participation in arbitration or adjudication[10] is justified by the need to redress the power imbalance between the parties (the counterpoise), defined as the third principle of fairness, and discussed in Chapter 2.[11] Hence the asymmetric obligation would be a procedural tool used to level the power imbalance between the parties.

It means that the individual *should* be able to choose between online extra-judicial adjudication and litigation, whereas the corporate entity *should* have to agree to submit to the extra-judicial adjudication procedure once a dispute arises. However, after a dispute has arisen, once the individual has agreed to extra-judicial adjudication, both parties *should* be bound by the decision of the adjudicator, provided the adjudication is fair.[12]

The challenge is to introduce such an asymmetric obligation into the relationship between the parties. This can be done through a contractual membership scheme and/or through making online extra-judicial adjudication compulsory by law.

### 8.2.1 Contractually mandated schemes

The first possibility is to bind corporate entities to online arbitration through a contractually mandated scheme operated by a trusted party.

---

[9] Doyle, Ritters and Brooker, *Seeking Resolution*, 78; this is also a requirement of the OFT's Consumer Code Approval Scheme, discussed at 8.2.1; see Condition 4d of the Consumer Code Approval Scheme, Core Criteria and Guidance, dated November 2006, OFT 390; see also Consumers International, 'Disputes in Cyberspace', 29–30 ('Recommendations'), and see also EC Recommendation 98/257/EC, Principle VI, 2nd sentence; see also AAA, *Consumer-Related Disputes: Supplementary Procedures* of 15 September 2005, available from www.adr.org/sp.asp?id=22014 [1 April 2008] and AAA, *Due Process Protocol for Consumers*, Principle 5, available from www.adr.org/sp.asp?id=22019 [1 August 2008]; BEUC position paper, 'Alternative Dispute Resolution' of 21 November 2002, BEUC/X/048/2002, 4.6; TACD (Transatlantic Consumer Dialogue), 'Alternative Dispute Resolution in the Context of E-Commerce', position statement of February 2000 E-comm 12–00, Resolution No. 4, available from www.tacd.org/cgi-bin/db.cgi?page=view&config=admin/docs.cfg&id=41 [1 April 2008]; Bamford, 'Shopping Around', 110; OECD Report, *Consumer Dispute Resolution and Redress in the Global Marketplace*, 20.

[10] The term 'adjudication' in this book is used as a neutral term to mean a form of dispute resolution involving a third party making a decision binding on the parties, and is to include arbitration, ombudsmen and litigation.

[11] See the third principle of fairness, i.e. the need to counter-balance pre-existing inequalities, at 2.2.3.

[12] See the fairness standards discussed at 8.3.

This is essentially a contract between one (or each) party and a trusted party, which contains an arbitration agreement covering the Internet disputes that may arise. On an abstract level, the principle behind this is that the trusted party has the power to entice the more powerful party (the corporate entity) to agree to arbitration of all Internet disputes, thus obviating the need for the parties entering into a direct arbitration agreement between themselves. In contract-law terms, there are two different models for contractually mandated schemes.

### Arbitration agreement between participants

This model is equivalent to a club or association making rules and conditions for all its members, agreed to by each member as a condition of membership and governing the contractual relationships *between* the members. Although such a contract cannot be neatly analysed into offer and acceptance, it is nevertheless a binding contract *between* each member.[13] If a dispute arises later between two members, this will be governed by the rules agreed between the trusted party and each member.

For example, the operator of an online marketplace (such as an online auction or a B2B trading platform) or an online discussion forum (such as a blog) could impose online arbitration on participants for the resolution of disputes *among* participants in the online marketplace or discussion forum. The operator would act as a trusted party, obliging each participant to agree to solve any disputes with other participants by online arbitration.[14] This agreement could be made when participants join the marketplace or forum, as a condition of membership.

In order to prevent any unfairness against individuals, such a scheme could provide that this obligation to submit to arbitration only applies to corporate entities. Individuals are encouraged to take part in online arbitration, but are free to choose litigation instead.

For example, eBay, the online auction platform, provides an internal dispute resolution mechanism through its 'Item Not Received or Significantly Not as Described', 'Unpaid Item' and 'Mutual Feedback Withdrawal'[15] programmes, which can be instigated by buyers or sellers against

---

[13] As in the rules for the regatta in *The Satanita* [1895], 248; *Clarke* v. *Dunraven* [1897] AC 59, mentioned in G. Treitel, *The Law of Contract*, 11th edn (London: Sweet & Maxwell, 2003), 47.

[14] Probably containing an escalation clause, providing first for online conciliation or mediation, and if this fails, using online arbitration.

[15] Feedback is a crucial tool for sellers on online auction platforms to enhance their reputation. Buyers are encouraged to leave feedback on a particular seller's performance, which

the other party respectively. These dispute resolution programmes consist of online, assisted negotiation between the parties, and also an insurance element,[16] but they do *not* include online arbitration.[17] For higher value disputes, buyers and sellers can use an escrow service.

However, there is no direct referral to online arbitration, and no obligation on either party to participate in arbitration of any kind. Arguably, eBay's dispute resolution could be given more teeth if corporate buyers and sellers agreed to submit to online arbitration as the ultimate redress mechanism, to be used as a last resort in an escalated procedure.

All online marketplaces, discussion forums and other interactive platforms should consider the incorporation of an obligation for corporate entities to agree to online arbitration.

### Arbitration agreement for the benefit of a third-party claimant

The second model incorporates online arbitration into the membership agreement for the benefit of a third-party claimant, used where a claim arises from an online activity, but the claimant is not a participant in the activity or a member of the organisation.

An example of this is a trade association whose members commit to solve any disputes with third-party buyers by online arbitration.[18] A second example would be a claimant who has been defamed on a discussion forum or other online platform but who is not a member of this forum. In either example, the third party will not be privy to that contractual agreement, so the question arises as to whether the third party could rely on and enforce this arbitration agreement.

In the United Kingdom, s. 1 of the Contracts (Rights of Third Parties) Act 1999 confers a right to enforce a contract term on a party not privy to the contract if the contract intentionally provides a benefit for that party, provided the party is at least identified as a member of a class

---

in turn informs future buyers about this seller's trustworthiness, and a seller with a bad feedback rating is unlikely to be able to sell. Hence there may well be arguments about the appropriateness of feedback, which this programme is intended to address.

[16] The eBay Standard Purchase Protection Programme, which provides reimbursement of a maximum of £105, subject to certain conditions; see http://pages.ebay.co.uk/help/tp/esppp-process.html [1 April 2008].

[17] See http://pages.ebay.co.uk/help/tp/problems-dispute-resolution.html [1 April 2008].

[18] This construction may raise problems regarding the independence of the online arbitration institution and/or the arbitrators; see the discussion of standards at 8.3.

in the contract.[19] Section 8(2) furthermore provides that if the contract contains an arbitration agreement for the benefit of the third party, and it is in writing, the third party may choose to use arbitration.[20]

Hence the third-party buyer could rely on an arbitration agreement concluded between a seller and a trade association if the arbitration agreement is expressed to be for the benefit of the buyer. Likewise, the person claiming defamation damages could also sue the defendant if the arbitration agreement concluded between the defendant defamer and the operator of the discussion forum had envisaged a class of claimants to which the claimant belongs.

This raises the question of how such contractually mandated schemes could work in practice.

### Contractually mandated schemes in practice

Two types of contractually mandated schemes could be established in practice: (i) codes of practice coupled with a trustmark incorporating online arbitration or (ii) online arbitration imposed by the rules and conditions of a platform.

**Codes of practice and trustmarks**    In the consumer E-commerce context, this construction requires a sponsoring organisation. One possibility is that a trade or consumer organisation sponsors a code of practice, to which E-commerce businesses subscribe and to the provisions of which they agree to conform.

In return for this subscription, business members are allowed to use a trademark protected logo ('trustmark'[21]) indicating to consumers that the

---

[19]  Contracts (Rights of Third Parties) Act 1999, s. 1(1)(b) and (3).

[20]  Treitel points out that arbitration is optional for the third party; see Treitel, *The Law of Contract*, 656–7. By contrast, if the third party wishes to enforce a substantive right arising under the contract, which also contains an arbitration clause, then s. 8(1) applies and the arbitration clause is binding on the third party: *Nisshin Shipping* v. *Cleaves* [2004] 1 Lloyd's Rep 38 (Comm Ct), paras. 38, 41 and 42.

[21]  Examples of trustmark schemes, which cannot be discussed here because of lack of space, are Trusted Shops (www.trustedshops.com/merchants/index.html) and Euro Label (www.euro-label.com/euro-label/ControllerServlet) [1 April 2008]; their codes, however, do not provide for online arbitration. The Austrian certification body for Euro Label, however, does require participation in the Austrian Internet Consumer Ombudsman for Austrian-certified member businesses, including compliance with a recommendation made by the Ombudsman; see the discussion at 5.3.2. Another example of a trustmark scheme is the BBB Online Reliability Code, which obliges members to agree to participate in binding arbitration under the BBB Rules of Arbitration (Binding) if the consumer also agrees: www.bbbonline.org/reliability/dr.asp [1 April 2008].

business is safe to transact with, thereby boosting the business' branding and the consumer confidence it attracts. If a business persistently offends against the terms of the code, it may be expelled from the scheme, so that a sanction exists for non-compliance. However, a trustmark scheme financed by membership fees can only afford to lose so many members.[22] One of the terms of the code of practice could be that eBusinesses submit to online arbitration.

An example of this is provided by the OFT's Consumer Code Approval Scheme.[23] The OFT has established a programme for the approval of codes of practice, and if a code is approved, the businesses concerned are allowed to use the OFT logo. One of the terms of the OFT's Consumer Code Approval Scheme is that the code must include the availability of an independent redress scheme, which is binding in respect of code members, and that the code member must accept any decision made under the scheme.[24]

However, trustmarks only work if they serve to distinguish the products of one provider from those of another, and for this to occur, consumers must be aware of a trustmark. Many well-known brands rely on their own branding, and trustmarks are being predominantly subscribed to by smaller businesses.[25] Hence more thought should be given to the question of how consumer awareness about a trustmark can be raised, thereby making the trustmark more attractive for businesses.[26]

**Disputes arising from a platform**    A second possibility would be that the operator of an online platform incorporates online arbitration in the membership terms. This second construction could be used where sellers and buyers engage in B2B or B2C E-commerce on an online platform, such as an auction platform.[27]

However, it is by no means limited to E-commerce. Contractually mandated online arbitration could be extended to oblige participants in a

---

[22] Calliess, 'Transnational Consumer Law', 9.

[23] This is, strictly speaking, a secondary mark, establishing standards for codes rather than being attached to a particular code.

[24] Condition 4d of the Consumer Code Approval Scheme, Core Criteria and Guidance, dated November 2006, OFT 390.

[25] Calliess, 'Transnational Consumer Law', 9.

[26] Albeit that the OFT's Consumer Code Approval Scheme was publicised by a £1 million advertising campaign; see OFT, *Consumer Code Approval Scheme Newsletter*, Issue 7, available from www.oft.gov.uk/oft_at_work/consumer_initiatives/codes/publications/#named6 [1 August 2008].

[27] See Calliess, 'Transnational Consumer Law', 13.

whole range of online activities to take part in online arbitration for disputes between themselves or with third-party complainants (provided the dispute resolution clause is for the benefit of third parties). Such schemes are not limited to contractual disputes related to E-commerce, but could encompass tort disputes such as defamation or copyright infringement.

An operator of an online forum, an online auction site, a site providing an opportunity for users to upload user-generated content (such as homemade videos), or indeed any other Internet service provider (ISP) hosting users' content, could make it a condition of participation that users agree to online arbitration if a claim is made by a third party, for example, for defamation or infringement of copyright.

For example, eBay has introduced a 'notice and take-down' complaints system called the eBay VeRO programme, which allows third-party owners of IP rights to complain about infringements of their rights through sales on eBay.[28] Once such a notice has been filed, eBay will take down the allegedly offending item, without checking the validity of the notification.

This 'take-down on notice' procedure has to be seen in the context of the EU rules on the liability of ISPs for hosting illegal materials. An ISP is immune from liability only if they have no actual knowledge of infringement and are not aware of any facts or circumstances from which infringement would be apparent, and if they receive notice of such infringement, they have to act expeditiously to remove the infringing material.[29] This means that the burden to litigate is shifted from the complainant IP owner, who can achieve the removal of allegedly offending items by mere notice, to the provider of the content, such as the seller on eBay, who has to litigate to reinstate the material.

An example of this is the recent case of *Quads4Kids* v. *Campbell*.[30] The defendant had notified eBay that the claimant was selling children's dirt bikes, allegedly infringing the defendant's registered design right. The claimant had to institute proceedings and obtained an injunction reinstating his sales on eBay on the basis that he had an arguable defence, and that the use of the notice procedure was a groundless threat of proceedings for infringement of a Community design right.[31]

Instead of using a mere 'notice and take-down' procedure, access to dispute resolution could be increased if the parties used online arbitration to solve such a dispute, instead of litigation. The use of online arbitration

---

[28] See http://pages.ebay.co.uk/vero/participants.html [1 April 2008].
[29] E-commerce Directive 2000/31/EC, Art. 14(1).    [30] [2006] All ER (D) 162 (Oct) (ChD).
[31] Community Design Regulations 2005 (SI 2005/2339), reg. 2; see also the similar provisions in Trade Marks Act 1994, s. 21; Patents Act 1977, s. 70.

in such cases may be quicker, possibly cheaper and more convenient to use[32] (especially if the seller has limited financial means or is located in a different jurisdiction than the ISP or in a jurisdiction without an efficient court system),[33] and effective dispute resolution can enhance the platform's commercial reputation.

Most of the examples discussed in Chapter 3[34] neatly illustrate the benefits and the limitations of contractually mandated dispute resolution clauses.

**The examples in Chapter 3**    In Chapter 3,[35] six examples have been used to illustrate the cross-border nature of some Internet disputes and the difficulties of redress where this is coupled with a power imbalance between the parties.

In example 1,[36] if the B2B E-commerce platform made online arbitration compulsory for all its members, with the threat of expulsion for members who do not participate in online arbitration or who do not comply with an award, this would make redress more likely for the trader concerned.

In example 2,[37] it is likely that the consumer would obtain a credit-card chargeback. However, if this is not available, then if the travel company had subscribed to a trustmark scheme providing for independent redress, the consumer would be more likely to obtain redress, but this presupposes that consumers are aware of trustmarks and therefore only contract with subscribing businesses in the first place.

Example 3[38] is an illustration for the proposition that online arbitration should be binding on the corporate entity in order to avoid the more

---

[32] See the discussion in 5.5 on the benefits of ODR/online arbitration.

[33] For a more detailed discussion of this topic, see J. Hörnle, 'Internet Service Provider Liability – Let's Not Play Piggy in the Middle' (2002) 7(3) *Communications Law* 85–8, arguing that there should be a 'put back' provision combined with online arbitration.

[34] See 3.3.    [35] See 3.3.

[36] A sole trader in Nigeria concludes a contract with a company – manufacturing locally in China and trading internationally – for some widgets through a B2B E-commerce trading platform. The widgets are defective and the sole trader seeks redress for breach of contract.

[37] A consumer in Chile enters into a contract with a large US travel company for a cruise holiday through an E-commerce website. However, the cruise is cancelled at the last minute and the deposit of US $2,000 has not been refunded. The consumer seeks a refund of the deposit paid.

[38] The owner of a bricks and mortar shop located in Dublin (sole trader) has named her shop 'Crate & Barrel', and she also operates a website connected to her shop under the domain www.crateandbarrel.biz. A large US company running an extensive chain of stores present in most states of the United States claims infringement of their US federal trademark in the same name, and commences infringement proceedings against the unincorporated Irish trader before a US district court. The owner cannot afford litigation in the United States,

powerful party electing to litigate in a local court before which the individual is not able to defend themselves. The procedure of the UDRP should be made fairer and be binding on corporate entities.[39]

In example 4,[40] the Egyptian individual could use online arbitration to obtain redress against the US news corporation if the online news platform had obliged all persons posting on the website to agree to online arbitration. Again, this shows the importance of online operators binding users to online arbitration.

However, not all Internet disputes can be covered by contractually mandated online arbitration, especially where there is no trusted third party involved. In example 5,[41] the dispute is not covered by a contractually mandated, online arbitration scheme, as the dispute does not arise from a platform, but from the content of a private individual's own website.

Likewise, in example 6,[42] since there is no trusted party, there is no possibility for redress by online arbitration. These last two examples show the limitation of the contractually mandated solution.

For such disputes, something else is needed over and above contractually mandated online arbitration.

### 8.2.2 Compulsory statutory arbitration

At first sight, the notion of compulsory online arbitration may appear to be an oxymoron – it has been pointed out above that arbitration is based on the *agreement* of the parties,[43] and this seems, prima facie, contradictory to the notion that arbitration is compulsory. However, it is possible to argue that the parties have *agreed* to arbitrate in a case where extra-judicial adjudication has been imposed by statute, for the purposes

---

and the US district court enters default judgment in favour of the US corporation. The domain name is transferred to the US corporation.

[39] See the discussion at 7.3.

[40] A US-based corporation publishes an online video clip on an interactive, online news platform, accusing a named Egyptian civil servant of belonging to a terrorist organisation. The Egyptian individual seeks redress for defamation.

[41] A US citizen uploads potentially defamatory comments about an internationally famous Australian film star on his own website. These comments are copied and downloaded widely and thus propagated on a global basis. The film star commences proceedings against the US citizen before his local Australian court for defamation.

[42] A large Russian company illegally hacks remotely into the server of an English inventor in order to obtain confidential, sensitive information. The English inventor seeks redress for damages arising from this unlawful action.

[43] See 4.2.2.

of classifying a form of dispute resolution as 'arbitration'.[44] This argument is substantiated below.[45]

Clearly, as has already been discussed, compulsory extra-judicial adjudication has to comply with the fair trial principles under Art. 6 of the ECHR, as the waiver doctrine does not apply.[46] This requires compliance with the due process standards discussed below.[47]

In the United Kingdom, there are two statutory, compulsory and extra-judicial adjudication schemes that may serve as a model for a dispute resolution scheme for Internet disputes: the ombudsman[48] schemes for communication disputes and for financial services.

### Ombudsman schemes for communication disputes

Sections 52 to 54 of the Communications Act 2003[49] impose a duty on communications companies to subscribe to a dispute resolution scheme, providing redress and remedies to residential and small-business customers[50] complaining about the provision of electronic communications services, such as complaints about billing, customer service, loss of service, equipment faults, mis-selling, privacy infringement or disconnection.[51] The two ombudsman/adjudication schemes that have been approved to provide dispute resolution services are Otelo (Office of the Telecommunications Ombudsman)[52] and CISAS (Communication and Internet Services Adjudication Scheme).[53] Otelo and CISAS provide conciliation and adjudication services to complainants. Communications companies

---

[44] Redfern and Hunter, *Law and Practice of International Commercial Arbitration*, 9, fn. 34, Tackaberry and Marriott, 'General Principles', 15, para. 2–010.

[45] See 8.2.2.        [46] See the discussion at 6.2.5.        [47] See 8.3.

[48] Ombudsman schemes in the United Kingdom were traditionally set up to investigate maladministration (i.e. disputes between the state administration and individual citizens), and many ombudsman schemes still perform this function, such as the Local Government Ombudsman or the Parliamentary and Health Service Ombudsman or the Prisons and Probation Ombudsman; in recent, modern ombudsman schemes, emphasis has moved away from investigation and report writing to dispute resolution, so that this new generation of ombudsman schemes are making binding decisions between private parties on the merits; P. Morris and R. James, 'The Financial Ombudsman Service' [2002] *Public Law* 640–8, 640.

[49] As required by Art. 8(4)(b) of the Framework Directive 2002/21/EC of 7 March 2002, and Art. 34(1) of the Universal Service Directive 2002/22/EC of 7 March 2002.

[50] Communications Act 2003, s. 52(2)(b) – a small business customer is defined as having fewer than ten employees; see s. 25(6)(b).

[51] See Otelo, *Annual Report 2008*, 12; CISAS, *Annual Report 2007*, 11.

[52] Office of the Telecommunications Ombudsman, a company limited by guarantee.

[53] CISAS, operated by IDRS Ltd, a division of CIArb.

can choose which of these two schemes to subscribe to in order to fulfil their obligations under the conditions set under s. 52(2)(b) of the Communications Act 2003. Once a communications company has become a member of either scheme, it *has* to participate in the dispute resolution scheme, whereas customers are not obliged to use these schemes and are (at least in theory) free to go to court instead.

Furthermore, once the adjudicator has reached a final decision, the customer has a choice as to whether or not to accept it.[54] If the customer accepts, the decision becomes binding on the company;[55] if the customer does not accept the decision, it will lapse.[56] The maximum award under these schemes is £5,000.[57] However, under the OTELO scheme, awards have been small, 74 per cent of complainants receiving less than £100.[58] Most awards under the CISAS scheme have been in the bracket of £100–£500, and the average award was £160.[59] If a communications company persistently refused to comply with awards, this would amount to a breach of their membership conditions and could lead to expulsion from the dispute resolution scheme, and could ultimately trigger the enforcement provisions[60] in the Communications Act 2003.

### Financial Ombudsman Service

The Financial Ombudsman Service (FOS) considers complaints from consumers or businesses with an annual turnover of less than £1 million[61] about financial services,[62] consumer credit,[63] banking and insurance. The

---

[54] This distinguishes these ombudsman/adjudication schemes from arbitration. However, under the scheme proposed under the model in this book, the decision of the ombudsman would be binding on both parties.

[55] Otelo, *Terms of Reference*, para. 9.12; Otelo, *Annual Report 2006* states that only forty-seven remedies of 8,500 (0.55 per cent) in the period 2003–2006 have not been complied with; CISAS Rules, r. 4(l).

[56] Communications Act 2003, s. 52(2)(b) and Otelo, *Terms of Reference*, paras. 7.1, 9.9, 9.10, 9.11, 9.12 and 13(a) and (b); CISAS Rules, r. 2(e).

[57] Otelo, *Terms of Reference*, para. 9.3(c); CISAS Rules, r. 2(i).

[58] Otelo, *Annual Report 2008*, 25; 57 per cent of awards were for an amount less than £100; the average award was about £100.

[59] CISAS, *Annual Report 2007*, 11; the average award was £160.

[60] Communications Act 2003, ss. 94–7.

[61] Financial Services Handbook, rr. 2.4.3 and 2.4.4.

[62] Compulsory jurisdiction covers all regulated firms; see Financial Services and Markets Act 2000, s. 225.

[63] Compulsory jurisdiction; see Consumer Credit Act 2006, s. 59; only individuals and partnerships consisting of no more than three partners can use the procedure to complain about consumer credit.

maximum award the FOS can make is £100,000.[64] Since the Consumer Credit Act 2006 came into force in April 2007, its jurisdiction covers 26,000 regulated firms and up to 100,000 firms that have consumer-credit licences issued by the OFT.[65] A complaint made to the FOS does not have to be determined according to the law only; the ombudsman may decide a complaint by reference to what, in his or her opinion, is fair and reasonable in all the circumstances.[66] The FOS initially issues an informal recommendation to the parties; if the parties do not accept the recommendation, an ombudsman will review the case and issue a final decision.[67] This final decision only becomes binding if the complaining consumer notifies the FOS that he or she has accepted the decision.[68] A decision accepted in this way can be directly enforced by the complainant as a court order (just like an arbitration award would be).[69]

Since the decisions made under these two adjudication schemes are not binding on the consumer or customer, it is doubtful whether they would classify as arbitration. However, it should be examined whether a similar online adjudication scheme for Internet disputes, leading to decisions binding on both paries, can be classified as arbitration.

### Classification of compulsory arbitration/ombudsman services as arbitration

For cross-border disputes, the question will be whether a statutory ombudsman or adjudication decision is an award enforceable under the New York Convention. In this context, it has to be examined whether a compulsory statutory adjudication scheme counts, or should count, as arbitration.[70]

**The position under English law**    In England, s. 94(1) of the Arbitration Act 1996 expressly provides that the substantive part (Part I) of the Act

---

[64] Financial Services Handbook, r. 3.9.5.

[65] See OFT, *Annual Report 2005/2006*, 3, 9 and 10; Morris and James, in 'The Financial Ombudsman Service', 641, have described this huge institution and resulting bureaucracy as a 'brave new world in ombudsmanry'.

[66] See Financial Services and Markets Act 2000, s. 228(2) and *R (on the application of IFG Financial Services Ltd)* v. *Financial Ombudsman Service Ltd* [2005] EWHC 1153 (Admin), para. 13.

[67] A final decision is only issued in about 8 per cent of all cases; see OFT, *Annual Report 2005/2006*, 36.

[68] Financial Services and Markets Act 2000, s. 228(5).

[69] Financial Services and Markets Act 2000, s. 229(8) and (9) and Part III Schedule 17.

[70] Under the model proposed here, unlike the adjudication schemes discussed above, the decision would be binding on both parties.

applies (with modifications[71]) to statutory arbitration. Section 95(1)(a) creates a legal fiction by implying that the parties have concluded an arbitration agreement. Therefore, if the ombudsman or adjudication service is based on statute, the English Arbitration Act 1996, including its enforcement provisions, applies.

In England, there is no inherent contradiction between compulsory arbitration and agreement. An example of this is the recent Court of Appeal case of *Stretford* v. *Football Association*.[72] In this case, even though the arbitration clause was imposed on all players' agents by the sport's regulatory body (the Football Association) in the compulsory licence, the court found that the dispute resolution was voluntary arbitration.[73] The Court of Appeal held that the arbitration procedure was imbued with sufficient due process to comply with Art. 6 of the ECHR.[74] Even though the agent had no choice but to enter into the licence agreement with the (self-) regulatory body, and it could therefore be described as compulsory (the Court of Appeal avoiding this term), the Court of Appeal said that it was a voluntary agreement to submit the dispute to arbitration, and therefore the English Arbitration Act 1996 applied.[75]

In a much earlier case of 1874, the House of Lords held that a contractual obligation of the parties to refer a dispute to arbitration is compulsory if it is based on statute.[76] In that case, the parties were bound to refer the dispute to arbitration because of the statutory underpinning of the arbitration agreement. Hence there is no inherent contradiction in saying that arbitration is based on an agreement and statute simultaneously.

Under English law,[77] an extra-judicial adjudication scheme, which is imposed by statute *but at the same time* based on an agreement, may qualify as arbitration, regardless of the name given to the scheme or its statutory basis.[78]

In the the two schemes discussed above, since the decisions are not binding on the 'weaker' party, these adjudication schemes do not constitute arbitration for this reason.

If the ombudsman scheme is based on statute, the English Arbitration Act 1996 will apply in England because of s. 94(1). The position under

---

[71] See English Arbitration Act 1996, ss. 95–98.
[72] [2007] All ER (D) 346 (Mar) (CA), Judgment of 21 March 2007.
[73] *Ibid.* para. 49.     [74] *Ibid.* para. 65.     [75] *Ibid.* para. 49.
[76] *Caledonian Railway Company* v. *Greenock and Wemyss Bay Railway Company* (1870–1875) LR 2 Sc 347 (HL), Judgment of 24 March 1874.
[77] And because of s. 94(1) of the English Arbitration Act 1996.
[78] Provided it involves binding dispute resolution as described at 4.2.2.

English law and the New York Convention can be summarised by the following table:

Table 2. *Relationship between extra-judicial adjudication and arbitration*

|  | Adjudication scheme imposed by statute/statutory instrument | Arbitration imposed by self-regulatory body, not on statutory basis |
|---|---|---|
| Recognition and enforcement under the New York Convention, Arts. II and V(1)(a) | Agreement required | Agreement required |
| Applicability of English Arbitration Act 1996 | s. 94(1) | Agreement required (*Stretford* case) |

**Enforcement under the New York Convention**    The question of whether an award resulting from a compulsory scheme, which is also based on agreement, is enforceable in a foreign jurisdiction under Art. III of the New York Convention depends on whether the law applicable to the arbitration agreement[79] recognises it as such. One of the factors that may make an award unenforceable is the lack of consent.[80] Whether sufficient consent exists will be determined by the applicable law[81] and depends on all the circumstances.[82] Furthermore, the conclusion as to whether compulsory arbitration can be based on agreement will ultimately

---

[79] See 4.3.1.

[80] New York Convention, Arts. II(1) and V(1)(a); A. Van den Berg, *The New York Arbitration Convention of 1958* (Deventer: Kluwer, 1981) 287–8.

[81] New York Convention, Art. V(1)(a).

[82] An example for quasi-compulsory arbitration is the US–Iran Claims Tribunal. This has been set up by a treaty between the United States and Iran (Algiers Accord). Individuals bringing claims before the tribunal are, of course, not a party to this treaty. However, the Court of Appeal of Paris, on 28 June 2001, has held that an individual bringing a claim before the tribunal agrees to arbitration at that point; (2002) XXVII *Yearbook Commercial Arbitration* 439, para. 14; by contrast, the English High Court has found otherwise (under Dutch law) in *Dallal* v. *Bank Mellat* (1986) XI *Yearbook Commercial Arbitration* 547, para. 2 (but even though there was no agreement, the court found the tribunal to be competent and therefore found *res judicata* and struck out the English proceedings as vexatious; para. 15).

vary between national laws.[83] However, there are precedents in sports arbitration that suggests that it can.[84] Furthermore, it is unclear from the drafting history of the New York Convention whether or not it was intended to apply to compulsory arbitration.[85] Therefore there is no clear-cut answer, and much will depend on the applicable law.

**An argument for classifying compulsory arbitration based on agreement as arbitration under the New York Convention**    Both traditional arbitration and ombudsmen services constitute adjudication by a private party outside of the ordinary courts.[86] They play a similar role, i.e. the resolution of a dispute between two private parties with a final decision imposed by a third-party adjudicator outside the courts, which has *res judicata* effect.[87]

Ultimately, the question of whether a particular[88] adjudication scheme could be described as arbitration depends on whether the parties have agreed to it (in which case it may be arbitration) or whether it has been imposed by statute or a regulator *in such a way* that it cannot be said that there is an arbitration agreement (in which case there is no arbitration). It is argued here that if arbitration is imposed by a regulator, the process

---

[83] In some jurisdictions, compulsory or mandatory arbitration may be regarded as unconstitutional and an infringement of the right to a fair trial; see, for example, the decision of the Italian Corte Constituzionale of 8 June 2005, where it held that a statutory provision providing for mandatory arbitration for waterworks disputes is unconstitutional; see Kluwer Arbitration Reports available from www.kluwerarbitration.com/arbitration/arb/home/ipn/default.asp?ipn=80640 [1 April 2008].

[84] See, for example, *Slaney* v. *IAAF*, where the US Court of Appeals (7th Cir), 27 March 2001, has recognised an award made by compulsory sports arbitration as *res judicata*, and did not recognise the defence that there was no written submission agreement: (2001) XXVI *Yearbook Commercial Arbitration* 1091, paras. 8–12.

[85] Van den Berg, *The New York Arbitration Convention of 1958*, 380; Art. I(2) of the New York Convention states that the Convention applies to arbitral awards made by permanent bodies to which the parties have submitted – the adverb 'voluntarily' was dropped before 'submitted'; this seems to suggest that compulsory arbitration is covered by the Convention.

[86] R. James, *Private Ombudsmen and Public Law* (Aldershot: Ashgate, 1997), 3: 'An ombudsman is an independent person who can receive complaints, investigate them and direct or recommend a remedy where the complaint is found to be justified.'

[87] If the rules of the ombudsman scheme provide for finality (as is the case of the schemes reviewed above, once the customer has agreed to it): *R (on the application of Towry Law Financial Services Plc)* v. *Financial Ombudsman Service Ltd* [2002] EWHC 1603 (Admin), para. 17; *Westminster City Council* v. *Haywood and Another (No. 2)* [2000] ICR 827 (ChD), 840 (*res judicata* effect of statutory ombudsman schemes); and *R (Bradley and Others)* v. *Secretary of State for Work and Pensions, The Times*, 27 February 2007 (finding of ombudsman binding on Minister if it complied with due process).

[88] There is no general blueprint for ombudsman schemes; each has to be evaluated according to its own rules and terms of reference; James, *Private Ombudsmen and Public Law*, 2–3.

could nevertheless qualify as arbitration.[89] The argument here is that arbitration can be compulsory *and* be based on agreement at the same time. There is no inherent contradiction in the notion of compulsory arbitration based on agreement.

Hence arbitration and ombudsman schemes share many similar features, and the discussion of fairness standards and how to implement them is equally relevant to ombudsman schemes and arbitration. Therefore, if an ombudsman scheme is based on an agreement,[90] it *should* amount to arbitration, and the New York Convention should apply for enforcement purposes in foreign jurisdictions.[91]

### Compulsory ombudsman/adjudication scheme for Internet disputes

The reason why statutory ombudsman/adjudication schemes imposing compulsory arbitration have been discussed here is that they compel the 'stronger' party to submit to arbitration and therefore show an example of how the 'stronger' party can be brought before the adjudicator.

An ombudsman or adjudication scheme for Internet disputes would effectively solve the Catch-22 situation described above, while still avoiding the complexity, delay and cost involved in litigation. Such a scheme would be an intermediary dispute resolution mechanism where non-statutory online arbitration is not available, in accordance with the proportionate model advocated in Chapter 7.[92]

In his preliminary report, 'Access to Justice' (Department of Constitutional Affairs, June 2005), Lord Woolf recommended that the government should consider creating more ombudsman schemes for consumer complaints.[93]

An ombudsman or adjudication scheme for Internet disputes would be necessary in a situation where there is a dispute between an individual and a corporate entity, and where there is no contractually mandated arbitration scheme applicable to the dispute. This would ensure access to fair dispute resolution (second principle of fairness[94]).

---

[89] See, for example, the *Malmö Taxi Association* case discussed at 6.2.5, where, in order to provide a taxi service, a driver had to obtain a license from the MTA, and this contained an arbitration clause. Even though the adjudication was imposed in this way, it was still considered to be voluntary arbitration; the same argument is made by J. McLaughlin in respect of the United States in 'Arbitrability: Current Trends in the United States' (1996) 12(2) *Arbitration International* 113–36, 134.

[90] And if the ombudsman's decisions are binding.

[91] However, the courts in different jurisdictions may take different views on this; see fn. 83, above.

[92] See 7.4.      [93] Lord Woolf, 'Access to Justice', para. 16.      [94] See 2.2.3.

The model outlined here would include an online adjudication scheme created by legislation as one piece of the jigsaw puzzle.[95] Such an Internet-disputes ombudsman office could not be created without legislative backing, as there is no single discernible self-regulatory body or even industry sector that could take the initiative and bind the parties into arbitration agreements.

The need for such an ombudsman scheme arises from the power imbalance described in Chapter 2, the jurisdictional issues pointed out in Chapter 3 and the inadequacy of arbitration as a form of dispute resolution for Internet disputes discussed in Chapters 6 and 7. It would provide for a fair dispute resolution mechanism, thereby enhancing trust and confidence in the Internet as a communications medium and in E-commerce generally, and it would overcome the difficulties of bringing both parties to the adjudicator. It would make dispute resolution accessible (second principle of fairness) and provide a counterpoise (third principle of fairness[96]) where the parties are of unequal bargaining power.

The scheme should be based on the agreement of both parties, so that the scheme is a form of online arbitration that would fall under the regime of the New York Convention. This would ensure that the decisions are awards that can be enforced in a foreign jurisdiction under the New York Convention.[97] It has already been argued, above, that a statutory, compulsory arbitration scheme can be based on agreement of the parties.[98]

The scheme should be funded by a mixture of a fee imposed on the parties and a state subsidy from general taxation, which is required to make the scheme accessible. The issue of costs and funding is further discussed below.[99]

The next section will outline the due process (first principle of fairness[100]) standards that any online arbitration or ombudsman scheme should comply with.

### 8.3 Standards for online arbitration of Internet disputes – findings from previous chapters

This section compiles the due process standards that *should* apply to online arbitration and any ombudsman scheme by extrapolating the findings made from the discussion of applicable law in Chapter 4, due process

---

[95] The model is fully outlined below, at 8.6.    [96] See 2.2.3.
[97] See the discussion at 6.2.5.    [98] See 8.2.2.    [99] See 8.5.    [100] See 2.4.

in arbitration in Chapter 6 and consumer arbitration and the UDRP as examples of non-consensual forms of arbitration in Chapter 7.

### 8.3.1 Applying the 'weaker' party's mandatory laws

In Chapter 4, it has been argued that, for cross-border Internet disputes, the mandatory laws of the 'weaker' party (such as a consumer, or an insured) should be applied if the corporate entity directed its activities to that party's jurisdiction, unless the 'weaker' party has misled the corporate entity as to his or her location.[101] If mandatory laws did not apply, this would seriously undermine the effectiveness of laws designed to protect the weaker party in a situation of power imbalance.[102]

### 8.3.2 Independence and impartiality of the provider and the arbitrators

Independence and impartiality have been generally discussed in great detail in Chapters 6[103] and 7.[104] In this context, a distinction must be made between independence of the institution and that of the arbitrators.

### Independence and impartiality of the arbitrators

The first point here is that the arbitrator should be impartial and have no conflicts of interest.[105] The arbitrator should be under a duty to disclose a CV and any relevant interests.[106] A relevant interest would be an interest of the arbitrator or of a person closely affiliated to the arbitrator,[107] such as a business, professional, financial or personal relationship with one of the parties (or someone affiliated to a party or its representative), or any interest in the subject matter or outcome of the dispute.[108]

However, this is not sufficient. In addition, the procedure should allow each party to *challenge* an appointment of an arbitrator on the basis of lack of independence or partiality, and the same standard as that observed

---

[101] See 4.3.5.  [102] See 4.4.5 and, in relation to consumer protection, 7.2.4.
[103] See 6.3.  [104] See 7.2.4 and 7.3.2.
[105] With a duty to recuse him or herself if there is a conflict of interest.
[106] AAA, *Due Process Protocol for Consumers*, Principle 3(e).
[107] Such as a spouse, relative or business partner.
[108] ABA, *Guidelines*, Principle VI A(3)(a) and (b).

by a court of law should apply. Such a challenge could take place before a specialist appeal panel.[109]

A more difficult issue to address is systemic bias. As far as the independence of the arbitrators themselves is concerned, arbitrators should be chosen from a variety of stakeholder groups (i.e. not only those representing trademark interests for IP disputes, or not only those representing consumer interests for consumer disputes, etc.).[110] Furthermore, it would be preferable if the arbitrators' income is not dependent on the number of appointments, as, again, there is a risk of a 'repeat player' effect if only one party refers cases for arbitration.[111] Hence, if arbitrators are paid a regular (part-time or full-time) salary (such as adjudicators working for an ombudsman scheme), they are less likely to be influenced by the prospect of repeat business. Furthermore, the adjudicators should have sufficient independence from the provider. If possible, the allocation of arbitrators to a particular case should be random, after certain practical considerations (such as technical expertise, language capability, neutral nationality and availability) have been taken care of.[112] If both parties can influence the appointment of the arbitrator(s), this would improve independence, albeit that the dominant repeat player is at an advantage, knowing the arbitrators better than the one-shot player. Hence random allocation is preferable for ensuring independence.

## Independence of the institution

The institution should clearly be independent of both parties.[113] As with the arbitrators themselves, the institution should also be under an

---

[109] On the unavailability of such a challenge under the UDRP, see 7.3.2, and see also the discussion at 6.3.2 on the lower standards of independence applied to commercial arbitrators; AAA, *Due Process Protocol for Consumers*, Principle 3(e).

[110] See 6.3.2, 7.2.4 and 7.3.2.      [111] See 3.5.2 and 6.3.2.

[112] See discussion of the UDRP at 7.3.2.

[113] Dispute resolution by a trade or consumer association is not fully independent and is therefore contrary to this principle; however, cf. both EC Recommendation 98/257/EC, Principles I and II and ABA, *Guidelines*, Principle VI A, which both settle for lower standards (the arbitrator must not have been employed by the association in the last three years before appointment, and full disclosure). For a detailed examination of trade associations' complaints procedures and a conclusion that they are ineffective, see D. Greenberg and H. Stanton, 'Business Groups, Consumer Problems: The Contradiction of Trade Association Complaint Handling', in L. Nader (ed.), *No Access to Law* (New York, NY: Academic Press, 1980), 193–231, 225–7; see also Condition 4d of the Consumer Code Approval Scheme, Core Criteria and Guidance, dated November 2006, OFT 390.

obligation to disclose any financial or institutional relationship with either party.[114]

If one party sets up and pays for the procedure and/or sets up the arbitration scheme, this creates a risk of systemic bias.[115] This risk arises, for example, where a trade or industry association (or a consumer association for that matter) sets up a self-regulatory dispute resolution scheme for disputes between its members and consumers (business).

This issue could be mitigated through the institutional organisation of the provider. All competing stakeholder interests should be represented by the body designing the scheme and the governing or oversight body of the dispute-resolution service provider. Furthermore, the entire membership of the executive of the redress scheme should be independent of any trade association or other body promoting the redress scheme.

The service should be funded in such a way as to prevent real or perceived bias.[116] Clearly, if online arbitration or an ombudsman scheme is funded by general taxation, no independence issue would arise. Considering that state courts are also subsidised, public funds should be used to subsidise online arbitration for Internet disputes, and in particular to fund some of the costs of setting up such schemes.

The two ombudsman schemes in the financial services and communications sector, described above,[117] have been funded by industry through an annual levy and a case fee.[118] Since the respective regulators[119] have controlled and approved the procedural rules and supervise the operation of the schemes, their independence has not been tainted by the fact that the dispute resolution is paid for by industry. Therefore it should be considered whether a regulator, such as the OFT or Ofcom, should set up an online arbitration or ombudsman scheme for Internet disputes, as this would avoid the conflict between funding coming from industry and independence of the scheme.

However, it should be pointed out here that funding cannot come from industry in the form of a regular levy, as there is no clearly identifiable,

---

[114] Such as a trader being paid a commission for referring cases to the dispute-resolution service provider; see ABA, *Guidelines*, Principle VI A(1) and (2).

[115] See 6.3.2 and 7.2.4.

[116] Consumers International, 'Disputes in Cyberspace', 16; Condition 4d of the Consumer Code Approval Scheme, Core Criteria and Guidance, dated November 2006, OFT 390.

[117] See 8.2.2.

[118] See Otelo, *Terms of Reference*, Art. 12; CISAS Rules, r. 6(a); FOS, *Annual Report 2005/2006*, 42.

[119] Ofcom and the FSA respectively.

regulated sector.[120] Ideally, the procedure should be financed by public funds.[121] This is the case for the Austrian Internet Ombudsman.[122]

Furthermore, if only one party selects the dispute-resolution service provider, this also creates a risk of systemic bias, as has been explained in Chapter 7.[123] The problem is completely avoided if there is only one institution providing online arbitration for particular types of disputes, as competition between different institutions may taint their independence, competing to appear friendly to the party selecting their services.[124] If there is more than one institution, this problem could be avoided if cases are allocated to a provider either randomly or through a third party. Alternatively, the problem could be alleviated[125] by ensuring that the procedural rules are the same for all providers, so that they only compete on cost.

### 8.3.3 Fair hearing

The principle of fair hearing requires that each party is given an opportunity to present his or her case and respond to the case of the other. Hence each party must be given an opportunity to advance legal argument and factual evidence, and be shown and given an opportunity to react to the legal argument and evidence of the other party.[126]

Several requirements flow from this principle. Very tight and inflexible word limits or deadlines for filing submissions might infringe a party's right to present his or her case.[127] An example of this has been discussed in Chapter 7 in relation to the UDRP, where the respondent has less than three weeks for filing a response to the complaint.[128] Furthermore, a strict limit on the number of submissions by the parties, such as categorically disallowing a reply to response, may also be an infringement of the principle of fair hearing.[129] Similarly, while an oral hearing is not always required, in some complex cases or cases requiring the evaluation of evidence, an oral hearing (possibly conducted using online technology such

---

[120] See discussion at 8.5.    [121] See 8.5.    [122] See description at 5.3.2.    [123] See 7.3.2.
[124] UDRP is discussed above at 7.3.2.
[125] But not completely avoided, as the competition may still influence the decision-making.
[126] See 6.4, 7.2.4 and 7.3.2; see also EC Recommendation 98/257/EC, Principle III; Condition 4d of the Consumer Code Approval Scheme, Core Criteria and Guidance, dated November 2006, OFT 390.
[127] See 7.3.2; Consumers International, 'Disputes in Cyberspace', 19.
[128] See 7.3.2.    [129] Discussed in relation to the UDRP at 7.3.2.

as Web- and video-conferencing) may be appropriate, and this should be left to the discretion of the arbitrator.[130]

In the international context, language barriers may deprive one party from obtaining a fair hearing. For this reason, it is important that procedural rules contain sensible stipulations about the language of the proceedings and translation.[131]

It is important for an arbitration or ombudsman procedure used between parties subject to a power imbalance that the 'powerful' party is not given more influence in designing the procedural rules as an effect of the 'repeat player' situation. In other words, the procedural questions should be decided either by the arbitrator in the case or, *ex ante*, for all disputes, by all stakeholders involved.[132]

In situations where the individual is likely to be unrepresented and therefore unable to present a case, an inquisitorial procedure, where the arbitrator takes the initiative in investigating and researching the evidence and law, may be more suitable than the 'pure' adversarial approach in order to reduce the need for costly legal representation.[133]

### 8.3.4 Reasons for decisions and transparency

Arbitrators should hand down reasoned decisions.[134] Like the UDRP, any online arbitration procedure should be fully transparent. This not only means that information about the procedure, the rules, its terms of reference, costs, the arbitrators' details and CV, and the procedure for selection and allocation of arbitrators should be accessible online, but that the

---

[130] See discussion of the UDRP at 7.3; AAA, *Due Process Protocol for Consumers*, Principle 12(a); see also Perritt, 'Dispute Resolution in Cyberspace', 680.

[131] See the discussion of the language issue in the context of the UDRP at 7.3.2; Consumers International, 'Disputes in Cyberspace', 18.

[132] See further the discussion of consumer arbitration at 8.2.

[133] See 6.4 and the discussion of the model below at 8.6.3; see also EC Recommendation 98/257/EC, Principle IV and Condition 4d of the Consumer Code Approval Scheme, Core Criteria and Guidance, dated November 2006, OFT 390; see also Richardson and Genn, 'Tribunals in Transition', and James, *Private Ombudsmen and Public Law*, 3; OECD, *Recommendation on Consumer Dispute Resolution and Redress* (July 2007), Recommendation II A 3, recognising the need for accessible procedures, avoiding the need for legal representation.

[134] See the explanation of the importance of reasons at 6.5, and, in the context of consumer arbitration, at 7.2.4; see also Condition 4d of the Consumer Code Approval Scheme, Core Criteria and Guidance, dated November 2006, OFT 390; AAA, *Due Process Protocol for Consumers*, Principle 15(c) and Consumers International, 'Disputes in Cyberspace', 19.

reasoned decisions should also be published online, and the principle of confidentiality should not apply.[135]

This standard, that decisions should be published, would be a departure from the traditional confidentiality of arbitration awards and is likely to be resisted by corporate entities who wish awards to remain confidential.

### 8.3.5 Judicial review/appeal

In order to allow for the correction of serious irregularities in the procedure (such as a challenge to the arbitrator's independence) and of mistakes of law, and in order to reduce the inconsistency of decisions, there should be a possibility of appeal to a superior body.[136] This superior body could be a panel of three or five senior arbitrators. However, because of the potential inherent in an appeal system to increase cost and delay, and hence its risk of reducing access to justice, appeals should be strictly limited by a leave requirement and a requirement for the appellant to pay (at least some of) the costs of an appeal. Appeals should only be allowed on important points of law or for procedural challenges.[137]

Having discussed the fairness standards that should apply to online arbitration, some thought should be given to how these standards can be implemented.

## 8.4 Implementation of the standards

As has been seen in Chapter 6, traditional arbitration is based on the principle of party autonomy. This principle does not work well where the parties are subject to a considerable power imbalance, as here it is likely that the 'stronger' party will seek to determine the rules to the detriment of the 'weaker' party, especially if the 'stronger' party is a repeat player. Therefore it is important that the fairness standards outlined above are incorporated into procedural rules. This can be done in four ways: through (i) the institutional rules, (ii) national framework legislation,

---

[135] The case for transparency has been made at 6.6, but see also the discussion in Chapter 7 in relation to consumer disputes (at 7.2.4) and the UDRP (at 7.3.2); Perritt, 'Dispute Resolution in Cyberspace', 682; Consumers International, 'Disputes in Cyberspace', 17; BEUC position paper, 'Alternative Dispute Resolution' of 21 November 2002, BEUC/X/048/2002, 10. Cf. the Austrian Internet Ombudsman, which keeps its rulings confidential; see www.ombudsmann.at/ombudsmann.php/cat/21/title/H%E4ufige±Fragen [1 April 2008].

[136] See 6.7 and 7.3.2.     [137] See the discussion at 6.7.

(iii) an international convention and (iv) a referral system, each of which will be discussed in turn.

### 8.4.1 Institutional rules

Arbitration organisations may find that Internet disputes, or certain types of Internet disputes, require different sets of procedural rules than those used in commercial arbitration and therefore formulate separate rules for particular types of disputes.

Tentative first steps in this direction have been made. For example, AAA formulated special rules for consumer disputes in 2005.[138] These Rules amended the rules for commercial arbitration and provided, for example, that consumers could still go to a small claims court,[139] and also provided for a low-cost fee schedule for consumers.[140] The AAA has also formulated the principles that are to govern its consumer arbitrations in its Consumer Due Process Protocol. The Protocol was drawn up by the AAA's National Consumer Disputes Advisory Committee, whose aim was to draw up principles reflecting broad consensus on standards for consumer arbitration, hoping that this will inform consumer rules generally and, ultimately, legislation and judicial opinions. Likewise, the CIArb also provides a dedicated set of rules for consumer arbitration/ adjudication.[141]

The argument of this book is that, for the Internet disputes under consideration, special institutional rules should be drawn up. Institutional rules are important for the development of arbitration law and are therefore important for the development of fairness standards.

However, a general awareness that arbitration between parties subject to a power imbalance may need special rules to deal with fairness issues[142] is only beginning to develop, and these efforts are largely confined to the B2C power imbalance. Therefore the second option, national framework legislation, dealing specifically with Internet disputes, is required.

---

[138] See *Consumer-Related Disputes: Supplementary Procedures* of 15 September 2005, replacing the rules of 1 July 2003, available from www.adr.org/sp.asp?id=22014 [1 April 2008].

[139] *Ibid.* r. C-1(d).

[140] *Ibid.* r. C-8: if the claim does not exceed $10,000, the consumer is responsible for fees not exceeding $125; if the claim is between $10,000 and $75,000, the maximum fee the consumer will be charged is $375.

[141] ICAS, rules available from www.idrs.ltd.uk/Consumer/PDF/ICAS_Rules_Application.pdf [1 April 2008].

[142] And other issues such as affordability.

## 8.4.2 National legislation

National legislation should set a framework amending the general legislation on arbitration for Internet disputes between a company and individuals in order to incorporate the minimum fairness standards discussed
above. A party should be able to challenge an award if these standards
have not been met. For example, tentative steps in this direction have
been made by the Californian Code of Civil Procedure, containing specific
due process standards for consumer arbitration, concerning the independence of the arbitrators and of the arbitration institution and disclosure
requirements.[143] The due process standards outlined above may serve as
a blueprint to draft a model law setting out the standards that could be
provided in national framework legislation for Internet disputes.

### 8.4.3 An international convention on enforcement of awards

It has been mentioned at 3.9 that the jurisdictional rules and the rules
on enforcement of court judgments pose real and substantial barriers to
the resolution of Internet disputes. By contrast, the New York Convention has facilitated the recognition and enforcement of foreign awards
by committing contracting states to recognising and enforcing foreign
arbitral awards, and by limiting the grounds on which recognition and
enforcement can be refused to international public policy.[144]

However, as has been discussed in Chapter 7, certain types of disputes
where the parties are subject to a power imbalance, such as consumer
disputes, are either not arbitrable, or the recognition or enforcement of
the award may be against public policy.[145] Furthermore, some states have
limited the application of the New York Convention to commercial relationships, as defined under the law of that state.[146] Furthermore, for an
adjudication/ombudsman scheme on statutory footing, in some jurisdictions a court may refuse recognition and enforcement on the basis that
the decision is not an award.[147]

---

[143] Californian Code of Civil Procedure, §§ 1281.92–1281.96; no systematic, comparative
research of all US federal and state arbitration legislation has been undertaken – the
Californian Code of Civil Procedure is only mentioned as an example.

[144] The reader is referred to 6.2.5 and 7.7.    [145] See 7.2.

[146] New York Convention, Art. I(3), 2nd sentence; forty-five (out of 142) states, including
the United States, have made such a declaration according to the author's count on the
UNCITRAL website on 25 March 2007.

[147] In this book, the view is taken that ombudsman decisions may be arbitration awards,
provided the submission to the ombudsman is based on the parties' agreement and the

Hence the political incentive for negotiating a convention is that it would make online arbitration (including certain adjudication and ombudsman schemes) of a variety of Internet disputes enforceable across international borders. If this is not practical on an international level, an attempt should at least be made on a regional level, such as in the European Union.

The notion of Internet disputes as defined in this book is wider than consumer disputes,[148] and therefore it is helpful to have a separate convention on Internet disputes. Such a convention should stipulate that, provided the minimum due process standards as defined above have been applied, the award is to be recognised and enforced in the states that have ratified the Convention. This would enable the cross-border recognition and enforcement of awards relating to Internet disputes, thus enabling cross-border Internet transactions and interactions, and it would help to incorporate the due process standards into arbitral procedure for Internet disputes.

### 8.4.4 Referral systems / clearing house

A referral or clearing-house system would provide a gateway through which individuals could find a fair online arbitration scheme. This system would provide an electronic whitelist of all existing online arbitration mechanisms complying with due process. A referral system is a website indexing, listing and linking to all dispute-resolution service providers providing arbitration compliant with the minimum due process criteria.[149] In other words, a referral system amounts to an accreditation system that, if sufficiently monitored, updated and promoted, channels consumers to fair dispute resolution.[150] This gateway could be hyperlinked from relevant websites and Internet forums. The gateway would not merely provide information about different dispute-resolution service providers, but, in addition, can provide *the* access point for individuals seeking redress. Its function would be to exclude all providers who do

decision is binding on both parties; see the discussion above, but see, for example, fn. 83, above.

[148] See the definition of relevant disputes at 3.6.

[149] It would also be necessary for the referral system to evaluate and monitor compliance on an ongoing basis.

[150] See Philippe, 'Where is Everyone Going with Online Dispute Resolution?', 183–4; Schultz, 'Does Online Dispute Resolution Need Governmental Intervention?', 94–100, makes a distinction between mere accreditation and clearing houses, but this distinction seems to be more a matter of degree than substance.

not comply with minimum due process standards, thereby regulating due process.

An example of such a system is the ECC-Net (European Consumer Centre Network)[151] set up in 2001 by the European Commission for cross-border consumer disputes.[152] At the heart of this system is a central consumer body (European Consumer Centre) in each Member State, providing advice and assistance to consumers and citizens in that particular Member State. In order to help individuals wishing to bring a claim against a company established in another Member State, the national centre will liaise with the equivalent centre in the other Member State in order to refer the consumer to the most relevant dispute resolution system in that other (foreign) Member State.[153] This could be a court using some sort of small-claims procedure, or it could be an ADR provider providing mediation or arbitration. For a dispute-resolution service provider offering arbitration to be included in the ECC-Net, it has to comply with Recommendation 98/257/EC.[154]

In this fashion, the ECC-Net provides a referral system for ADR in all EU and EEA Member States, providing a one-stop shop for cross-border dispute resolution complying with minimum fairness standards. By directing the consumer to the dispute-resolution service provider in the business' Member State, the ECC-Net also overcomes any jurisdictional and enforcement issues.

However, it has already been pointed out[155] that this Recommendation is insufficient and needs to be further developed. Furthermore, the European consumer organisation, Bureau Européen des Unions de

---

[151] See, for example, www.eej-net.org.uk; this network was established under the name EEJ-Net in 2001. The EEJ-Net merged with the Euroguichets and was renamed ECC-Net in 2005. A similar, parallel organisation is the FIN-Net, a network of dispute resolution for financial services disputes; see http://ec.europa.eu/internal_market/finservices-retail/finnet/index_en.htm#network [1 April 2008].

[152] *The European Online Marketplace: Consumer Complaints 2007*, published by ECC-Net (2008), (available from http://ec.europa.eu/consumers/redress_cons/docs/ECC_E-commerce.pdf [1 August 2008]), states that 8,834 complaints were received in 2007 (at 1).

[153] For more detail, see Bamford, 'Shopping Around'; J. Hörnle, 'The European Extra-Judicial Network – Overcoming the Obstacles' (2002) 7 *Communications Law* 143–5.

[154] And with Recommendation 2001/310/EC on the Principles for Out-of-Court Bodies Involved in the Consensual Resolution of Consumer Disputes for mediation and other forms of consensual resolution. The 1998 Recommendation only applies to binding arbitration procedures, whereas the 2001 Recommendation is applicable to consensual, non-binding forms of consumer dispute resolution.

[155] See 6.2.2.

Consommateurs (BEUC), reported that not all ADR bodies notified by the Member States, which are listed on the ECC-Net referral system, are in fact complying with the principles enunciated in the Recommendation.[156]

Another issue with the current set up of the ECC-Net is that its coverage is far from being comprehensive.[157] The ECC-Net does not oblige the Member States to create any new ADR schemes, but merely links up the already existing provision of ADR schemes.[158]

Some Member States have ADR initiatives focused on particular towns or regions,[159] whereas others have very specific ADR schemes only covering a particular type of business or sector.[160] Only a very few Member States have a general, consumer ombudsman scheme.[161] Austria has a dedicated Internet Ombudsman Service, which has already been discussed in Chapter 5,[162] and which is further mentioned below.[163] Some Member States have not notified any compliant ADR schemes.[164]

Hence, for many types of Internet disputes, there will be no relevant ADR scheme in the respondent's home Member State. Therefore the establishment of a specific Internet-dispute ombudsman/adjudication scheme should be considered at European or Member State level.[165]

## 8.5 Proportionality, costs and state funding

In Chapter 2 the conflict between due process and effectiveness has been pointed out, and it has been explained that a compromise has to be found

---

[156] BEUC position paper, 'Alternative Dispute Resolution' of 21 November 2002, BEUC/X/048/2002, 3.

[157] Ibid.

[158] Bamford, 'Shopping Around', 109. Another issue is that traders may not agree to arbitration; this has already been discussed above at 8.2.

[159] For example, in Belgium, Portugal, Germany and Spain; see http://ec.europa.eu/consumers/redress/out_of_court/adrdb_en.htm [1 April 2008].

[160] For example, Ireland and the United Kingdom; see http://ec.europa.eu/consumers/redress/out_of_court/adrdb_en.htm [1 April 2008].

[161] Norway, Sweden, Denmark, Estonia, Finland and Greece have some sort of general dispute resolution scheme for consumer disputes; see http://ec.europa.eu/consumers/redress/out_of_court/adrdb_en.htm [1 April 2008].

[162] See 5.3.2.      [163] See 8.5 and 8.6.

[164] Notably at the date of writing: the Czech Republic, the Slovak Republic, Lithuania, Hungary, Slovenia and Malta; see http://ec.europa.eu/consumers/redress/out_of_court/adrdb_en.htm [1 April 2008].

[165] The only country that seems to have a dedicated Internet ombudsman is Austria, which provides online mediation services for B2C E-commerce disputes; see www.ombudsmann.at [1 April 2008].

by balancing due process with effectiveness.[166] This book proposes four possible solutions to this conflict: (i) the use of online technology[167] to increase access (so that more due process can be 'afforded'); (ii) the use of the proportionate model of dispute resolution, creating a model of online adjudication that (in terms of due process) is positioned between litigation and commercial arbitration; (iii) recognising that some disputes are *de minimis*, i.e. of such small value that they cannot be solved by online arbitration or other forms of binding dispute resolution; and (iv) a state subsidy for some disputes to increase access, paid for by general taxation.

The first solution, the use of online technology to increase access and efficiency has already been discussed at length in Chapter 5, and will not be further discussed here.

The second possible solution to this conflict is the concept of proportionate dispute resolution discussed in Chapter 7 – the idea that procedures should be appropriate to the nature of the dispute.[168]

This concept of proportionate dispute resolution entails that, for high-value claims, formal litigation may be appropriate. For small disputes, especially if the disputants are located in different jurisdictions, online arbitration / an ombudsman scheme may be the only appropriate form of dispute resolution. It has been argued that, if there is a power imbalance between the parties, in order to make such procedures meaningful, minimum due process standards, as outlined above, should be followed. This is in accordance with the principle of proportionate dispute resolution, as these minimum due process requirements are less formal and allow for some abbreviation of procedural complexities compared to the procedure before the courts.[169] The model of online arbitration envisaged here is, in terms of due process, somewhere between litigation and commercial arbitration.

However, this raises the question of whether there should be a *de minimis*, whether disputes below a certain value can be solved at all by online arbitration. For example, if an individual pays £7 by credit card for a book from an online company, which is never delivered, the question arises as to whether such a dispute could ever be solved by online arbitration that satisfies the procedural due process outlined above – the answer is likely

---

[166] See 2.6.    [167] See Chapter 5.    [168] See the discussion at 7.4.

[169] Even if they entail 'more' due process than traditional arbitration, where the parties are of more equal bargaining power and can therefore curtail procedural protections on the basis of the principle of party autonomy and the waiver principle.

to be no. It could be argued that, for disputes below a certain threshold value, payment-card chargeback or negotiation are the only feasible forms of dispute resolution. If the dispute cannot be solved by such means, the party affected has to write off the loss.

Even if, however, a claim is trivial, but the problem is widespread and systemic, so that a large number of individuals suffer (small) harm, this should be addressed, but by regulatory compliance[170] through state enforcement or through criminal law in the case of fraud, rather than individual redress. However, since this book is only concerned with individual redress, this issue will not be discussed here.

The difficulty, however, is to state what this *de minimis* threshold should be. As a ballpark measure, one could say that this should be 10 per cent of the monthly average disposable income. Arguably, 10 per cent of the monthly average disposable income is roughly the amount any household can afford to lose without substantially damaging its standard of living. It could be argued that if the average household lost this money on an Internet transaction, this could be written off without severe financial consequences. In other words, this could be described as an acceptable risk. For the United Kingdom, the yearly average disposable income in 2005 was £13,300.[171] Twenty per cent of the average monthly disposable income is about £100. So, for claims below a value of £100,[172] it may be argued that online arbitration is not appropriate in any event, and that persons transacting online need to accept that there is a minimum level of financial risk for which redress cannot be achieved in all cases. This argument may run counter to intuition at first glance, as it seems that, currently, many Internet disputes are of small value.[173] The purpose of this book, however, is to construct a model for *fair* dispute resolution, and it has to be recognised that online arbitration that complies with due process standards will only be proportionate for certain disputes. Hence, for claims of very small value, different methods – such as negotiated assistance,

---

[170] In the United Kingdom, the OFT has enforcement powers under the Enterprise Act 2002 and in the United States the FTC has enforcement powers under the Federal Trade Commission Act.

[171] Statistics from National Statistics Online; see www.statistics.gov.uk/cci/nugget. asp?id=1552 [1 April 2007].

[172] This is only a rough estimate; it could be argued that a maximum of 5 or 20 per cent of the monthly income is the maximum that is affordable – this is not a point that is further examined.

[173] See, for example, the average claim of £87 for the Austrian Internet Ombudsman in 2006, quoted above at 5.3.2.

online mediation or resolution through payment-reverse mechanisms – must be used.

However, even for higher-value claims, the question of costs is an issue. For high-value claims, the costs of online arbitration may well be proportionate, but there is likely to be a middle ground – where the claim is above the *de minimis* (which has been argued to be in the region of £100) but below the threshold – that makes online arbitration worth pursuing. It is therefore argued that a state subsidy is needed.

In order to illustrate this argument further, it is necessary to consider how much online arbitration costs with due process incorporated. Online arbitration involves paying for the time of the arbitrator, the cost of the administration of the dispute (assuming that the administrator of the online arbitration scheme would provide the technology) and legal advice and representation. The cost will clearly vary enormously, depending on how these tasks are carried out and by whom.

Assuming, for the sake of argument, that, in a single case, an arbitrator can be found who is willing to act for a fee of £500, the administration fee is £500 and legal representation does not exceed £500 for each party, the total aggregate cost would amount to £2,000 in a not-too-complex scenario.[174]

Looking at the AAA's 'Consumer Arbitration Costs',[175] a case with a claim value below US $75,000 but above US $10,000 attracts an administrative fee of US $950 and an additional US $300 if an in-person hearing is held, an arbitrator fee of US $250 for a documents-only arbitration[176] and an arbitrator fee of US $750 if an in-person hearing is held. Hence the total for such a claim would be US $1,200 (about £600) for documents-only arbitration and US $2,000 (about £1,000) for arbitration with a hearing. If the value of the claim does not exceed US $10,000, the administrative fee is US $750, and an additional US $200 if a hearing is held, and the arbitrator fees are the same. Hence, for a claim of up to US $10,000, the total is US $1,000 (about £500) for documents-only arbitration, and US $1,700 for arbitration with an in-person hearing (about £850).[177] These figures work out between £500 and £1,000 *plus* any legal costs for both

---

[174] This is, of course, only a vague estimate of what it would cost to conduct an online arbitration. Since there is no travelling involved, and administration through an online platform is more efficient, the procedure conducted offline would be even more expensive.

[175] Effective 1 July 2003, available from www.adr.org/sp.asp?id=22039 [1 April 2008].

[176] This may include a telephone or online hearing.

[177] The arbitrators' fees are only estimates for the purposes of the deposit; however, the consumer's contribution is capped at US $125 for disputes not exceeding US $10,000,

parties.[178] If the parties choose to be legally represented, and the legal costs are about £500 for each party, the total costs for the procedure are between £1,500 and £2,000.

Another example is the CIArb arbitration scheme for disputes involving consumers or a small business in dispute with companies, for which a registration fee of £500 plus VAT is payable by the company.[179] This scheme is a documents-only arbitration. Again, there may be additional costs for legal advice and/or legal representation.

Straightforward arbitration, supported by online technology,[180] is efficient but nevertheless requires the time of a professional arbitrator, an administration institution and a legal adviser/representative, and, on the figures illustrated above, may well involve total costs in the region of somewhere between £500 and £2,000.[181]

This raises the question of whether the parties can foot this bill or whether the cost of online arbitration means that the parties will, to a large extent, be deprived of online arbitration. If a claim is smaller than, say, £5,000, the cost of online arbitration may simply be too expensive for the parties.

It should be recognised that fairness, due process, access to justice and, ultimately, the rule of law are important values that should be supported by public funding, through tax. After all, the courts are financed by the public purse, so it does not seem illogical to argue that this should also apply to online arbitration.

An alternative could be some form of insurance. However, insurance is only functional if the risk is spread widely, and if an insurance levy were imposed on E-commerce, or even Internet access, this would amount to a form of taxation that would hinder this form of technology and be contrary to the policy that the Internet should not be subject to special forms of tax. Therefore an insurance scheme is likely to be politically unacceptable. Finally, this funding could come through regulatory action – imposing a regular levy on industry to at least partially fund an Internet ombudsman service – in a similar fashion to the communications services

and at US $375 for disputes between US $10,000 and US $75,000. The business has to pay the remainder.

[178] The parties may use the AAA online platform, but the costs are the same.

[179] ICAS Rules for the scheme, para. 1.3, available at www.idrs.ltd.uk/Consumer/PDF/ICAS_Rules_Application.pdf [1 April 2008].

[180] For forms of technology, see 5.4.5.

[181] Depending on the degree of technology used, the efficiency of the administration, complexity and duration of the cases and whether the parties are legally represented/advised.

ombudsman and the financial services ombudsman. While such a scheme should be considered, at the present point in time it seems unlikely to be politically acceptable, as the Internet, unlike the areas of financial services or telecommunications, is not heavily regulated but only subject to light-touch regulation. Furthermore, the Internet sector is not homogeneous, and thus it would be hard to identify who should pay.

Therefore, funding should come from general taxation to ensure access to justice for Internet disputes. A good example for a dispute resolution procedure financed by public funds is the Austrian Internet Ombudsman, described in Chapter 5.[182]

This leaves the final issue to be considered, i.e. the question of how the costs of online arbitration should be distributed between the parties. The distribution of costs can serve as an important counterpoise to pre-existing inequality between the parties.

If the loser pays the winner's costs, an individual may be barred from access to online arbitration if costs are so high that he or she may not be able to take the risk of losing the case and having to pay the costs.

Therefore it is proposed here that, under an online arbitration scheme for Internet disputes, individuals (as the 'weaker' party) should pay a certain amount towards the cost of online arbitration, possibly capped at a maximum of between £20 and £100 depending on the value of the claim,[183] in order to deter vexatious claims. However, it is submitted that individuals, when claiming against companies, should not have to pay the full cost, even if they lose their case, in order to increase access to justice and to level the power imbalance in such cases. Companies should have to pay a larger share of the cost of online arbitration on a case-by-case basis.[184] If a dispute is between individuals, they have to share the costs equally, hence there is an even greater need for a state subsidy to increase access to dispute resolution.

## 8.6 The model: resolution of Internet disputes

The model for the resolution of Internet disputes proposed in this book is a jigsaw puzzle with different elements. The main elements proposed

---

[182] See 5.3.2.

[183] See, for example, OECD, *Recommendation on Consumer Dispute Resolution and Redress* (July 2007), Recommendation II A 1, which recognises that some costs *may be* imposed on the consumer, but that this cost must not be disproportionate to the claim.

[184] This contribution could be tapered according to the size of the corporate entity; see 3.6.1.

are: (i) non-binding forms of ODR, (ii) redress against online merchants provided by payment providers, (iii) online arbitration provided by private schemes, (iv) a statutory online adjudication or ombudsman scheme and (v) litigation. While this book focuses on online adjudication (online arbitration and online ombudsmen) and its benefits for Internet disputes, it acknowledges the role of other forms of ODR and litigation as parts of this jigsaw puzzle. Hence this book does not propose that online arbitration is the only form of dispute resolution. The significance of online arbitration is that it widens the availability of (and access to) binding dispute resolution.[185] The following outlines the essential elements of the model, and how they each fit into the puzzle.

### 8.6.1 Non-binding forms of ODR

Non-binding forms of dispute resolution can terminate a dispute without the need for a binding decision. It has been discussed in Chapter 4 that online mediation should be used as a mechanism before online arbitration, to filter out the disputes where a compromise can be found.[186] Non-binding forms of ODR are complementary to online arbitration, and may, in particular, solve disputes that fall below the *de minimis* threshold for online arbitration.

### 8.6.2 Payment-reverse mechanisms

Payment-reverse mechanisms, such as credit-card chargebacks, have been outlined in Chapter 3.[187] They can provide a remedy where a party claims that payment should be reversed.

### 8.6.3 Online arbitration

Online arbitration is the most important jigsaw piece for the model proposed, and this section outlines, by way of summary, the main issues.

#### De minimis

In recognition of the principle of proportionality, it has been argued in this chapter[188] that there should be a *de minimis* threshold below which disputes cannot be solved by online arbitration. This has been set at a

---

[185] See 5.5.      [186] See 4.2.      [187] See 3.8.      [188] See 8.5.

figure of approximately £100 on the basis of affordability.[189] Disputes below this threshold should be solved by non-binding forms of dispute resolution or payment-reverse mechanisms.

## Due process standards and their implementation

The main concern of this book is the *fair* resolution of Internet disputes, and it has been argued that, in order to achieve this, minimum due process standards, set at a higher level than those pertaining to traditional arbitration, should be incorporated in all online arbitration procedures. They could be implemented by professional bodies and arbitration institutions, national legislation, a clearing-house referral system and, on the international plane, a new convention.[190]

## Contractually mandated online arbitration

The greatest challenge for online arbitration is how to bring the parties before the online arbitrator. As has been discussed in Chapter 4,[191] arbitration is based on the *agreement*[192] between the parties, and this raises the question of how to make this form of dispute resolution available against an unwilling party, to protect the 'weaker' party in dispute resolution. Essentially, a trusted party who commits the parties to use online arbitration is needed. As has already been discussed,[193] there are two ways to achieve this.

Firstly, if the dispute arises from the activities of a platform (such as an online auction,[194] a social networking site[195] or a video-sharing site[196]), arbitration could be made a condition for participation in the activity. Participants would agree to online arbitration for the benefit of other participants or third parties. The platform operator could refer the parties

---

[189] See the discussion above at 8.5.     [190] See 8.4.     [191] See 4.2.2.

[192] With the exception of statutory arbitration, for example in England.

[193] See the discussion above at 8.2.

[194] eBay, for example, does not bind buyers and sellers on its auction platform to (online) arbitration.

[195] Facebook, for example, provides for arbitration of disputes between itself and its users, but not for disputes between users or between a user and a third party. The terms expressly state: 'no disputes or claims relating to any transactions you enter into with a third party through the Facebook Marketplace may be arbitrated'; see 'Terms of Use' (24 May 2007), available from www.facebook.com/terms.php [1 April 2008].

[196] YouTube, for example, also does not include arbitration between users, or between users and third parties, in its terms and conditions; see 'Terms of Use', available from www.youtube.com/t/terms [1 August 2007].

to online arbitration (maybe after online mediation has been attempted but failed) at no cost to the operator.

Secondly, companies engaging in business activities on the Internet should consider joining a trustmark scheme, which incorporates online arbitration (possibly as part of an escalated dispute resolution procedure, moving from assisted negotiation to online mediation and then to online arbitration).[197]

For both ways of contractually mandated online arbitration, the costs should be shared between the parties, and the company should pay a greater share than the individual.[198] Both online platforms and online companies would benefit from such referral, as it would make their activities 'safer' and more reliable, as participants would know that binding dispute resolution and redress are available. Therefore it is highly recommended that online platforms and individual online companies refer the participants in their activities to online arbitration *before* a dispute arises.

## UK National Online Ombudsman Office

The second answer to the challenge of bringing the parties before the online arbitrator is the creation of a national online adjudication or online ombudsman scheme on a statutory footing ('Online Ombudsman Office' or 'OOO'). The legislation should provide for the procedural rules of the OOO, incorporating the due process standards outlined above[199] and addressing costs and payment issues. In order to keep costs down and avoid the need for legal representation, the procedure should be inquisitorial – the ombudsman should be in charge of managing the evidence and submissions.

One design issue is whether there should be only one OOO (similar to the Financial Ombudsman or the Austrian Internet Ombudsman) or whether there should be several providers (similar to the UDRP). The advantage of having more than one provider is that competition between providers reduces costs and means that companies have a choice as to which scheme to join (which makes it easier to argue that there is an arbitration agreement).[200] However, the disadvantage is that due process may seriously be compromised, as the providers will not only compete on the basis of cost but also on whether they effectively represent the interests

---

[197] See the discussion above at 8.2.1.    [198] See the discussion above at 8.5.
[199] See 8.3.    [200] See the discussion above at 8.3.2.

of the companies.[201] For this reason, it would be preferable to have only one OOO.

In order to bring the parties before the online arbitrator, it will be necessary to make it compulsory for companies conducting business online to join the OOO scheme.[202] This would address the problem of companies avoiding the jurisdiction of the OOO. The scheme should be asymmetrical – compulsory for companies to join but voluntary for individuals in the sense that they can opt to agree to the OOO online arbitration *after* the dispute has arisen, by submitting the dispute to the OOO or by agreeing (or refusing) to defend a dispute brought against them before the OOO. Only if an individual refuses to agree to online arbitration before the OOO should the company be able to litigate before the courts. Individuals would be encouraged (but not forced) to use the OOO. However, once a case has been brought before the OOO, any decision should be binding on and enforceable by both parties, including the individual.

The legislation should impose an obligation on companies to join the OOO online-arbitration scheme, by entering into an agreement with the OOO. If a company flouts this statutory obligation, it would be in breach of law, and regulatory enforcement action could be taken.[203] Such enforcement action could include undertakings by the company that it will join the OOO online-arbitration scheme and, if this is not complied with, a power of the regulator to apply for an injunction to compel membership in the OOO scheme. However, the OOO would have no jurisdiction unless and until the company has agreed to the OOO online-arbitration scheme. This is important, as, for the New York Convention, arbitration must be based on agreement. Under this construction, the OOO scheme would be arbitration, with the consequence that an OOO award can be enforced in a foreign jurisdiction under the New York Convention.[204]

Another design question relates to the jurisdictional reach of the OOO.[205] In particular, the question arises as to whether the statute could

---

[201] Examined in the context of the UDRP.     [202] See the discussion above at 8.2.2.

[203] The Enterprise Act 2002 could be amended to bring this within the remit of the OFT. The issue with this construction would be that, for the model, the definition of the 'weaker party' not only includes consumers but all individuals. Another alternative would be to amend the Communications Act 2003 and establish the OOO under OFCOM's supervision; or a new piece of legislation might establish a new regulator, creating and supervising the OOO and enforcing the statutory obligations of companies conducting online activities.

[204] See the discussion above.

[205] The Austrian Internet Ombudsman covers consumers resident in Austria who claim against companies in Austria or abroad (this reach is limited to the European Union).

bind companies *established* in a foreign jurisdiction to join the OOO scheme. If the foreign company can be said to have directed or targeted its online activities to the territory, the United Kingdom could assert prescriptive jurisdiction on the basis of the territoriality principle.[206]

Even if the United Kingdom were justified in applying the statute to foreign companies under international law, nevertheless the question arises as to whether this assertion of jurisdiction would be practical or effective. If a foreign company did not join the OOO scheme, and if it refused to take part in any proceedings before the OOO, the OOO would have no jurisdiction. A UK-based individual wishing to bring a case against the foreign company would be limited to bringing a complaint before the regulator. Although the company's local regulator is unlikely to enforce that regulatory action by the UK body, it would, in itself, involve negative publicity and put pressure on the company to join the scheme. At this stage, it should be pointed out that the OOO would effectively be providing a valuable service for online companies by providing subsidised, fair dispute resolution, which should enhance the reputation and branding of the companies involved. Therefore, once foreign companies are aware of the scheme, they are likely to join.

Another question arises as to whether the OOO scheme as outlined above would be in breach of the country-of-origin rule in Art. 3(2) of the E-commerce Directive 2000/31/EC. However, it is doubtful that it could be argued that a dispute resolution scheme is a *restriction* of the provision of online services. As has been pointed out in the previous paragraph, the scheme's purpose is to promote cross-border services by providing subsidised online arbitration.

### New convention to overcome two potential obstacles to the New York Convention

In the context of Internet dispute resolution, there are important limitations to the enforceability of foreign awards under the New York

The difference is, of course, that the Austrian Internet Ombudsman is not compulsory; see the discussion at 5.3.2.

[206] States have asserted jurisdiction in cases where all the relevant acts were carried out in another jurisdiction and all the relevant actors were located outside the jurisdiction, on the basis that the effects of those acts were felt within the jurisdiction. International law has recognised for some time that states have authority to regulate activities that originate abroad but which cause local harms; V. Lowe, 'Jurisdiction', in M. Evans (ed.), *International Law* (Oxford University Press, 2003), 329–55, 338–9.

Convention. These limitations apply to consumer arbitration[207] and may apply to statutory ombudsman decisions.[208] It is therefore suggested that a new convention should be negotiated that, on the one hand, incorporates strict minimum due process standards into online arbitration procedures for Internet disputes,[209] but, on the other hand, provides for enforceability of online arbitration awards and ombudsman decisions across borders. Politically, such a convention may have greater success than the Hague Jurisdiction Convention, as, in the United States, consumer arbitrations are common, and their enforceability in the European Union may be desirable from a US point of view, whereas the European Union may be interested in increasing due process for the arbitration of consumer and other Internet disputes as a safeguard against exploitation of the 'weaker' party.

### 8.6.4 Litigation

The final piece of the jigsaw is, of course, litigation. This is only available for the largest of claims.

### 8.7 Conclusion

This book has (hopefully) shown that there is a need for online arbitration and a statutory online adjudication/ombudsman scheme for the resolution of Internet disputes, particularly for disputes between individuals and/or where the parties are subject to a power imbalance.

The issue here is that there is a great potential for providing greater access to justice through ODR, which has not been exploited. The main problem is bringing the parties to the dispute before the online arbitrator, since pre-dispute arbitration clauses are prejudicial to individuals pitched against a corporate entity, and since companies may not agree to participate in arbitration after the dispute has arisen. This chapter has suggested two solutions to this: (i) the creation of a compulsory scheme for Internet disputes and (ii) online arbitration schemes contractually mandated by the operator of the online activity.

This chapter has also set out the minimum standards that should apply to such online arbitration schemes, drawing on the conclusion from the previous chapters, and has discussed how these could be implemented. For implementation, a mixture of institutional rules, national

[207] See 7.2.    [208] See the discussion above at 8.2.2.    [209] As defined at 3.6.3.

framework legislation, an international convention to deal with recognition and enforcement and a regional or international referral system has been suggested.

While the combination of cross-border litigation and traditional arbitration (the latter curtailing due process on the basis of the principle of party autonomy and the waiver principle) is not sufficient as a model for the resolution of such disputes, this book has proposed a new model, adding online arbitration and an online ombudsman or adjudication scheme with minimum due-process guarantees to the existing methods. Hopefully this would avert any Michael Kohlhaases from making an appearance on the Internet.[210]

## 8.8 Recommendations

### 8.8.1 For online platforms

It is recommended that online platforms hosting content (such as online auctions, marketplaces, content-sharing websites, blogs, wikis or virtual-reality websites) bind their users to an escalated dispute resolution scheme, starting with online mediation and moving to fair and binding online arbitration. The dispute resolution clause should be expressed to be for the benefit of third parties. It should be binding on corporate entities, and optional for individuals.

### 8.8.2 For Internet access providers

Internet access providers should likewise consider including an escalated dispute resolution scheme, starting with online mediation and moving to fair and binding online arbitration in their contracts with subscribers. This could deal with issues such as copyright infringement by peer-to-peer file-sharing between users. The online arbitration could be carried out by a third-party provider at no cost to the Internet access provider, relieving the Internet access provider from having to deal with dispute resolution.

### 8.8.3 For E-commerce websites generally

It is advisable that the operators of E-commerce websites subscribe to fair and binding ODR schemes by including a dispute resolution clause in

---

[210] See start of Chapter 1 for the story of Michael Kohlhaas.

their contracts (although an online arbitration clause may not always be enforceable against a consumer).

### 8.8.4 For payment service providers

Payment service providers are the intermediary handling the money, and are therefore in a position to 'enforce' a dispute resolution outcome. At present, payment service providers have developed some mechanisms to prevent fraud and to provide for chargebacks. It should be considered how this could be integrated into more sophisticated forms of fair and binding ODR, including online arbitration, that could be carried out by a different institution.

### 8.8.5 For providers of dispute resolution services

It is recommended that providers of dispute resolution services set up online arbitration schemes and establish rules for online arbitration for Internet disputes that comply with the due process standards developed in this book.

### 8.8.6 For governments and regulators

Governments should consider the large-scale promotion of trustmarks providing for fair dispute resolution to make users aware of them, and in order to enable users to distinguish between websites that provide for fair dispute resolution and those that do not; the OFT Consumer Code Approval Scheme provides a useful precedent for this. Governments should consider joint liability of credit-card providers (as is the case for consumer credit cards in the United Kingdom). This would make payment card services more expensive, but would provide greater access to redress for buyers. However, this system may burden small business merchants. It is also recommended that governments consider the introduction of a compulsory online adjudication or ombudsman scheme that should be subsidised. Governments should also legislate on standards for online arbitration used in Internet disputes. If an individual enters into an online arbitration agreement after the dispute arises, provided the rules comply with due process, the award should be binding. Governments should consider providing for a referral system, providing for online arbitration for all Internet disputes and incorporating the due process standards outlined in this book. Legislating for online arbitration and providing for a comprehensive referral system should probably be done at EU level. Finally, on an international level, it is advisable that governments agree a convention allowing for the mutual recognition and enforcement of foreign online arbitration awards (even where one or both parties are consumers), provided the online arbitration complies with due process.

# BIBLIOGRAPHY

Abdel Wahab, M. S. 'Does Technology Emasculate Trust? Confidentiality and Security Concerns in Online Arbitration' [September 2004] (Special Supplement: Using Technology to Resolve Business Disputes) *ICC International Court of Arbitration Bulletin* 43–51

Alderman, R. 'Pre-Dispute Mandatory Arbitration in Consumer Contracts: A Call for Reform' (Winter 2001) 38 *Houston Law Review* 1237–68

Allison, J. 'A Process Value Analysis of Decision-Maker Bias: The Case of Economic Conflicts of Interest' (1995) 32 *American Business Law Journal* 481–540

Bagner, H. 'Confidentiality – A Fundamental Principle in International Commercial Arbitration?' (2001) 18(2) *Journal of International Arbitration* 243–9

Bailey, S. H., Ching, J. P. L., Gunn, M. J. and Ormerod, D. C. *Smith, Bailey and Gunn: On the Modern Legal System*, 4th edn (London: Sweet & Maxwell 2002)

Bamford, R. 'Shopping Around: Dealing with Cross-Border Complaints' (2004) 14(4) *Consumer Policy Review* 108–12

Barak, A. 'Constitutional Human Rights and Private Law', in D. Friedmann and D. Barak-Erez, *Human Rights in Private Law* (Oxford: Hart Publishing, 2001), 13–42

Beyleveld, D. and Brownsword, R. *Consent in the Law* (Oxford and Portland, Oreg.: Hart Publishing, 2007)

Bingham, L. 'On Repeat Players, Adhesive Contracts and the Use of Statistics in Judicial Review of Employment Arbitration Awards' (1998) 29 *McGeorge Law Review* 223–59

Black, W. 'The Domain Name System', in L. Edwards and C. Waelde, *Law & the Internet*, 2nd edn (Oxford: Hart Publishing, 2000), 125–32

Blessing, M. 'Mandatory Rules of Law Versus Party Autonomy in International Arbitration' (1997) 14 *Journal of International Arbitration* 23–40

Brisby, P. 'Dispute Resolution in Telecoms – The Regulatory Perspective' (2005) 11(1) *Computer and Telecommunications Law Review* 4–9

Brown, H. and Marriott, A. *ADR Principles and Practice*, 2nd edn (London: Sweet & Maxwell, 1999)

Budnitz, M. 'Arbitration of Disputes between Consumers and Financial Institutions: A Serious Threat to Consumer Protection' (1995) 10 *Ohio State Journal on Dispute Resolution* 267–342

Burnstein M. 'A Global Network in a Compartmentalised Legal Environment', in
K. Boele-Woelki and C. Kessedjian (eds.), *Internet: Which Court Decides?*
*Which Law Applies?* (The Hague: Kluwer Law International, 1998), 23–
34

Calliess, G.-P. 'Transnational Consumer Law: Co-Regulation of B2C E-Commerce'
(2007) 3(3) *Comparative Research in Law & Political Economy* 2–54

Cappelletti, M. 'Alternative Dispute Resolution Processes within the Framework
of the World-Wide-Access-to-Justice Movement' (1993) 56 *The Modern Law
Review* 282–96

Carbonneau, T. 'Arbitral Justice: The Demise of Due Process in American Law'
(1996) 70 *Tulane Law Review* 1945–67

   *Cases and Materials on the Law and Practice of Arbitration*, 2nd edn (Huntington,
NY: Juris Publishing, 2000)

   *The Law and Practice of Arbitration* (Huntington, NY: Juris Publishing, 2004)

Carrington, P. 'Regulating Dispute Resolution Provisions in Adhesion Contracts'
(Winter 1998) 35 *Harvard Journal on Legislation* 225–31

Chatterjee, N. 'Arbitration Proceedings under ICANN's Uniform Domain Name
Dispute Resolution Policy – Myth or Reality?' (2006) 10 *Vindobona Journal
of International Commercial Law & Arbitration* 67–90

Clark, E., Cho, G. and Hoyle, A. 'Online Dispute Resolution: Present Realities,
Pressing Problems and Future Prospects' (2003) 17(1) *International Review
of Law, Computers & Technology* 7–25

Clarkson, C. M. V. and Hill, J. *The Conflict of Laws*, 3rd edn (Oxford University
Press, 2006)

Cobb, S. and Rifkin, J. 'Practice and Paradox: Deconstructing Neutrality in Mediation' (1991) 16 *Law and Social Inquiry* 25–63

Collins, L. *Dicey, Morris & Collins: The Conflict of Laws*, 14th edn (London: Sweet
& Maxwell, 2006)

Conley-Tyler, M. 'One Hundred and Fifteen and Counting: The State of Online
Dispute Resolution 2004', in M. Conley-Tyler, E. Katsh and D. Choi
(eds.), *Proceedings of the Third Annual Forum on Online Dispute Resolution 2004*, available from www.odr.info/cyberweek2004_library.php [1 April
2008]

Consumers International. 'Disputes in Cyberspace' (December 2000) ISBN
19023913162, available at www.consumersinternational.org [1 August 2008]

Department of Commerce and Federal Trade Commission. *Alternative Dispute Resolution for Consumer Transactions in the Borderless Online Marketplace* (June
2000), available from www.ftc.gov/os/2000/02/altdisputeresolutionfrn.htm
[1 July 2008]

Donahey, M. Scott. 'A Proposal for an Appellate Panel for the Uniform Domain
Name Dispute Resolution Policy' (2001) 18(1) *Journal of International Arbitration* 131–4

'The Uniform Domain Name Dispute Resolution Process and the Appearance of Partiality – Panelists Impaled on the Horns of a Dilemma' (2002) 19(1) *Journal of International Arbitration* 33–8

Doyle, M., Ritters, K. and Brooker, S. *Seeking Resolution* (research report published by the DTI and the National Consumer Council, January 2004, URN 03/1616)

Drahozal, C. and Friel, R. 'A Comparative View of Consumer Arbitration' (2005) 71 *Arbitration* 131–39

ECC-Net. *The European Online Marketplace: Consumer Complaints 2005* (Stockholm, 2006), available at http://ec.europa.eu/consumers/redress/ecc_network/european_online_marketplace2006.pdf [1 August 2008]

*The European Online Marketplace: Consumer Complaints 2007* (2008), available at http://ec.europa.eu/consumers/redress_cons/docs/ECC_E-commerce_report.pdf [1 August 2008]

Edwards, H. 'Alternative Dispute Resolution: Panacea or Anathema?' (1986) 99 *Harvard Law Review* 668–84

Edwards, L. 'Defamation and the Internet', in L. Edwards and C. Waelde, *Law & the Internet*, 2nd edn (Oxford: Hart Publishing, 2000), 249–73

Emerson, C. 'Wasting Time in Cyberspace: The UDRP's Inefficient Approach toward Arbitrating Internet Domain Name Disputes' (2004) 34 *University of Baltimore Law Review* 161–97

Fietkau, H.-J. 'Unscharfe Kommunikation und verzerrte Entscheidungen in der Online Mediation', in O. Märker and M. Trénel, *Online Mediation* (Berlin: Edition Sigma, 2003), 82–104

Fisher, R. & Ury, W. *Getting to Yes: Negotiating an Agreement Without Giving In*, 2nd edn (London: Random House, 1992)

Fiss, O. 'Against Settlement' (1984) 93 *Yale Law Journal* 1073–90

Flick, G. *Natural Justice Principles and Practical Application*, 2nd edn (Sydney: Butterworths, 1984)

Foskett, D. *The Law and Practice of Compromise*, 4th edn (London: Sweet & Maxwell, 1996)

Fouchard, P. 'La Porteé Internationale de l'Annulation de la Sentence Arbitrale dans son Pays d'Origine' (1997) 3 *Revue de l'Arbitrage* 327–52

Freeman, J. 'The Private Role in Public Governance' (2000) 75 *New York University Law Review* 543–675

Freyhold, H. van, Gessner, V., Vial, E. and Wagner, H. (eds.). *Cost of Judicial Barriers for Consumers in the Single Market, A Report for the European Commission*, Zentrum für Europäische Rechtspolilik an der Universität Bremen (October/November 2005)

Friendly, H. J. 'Some Kind of Hearing' (1975) 123 *University of Pennsylvania Law Review* 1267–317

Froomkin, A. M. 'ICANN's Uniform Dispute Resolution Policy – Causes and (Partial) Cures' (2002) 67 *Brooklyn Law Review* 608–718

Fuller, L. 'Mediation – Its Forms and Functions' (1971) 44 *Southern California Law Review* 305–39

'The Forms and Limits of Adjudication' (1978–1979) 92 *Harvard Law Review* 353–409

Gaillard, E. 'Transnational Law: A Legal System or a Method of Decision-Making' (2001) 17(1) *Arbitration International* 59–71

Galanter, M. 'Why the "Haves" Come Out Ahead: Speculations on the Limits of Legal Change' (1974) 9 *Law and Society Review* 95–160

Galanter, M. and Cahill, M. 'Most Cases Settle: Judicial Promotion and Regulation of Settlements' (1994) 46 *Stanford Law Review* 1339–91

Galligan, D. J. *Due Process and Fair Procedures* (Oxford: Clarendon Press, 1996)

Geist, M. 'Fair.com? An Examination of the Allegations of Systemic Unfairness in the ICANN UDRP' (2002) 27 *Brooklyn Journal of International Law* 903–37

Genn, H. *The Central London County Court Pilot Mediation Scheme Evaluation Report* (London: Lord Chancellor's Department, July 1998)

Gibbons, L. J. 'Private Law, Public "Justice": Another Look at Privacy, Arbitration and Global E-Commerce' (2000) 15 *Ohio State Journal on Dispute Resolution* 769–93

Gibbons, L., Kennedy, R. and Gibbs, J. 'Cyber-Mediation: Computer-Mediated Communications Medium Massaging the Message' (2002) 32 *New Mexico Law Review* 27–72

Gillies, L. 'A Review of the New Jurisdiction Rules for Electronic Consumer Contracts within the European Union' [2001] *Journal of Information Law & Technology* (eJournal), available from www2.warwick.ac.uk/fac/soc/law/elj/jilt [8 July 2008]

'European Union: Modified Rules of Jurisdiction for Electronic Consumer Contracts' (2000) 17 *Computer Law & Security Report* 395–8

Girsberger, D. and Schramm, D. 'Cyber-Arbitration' (2002) 3 *European Business Organization Law Review* 605–22

Gordon, R. 'The Electronic Personality and Digital Self' [February/April 2001] *Dispute Resolution Journal* 8–19

Greenberg, D. and Stanton, H. 'Business Groups, Consumer Problems: The Contradiction of Trade Association Complaint Handling', in L. Nader (ed.), *No Access to Law* (New York, NY: Academic Press, 1980), 193–231

Guiliano, M. and Lagarde, P. *Report on the Convention on the Law Applicable to Contractual Obligations*, OJ C282 of 31 October 1980

Gunn, J. and Roebuck, W. 'White Paper on Alternative Dispute Resolution in a Supply Chain Transformed by On-Line Transactions' (May 2001), available from the eCentre Legal Advisory Group

Habermas, J. *Faktizität und Geltung* (Frankfurt am Main: Suhrkamp, 1992)

Halpern, M. and Mehrotra, A. 'Exploring Legal Boundaries within Cyberspace: What Law Controls in a Global Marketplace?' (2000) 21 *University of Pennsylvania Journal of International Economic Law* 523–61

Hart, H. L. A. *The Concept of Law*, 2nd edn (Oxford: Clarendon Press, 1994)

Heiskanen, V. 'Dispute Resolution in International Electronic Commerce' (1999) 16 *Journal of International Arbitration* 29–44

Helfer, L. 'Whither the UDRP: Autonomous, Americanized or Cosmopolitan?' (2004) 12 *Cardozo Journal of International and Comparative Law* 493–505

Hochstrasser, D. 'Choice of Law and "Foreign" Mandatory Rules in International Arbitration' (1994) 11 *Journal of International Arbitration* 57–86

Hörnle, J. 'Internet Service Provider Liability – Let's Not Play Piggy in the Middle' (2002) 7(3) *Communications Law* 85–8

  'Online Dispute Resolution', in J. Tackaberry and A. Marriott, *Bernstein's Handbook of Arbitration and Dispute Resolution Practice*, 4th edn (London: Sweet & Maxwell, 2003)

  'Private International Law and E-Finance: The European Perspective' (2001) 8 *The EDI Law Review* 209–29

  'The European Extra Judicial Network – Overcoming the Obstacles' (2002) 7 *Communications Law* 143–5

  'The Jurisdictional Challenge of the Internet', in L. Edwards and C. Waelde, *Law & The Internet*, 3rd edn (Oxford: Hart Publishing, forthcoming 2008)

Houlden, P., La Tour, S., Walker, L. and Thibaut, J. 'Preferences for Modes of Dispute Resolution as a Function of Process and Decision Control' (1978) 14 *Journal of Experimental Social Psychology* 13–30

ITAA, *E-Commerce Taxation and the Limitations of Geolocation Tools*, available from www.itaa.org/taxfinance/docs/geolocationpaper.pdf [1 April 2008]

Jaksic, A. *Arbitration and Human Rights* (Frankfurt am Main: Peter Lang, 2002)

James, R. *Private Ombudsmen and Public Law* (Aldershot: Ashgate, 1997)

Jarrosson, C. 'L'Arbitrage et la Convention européenne des droits de l'Homme' [1989] *Revue de l'arbitrage* 573–607

Johnson, D. and Post, D. 'Law and Borders – the Rise of Law in Cyberspace' (1996) 48 *Stanford Law Review* 1367–402

Katsh, E. and Rifkin, J. *Online Dispute Resolution* (San Francisco, Calif.: Jossey-Bass, 2001)

Kaufmann-Kohler, G. and Schultz, T. *Online Dispute Resolution: Challenges for Contemporary Justice* (The Hague: Kluwer Law International, 2004)

Kouris, S. 'Confidentiality: Is International Arbitration Losing One of Its Major Benefits?' (2005) 22(2) *Journal of International Arbitration* 127–40

Kronke, H. 'Applicable Law in Torts and Contracts in Cyberspace', in K. Boele-Woelki and C. Kessedjian (eds.), *Internet: Which Court Decides? Which Law Applies?* (The Hague: Kluwer Law International, 1998), 65–87

Kurkela, M. *Due Process in International Commercial Arbitration* (New York, NY: Oceana, 2005)

Lessig, L. 'The Law of the Horse: What Cyberlaw Might Teach' (1999) 113 *Harvard Law Review* 501–49

*Code and Other Laws of Cyberspace* (New York, NY: Basic Books, 1999)

Lew, J. D. M., Mistelis, L. A. and Kröll, S. M. *Comparative International Commercial Arbitration* (The Hague: Kluwer Law International, 2003)

Liebscher, C. *The Healthy Award* (The Hague: Kluwer Law International, 2003)

Lind, E. A., Erickson, B. A., Friedland, N. and Dickenberger, M. 'Reactions to Procedural Models for Adjudicative Conflict Resolution: A Cross-National Study' (1978) 22(2) *Journal of Conflict Resolution* 318–41

Lloyd, I. *Legal Aspects of the Information Society* (London: Butterworths, 2000)

Lodder, A. and Zeleznikov, J. 'Developing an Online Dispute Resolution Environment: Dialogue Tools and Negotiation Support Systems in a Three Step Model' (2005) 10 *Harvard Negotiation Law Review* 287–337

Lowe, V. 'Jurisdiction', in M. Evans (ed.), *International Law* (Oxford University Press, 2003), 329–55

Lowenfeld, A. 'The Mitsubishi Case: Another View' (1986) 2 *Arbitration International* 178–90

Mackie, K., Miles, D., Marsh, W. and Allen, T. *The ADR Practice Guide* (London: Butterworths, 2000)

Mann, F. A. 'The Proper Law in the Conflict of Laws' (1987) 36 *International Comparative Law Quarterly* 437–53

Marsden, C. 'Introduction: Information and Communications Technologies, Globalisation and Regulation', in C. Marsden (ed.), *Regulating the Global Information Society* (London: Routledge, 2000), 1–40

Matscher, F. 'Schiedsgerichtsbarkeit und EMRK', in W. Habscheid and D. Schwab, *Beiträge zum internationalen Verfahrensrecht und Schiedsgerichtsbarkeit* (Münster: Festschrift für Heinrich Nagel, 1987)

Mayer, P. 'Mandatory Rules of Law in International Arbitration' (1986) 1 *Arbitration International* 274–93

McClean, D. and Beevers, K. *Morris on the Conflicts of Law*, 6th edn (London: Sweet & Maxwell, 2005)

McLaughlin, J. 'Arbitrability: Current Trends in the United States' (1996) 12(2) *Arbitration International* 113–36

Menkel-Meadow, C. 'Toward Another View of Legal Negotiation: The Structure of Problem-Solving' (1983–1984) 31 *UCLA Law Review* 754–842

Merry, S. and Silbey, S. 'What Do Plaintiffs Want? Reexamining the Concept of Dispute' (1984) 9(2) *Justice System Journal* 151–78

Mnookin, R. H. 'The Public/Private Dichotomy: Political Disagreement and Academic Reputation' (1982) 130 *University of Pennsylvania Law Review* 1429–40

Mnookin, R. H. and Kornhauser, L. 'Bargaining in the Shadow of the Law: The Case of Divorce' (1979) 88 *The Yale Law Journal* 950–97

Morris, P. and James, R. 'The Financial Ombudsman Service' [2002] *Public Law* 640–8

Mueller, M. 'Rough Justice – An Analysis of ICANN's Uniform Dispute Resolution Policy' (research report published by the Convergence Center, Syracuse University School of Information Studies, dated November 2000). Also published as 'Rough Justice: A Statistical Assessment of ICANN's Uniform Dispute Resolution Policy' (2001) 17(3) *The Information Society* 153–63

Mustill, L. J. 'The New Lex Mercatoria – The First Twenty-Five Years' (1987) 4(2) *Arbitration International* 86–119

Nader, L. 'Alternatives to the American Judicial System', in L. Nader, *No Access to Law: Alternatives to the American Legal System* (New York, NY: Academic Press, 1980)

Nader, L. and Shugart, C. 'Old Solutions for Old Problems', in L. Nader, *No Access to Law: Alternatives to the American Legal System* (New York, NY: Academic Press, 1980), 57–102

Nobles, R. 'Keeping Ombudsmen in their Place' [2001] *Public Law* 308–28

North, P. and Fawcett, J. *Cheshire and North's Private International Law*, 13th edn (London: Butterworths, 1999)

OECD. 'Guidelines for Consumer Protection in the Context of Electronic Commerce' (9 December 1999), available from www.oecd.org/document/ 51/0,2340,en_2649_34267_1824435_1_1_1_1,00.html

'Online Payment Systems for E-Commerce' (2006 Report, 18 April 2006), available from www.oecd.org/dataoecd/37/19/36736056.pdf [1 April 2008]

OFT, *Unfair Contract Terms Guidance* (February 2001)

Park, W. *Procedural Evolution in Business Arbitration* (Oxford University Press, 2006)

Partasides, C. 'International Commercial Arbitrations', in J. Tackaberry and A. Marriott, *Bernstein's Handbook of Arbitration and Dispute Resolution Practice*, 4th edn (London: Sweet & Maxwell, 2003), 651–706

Patel, A. 'Consumer Protection and Redress – The Wider Context' (2000) 3 *Electronic Business Law* 9–10

Paulsson, J. 'Delocalisation of International Commercial Arbitration: When and Why It Matters' (1983) 32 *International and Comparative Law Quarterly* 53–61

Perritt, H. 'Dispute Resolution in Cyberspace: Demand for New Forms of ADR' (2000) 15 *Ohio State Journal on Dispute Resolution* 675–703

'The Internet is Changing the Public International Legal System' (1999–2000) 88 *Kentucky Law Journal* 885–955

Petrochilos, G. *Procedural Law in International Arbitration* (Oxford University Press, 2004)

Philippe, M. 'NetCase: A New ICC Arbitration Facility' [2004] (Special Supplement) *ICC International Court of Arbitration Bulletin* 53–61

'Where is Everyone Going with Online Dispute Resolution?' (2002) 2 *International Business Law Journal* 167–210

Ponte, L. and Cavenagh, T. *Cyberjustice* (New Jersey, NJ: Pearson Prentice Hall, 2005)

Price, M. E. and Verhulst, S. G. 'In Search of the Self', in C. Marsden, *Regulating the Global Information Society* (London and New York, NY: Routledge, 2000)

Protopsaltou, D., Schultz, T. and Magnenat-Thalmann, N. 'Taking the Fourth Party Further? Considering a Shared Virtual Workspace for Arbitration' (2006) 15(2) *Information & Communications Technology Law* 157–73

Qureshi, K. 'Conflict of Interest' (2004) 154 *New Law Journal* 1400–1

Rau, A. S. 'Integrity in Private Judging' (1997) 38 *South Texas Law Review* 485–539

Rawls, J. *A Theory of Justice*, revised edn (Oxford University Press, 1999)

Redfern, A. and Hunter, M. *Law and Practice of International Commercial Arbitration*, 4th edn (London: Sweet & Maxwell, 2004)

Redish, M. H. and Marshall, L. C. 'Adjudicatory Independence and the Values of Procedural Due Process' (1986) 95 *Yale Law Journal* 455–505

Reed, A. 'Jurisdiction and Choice of Law in a Borderless Electronic Environment', in Y. Akdeniz, C. Walker and D. Wall (eds.), *The Internet Law and Society* (Harlow: Longman, 2000), 79–106

Reed, C. *Internet Law*, 2nd edn (Cambridge University Press, 2004)

Reidenberg, J. 'Governing Networks and Rule-Making in Cyberspace' (1996) 45 *Emory Law Journal* 911–30

Reuben, R. 'Constitutional Gravity: A Unitary Theory of Alternative Dispute Resolution and Public Civil Justice' (2000) 47 *UCLA Law Review* 949–1104

Richardson, G. and Genn, H. 'Tribunals in Transition: Resolution or Adjudication' [2007] *Public Law* 116–41

Riddall, J. G. *Jurisprudence* (London: Butterworths, 1999)

Robinson, P. 'Centuries of Contract Common Law Can't Be All Wrong' [2003] *Journal of Dispute Resolution* 135–73

Robinson, W. and Kasolowsky, B. 'Will the United Kingdom's Human Rights Act Further Protect Parties to Arbitration Proceedings?' (2002) 18(4) *Arbitration International* 453–66

Ross Saxer, S. 'One Professor's Approach to Increasing Technology Use in Legal Education' (1999–2000) 6 *Richmond Journal of Law and Technology* 21–57

Rule, C. *Online Dispute Resolution for Business* (San Francisco, Calif.: Jossey-Bass, 2002)

Rutherford, M. 'Documents-Only Arbitrations in Consumer Disputes', in J. Tackaberry and A. Marriott, *Bernstein's Handbook of Arbitration and Dispute Resolution Practice*, 4th edn (London: Sweet & Maxwell, 2003)

Samuel, A. 'Arbitration, Alternative Dispute Resolution Generally and the European Convention on Human Rights' (2004) 21(5) *Journal of International Arbitration* 413–38

Schiavetta, S. 'The Relationship between e-ADR and Article 6 of the European Convention of Human Rights Pursuant to the Case Law of the European Court of Human Rights' [2004] (1) *Journal of Information Law and Technology*, available at www2.warwick.ac.uk/fac/soc/law/elj/jilt/2004_1/schiavetta [1 August 2008]

Schlosser, P. 'Jurisdiction and International Judicial and Administrative Co-operation' (2000) 284 *Recueil des Cours* 9–430

Schu, R. 'The Applicable Law to Consumer Contracts Made over the Internet: Consumer Protection through Private International Law?' (1997) 5 *International Journal of Law and Information Technology* 192–229

Schultz, T. 'Does Online Dispute Resolution Need Governmental Intervention?' (2004) 6 *North Carolina Journal of Law & Technology* 71–106

  'Human Rights: A Speed Bump for Arbitral Procedures?' (2006) 9(1) *International Arbitration Law Review* 8–23

Shaw, M. N. *International Law*, 5th edn (Cambridge University Press, 2003)

Sternlight, J. 'Panacea or Corporate Tool?: Debunking the Supreme Court's Preference for Binding Arbitration' (Fall 1996) 74 *Washington University Law Quarterly* 637–712

Summers, R. S. 'Evaluating and Improving Legal Processes – A Plea for "Process Values"' (1974) 60 *Cornell Law Review* 1–52

Susskind, R. *Transforming the Law* (Oxford University Press, 2000)

Tackaberry, J. and Marriott, A. 'General Principles', in J. Tackaberry and A. Marriott, *Bernstein's Handbook of Arbitration and Dispute Resolution Practice*, 4th edn (London: Sweet & Maxwell, 2003)

Tedeschi, B. 'E-Commerce: Borders Returning to the Internet', *New York Times* (2 April 2001)

  'Putting It in Its Place', *The Economist* (9 August 2001)

Teitz, L. 'Providing Legal Services for the Middle Class in Cyberspace: The Promise and Challenge of Online Dispute Resolution' (2001) 70 *Fordham Law Review* 985–1016

Thiessen, E. and McMahon, J. 'Beyond Win-Win in Cyberspace' (2000) 15 *Ohio State Journal on Dispute Resolution* 643–67

Thornburg, E. 'Fast, Cheap and Out of Control: Lessons from the ICANN Dispute Resolution Process' (Spring 2002) 6 *Journal of Small and Emerging Business Law* 191–233

'Going Private: Technology, Due Process and Internet Dispute Resolution' (Fall 2000) 34 *UC Davis Law Review* 151–220

Treitel, G. *The Law of Contract*, 11th edn (London: Sweet & Maxwell, 2003)

Tschentscher, A. 'The Function of Procedural Justice in Theories of Justice', in K. Röhl and S. Machura (eds.), *Procedural Justice* (Aldershot: Ashgate, 1997), 105–19

Tweedale, A. 'Confidentiality in Arbitration and the Public Interest Exception' (2005) 21(1) *Arbitration International* 59–70

Van den Berg, A. *The New York Arbitration Convention of 1958* (Deventer: Kluwer, 1981)

Vidmar, N. 'Procedural Justice and Alternative Dispute Resolution', in K. Röhl and S. Machura (eds.), *Procedural Justice* (Aldershot: Ashgate, 1997), 121–36

Voser, N. 'Mandatory Rules of Law as a Limitation on the Law Applicable in International Commercial Arbitration' (1996) 7 *American Review of International Arbitration* 319–57

Wallace, R. *International Law*, 4th edn (London: Sweet & Maxwell, 2002)

Ware, S. 'Default Rules from Mandatory Rules: Privatizing Law through Arbitration' (1999) 83 *Minnesota Law Review* 703–54

'Domain Name Arbitration in the Arbitration-Law Context: Consent to, and Fairness in the UDRP' (2002) 6 *Journal of Small and Emerging Business Law* 129–65

Wiener, A. 'Regulations and Standards for Online Dispute Resolution', dated 15 February 2001

Wiener, J. *Globalisation and the Harmonization of Law* (London and New York, NY: Pinter, 1999)

Woolf, The Right Honourable Lord. 'Access to Justice' (Department of Constitutional Affairs, June 2005)

# INDEX

transparency versus (*cont.*)
  case for transparency, 145–9
  contract and institutional rules,
    150–2
  inadequate balance under English
    law, 159–60
  presumption of confidentiality,
    149
  what should be kept confidential,
    149
  who is under duty of
    confidentiality, 150
  waiver of right to go to court, 171,
    183
  absolute-waiver theory, 104–6
  proportionate model of online
    dispute resolution, 215–17
  requirements for waivers, 107–8
  significance of waiver, 106–7
artificial intelligence, 88
Asian Domain Name Dispute
  Resolution Centre, 189, 195–6,
  200, 203, 209
Astbury, John, 220
*audi alteram partem*, 98
Australia
  confidentiality in arbitration,
  158
Austria
  Internet Ombudsman, 76–8, 242,
  249
automated negotiation
  blind bidding, 81–2
  negotiation assistance, 81
awards
  appeals, 160–7
  default awards, 59
  fairness of, 12
  international conventions and,
    246–7, 259
  judicial review, 160–7
  as *res judicata*, 59, 60, 101

Barak, Aharon, 100
bargaining, 47
Bentham, Jeremy, 147
bias *see* impartiality and independence
Bingham, Lisa, 12, 30, 124, 126
blind bidding, 81–2

breach of contract
  joint liability, 39–41
bringing parties to arbitration,
  221–38
  compulsory statutory arbitration,
    230–8
  classification, 233–7
  Financial Ombudsman Service,
    232–3
  Internet disputes, 237–8
  National Online Ombudsman
    Office, 257–9
  ombudsman schemes for
    communication disputes,
    231–2
  contractually mandated schemes,
    223–30, 256–7
  agreements between participants,
    224–5
  agreements for benefit of
    third-party claimants, 225–6
  agreements in practice, 226–30
browse-wrap contracts, 180
business people
  arbitrators as, 122–4

Canada
  online dispute resolution in, 75
Carbonneau, Thomas, 97
chargebacks by payment service
  providers, 38–44, 255
  credit-card chargeback and joint
    liability, 38–42
  PayPal, 42–3
Chartered Institute of Arbitrators, 34,
  245
  arbitration costs, 252
choice of law
  arbitration, 63–5
clearing houses
  implementation of standards for
    online arbitration, 247–9
click-wrap contracts, 180
codes of conduct, 226–7
  arbitration, 92–3, 125, 127
coercive powers of government, 13
collaborative workspaces, 85
common law
  arbitration and, 97–8